LAW AND

Law and Philosophy Library

VOLUME 35

Managing Editors

FRANCISCO J. LAPORTA, *Department of Law,*
Autonomous University of Madrid, Spain

ALEKSANDER PECZENIK, *Department of Law, University of Lund, Sweden*

FREDERICK SCHAUER, *John F. Kennedy School of Government,*
Harvard University, Cambridge, Mass., U.S.A.

Former Managing Editors
AULIS AARNIO, MICHAEL D. BAYLES†, CONRAD D. JOHNSON†, ALAN MABE

Editorial Advisory Board

AULIS AARNIO, *Research Institute for Social Sciences,*
University of Tampere, Finland
ZENON BANKOWSKY, *Centre for Criminology and the Social and Philosophical*
Study of Law, University of Edinburgh
PAOLO COMANDUCCI, *University of Genua, Italy*
ERNESTO GARZÓN VALDÉS, *Institut für Politikwissenschaft,*
Johannes Gutenberg Universität Mainz
JOHN KLEINIG, *Department of Law, Police Science and Criminal*
Justice Administration, John Jay College of Criminal Justice,
City University of New York
NEIL MacCORMICK, *Centre for Criminology and the Social and*
Philosophical Study of Law, Faculty of Law, University of Edinburgh
WOJCIECH SADURSKI, *Faculty of Law, University of Sydney*
ROBERT S. SUMMERS, *School of Law, Cornell University*
CARL WELLMAN, *Department of Philosophy, Washington University*

The titles published in this series are listed at the end of this volume.

EMILIOS A. CHRISTODOULIDIS
*The University of Edinburgh,
Scotland, U.K.*

LAW AND REFLEXIVE POLITICS

KLUWER ACADEMIC PUBLISHERS
DORDRECHT / BOSTON / LONDON

A C.I.P. Catalogue record for this book is available from the Library of Congress.

ISBN 1-4020-0283-1
Transferred to Digital Print 2001

Published by Kluwer Academic Publishers,
P.O. Box 17, 3300 AA Dordrecht, The Netherlands.

Sold and distributed in the North, Central and South America
by Kluwer Academic Publishers,
101 Philip Drive, Norwell, MA 02061, U.S.A.

In all other countries, sold and distributed
by Kluwer Academic Publishers,
P.O. Box 322, 3300 AH Dordrecht, The Netherlands.

Printed on acid-free paper

All Rights Reserved
© 1998 Kluwer Academic Publishers
No part of the material protected by this copyright notice may be reproduced or
utilized in any form or by any means, electronic or mechanical,
including photocopying, recording or by any information storage and
retrieval system, without written permission from the copyright owner

Στο γιο μου Θοδωρο,
τον αναγνωστη

CONTENTS

Preface and Acknowledgements   xi

Introduction   xiii

PART I

Republican Constitutionalism

Chapter 1. **Citizenship, Passive and Active**	3
Chapter 2. **Republicanism and its Legacy**	10
Chapter 3. **Habermas on the 'Interpenetration' of Law and Politics**	19
Chapter 4. **American Civic Republicanism**	31
Ackerman and the 'Discovery' of Constitutional Politics	31
Sunstein and Michelman: 'Empathy' in 'Law's Republic'	36
Deliberation, Distance and Empathy	37
Institutional Deliberative Politics	42
Sunstein's Institutional suggestion	43
Michelman's Institutional suggestion	45
The Critique of Elitism and the Retreat from the Institutional Dialogue	48
Chapter 5. **Dworkin and the Law as Forum of Principle**	52
The Interpretive Thesis	53
Integrity: The Right Answer	55
Integrity, Coherence, Narrative	57
Dworkin Republican	59
Chapter 6. **The Containment Thesis**	61

PART II

Political Conflict Under Legal Categories: A systems-theoretical critique of Republican Constitutionalism

EXCURSUS: **Luhmann's Systems Theory: An Introduction**	73
Operations	74
System and Meaning	78
Observation	81
Observation: system-centric and system-specific	81
The Reduction of Complexity	83
Society and Sub-systems	84
Guiding Distinctions	88
Chapter 7. **Law, Society and Conflict**	96
The Juridification of Conflict	97
Chapter 8. **Law and the Double Contingency of Conflict**	102
* *Thesis [1] against Republicanism*	112
Chapter 9. **Legal Expectations**	116
The Function of Law	117
The Generalisation of Expectations as Legal	120
The Temporal dimension	121
The Social Dimension	122
The Material Dimension	124
Chapter 10. **The Relationship of Conflict and Law**	129
Chapter 11. **Conflicts Conflated**	136
* *Thesis [2] against Republicanism*	137
* *Thesis [3] against Republicanism*	141
* *Thesis [4] against Republicanism*	145
Chapter 12. **Conflict Re-enacted**	149
* *Thesis [5] against Republicanism*	157
* *Thesis [6] against Republicanism*	163

Incitement to subvert	168
Contempt of Court	173

Chapter 13. **Conflict Severed** 187
The Material Dimension 187
  * Thesis [7] against Republicanism 188
The Social Dimension 192
  Touraine and Melucci: Identity and Constitutive Conflict 193
  Simmel and Coser: Identity and 'Phenomenal' Conflict 197
  * Thesis [8] against Republicanism 200
  * Thesis [9] against Republicanism 206
  * Thesis [10] against Republicanism 209

Chapter 14. **Conflict Normalised** 211
  * Thesis [11] against Republicanism 220

PART III

Reflexive Politics

Chapter 15. **The Exclusionary and the Reflexive** 227

Chapter 16. **Theories of Political Reflexivity** 234
  Cover: Reflexivity and Anarchy 235
  Lyotard: Reflexivity as the threat of the Différend 237
  Unger: Reflexivity as Negative Capability 242

Chapter 17. **Luhmann on Political Reflexivity** 248

Chapter 18. **On Love, Marriage, Law and Politics** 256
  The Facilitative Side of Marriage 257
  The Incompatibilities of Love and Marriage 259
  Exclusionary Reasons and the Community of Marriage 265
  Back to Politics 269

Chapter 19. **Contingency as Eigen-value of Politics** 273
  [Reflexivity as second-order observation]

Chapter 20. **Politics 'As Passion'** 283
  [Reflexivity as Self-Reference]

Conclusion 287

Bibliography 289

Index 305

PREFACE AND ACKNOWLEDGEMENTS

I began work on the thesis that became the book through a three-year Scholarship of the Faculty of Law of the University of Edinburgh and I am grateful to the University for making it possible financially and for providing such a welcoming environment for research. Parts of this research were carried out at the European University Institute in Florence and the Academy for Legal Theory in Brussels and I am grateful for the hospitality that both institutions extended to me.

I have many important debts to acknowledge. To Zenon Bankowski for his true involvement and help, our many long discussions on the nature of legal reasoning, on what it means for something to be reflexive, what 'exclusionary'; I have benefited greatly from his insights, teaching and guidance over the years. To Beverley Brown for her hugely perceptive and very encouraging comments on earlier drafts that made the final product much better than it would have otherwise been. To Wilson Finnie who helped me not lose sight of the serious civil liberties implications of much of what I was arguing and whose perseverance saved me from certain loosely argued legal points. To David Garland who read this more closely than anyone and to whose advice and comments I owe not only that the end product makes (some) sense sociologically but also that it is not all too convoluted and empty in its abstraction. To Günther Teubner who saw me through many of the complexities of systems theory and who, at a very early meeting years ago, during which I was struggling to explain what my conception of politics entailed, put it to me so clearly and concisely: 'a theory of reflexive politics, then.' To Neil MacCormick, not only because of his valuable suggestions as to how to turn the thesis into a book, but also for his encouragement and guidance. To Scott Veitch, in discussion with whom many of the ideas here developed at the time that we were doctoral students at Edinburgh, for his friendship and the clarity he brings to difficult ideas. To Maurice Glasman, whose commitment to the ideals that have motivated my own work, community *with* freedom, freedom *in* interdependence, socialism with democracy, the true empowerment of people - beautifully defended in his *Unnecessary Suffering* - has been such an inspiration to me. And to Sean Smith whose understanding of systems theory makes it so refreshing and powerful, for his willingness to re-open the debate at every chance. I have also benefited greatly from discussions with many other people, all of whom I could not possibly include here. But I would like in this respect to thank

Lindsay Farmer, Anne Barron, Peter Young, Ioannis Tassopoulos, Vikki Bell, John Holmwood, Kimberly Hutchings, Russell Keat, Liz Kingdom, John Touchie as well as all the people at the Centre of Law and Society in Edinburgh and many at the Institute in Florence. I would like to thank them all for making the work so challenging and the challenge so rewarding.

My overriding debt is to my parents for their loving and generous support, always. And to Jane, for hers; I can now finally restore what was previously censored, and dedicate the piece on love and marriage to her, with *love*. The book itself I would like to dedicate to our wee man Theo, my gentle, troubled and oh so thoughtful one.

INTRODUCTION

Law is the great concealer; and law is everywhere. Or so claimed Marxists once upon a time.

[Law] was imbricated within the mode of production and productive relations themselves ... it intruded brusquely within alien categories, re-appearing bewigged and gowned in the form of ideology; ... it was an arm of politics and politics was one of its arms; it was an academic discipline, subjected to the rigour of its own autonomous logic, it contributed to the definition of the self-identity of both the rulers and the ruled.[1]

Does the old critique of domination still hold any sway?

Apparently not. Or so even scholars of the far Left keep reminding us in their eagerness to embrace law and proclaim their allegiance to the new constitutional politics of civil society. Old Marxists now describe popular sovereignty as 'co-original' with, and democracy 'internally linked' to constitutional rights[2] and find it hard to remember what it was they once disagreed with liberals about. No *tension* left between emancipatory politics and oppressive law; instead we have *reciprocal constitution*, simultaneous realisation. In the Left's embracing of the new constitutionalisms its old critique of law - the critique of the law's concealment of class inequality, class conflict and class action - is left behind. In a way that is indicative of the odd embarrassment with which the West European Left faces up to its tradition today, it is now all too willing to abandon all that it once held with such commitment, too busy shouldering responsibility for the aberrations of state coercion and central planning to remember that it has been *its* ideals, commitments, achievements and negotiated compromises of the last half century that have made our western societies humanly functional.[3]

Against so grand a coalition I will attempt to make a case for the critique of legal ideology. I will claim that the law *does* conceal and that its ideology does mask the exclusion and the compulsion of meanings. I will claim that this compulsion is not external but structural and occurs at the very point of the recovery of meaning. In effect to treat law, as many advocates of (what I will call) *'republican'* constitutionalism do, as a lever and substitute for politics depletes the emancipatory potential of politics. I argue against impoverishing politics in this way. My argument draws - selectively and sometimes 'heretically'- on Luhmann's version of systems theory.

---

[1] Thompson, E P, 1978, 288
[2] E.g. Habermas (1992b)
[3] See Glasman's excellent (1994) and (1996)

Constitutionalism is about the intersection of law and politics. Through recourse to Luhmann I will explore what kind of intersection this is, and why it makes the republican celebration of constitutional politics somewhat hollow, and to the extent that ideology is at play, somewhat dangerous. Then, in place of legal politics, I will put forward a suggestion for *reflexive* politics, that is emancipatory, utopian and an-archistic.

Before I explain in more detail how I will set out the argument, I want to establish at the outset that not for a moment am I suggesting that constitutionalism does not have a place - an important and indeed valuable place - in the politics of civil society in guaranteeing limitations on State power. That aspect of its value, associated with the rule of law ideal, is not in dispute. What I am arguing is that the law cannot, as the republicans would have it, *contain* the politics of civil society and exhaust what these politics are about. The law cannot contain and voice our strivings for the communities we want to have and our aspirations for the people we want to be.[4] In effect, the constitutional arrangements, that purport to provide merely the organising principles within which societal self-determination would take effect, simultaneously facilitate and frustrate the political. Constitutional processes *do* allow for constitutional deliberation and self-determination *but* in a significantly limiting and limited way; they simultaneously lend resilience and opacity to what remains unchallenged. My project thus addresses the ideological function of law and its ideological use by republican theory.

The book is divided into three parts. The first is an exposition of the 'republican' argument culminating in the 'containment thesis'. This is a thesis about legal politics that unites theorists as diverse as Dworkin, Habermas, Unger, Ackerman and the other 'civic republicans'. The second part is a critique of the republican thesis undertaken with the help of Luhmann's version of systems theory. The third part advances a suggestion for a definition, or re-conceptualisation, of the political as 'reflexive', one that cannot be captured or contained in law.

More specifically:

Part I explores the foundational notion of popular sovereignty as guiding ideal - or at least key precondition - of constitutionalism. By sanctioning the public political sphere, constitutional law maps out a universe of politics. I will approach the intersection of law and politics from the republican perspective, where the role of law is seen as substantiating the ideal of

---

[4] The allusion is to Dworkin, 1986, opening and closing phrases.

popular sovereignty and as empowering politics. Constitutionalism, here, is above all about self-determination and sovereignty and the sanctioning of the processes where the sovereign will is formed. I review the theories of some key advocates of republicanism and conclude this part with an account of their institutional suggestion for the 'containment' of the politics of civil society. Those familiar with the recent arguments of Habermas, Dworkin and the American 'civic republicans' need only refer to chapter six of this part, which summarises what I take to be the crux of the republican theory of 'legal politics', and thus what I take to be at stake. The rest of the book is a critique of this position.

Part II draws from systems theory to confront the republican claim that the politics of civil society can be contained (and empowered) by the law.

It begins with a short *introduction* to some very basic premises of autopoietic theory. This introduction only aims to kickstart the analysis and has absolutely no aspirations to completeness; aspects of the theory will be visited at much greater depth later in the book. This expositional structure is justified for the following reason. All too often autopoiesis, in truth much too rapidly marketed,[5] is recruited to back empirical studies of regulatory failures without any serious attempt to fill in the middle ground. From a theoretical account of why the logics of systems do not, and cannot, meet we are transported to a practical account of, say, social workers who misunderstand their clients' needs. This is regrettable because systems-theory is invaluable in probing what is precisely missing in these analyses: it makes available a heuristic device of great power and precision that can lend insights into the mechanisms of the construction of meaning, the dynamics of overlapping and mutually undercutting accounts of problems, of the communicative media that 'seduce' certain linkages at the expense of others, the simultaneity of coupling and closure of communications, that are at once 'the same and different'.[6] My expositional structure thus denotes my intention to work *with* the theory and not *from* its already given conclusion of incommunicability across systems.

Law is an index of how much conflict has to be suppressed. That is how Alasdair MacIntyre describes the main function of the law of liberalism.[7] My own venture into the relationship between conflict and law, in chapters seven to fourteen, aims to explore the degree to which dissensus can be represented in law. I suggest here that law allows for conflict selectively, by setting the thresholds of valid dissensus, the *when* and *how* of possible conflict. In the process not only is much repressed but much is appropriated as well, as

---

[5] 'Autopoietic theory has been perhaps truly too rapidly marketed' says Luhmann (1985b, 389)
[6] Glanville (1981)
[7] MacIntyre, 1981, 253

political conflicts are forced to meet criteria of legal relevance in order to be represented. But if law is to be the vehicle and guarantor of the public deliberative processes it must host people's entry and engagement in public life and guarantee that their dissenting voices will be heard. It must be able to voice conflict over the terms of social life - the expression of our disagreements, griefs and angers. If it fails to do that, by allowing only certain conflicts to register, it is not containing but instead selectively privileging and suppressing. And if that is so, then our legal democracy is prejudicial and deaf to genuine aspirations expressed in civil society - aspirations which are manifest in political conflict *but not* in legal argument. Or so I will argue.

And I will argue this via eleven inter-related theses against republicanism. In each of these theses I will discuss one aspect of this silencing or depletion of political conflict. I will suggest that at crucial junctions where constitutive political connections are made, republicans advocate a containment of politics in law that is either arbitrary, question-begging or self-defeating. To this end I will discuss the 'generation' and consolidation of political identity through conflict, the question of participation in conflict, symbolic conflict, the legal depiction of conflicting political interests, the impossibility of legally institutionalising solidarity, the law's mode of 'empathy' to dissenting voices, etc. In all, law's claim to *contain* the politics of conflict in its own meta-politics of order will be shown instead to *conflate* (theses two to four), *re-enact* (theses five and six), *sever* (theses seven to ten) and *normalise* (thesis eleven) political conflict in ways which impoverish its meaning.

Amongst these eleven moments of the legal mis-recognition of politics, I place special emphasis on thesis six, on subversive speech. It is meant as an inquiry in depth into one of the aspects of conflict depleted in law. Subversive speech is both an example and a test case. It is a test case because of the paramount importance of free speech in the construction of the public sphere. Speech undergirds the conception itself of democratic politics. The constitutive moment of participation as discussion of the terms of our public life cannot afford the displacement that I claim law inflicts on political speech. It is a displacement that occurs as the law re-aligns and re-enacts our political claims when these tap the seam of subversion of the constitutional processes. As I will explain it is not the verdict that matters here but rather the deployment of the operative distinction that views subversion as the opposite of politics. In the process law works out a concept of political speech for itself through self-reference and then, on this basis, renders every challenge to its rendering invisible.

What motivates my critique of republicanism is a perception that politics is neither contained, nor empowered through law but instead silenced by it. In every aspect discussed in Part II fundamental aspects of the political are submerged, litigated away, obliterated. In the final **Part III** of the book I will attempt a re-construction by suggesting elements of a theory of reflexive politics that will re-politicise all the assumptions behind conflict, action and identity that the law takes for granted. What is 'stilled' by law here becomes contested terrain again and, as such, political.

Having tentatively defined the reflexive as the opposite of the 'exclusionary', I visit certain key theorists to retrieve elements of reflexivity in their writings; I find them all wanting in some respect or other. Then I look at Luhmann from this perspective; why does his theory appear so incompatible with emancipatory politics? While criticising the theory in some respects I again extract and exploit key elements of systems-theory to ground a theory of reflexive politics.

To make a case for reflexive politics I advance an argument about how politics is like love. Both are reflexive and self-referential in the same way, and moreover, in both cases, this reflexivity and self-reference is of constitutive importance. I cannot anticipate the full implications of this argument at this stage save to say that, as a consequence, both love and politics do not admit of any middle range, 'exclusionary' reasons - such as legal ones - that stand in the way of constant revisability and re-evaluation of reasons to act.

I claim for reflexivity that it is the constitutive moment of politics. In a sense the argument for reflexive politics straddles both the descriptive and the normative. On the one hand I argue that politics should best be understood as reflexive. But my argument is also descriptive because my claim is that the constitutional forms celebrated by the republicans silence meanings that *are* political *not* that *ought* to be that. What is lost in the republican argument can only be assessed in the light of what it means, aspirationally, for politics to be reflexive.

What is reflexive politics? It is a politics that keeps the question of its revisability always open and where the political constellation of meanings is always disruptable: only in that does it gain its quality as political. By replacing the reflexive with the exclusionary, which dictates its own limited mode of revisability, law dictates the terms of closure of the field of political possibility. Reflexive politics is an attempt to recover it.

The autological consequence of this line of argument is that the definition of politics itself has to understand itself reflexively as contingent, as always subject to revision. A theory of reflexive politics does not cower from such reflexive risk, but - since the riskiness involved expands the field of political possibility - assumes it and embraces it.

PART I

Republican Constitutionalism

CHAPTER ONE

CITIZENSHIP, PASSIVE AND ACTIVE

The last few years have witnessed a remarkable renewal of interest in citizenship. The ideal of an active citizen has made a spectacular return to the political agenda of both the Left and the Right.[1] On the Right the active citizen is resurrected along the lines of 'the more Victorian concepts' of charity, philanthropy and self-help and called upon to compensate for the gradual abolition of the Welfare State. The Left has viewed it as an appropriate lever to retrieve its tradition of solidarity. Indeed, rarely in recent years has a theory gripped the imagination of legal scholars of the political Left with such force as the new republicanism. The Left appears increasingly attracted to the promise of a republican constitutionalism as the site where the politics of the people will be redeemed. And citizenship-talk has become so pervasive that conceptions of republican 'empowered' citizenship have come to signify not only political involvement and popular sovereignty as such but also individual self-government and even self-fulfilment. Why? On the face of it the answer seems simple. The republicans are advancing a theory about the self-legislating political community. The emphasis has been shifted from rights and individualism to duty and care; from myopic bargaining to public disinterested deliberation; from self-interest to 'empathy'; from compromise to the pursuit of common collective values. The theory professes to fulfil the promise of what Habermas calls a 'constitutional patriotism' or even the more elusive one of social solidarity, which, as Walzer once said, is the patriotism of the Left.[2] In all, it exerts the appeal of an emancipatory project that is ambitious and all-inclusive.

If one contrasts the promise of the new politics with the otherwise poor condition of contemporary political imagination, one can discern the source of their appeal. After the popular mobilisations of the late 1960s theorists like Donzelot described the retreat of the political - the decline of political passions - as 'nous détachant de la chose politique au lieu de nous offrir sur elle la prise renouvellée que nous escomptions.'[3] 'Liberal democratic politics,' writes Wolfe in a similar vein, 'has given many citizens of Western societies [the] unique gift [of] liberation from politics .. Released by politics

---

[1] On the revival of the notion of citizenship in British politics, see Heater (1991), Oliver (1991), Oldfield (1990)
[2] Walzer, 1970, 191
[3] Donzelot, 1984, 9

from politics [Western societies] can remain unaware of power struggle.'[4] But now civil society has been 're-discovered', claim the new democratic theories, in their numerous strands of 'strong democracy',[5] 'adversary democracy', 'constitutive democratic theory', e.t.c.[6]

Within the ambit of the 're-discovery' of civil society there is a crucial split. This split has too often been ignored. It divides the re-discoverers into, on the one hand, advocates of associational democracy, on the other, advocates of republicanism. I employ both terms in a loose, broad sense to cover also strands that do not describe themselves in these terms. But what is crucial to the division is the distinction that each broad category employs as significant to the re-discovery they claim.

Associational democracy views the State as the significant other of civil society. Theorists of associational democracy focus on social groups and voluntary associations as embodiments of partisan solidarities, ideological and interest group affiliations, partisan beliefs and interests, competing, overlapping, even mutually undercutting. This commitment to a pluralist democratic culture unites theorists that warn against subsuming this heterogeneity under statal institutions and processes[7] and writers from and on eastern Europe whose obvious target is still the nightmare of collective harmony under the watchful State.[8] What is significant to this position is that it does not view dissonance and fragmentation as undermining civil society's self-discovery and therefore assigns no integrative function to State-sanctioned processes; in fact the latter would prove erosive to that heterogeneity that is constitutive of civil society.[9] In this view associations are conceived of primarily as countervailing forces to the State.

The civil society that *republicans* have in mind is one that conceives of *the State and civil society on a continuum*. Michael Walzer writes characteristically: 'Only a democratic state can create a democratic civil society; only a democratic civil society can sustain a democratic state.'[10] Far from being the significant Other of civil society, the state is its pre-supposition in this formulation. Walzer's argument here is reminiscent of that powerful current in communitarian theory that understands deep allegiance to the State and commitment to one's community as interchangeable. Instead of the State it is now the 'atomism' of liberalism and pluralism that become civil society's significant other. The individualist

---

[4] Wolfe, 1989, 1

[5] Barber (1984)

[6] For an overview, see Rosenblum 1994, esp 68-75

[7] Typically here the British pluralist tradition, see Hirst (1989)

[8] See amongst many Gordon-Skilling (1988) and Lukes (1989)

[9] In this respect see Sullivan, 1988

[10] Walzer, 1991, 302

underpinning of both liberalism and pluralism, claim the republicans, with the consequent emphasis on issue-based memberships and pre-political interests, misunderstands the value of the integrative function of political participation itself. [11]

What is perhaps the single most surprising feature this strand shares is that the re-discovery of civil society is accompanied not by a rejection of the State but by the latter's re-conception and endorsement as benign guarantor of the democratic process. No resonances here of the 'bourgeois state' to 'be seized', 'occupied' or to 'wither away'. Radical democracy here no longer needs to be pitted against State institutional structures. Instead the empowerment of civil society gains its leverage from the State and its law and indirectly thus recognises state law as guarantor and vessel of the political discursive process. Republican constitutionalism builds on substantiating precisely this connection.

If we turn to the concept of *citizenship* we will see not only the split between the two conceptions of democracy replicated, but importantly also the origin of a significant tension: with its roots in both the ideas of *State membership* and *political participation*, 'citizenship' stands in an important way witness to a tension between the two, having evolved from the former to the latter and now accommodating uneasily within it strands of both.

For a long time 'citizenship', 'citoyenneté' or 'Staatsbürgerschaft' meant political membership as understood in the language of the law. Membership was conferred from above and citizenship was the legal link with a State that exercised effective power over a given territory. Membership was established through a network of duties and rights that connected citizen and State. While the element of membership did not change, as a result of the dramatic events of the late 18th Century sovereignty was transferred from the king to the people. The transferral enriched the liberal moment of civil liberties with rights of participation in the formation of the people's sovereign will.[12] There

---

[11] Neither is membership in civic associations - as constant source of democratic socialisation - confined to political institutions stricto sensu. Michael Sandel, for example, suggests reading republican potential in existing institutions like 'the family and neighborhood, religion and patriotism.' (Sandel, 1988, 20).

[12] Marshall's famous work on citizenship still stands as departure point of any discussion of rights in Britain. Marshall locates in the 18th C a development of civil rights in Britain, targeted primarily at the acquisition of legal status, equal access to the legal system and fair trial. The 19th C witnessed the emergence of political rights in terms of more immediate access to the halls of power and the parliamentary process (electoral rights and provisions for political parties.) Finally in the 20th C he located the emergence of a series of social welfare rights establishing entitlements to social security and compensation for unemployment, illness or accidents, 'abating' the prerogatives of property and wealth established during the previous centuries. (Marshall (1950))

was a shift of emphasis from membership to participation. The shift is so decisive as to alter the understanding of the status of citizen and establish the participatory element as the decisive one.[13]

Citizenship is a status that confers a set of rights upon individuals. Citizenship, in other words, is the right to have rights.[14] The ascription of the legal status grants the capacity to operationalise rights of political participation. Sovereignty means self-government and freedom of speech underpins it in this sense: the speech of the individual citizen is the input into the formation of public opinion that gears self-government. The status of citizenship is realised in this contribution. Citizenship is not a pre-condition to the freedom to speak. The right to speak, as input into the collective self-determination is the vessel of citizenship; only in that process is citizenship realised. The internal connection between speech and citizenship is essential if the argument from citizenship is to be understood properly: *speech is the mode of existence of the citizen; free speech makes the citizen sovereign.* Freedom of speech is integral to rather than a result or a condition of democracy; it defines the democratic conception of politics.[15]

Bearing in mind these initial remarks on the freedom of speech as mode of participation in democratic politics, it is of paramount importance to stress that whether the emphasis falls on membership or participation, the link with the State - membership - is crucial to citizenship and cannot be severed.[16] A

---

[13] The transfer of sovereignty from the body of the king to the body politic of citizens has found only partially an institutional expression in the U K that still adheres to the old formulations of the 'Crown in Parliament' for the sovereign body, and 'subject of the Crown' for the citizen. The notion of citizen, developed in most constitutions is only a term of art in the UK for the British concept of subjecthood. It is indicative that the 1948 British Nationality Act continued to refer to the subject as fundamental category (Dummet & Nicol (1990)). Even where the term "citizen" is employed it is done to distinguish from "aliens", those who lack the national status. One should note that the retention of the archaic notion of subjecthood is not irrelevant to the secrecy under which the business of government is conducted in Britain and the rapid decline of civil liberties in recent years. In this vein, Charter 88 demanded "a clear legally defined status of citizenship" enshrined in a Bill of Rights that would enhance Britain's position as a democratic polity.

[14] In the words of Chief Justice Earl Warren in *Trop v Dulles*, 356 US 100-2 (1958)

[15] 'A community is a universe of discourse in which the members participate by speaking and listening ... the individual can feel free by participating in this enterprise. The First Amendment takes the universe of discourse for granted.' (Chaffee, 1947, 21-2)

[16] Of course one of the major pre-occupations of the last few years in legal and political theory has been the demise of the State and the need to re-think many assumptions underlying political community and the very concepts we used to describe its sovereignty, its politics and its law. In respect to the latter, see Neil MacCormick's overview of the repercussions of the demise of the sovereign State on legal theory (1993). However, my own argument here concerning the relation between membership and participation would not be substantially different whether membership is conceived in the Nation State or a supra-national entity like

double connection underlies citizenship: on the one hand the connection to political participation; citizenship is the status or office that can operationalise political rights. On the other hand, the connection with the State *defines the contours of the relevant political community and in effect the circumference of political space.*[17] Citizenship not only involves a common membership but relies on that membership to initiate and direct participatory undertakings. The civic republican tradition, that we will turn to shortly, that purports to re-invigorate citizenship as praxis has located itself in this space.[18] Habermas's notion of 'constitutional patriotism' pronounces its ties to both active participation and membership in the State; as does Turner's concept of 'revolutionary citizenship', that relies on the 'horizontal' connection between members (or connection from below) proclaims the citizen as 'an active bearer of effective claims against society via the state,'[19] because it is the State that grants the capacity to act politically.

And it is by probing the dynamic of that connection between participation and membership that we may appreciate how acute an ambivalence inhabits the notion of citizenship. There is no shortage of accounts of the opposition: citizenship 'active and passive',[20] liberal/pluralist and 'republican',[21] 'instrumental' and 'political',[22] 'individualist' and 'communitarian', between 'participant' and 'participator'[23] and underlying them, between freedom negative and positive.[24] The following two accounts of the opposition are by Jürgen Habermas and Charles Taylor respectively:

---

the EU. My argument relies, instead, on the fact that whether at the statal or supra-statal level it is the law that constitutes and underpins participation in the politics of the community.

[17] For a notion of 'political space' see Wolin, (1960). Briefly, political space includes both objective and subjective elements; on the one hand institutional practices and processes. On the other, subjective perceptions and shared political meanuings, including hierarchies of valued priorities.

[18] It is worth stressing that Habermas appends the importance of constitutional forms to their integration into a system of political expectations, to remind us that, 'the institutions of constitutional freedom are only worth as much as the population makes of them ... [T]he legally institutionalized role of a citizen has to be embedded in the context of a political culture imbued with the concept of freedom.' (1992, 10) Under the structural conditions of late modernity, Habermas was initially very pessimistic about whether the availability of the fora will make the public critically attentive to politics. Paradoxically, perhaps, he is far less so in his recent work.

[19] Turner, 1990, passim and 200

[20] ibid.

[21] See following chapter

[22] Theorists in the Aristotelian tradition of politics, principally Arendt, Wolin, Strauss, e.t.c.

[23] Pranger, 1968, 91

[24] Crick (1969). The opposition has even found a resonance in law, with the introduction of active citizenship (Aktivbürgerschaft) in the text of the Swiss constitution and re-interpretations of Article 33 of the German Constitution in this light. (Habermas, 1992, 5)

'From the first perspective, citizenship is conceived in analogy to the model of received membership in an organisation which secures a legal status. From the second, it is conceived in analogy to the model of achieved membership in a self-determining ethical community. In the one interpretation, the individuals remain external to the State, contributing only in a certain manner to its reproduction in return for the benefits of organisational membership. In the other, the citizens are integrated into the political community like parts into a whole.'[25]

'One model focuses mainly on individual rights and equal treatment, as well as on government performance which takes account of citizen preferences. This is what has to be secured. Citizen capacity consists mainly in the power to retrieve these rights and ensure equal treatment, as well as to influence the effective decision-makers. These *institutions have an entirely instrumental significance ... No value is put on participation in rule for its own sake.* The other model by contrast, defines participation in self-rule as of the essence of freedom, as part of what must be secured. This is an essential component of citizen capacity. Full participation in self-rule is seen as being able ... to have some part in the forming of a ruling consensus, with which one can identify along with others.'[26]

While the distinction between the two models is usually assumed to correlate to a liberal/communitarian divide, what is significant for present purposes is the connection with *law* underlying both models. It is a pre-requisite of this divide to see constitutionalism as the inclusive whole within which the divide is located. By saying this I do not mean to pre-empt what the republicans argue against liberalism. I merely mean to designate, in a language that I hope does not already inhibit either claim, what in the course of history has emerged as the category that encloses and circumscribes the outer limits of political action, both liberal and republican. Like Habermas, we must understand constitutionalism as the institutional expression of the Public Sphere in the era since the emergence of the democratic constitutional state. 'Institutional expression' because a political Public Sphere - Habermas stresses this too as we will see - exists as institutionalised rational discussion. It exists in the rational discussion of public matters by individuals who are organised as a body politic according to legal rules of inclusion/exclusion in citizenship. Constitutionalism provides the institutional form (and guarantee) of political communication through freedom of speech and the press, assembly, association and petition, suffrage and the right to form and join political parties. Within the contours of this constitutionalism, liberal and republican accounts of Public Opinion can be accommodated. The existence of the constitutional framework underpins both competing positions because neither transcends the language of citizenship and rights and both seek their

---

[25] Habermas, 1992, 8-9
[26] Taylor, 1989, 178

anchorage, ultimately, in law. It is from that shared premise that they then diverge, and it is that shared premise - the constitutional context - that centres the opposition. Having shared the pre-supposition the positions then diverge greatly. Where the liberal sees accommodation of interest the republican sees the grounds for an intersubjectively shared praxis. Where the liberal sees a one-way process of feeding his/her contribution into the collective Public Opinion, the republican sees also a feedback, in that participation in debate serves to situate the lone political actor in shared intersubjectivity. Where in liberal constitutionalism the constitution is primarily a framework of constraint for politics, in the republican variant the constitution becomes the vessel of politics. But underpinning both positions is a shared legal/constitutional premise, seen in the one case (liberal) as a safeguard from the collective will, in the other (republican) as a springboard for collective praxis.

CHAPTER TWO

REPUBLICANISM AND ITS LEGACY

I must begin with a clarification of my use of the term *republicanism*. As I have already indicated, to some extent at least I use it as a term of art to cover all theories that stipulate a certain internal relationship between law and politics. The term covers theories that explicitly call themselves republican, but is also broader and covers theories that don't necessarily describe themselves by that term *yet* stipulate the same relationship between law and politics. I will therefore, at the outset, put forward the criterion that at the expense of other criteria groups 'my republicanisms' together. I hasten to say that this designation will not be uncontroversial; and while very few may contest, say, the recent convergence of the theories of Dworkin and Habermas on the subject of law and democracy, Dworkin and Unger would justifiably appear to most as very odd bedfellows. Indeed, in all but one respect, but it is that which is the one crucial here.

Republicanism is a theory about how political sovereignty finds expression in law. Law, claim the republicans, substantiates popular sovereignty by lending it constitutional provisions as vehicle or 'home' of political deliberation. It is this double connection, of law to politics and the community that defines republicanism in my use of the term, and it is with this double connection that I will take issue. While republicanism is a theory that is all about the empowerment of political community through law, my concern is, perhaps paradoxically, to rescue a notion of the political that is reflexive and a notion of community that is interpretative, these notions, I will claim, being true to the authentic nature of the political and the communal.

While avoiding going into the contentious liberal/republican dichotomy at this point, I want to stress again at the outset the limited yet important way in which liberal and republican constitutionalism are at one. Both seek a home for political deliberation in the Constitution. It is as freedom of speech, broadly understood,[1] that both see political sovereignty substantiated in law. The citizen is free and sovereign in that his/her speech is uncompromised. Both liberal and republican constitutionalism begin from this premise. While both locate the site of political deliberation in the Constitution, the republicans attribute far more decisive functions to constitutional political deliberation. For them, the political is rooted in law, and it is from the constitution that it draws for backing and aspiration.

---

[1] *Supra* about downplaying the formal boundaries between rights of participation.

Republicanism, of course, is not a new idea. What characterises this re-working of older ideas of civic participation in politics is the commitment to a notion of active citizenship as well as the suggestion of a plausible scheme about how this engagement can be institutionally realised in law. The suggestion is of an intimate, mutually nurturing relationship between law and politics. But that is not all. The writings of republicans are all the more appealing because they are highly ambitious; today's republicanism is not simply a theory about how law and politics merge in a new synthesis - it is also a theory about 'retrieving the self' in the process. The citizen actively participates in forming the political future and this active involvement, in turn, feeds back and situates the self-in-community. Tying the argument together, the republicans purport to point the way to self-fulfilment and self-determination through institutionalised political participation. It is by drawing this interconnection that we may appreciate the enormity of the republican project that ties human fulfilment to law by driving it through community and politics, expressed eloquently by Dworkin in the very first and last lines of *Law's Empire*:

'We live in and by the law. It makes us what we are. We are subjects of law's empire, liegemen to its methods and ideals, bound in spirit while we debate what we must therefore do ...
[Law] is a fraternal attitude, an expression of how we are united in community ... That is anyway what the law is for us: for the people we want to be and the community we aim to have.'

The complex interrelationship is established by the republicans through a number of stages of argumentation and there are of course variations between the major exponents as to how the interrelationship is to be understood precisely. I will introduce the argument here in terms of premises the major exponents share and to simplify things slightly I will distinguish two stages in their central argument, a moment of critique and a moment of reconstruction.

The *first stage, of critique,* involves them arguing against a view of the interrelationship between law, politics and community that they oppose. More accurately the view they oppose cannot sustain their preferred interrelationship at all. This is an argument very much on communitarian lines, in the way that the communitarians set up liberalism to argue against it. The republican twin targets here are *liberalism and pluralism*.

With the first I will deal only briefly, partly because I am personally doubtful that there is much mileage left in the communitarian/liberal opposition, partly because not all republicans share it (e.g. Sunstein and obviously Dworkin do not), but most importantly because the civic republican attack here appears to me either too thin or directed at a straw man[2] and thus does not serve to set up their position adequately. While the philosophical controversy between liberal theory and its critics is multi-faceted and ever shifting, the republican attack targets primarily the liberal 'thin' theory of the self. Often their communitarian argument here is inadequate, a forgery even.[3] The most eloquent account draws its inspiration from Michael Sandel. The liberal image of the individual, says Sandel, is one of the 'unencumbered self', whose values and convictions - as attributes of the self - become relegated to the external and the contingent 'as features of my condition rather than as constituents of my person.'[4] In this way liberal theory mis-construes communities that generate value and commitment because it remains blind to the intricate ways in which these values and beliefs impinge upon the very constitution of the self. For liberals, already constituted selves 'enter' the community they inhabit in the same way that they would enter a voluntary association. Sandel contrasts this with his 'constitutive' conception of community whose members understand it as describing 'not only what they *have* as fellow citizens but also what they *are*, not a relationship they choose but an attachment they discover, not merely an attribute but a constituent of their identity.'[5] The recourse to communitarian theory allows republicanism to confront liberalism first and foremost on an epistemological basis. This in turn allows them to argue the fundamental importance of participation in politics as constitutive of both communities and selves.

As I have mentioned already, it would be wrong to view this opposition to liberalism as the significant one for republicanism not only because the republicans are not united in their rejection of liberalism but because it does not yet allow them to establish other significant tenets that, alongside participation, are central to republicanism.[6] For this they will confront the tradition of *political pluralism*.

---

[2] It is often without doubt a liberal straw man that the republicans set up. The new liberalisms also condemn the abstraction that the traditional liberal 'dispossession of the self' entails. Indicatively Dworkin, 1989, Kymlicka, 1991, or Raz, 1986. As Raz argues (1986, 18): 'If there is one common thread to the argument of this book it is its critique of individualism and its endeavour to argue for a liberal morality on non-individualistic grounds.'

[3] Most significant here is Dworkin's counter-attack; one example is his critique of Tushnet's 'forgery' of liberalism in 1986, 440, n.19

[4] Sandel, 1982, 94

[5] ibid, 150

[6] Significantly here, those of civic virtue and the common good. For the new emphasis on civic virtue even outside mainstream republicanism see Heater (1991). What he defines as civic virtue is '[that] psychic side to citizenship [that is] expressed as commitment.'

What needs to be resisted, say the republicans, is the pluralist assumption that politics is a bargaining process where interests battle for recognition and superiority. According to the republicans, the pluralists view the public sphere as a political market that functions on the lines of the economic market.[7] Here, individual preferences and interests seek a mechanism to best accommodate their competition. Groups are nothing more than organisational forms through which individuals pursue their individual interests more effectively. What wins the 'democratic competition' is conceived as approximating public interest, and the market logic underpinning the political process guarantees democracy's self-correcting capacity. What the republican most opposes is this conception of the political actor projected from within the logic of the *homo economicus*, that pulls away the ground from any possibility of conceiving an objective public interest in politics that transcends individual and group interests.[8]

So what is wrong with political pluralism? Nancy Rosenblum summarises it:

'Individuals bring interests ready-formed to groups, which simply amplify them; interests are partial and contingent and thus without significance to moral identity; liberal pluralism is based on scepticism about our ability to communicate needs and values in a fashion that moves others towards consensus.'[9]

And, I would add, the republicans are very sceptical of the pluralist commitment to the sovereignty of associations and their superiority over state sovereignty, because this would erode the fundamentally *integrative* role of the democratic deliberative process and the production of authoritative public norms.

Having established their opposition to the theory of political pluralism in the broader framework - and still within the first, critical, stage of their argument - the republicans then direct the debate to constitutional theory. The republicans oppose an understanding of constitutional provisions as simply placing limits on political bargaining. Instead politics is the site where

---

[7] The market-place of ideas formula has dominated Constitutional theory and practice and motivates much First Amendment literature. Typically associated with Holmes, the market place of ideas is conceived as the medium of competition of ideas and the mechanism of striking a balance.

[8] This is a pluralism most associated with Bentley, Buchanan and Tullock. Obviously the question arises, as it arose with liberalism too, whether it is not a straw man the republicans are setting up here. Why, for example, are there practically no references in their work to Dahl, Laski and the important British school of political pluralism? The question is not irrelevant to how under-explicit political pluralism is as a theory.

[9] Rosenblum, 1994, 74

communities strive for self-determination, and the constitution, claim the republicans, hosts the political process.

In this context the republican rebuttal of pluralism is a rebuttal of a misconception that understands law as external to politics and community. The Constitution is misconstrued as a mechanism of checks and balances for - but external to - the bargaining process that is politics. The rebuttal of the pluralist mis-conception keys into a constitutional issue of the greatest importance. It underpins, claim the republicans, the contradiction that has haunted constitutional theory. The contradiction is generally referred to, following Alexander Bickel, as the '*counter-majoritarian difficulty or paradox.*'[10] In a nutshell, the problem is that the constitution at once proclaims popular sovereignty and at the same time establishes limits - rights - and a mechanism - judicial review - that may override what the populace may wish at a particular time.

The paradox has so dominated American constitutional theory as to have been occasionally identified with constitutionalism itself,[11] and underlies many other famous distinctions. In early American history we encounter it as the opposition between federalists and anti-federalists (Madison v. Jefferson), later as the contrast schemata of 'democracy (as majority will) and rights' (and consequently the liberal opposition of 'policy and principle'), as 'will and reason', as 'government based on political consent and government based on political science', etc. However the opposition is identified, it currently finds its most urgent expression in the suspect legitimacy of judicial review or, as Bickel put it, in the fact that judicial review remains a 'deviant institution' in democratic thinking.[12] Because how can it be consistent with basic democratic principle that the Court should be able to invalidate decisions of 'Us The People' as expressed through our representatives?[13]

There have been (at least) two lines of argument out of the quandary. The first, 'fundamental rights theory', is more a blatant admission of the tension rather than an attempt to overcome it, although the paradoxical dimension of the tension is downplayed. This line of argument subordinates democracy to

---

[10] Bickel 1962, 16

[11] At least in the US context: 'Constitutionalism: that is, restricting the choices open to a current majority' (Klarman, 1992, 796)

[12] Bickel, 1962, 18

[13] In an interesting article Leubsdorf suggests a deconstruction of the Constitution in a way that reveals these tensions as inherent in the text itself. Then it is no paradox that the Constitution is at once a Constitution of power and a Constitution of limits. 'Any Constitution,' he writes, 'participates in the tensions oppositional goals create and in the tensions that attend its own creation.' (1987, 201)

rights and maintains that individual rights should always outweigh - or 'trump' - democratic choices when the two compete. But this does not automatically translate as a privileging of law over politics because, as fundamental rights theorists argue, our very political culture incorporates both rights and democracy as of fundamental value. Western democracy has developed a commitment to upholding fundamental rights as an inherent and constitutive feature; therefore no externality and therefore no paradox. Dworkin is considered one of the most prominent figures in this camp, on account of his *Taking Rights Seriously,* although I would argue that his recent work has brought him closer to the second line of argument.

The second line of argument subordinates judicial review to democracy. John Ely[14] is usually hailed as the first major exponent of this orientation though many variations on that argument have since appeared. Judicial review exists, according to Ely, to 'unblock stoppages in the democratic process'[15] and maintain open the channels of political change, by, for example, facilitating the representation of minority interests. By securing political freedoms, judicial review secures what is integral to the function of 'an open and effective democratic process.'[16] Ely's path-breaking work could thus, more broadly be seen as suggesting that democracy provides a kind of master-narrative that gives content and meaning to provisions about rights and lends the perspective through which rights may be interpreted.[17] Thus understood there is little doubt that Dworkin of *Law's Empire* falls within this category[18] and so do, if less straightforwardly, the civic republicans.

As far as I know many of the republican arguments to follow have not been explicitly tied to the democratic grand narrative approach. Ackerman,

---

[14] Ely, 1981, and its forerunner under the eloquent title 'Toward a Representation-reinforcing Model of Judicial Review' (1978)

[15] ibid., 117

[16] ibid., 103

[17] Cf. MacCormick (1993, 143): 'The advantage of of insisting on rights as constitutionally derivative is, as we now see, that this leaves them in the end subject to democratic processes ... It is to the people as a whole that belongs the decision about the exact specification of those rights, and about the other essential elements of constitutional structure and distribution of constitutional authority. In this way democracy acquires a self-referential character.'

[18] The question admittedly needs to be changed from Ely's articulation of it. Ely subordinated judicial review to the democratic narrative that first gives it perspective. Dworkin seeks that perspective in a reconstruction of constitutional history that first enables and constrains legal meaning, and thus judicial interpretation as well. Integrity provides the grand narrative here rather than Ely's democratic ethos. But thus seen, Dworkin's is a specification rather than a qualification. And so too, one might claim, is that of Stanley Fish. In each case, an 'ethos' (Ely), a commitment to coherence (Dworkin), or the constraints to a logic internal to an interpretative community (Fish) supply a kind of master narrative that first enables legal meaning as such in the broadest sense and thus neutralises the 'deviant' nature of judicial review.

for example, criticises Ely for cloaking rather than dispensing with the paradox and is careful to proclaim he is steering a different course.[19] In spite of the disclaimer, the republicans are putting forward a grand democratic narrative even if it is a different one from the one Ely, the 'monist',[20] has in mind. It is by claiming a special role for law in the democratic deliberative process that the republicans 'dissolve' the constitutional paradox and disprove thus the externality of law to politics.

Having argued against conceiving law and politics as mutually opposing forces (as the pluralists would have it), the republicans proceed to the *second, reconstructive, stage* of their argument and suggest a different function for law. They will claim that the constitution provides for the possibility of politics and the substantiation of community. By inserting law into the picture they add a new and decisive variable to the communitarian interconnection we saw them putting forward earlier. For the republicans it is the Constitution that underpins the community's politics, in one and the same stroke, promoting 'participation, capacitation and emancipation.'[21] The communitarian connection lingers here not only in the argument about the social construction of the embedded self, but also in the argument that although citizenship is a universal category the dialogue into which it facilitates entry is specific to the historical community.[22] There are strong resonances here of the 'Aristotelian' politics of the *polis*, a tradition that envisages man as a 'political being' who could only realise his telos in a *vivere civile*, a republic, as there are of Rousseau's concept of politics as the expression of the civic will of the people, and the republicanism of Hannah Arendt and Leo Strauss.[23] The debt to these theorists runs deep. Arendt's

---

[19] Ackerman, 1985, pp737ff

[20] Ackerman describes 'monist democrats' (1989, pp7-13, 23) as those who take this line, and has Ely as his primary target here.

[21] Michelman, 1986, 43

[22] Michelman draws from Pitkin, 1984, 276, to stress 'the simultaneous discovery of our particular, historically selves, and the particular, historically shaped way of life of our community. The community, like the choosing self, already exists in its historical particularity.'

[23] Despite their reliance on the concepts of civic virtue, participation and the common good, it would be wrong to assume that for the new republicans, the modern political process is identifiable with the classical politics of the polis. There is little doubt that the background to new republican theory is a tradition of political thought with roots in Aristotle's *Politics*, Cicero's *Res Publica*, Macchiavelli, Harrington, a tradition renewed by Hannah Arendt and Leo Strauss. The new republicans may retain the key notions but reject the ancient view. The republicans reclaim the idea from its original context and 'do not share in its nostalgia' as do modern theorists like Arendt or Leo Strauss. Republicanism must be divorced once and for all from 'organicist, solidaristic communities.' (Michelman, 1988 1526) Instead, as a 'tradition in political thought, republicanism figures less as a canon than ethos, less as blueprint than as

own definition of politics sounds very apposite: '[t]he realm of politics,' she says, 'is the organisation of the people as it arises out of acting and speaking together, and its true space lies between people living together for this purpose.'[24] Like Arendt, the republicans conceive society as a politically constituted system. The most important element here is that membership in the political community is not seen - as the liberals and pluralists would have it - as means to an end, the pursuit of partisan choice, but instead it is in the very process of participation as its own end that perspectives engage with one another and conceptions of a good that is common are shaped. Whereas in the liberal/pluralist world-view, politics is about promoting diverse goods and thus relies on bargaining within a framework of rules neutral to the bargaining parties, the republican picture of politics is one of the pursuit of the *common good*. In their account, the heterogeneity of interest (of the Hobbesian rent-seekers), associated with liberalism, gives way to the heterogeneity of perspective. Bargaining gives way to arguing, and this shift allows republicans to claim *civic virtue* for their politics, a tenet so central as to be characterised by both Michelman and Sunstein as the 'animating principle' of civic republicanism. [25]

This is a re-statement of popular sovereignty in no uncertain terms. Having argued the meaning and significance of their key notions, the republicans can now celebrate having established a connection between the *embedded self*, where the form of that embeddedness is participation in a dialogue, that at once both constitutes the realm of *politics* and substantiates *community*, and finally *law* as enabling the dialogue in the constitutional forum. It is this final connection to law that the republicans are called most urgently to establish. What they need to prove is the nature of the connection between the political and the legal, their recourse to constitutional-legal discourse *as* communal, political discourse.

In order to do justice to a relative divergence, here, in the way in which the internal connection of politics to law is drawn, I will distinguish and give separate accounts of a number of prominent theorists that share the basic republican thesis. I will begin with Habermas's theory of the public sphere,

---

conceptual grid, less as settled institutional fact than as semantic fields for normative debate and constructive imagination.' (Michelman, 1986, 17)

[24] Arendt, 1958, 198

[25] Michelman, 1986, p18, Sunstein, 1985, p31. For an attempt to make a feminist case of civic virtue see Sherry: 'Where liberalism finds the primary purpose of government to be promotion of the diverse goods of its individual citizens, republicanism finds its primary purpose to be the definition of community values and the creation of public and private virtue necessary for societal achievement of those values.' (1986, 551)

recently unconditionally turned republican. I will then give relatively short expositions of the theories of three of the leading figures of the 'civic republican' movement in American Constitutional theory, Bruce Ackerman, Frank Michelman and Cass Sunstein. I will follow this up with a look at the legal theory of Ronald Dworkin that I consider 'republican' in spite of much literature that would contest this classification. The sections of the present part are *only an exposition* of the republican argument, and the occasional critique that I include aims to clarify the exposition, either because it brings critical aspects of the theory into relief, or because it is a critique to which the republicans themselves have responded by qualifying their positions. This way of proceeding does justice to republicanism as a project in progress - which also explains why the positions are often related as in a dialogue, and why there are occasional interruptions and overlaps in the narrative. The aim of the exposition is to explore the republican deep connection of law to community and to politics. I will explain this as **the containment thesis**. It is this thesis that the chapters to follow will take issue with and which the prime objective of this book is to counter.

CHAPTER THREE

HABERMAS ON THE 'INTERPENETRATION' OF LAW AND POLITICS

Within the affluent democracy the affluent discussion prevails and, within the established framework, it is tolerant to a large extent. All points of view can be heard: the Communist and the Fascist, the Left and the Right, the White and the Negro, the crusaders for armament and disarmament. Moreover, in endlessly dragging debates over the media, the stupid opinion is treated with the same respect as the intelligent one, the misinformed may talk as long as the informed, and propaganda rides along with education, truth with falsehood.
(Marcuse)

The debate over the meaning, functions and limits of the public sphere is as old as politics itself. The notion of the public sphere has a peculiar dynamic of its own for it includes the debate over what it is about. Our very activity of entering public life to debate and provide competing interpretations over the meaning of 'the public', political and social life, turns the public sphere into an 'essentially contested concept.'[1] One of the reasons that Jürgen Habermas has, in recent years, been held as a major theorist of the public sphere[2] is because he not only provides a theory of the public sphere, but a theory of rational discourse as a means to substantiate it.

When Habermas wrote his *Structural Transformation of the Public Sphere* in 1962, it was hailed almost immediately as a major work in the tradition of the Frankfurt School,[3] and contributed to shaping many of the main ideas of the then emerging New Left. The book was an exploration into the formation and demise of the public sphere (Öffentlichkeit), a category that has since remained a central focus of Habermas's work.

Habermas claims that the public sphere - as a sphere of rational, critical debate about society - is central to our understanding of modern society and its evolution since the 18th Century. Habermas locates its origin in such fora of public discussion as clubs, cafés, and most importantly, the press. When the State drifts apart from the (newly depoliticised) private realm following the expansion of market economies, the public sphere emerged as a specific sphere *between* those of State and civil society, its structure and more

---

[1] In the sense of Gallie (1956), later Connolly (1974)
[2] On this see Thompson (1993), Rasmussen (1985)
[3] By everybody except the Frankfurt school that is; in fact so unenthusiastic was its reception by Horkheimer and Adorno that Habermas had to submit the work to Marburg as his Habilitationsschrift.

importantly its function determined by the nature of the confrontation between the absolutist State and a bourgeoisie in the process of emancipation from the old regime.[4] The function of this public sphere was to oversee the absolutist State in order to make political decisions transparent. And what was the medium of making them transparent? It was the *public use of reason* that Habermas, anticipating much of his later writings, defines as free and unconstrained. Habermas says:

'Between State and civil society [lies] the realm of people assembled into a public, which as a citizenry mediates the government with the needs of bourgeois society in such a way that, ideally, political authority of this kind is gauged in the medium of the public realm.'[5]

In the book Habermas traces the emergence and the demise of the public sphere. While he locates the emergence and flourishing of the public realm in the constitutional enactment of rights in the era of liberal constitutionalism, he stresses that the ideals of free speech and discursive will-formation were not fully realised in the politics of capitalist society. What was not realised then, he subsequently goes on to say, is today no longer feasible because of structural constraints: the critical nature of public political discussion has been usurped and depleted by the functional imperatives of capitalism. Much of the book is taken up with analysing this demise of the public sphere, but I will say very little here on this. The demise is described in terms of a regress to a 'refeudalisation', which is due to the withdrawal, in late capitalism, of the 'space' between State and society that the public sphere occupied. Due to the increasing involvement of the State in the workings of civil society, their strict separation began to break down. Later, in *The Theory of Communicative Action,* Habermas described this as the State's *systemic* impingements on the *lifeworld,* that prevent the articulation of a *critical logos.* Here 'refeudalisation' was renamed 'colonisation', to describe the process in late modernity whereby 'systemic' exigencies - monetarisation and expanded administrative control - take over the public sphere-as-lifeworld and imbue it with their logic.[6] This logic is alienating for the political actor and destructive of the kind of communication that Habermas views as undergirding his 'discursive' democracy. Due to the depletion of the public sphere, politics is reduced to the occasional recourse to a public opinion that is little more than a 'acclamatory assent' managed by public relations managers.[7] Perhaps one of the most noticeable features of

---

[4] Hohendal, 1974
[5] Habermas, 1962, 263-4
[6] Habermas, 1987a, vol 2, passim, esp pp345ff
[7] Thompson (1993), and Habermas 1962, final chapter

constitutionalism as an ideology is its reluctance, in the face of rapidly declining participation and the erosion of the political lifeworld, to distance itself from the now redundant categories that once described the public sphere.[8] Because while, as Habermas explains, the political public sphere of the social Welfare state is characterised by a peculiar weakening of its critical functions, the State professes to be committed to making politics public and subjecting affairs to public reason. This disparity between structural conditions and rhetoric can be fruitfully elaborated as one of the principal sites of 'constitutionalist' ideology. As Mark Warren puts it, 'by evoking the image of rational discussion in a public space, liberal constitutions legitimate this progressive principle of politics.'[9] It must be stressed that Habermas's position in relation to this is ambiguous and shifting. His strong stance against the legitimating function of constitutionalist ideology - as one of the mechanisms through which capitalism offsets legitimation crises - is gradually abandoned after *Legitimation Crisis*. Initially he replaces his oppositional stance with a qualifying distinction (law as medium/institution) and most recently he abandons it altogether as we will see. In his recent 'republican' tour de force - *Faktizität und Geltung* - his account of the demise of the critical function of the public has been 'rectified' in favour of a much more optimistic theory of democracy.[10]

But let's return to the fundamentals of Habermas's concept of the public sphere. He defines it as a realm of rational argumentation where differences of opinion from across society can be discussed and settled. It is important to note that Habermas does not equate the public sphere with the public as such; rather 'the concept is directed at the *institution* which assumes concrete form through participation.'[11] In Habermas's own words, the public sphere is to be defined as 'a sphere that mediates between State and Society, in which the public *organises* itself as bearer of public opinion.'[12] The decisive moment here is the institutional one, the key formulation is 'organises as public opinion.' What does this 'organising' involve? It involves what MacCormick and Weinberger call the *institutive rules*[13] that set up the realm

---

[8] In this mode, Douzinas (1983) on a study of the legal construction of the category of freedom of speech, questions the discursive representations of power, law and legitimation that are embodied in the constitutional mode of discourse as remnants of an era long gone, whose present function is to conceal the realities of the operation of power and the law and by concealing them, legitimate them.
[9] Warren, 1989, 519
[10] For a concise and clear account of Habermas' trajectory see Delanty (n.d.)
[11] Hohendal, 1974, 45
[12] Habermas, 1974, 53
[13] MacCormick (1974)

of political participation as a legally constituted public sphere. In his later work Habermas explores institutionalisation historically, as a process of organising that involves a succession of steps, which, in *The Theory of Communicative Action*, he identifies as 'juridification thrusts'. We should understand this as a process whereby the realm of the social, more generally, and the realm of the political, more particularly, come under legal sway.

'Juridification [Verechtlichung],' says Habermas, 'refers quite generally to the tendency toward an increase in formal (or positive) law that can be observed in modern society.' Juridification includes both an expansion of legal provisions into hitherto unregulated areas of social life and an increase in the 'density' of the law. In this process, general formulas, characteristic of the Rule of Law ideal, are broken down into particularised regulation.[14] As we shall see later this account of Juridification tends to collapse upon closer scrutiny. However this very general formulation of the concept allows Habermas to treat juridification as a generic descriptive category that includes *all* communication through law, and not just the pathological aspects of law's 'distorted' communication, which is the usual reference of 'juridification' when used as a critical term. The pathology is instead, for Habermas, tied more narrowly to the phenomenon of 'colonisation' and has to do not with the communicative medium of law as such but the form of law specific to the Welfare State.[15] It is only the latter that impinges upon the lifeworld, leading to - what is Habermas's major pre-occupation throughout his later work - an 'un-coupling' of system and lifeworld.

'Juridification thrusts' are epochal processes - Habermas identifies four of them - whereby certain areas of the social realm come under legal sway. The first led to the bourgeois State, the rise of the absolutist Nation-State in Europe. The second wave led to the Constitutional State [Rechtstaat]. The third wave led to the Democratic Constitutional State,

'which spread in Europe and N. America in the wake of the French Revolution. The last stage (to date) led finally to the Democratic Welfare State which was achieved through the struggles of the European workers' movement in the course of the twentieth century.'[16]

Of the four waves of juridification, it is the second and third that concern the emergence of the Public Sphere as we know it. The second wave introduces constitutional regulation of the State's executive power. This marks the liberal moment of constitutionalism. The citizens are given actionable rights against the sovereign even if they do not yet participate in the sovereign will.

---

[14] Habermas, 1987a, vol 2, 357
[15] ibid., 367ff
[16] ibid., 357

With the third wave sovereignty is transferred from the person of the king to the collective person of the citizenry. With it

'[c]onsitutional power was democratized; the citizens, as citizens of the state, were provided with rights of political participation. Laws now come into force only when there is a democratically backed presumption that they express a general interest and that all those affected could agree to them. This requirement is to be met by a procedure that binds legislation to parliamentary will-formation and public discussion.'[17]

Underpinning this form of political participation are equal suffrage and political rights of expression and association. The third 'juridification thrust' is crucial to this discussion. Of course the liberal moment of protection against State power is maintained (and integrated) in the new constitutionalism; but now, through the extension of the vote and political rights, a new concept of political action emerges to give expression to participation in the public sphere. The Public Sphere is reconceived as a body politic comprising of citizens who contribute equally to the formation of Public Opinion, which is uncoerced and sovereign to the extent that the contributions are uncompromised. *Free speech* underpins participation in the public sphere in that very important sense. There are a number of key concepts here that need to be more precisely distinguished from each other:

(i) The protection of the *freedom of Speech* underpins freedom as political self-determination because it guarantees the integrity of the democratic process, and thus of democratic self-government. This justification from the argument for democracy is by no means the only one for the protection of speech. Thus the need to protect speech as contribution to the formation of *Public Opinion* needs to be distinguished from the protection of speech that is dictated by other rationales. These are far from straightforward delineations. Suffice it to say here that the literature on the question of freedom of speech includes a multitude of cross-cutting and mutually undercutting categorisations of speech, stemming from a multitude of rationales for protecting speech.[18] To complicate things further, judicial practice has also developed a multitude of legal tests both for delineating categories and identifying rationales. Not all this is relevant to Public Opinion as it is understood here, and in that sense freedom of speech is a broader category: the protection of the freedom of speech is motivated by reasons not all of which are relevant to the formation of a Public Opinion that can be claimed to be sovereign.

---

[17] ibid., 360
[18] Indicatively Schauer, 1982, Barendt, 1985, Greenawalt, 1989

CHAPTER THREE

(ii) The concept of the *Public Sphere*, as employed in Habermas, is also broader than that of *Public Opinion*. Because the Public Sphere is the framework within which 'the public organises itself as the bearer of Public Opinion.' The Public Sphere is the mode of that 'organisation'. It is the institutional framework and support of the realm of political participation, the institutional matrix for the formation of Public Opinion, and as such includes also procedures and practices; for example, the distribution and access to the means of communication are elements of the Public Sphere, which although relevant to the formation of Public Opinion are not reducible to it.

(iii) The notion of *Popular Sovereignty* is also internally linked to but not interchangeable with both the notions of the *Public Sphere* and of *Public Opinion*. Uncoerced Public Opinion, the ideal that the citizenry is free and self-determining, finds its institutional expression in the notion of popular sovereignty inscribed in constitutions. By providing the mode in which Public Opinion becomes enacted as 'sovereign' public will, the notion of the Public Sphere mediates between the two and underlies both.[19]

The crucial linkage is, thus, between the concepts of public sphere, public opinion and popular sovereignty. Constitutionalism meets the aspiration of popular sovereignty by providing the institutional moment for participation and political praxis. The equal distribution of political rights of participation[20] and their entrenchment at the constitutional level guarantees that Public Opinion can be expressed and enacted as law, sovereign because shielded from State inhibition. In sanctioning the channels of representation, the Constitution provides the institutional vessel for Public Opinion to be communicated to the State in the ultimate expression of self-government: law-making. The sovereign will of the citizenry thus translates into the sovereign will of the State. The Constitution guarantees that the transition is an authentic one through the principles of open government, publicity, and underpinning those, freedom of the press, administrative review, e.t.c. By institutionalising the political process along these lines, constitutionalism

---

[19] Popular sovereignty finds other constitutional outlets too. The sovereignty principle is also exemplified in the status of the Constitution as supreme law. It is exemplified also in the fact that Constitutions are to varying degrees 'fixed': they cannot be amended through ordinary legislative majorities but only special majorities in the form of constitutional referenda, constitutional Conventions, or constitutional legislative majorities

[20] And at the fringes of rights, the neo-liberal concern to accommodate some expressions of direct action and civil disobedience (Rawls (1973), Dworkin (1977, pp206ff), Pope ('Read in context the first amendment carves out the constitutional space for direct popular power', 1990, pp366-8), Carter (1973).

promises that Public Opinion will, at all times, be an authentic expression of popular sovereignty.

Hence for Habermas too, *free speech is the supreme form and index of political action*. Firstly because the legal regulation of the protection of free speech is precisely the kind of institutional achievement that '*organises* the public as bearer of public opinion.' In MacCormick's and Weinberger's sense the right to free speech is the core 'institutive' rule of popular sovereignty as inscribed in institutions.[21] Even in constitutional practice this *prima facie* reduction of 'political action' to 'freedom of speech' is not illegitimate.[22] The insistence on centring this whole analysis on speech is not intended to the exclusion of, but rather on behalf of, other political rights of participation. Viewed from the perspective of participation and contribution to the deliberative process, rights of assembly, association and petition are facilitative of and thus secondary to the core organising political right of freedom of speech; they should be seen in the context of the deliberative process as the Public Sphere's organisational patterns of participation in politics. Consequently, with Habermas and others,[23] I will downplay the formal distinctions and use the formula freedom of speech to cover all of these rights.

But there is a second reason why for Habermas the legal protection of free speech is of such importance. It is because Habermas centres politics on discourse. By evoking the image of rational discussion in a public space the legally protected political speech of the individual actor becomes a contribution to the institutional process that conveys the rationally formed deliberative will of the people to the State for execution. The State thus becomes the agent of the people's self-government. As Habermas puts it: 'Although construed as power, legislation ... issues not from political will, but rational agreement.' Later, in *The Philosophical Discourse of Modernity*, he will claim:

'According to the normative ideas of our political tradition, the democratically legitimated apparatus of the State ... is supposed to be able to put into effect the opinion and will of the citizenry as a public. The citizens themselves participate in the formation of collective consciousness but they cannot act collectively. Collective action means that the government would transpose the intersubjectively constituted self-knowledge of society organizationally into the self-determination of society.'[24]

---

[21] MacCormick and Weinberger, 1976

[22] For a judicial decision to this effect see *NAACP v Button*, 371 US 415, 429-30, (1963)

[23] For theoretical backing for this reduction, I draw, among others, from Nowak et al (1986, s.16.53 at 1004)

[24] Habermas, 1987b, 360, my emph.

Habermas is still careful to point out that this is an aspiration, realised only imperfectly throughout modernity. But as an ideal, the Public Sphere as the institutional expression of critical and rational public deliberation is elevated by Habermas to no less than 'the normative content of Modernity.' [25]

With the last traces of the kind of radical socialism that inspired earlier work finally and completely abandoned now, Habermas's discursive democracy receives its republican baptism in the latest work, *Faktizität and Geltung*. I will refrain at this stage from commenting on how non-radical I find Habermas's latest rendering of 'radical democracy'. This is properly the subject of later chapters. What is important here is to establish and explore the 'republican' deep premise of this theory of democracy, the way it is premised on law and gains its leverage from law. I will take issue with what - in the last instance at least - inspires and organises the whole undertaking : the embedding of democracy, discourse and political self-determination in law.

The distinction that gives the work its title is that between the 'social facticity' of the law and its 'normative validity'. Law's facticity is explained by the fact that law is a product of politics and thus of power. It is a product of the will of a political law-giver and as an exercise of will it is changeable, contingent and arbitrary. But,

'the formal properties of coercion and positivity are associated with a claim to legitimacy ... this expectation of legitimacy is intertwined with the facticity of law-making and law enforcement. And this connection is in turn mirrored in the ambivalent mode of legal validity.'[26]

This ambivalence carries through to the fundamental modes of understanding action. As '*facticity*', as power and as command, the law invites the *strategic* mode of action from citizens, i.e. action oriented to success rather than understanding;[27] citizens, here, view rules as factual constraints on the scope of possible courses of action. But of course Habermas wants to reserve for

---

[25] ibid., last chapter. According to Thompson, 'Habermas wishes to maintain that, despite the decline of the bourgeois public sphere which provided a partial and imperfect realization of this idea, the critical principle of publicity retains its value as a normative ideal, a kind of critical yardstick by means of which the shortcomings of existing institutions can be assessed. The critical principle of publicity is the core concept of a theory of democracy and of democratic will-formation.'(1993, pp178-9)

[26] Habermas, 1996, (Postscript) 135

[27] For the differentiation of types of action see Habermas, 1987a, pp75ff

legal norms the function of allowing *communicative* action, mutual understanding, and on the basis of that *'validity'*, rationality and rightness.

Law's ambivalence, its straddling the strategic and the communicative, the 'factual' and the 'valid', derives from a tension. On the one hand there is in law a decisionist imperative; decisions need to be made, not avoided (*non liquet*), they need to be reached under the pressure of time, and once reached they need to be enforced. Each of these moments of decision signals an abrupt curtailment of the processes of reason and communicative rationality. And yet it is precisely in communicative rationality that law finds its footing in justice and can establish its claim to be a form of rational discourse.

Now what Habermas takes to be rational discourse is well known and requires only brief mention here. A rational discourse that guarantees rightness (and the truth of normative propositions) is one that involves complete transparency and freedom of communication; participants in discourse must be prepared to attempt to understand the contributions of all others and subject their own claims to the scrutiny of all others, be prepared to defend their claims and accept what prevails on the mere persuasive force of the better argument even if it is not what they had set out to convince others about.

It is obvious that the decisionist imperative of law pulls away from the limitless pursuit of consensus, and it is in that sense the law could be seen not to guarantee but to potentially undermine rational discourse. Yet to the extent that present legal decisions and norms are fallible, open to future scrutiny and revisable, the institutions of legality, for Habermas, hold out the promise of institutionalising communicative reason. This is how he states the 'discourse principle':

'The only regulations and ways of acting that may claim legitimacy are those to which all who are possibly affected could assent as participants in rational discourses ... As legal subjects they must anchor this practice of self-legislation in the medium of law itself; they must legally institutionalize those communicative presuppositions and procedures of a political opinion- and will-formation in which the discourse principle is applied ... *In this way the discourse principle acquires the legal shape of a democratic principle.*'[28]

This is the moment of republican baptism. The principle of democracy derives from the 'interpenetration' of the discourse principle and the legal form. Discourse and legality become mutually enabling in this internal linking and find expression in a 'radical' theory of democracy. Of course given the constraints on discourse exerted by 'facticity', reason finds its opportunities only partly realised in law. It is still held back both by the

---

[28] Habermas, 1996, 144

'old' pathologies like the instrumental use of 'law as medium' and administrative imperatives not transparent to democratic scrutiny on the one hand,[29] on the other by rigid formal rules of interpretation and 'recognition' that guarantee certainty of law at the expense of its discursive revisability.[30] But in spite of all this, law holds out a claim that goes beyond the contingency of power to rationality and the aspiration that citizens are free authors of their law and free to revise their normative standards in an uncoerced, rational way. This normative validity of law Habermas identifies as primarily residing in Constitutional law; here facticity does not constrain validity. The Constitution is for Habermas an 'unfinished project' an 'ongoing process of self-organisation in which [the citizenry] defines itself'[31] through the opportunities that law offers radical democracy.

What are these opportunities that (Constitutional) law supposedly gives to politics?

Firstly, law offers a citizenry the safeguards, guarantees and medium through which its self-determination may be realised; the protection of free speech and the safeguarding of the processes and milieux in which 'validity claims' are shaped and expressed (political rights and freedoms more generally). The above take us back to Habermas's theory of the public sphere as public political dialogue; here legality provides the external guarantees that the discourse will not be coerced. This is an argument very close to John Ely's about rights 'unblocking' the channels of political participation. As Habermas puts it, rights 'should not only institutionalize a rational political will-formation, but should also guarantee the very medium in which this will-formation can express itself as a common will of freely associated consociates under law;'[32] moreover 'communicative and participatory rights constitutive of democratic will-formation acquire a privileged position.'[33] Habermas's defence of constitutional rights as 'opportunity structures' is very much undertaken on the grounds that they establish the conditions of rational discourse by safeguarding the integrity of the democratic process.

Thus Habermas's theory of rightness as uncoerced consensus remedies this otherwise '*external*' connection between law and politics - the law protecting and accommodating politics by providing a framework - with an

---

[29] See above, text accompanying fns 4-6.

[30] 'How can the application of a contingently emergent law,' asks Habermas, 'be carried out with internal consistency and grounded in an externally rational way so as to guarantee simultaneously the certainty of law and rightness?' (Habermas, 1996, 243)

[31] ibid., 384

[32] ibid., 143

[33] ibid., 321

'*internal*' connection, where law contains and carries politics understood as contributions to a common dialogue. But it may be worth stressing the point that democracy on these terms must be understood as wider than the purely institutional. After their 'public struggle for recognition,' the freely contested validity claims 'will be taken up by the responsible political authorities, put on the parliamentary agenda, ... worked into legislative proposals and binding decisions.'[34] We will return to this connection of informal and formal processes (that informs a number of other republican positions too) as an important aspect of the 'containment thesis', in order to show that it is far more problematical than Habermas assumes it to be. The republicans must establish that the citizens are the free authors of their laws. As we will see in the following chapter, this central thesis takes many forms. Sometimes the authorship is undertaken in exceptional moments of popular mobilisation (Ackerman), sometimes it relies on an identification of the People's will with that of delegates (Sunstein) or judges (Michelman, Dworkin); in Habermas's case the authorship is re-conceived as the ideal *of an open society of interpreters of the constitution*. 'Openness' may satisfy the conditions of rational discourse but 'authorship' *must* involve a congruence of informal and formal processes, a 'meeting' of legal and lay discourses, a connection which, I will argue, Habermas like the rest of the republicans can only postulate or assume *a priori*.

I have given a very broad outline of Habermas' claim that radical democracy can be understood best as internally connected to law. My summary of the 'containment thesis' in the last section of this part continues this argument. Of course there are many points at which Habermas would disagree with other republicans; for example he is at pains to establish that his theory does not assume the unity of civil society and any concept of a common good that might build on that. In answering what he perceives to be the major challenge of theories of functional differentiation, such as Luhmann's, he will concede that complexity and differentiation must impose a qualification on older ideals of popular sovereignty. His discursive 'take' on this avoids the postulation of an *a priori* 'unity'. At the same time, by establishing rational discourse as the centrepiece of politics, and law as the prime instance and grand enabler of rational discourse, he bridges the counter-position of law and politics (that we saw earlier in its many expressions). Now the 'universality' of his founding premise bridges democratic will with democratic reason: 'just those norms deserve to be valid that could meet with the approval of those potentially affected, insofar as the latter participate in rational discourse.'[35] In this and many other respects this

---

[34] ibid, 314
[35] ibid., 127

is a work quite awesome in its undertaking; at the same time and most significantly underlying it all is a deep endorsement of law as the potential site of the rational redemption of politics, its siting as centrepiece and watchman of the political. It is this that connects him to the other advocates of republicanism and this central claim alone that I will attempt to refute.

CHAPTER FOUR

AMERICAN CIVIC REPUBLICANISM

It is at the constitutional junction of law and politics, that a number of prominent American public lawyers have located their 'civic republicanism' as a theory about the empowerment of civil society. Civic republicanism is a theory that draws on a number of disciplines and integrates the insights into constitutional theory to suggest a thorough rethinking of the premises of constitutionalism. While the republicans all share the basic premise of the interrelationship I described between self, community, politics and law, they diverge in their accounts of the precise institutional vessel of the political dialogue. They disagree about where to locate the constitutional 'home' of the deliberative practice. One of them designates the Supreme Court as the most appropriate forum of the deliberative practice, another the Congress, while a third seeks to locate his republican politics in the 'constitutional' mobilisation of the citizenry at large. The initial disparity between the theorists, between elite and populist institutional solutions, has given way, more recently, to some convergence. But the problem of designating the appropriate constitutional realm of the political dialogue still remains the issue that most sharply divides civic republicans. The following sections will explore the answers they give to the problem independently. I will in each case, rehearse the basic premise only briefly and focus more extensively on the various suggested constitutional outlets of the political dialogue to explore how it is that they perform the function of 'carrying' the political dialogue onto legal-institutional ground.

ACKERMAN AND THE 'DISCOVERY' OF CONSTITUTIONAL POLITICS

Ackerman launches his grand scheme to 'discover' the constitution in order to map out the contribution of American constitutionalism to no less than 'the rebirth of Democracy in the modern era.'[1] His discovery is a most ambitious one, suggesting that the constitution's past and present role has been to serve as a lever for politics in a way that compounds a sense of community among citizens. To advocate his republican grand synthesis of law and politics, however, he first needs to argue against a position - already discussed - that understands the two as external and even incompatible to each other. He argues against this mis-conception by confronting the

---

[1] Ackerman, 1991, 295-6

traditional constitutional problem that we have already discussed, the counter-majoritarian paradox. 'The root difficulty,' Ackerman explains, 'is that judicial review is a counter-majoritarian force in our system. There are various ways of sliding over this ineluctable reality.'[2] But under whatever formulas the sharp edge of the paradox has been removed, this limitation upon popular sovereignty is impossible to deny. Whenever the Supreme Court reverses a legislative decision, it 'thwarts the will of the representatives of the actual people of the here and now; it exercises control not on behalf of the prevailing majority but against it.'[3] There is, says Ackerman, a tension here between politics (the overturned legislative decision) and law (the Court decision) and this tension gives rise to a mis-conception: the externality of law to politics.[4] This misconception, he claims, must be attributed to liberalism, to the 'liberal democratic compromise that is *levelling* democracy.'[5] In place of the liberal understanding, he places his own republican 'promise of the *dualist* constitution,'[6] the linchpin of his theoretical enterprise. The levelling accounts for the paradox; the dualist constitution *dissolves* it. By dissolving the paradox Ackerman steers his republican project clear of the impasses that have blocked both the liberal 'rights-foundationalist' and the 'monist democrat' positions in dealing with the paradox (see above).[7]

The liberal 'levelling' understanding of democracy fails to distinguish two quite distinct levels of political conduct, says Ackerman. 'The leveller treats all acts of political participation as if they were accompanied by the same degree of civic seriousness.'[8] Ordinary or normal politics consists in advancing private ends. But the liberal leveller's 'impoverished constitutional vocabulary' does not give form to those 'constitutional moments' in a people's history when 'the people sacrifice their private interests to pursue the common good in transient and informal political association.'[9] It is

---

[2] Ackerman, 1984, 1013

[3] ibid.

[4] 'If Ackerman is right,' comments Simon, 'then the most contentious issues of modern constitutional theory have been fought out on a map that misses the most significant features of our political landscape.' (1992, 501)

[5] Ackerman, 1984, 1038, my emph.

[6] ibid., 1039

[7] I find it far from obvious that Ackerman's position is incompatible with Ely's treatment of the paradox. But Ackerman insists that Ely's theory cloaks rather than dispenses with the problem (Ackerman 1985, pp737ff). I think that Ackerman would find it difficult to sustain this critique that Ely simply passes over judicial value judgements, in view of the position he too reseves for the Court in times of 'ordinary politics'.

[8] Ackerman, 1984, 1038

[9] ibid., 1020

during such moments that the true voice of 'The People' is heard. It is in such moments that citizens act in their capacity as sovereign populace. As Paul Kahn puts it concisely,

'"Levelling" represents a political world-view that simultaneously drains the Constitution of any special, public meaning, undermines the conditions of the democratic legitimacy of a substantive judicial review and reduces citizens to private individuals using politics for the pursuit of purely personal ends.'[10]

What is a constitutional moment?[11] According to Ackerman's definition, it is an occasion upon which The People exercise deliberative, 'considered judgements regarding the rights of citizens and the permanent interests of the community.'[12] The appeal to the common good 'ratified by a mobilized mass of American citizens expressing their assent through extraordinary institutional forms'[13] defines Ackerman's republican vision. He is prepared to concede that these moments of exceptional politics occur rarely and 'should become pre-eminent only under well-defined historical situations. When these conditions do not apply, the claim of the legally established authorities to speak in the name of the people must be conceded by all thoughtful citizens.'[14] Normal politics must be tolerated in the name of individual liberty; it is however 'democratically inferior to the intermittent and irregular

---

[10] Ackerman, 1989, 19

[11] And how do we identify an instance of popular mobilisation as a constitutional moment? In (1991) Ackerman designates criteria for this task in a detailed and precise account of a set of formal stages that the 'moment' must pass through to qualify as a constitutional one. Very briefly these involve (i) that one branch of government alleges a mandate to transformative policy (ii) opposition to this by another branch of government leading to stalemate (iii) a critical election which addresses the choice to a deliberating citizenry and (iv) acquiesence to the will of The People by the initially reactionary branch, followed by the sanctioning of the new state of affairs by the Supreme Court (Ackerman, 1991, ps 48ff, 266ff, 272ff). In those few constitutional moments that Ackerman has identified and discussed (the Founding - Philadelphia Convention, in (1991), and the Reconstruction and New Deal in the two volumes to follow (1991)) he claims the formal criteria were fulfilled and furthermore there was clear proposal, long deliberation and super-majoritarian consent. There have been, however, he acknowledges, also 'lesser' constitutional moments such as the Civil Rights movement and the 'Reagan revolution' (1991, 108ff, 51) that did not fulfil all the conditions. For a well-argued charge of inconsistency at this point, see Klarman (1992, pp769-70). If Ackerman abandons his constraining formal criteria and characterises as 'near-miss' constitutional (moments), episodes that scarcely fulfil those criteria, how will he insulate his 'moments' from every case of popular mobilisation? 'If the 60s Civil Rights movement why not the 20s Ku Klux Klan crusade?' Especially since Ackerman obviously inserts no evaluative threshold or premise (and explicitly- 1991, 308, does not include 'political correctness') in his criteria of a constitutional moment.

[12] Ackerman, 1991, pp240, 272-4

[13] Ackerman, 1984, 1042

[14] ibid., 1020

politics of public virtue associated with moments of constitutional creation.'[15] During these moments of profound rupture, citizens re-claim their delegated sovereignty through direct popular action.[16]

According to Ackerman's account of this dualism, constitutional regimes designate two levels of politics: a level of representational politics, and a level of politics of direct participation. During the latter the political community re-emerges to re-define itself. As Simon writes, 'Ackerman sees our history as the periodic efforts of our people to break through the structures created in one democratic process into another democratic process.'[17] What this means more precisely is the following: because the constitutional provisions do not license these moments of creativity,[18] the amendment that the constitutional moment carries is also not, legally speaking, democratically licensed. Yet constitutional moments are democratic in a more fundamental sense as exercises of political sovereignty. These moments are moments of 'constitutional creativity'[19] and re-birth of democracy[20] in the sense that the populace as sovereign periodically instigates transformations of such depth that they can be credibly claimed to have re-situated the meaning of freedom and democracy.

It is within this 'two-track democracy' that Ackerman places the important function of the *Supreme Court*. The role of the Constitutional Court is to safeguard prior moments of constitutional politics. This means that during the long periods of normal politics, the Court remains the sole bearer of that constitutional momentum that marked past achievements of

---

[15] ibid., 1022

[16] Even in Ackerman's major examples of constitutional moments, there is always a question of precisely what level of national participation is necessary to the occurence of a constitutional moment. Historically it has been overwhelmingly the case that Ackerman's constitutional moments have been initiated and pursued by active minorities of the population who have come up against and managed to curb the 'normal-political' attitude of large indifferent majorities. These majorities were conducting business as usual, in a non-constitutional, non-identity-generating mode. If this is the case, do we identify the politics of the minority as 'constitutional' on a qualitative basis, or do we compromise the notion by projecting it on the indifferent majorities? If we opt for the latter - without mobilisation and the rest - the argument for the two degree democracy is hardly sustainable; if we opt for the former and accept that minorities can conduct constitutional politics then what happens to the question of identity in community? If, that is, we abandon the criterion of We The People - as a whole - mobilising around community issues, how will the identity-generating involvement of the few spill over to furnish the sense of identity of the Nation/citizenry as such? (I run nationality and citizenship together intentionally, because Ackerman draws no significant distinction between We The People (the legal capacity) and We Americans (nationality).)

[17] Simon, 1992, 512

[18] I am referring here the the constitutional provisions that designate the conditions and the procedure of Amendment of a Constitution.

[19] Ackerman, 1991, pp314ff

[20] ibid., 1991, pp295-6

heightened politics. To fulfil its role it must interfere in interest-geared politics (through judicial review) and remind the factions of the meaning of the Constitution, that is, of the meaning that 'the people' as community ascribed to their acts.

'[The Court] signals to the mass of private citizens in the U S that something special is happening in the halls of power; that their would-be representatives are attempting to legislate in ways that few political movements in American history have done with credibility'[21]

What is it that defines this 'highest kind of politics' and how does it substantiate the claim for individual self-realisation through politics? As Kahn writes:

'[t]he difference between these two forms of politics is the difference between a politics founded on a community of discourse and a politics of private individuals. Republicanism reconceptualizes the character of public order as a domain in which individuals construct their identity through the dialogical creation of a community.'[22]

It is indeed in informal association, 'in sustained debate and struggle, [that Americans] hammer out new principles to guide public life,' and it is in this 'transient' form that that the citizen crosses the threshold from private to public life.'[23]

'What does the Constitution constitute?' asks Ackerman towards the end of the Storrs lectures. The link he attempts is with the constitution of self-identity. Constitutionalism now extends into the politics of identity. This is a crucial link with the deep premise of republicanism. Ackerman begins with the 'private citizen' with the emphasis on the 'private'. This citizen is immersed in the private spheres of family, profession, friendship and only views politics as a 'sideline'. There is however a point at which this citizen, without reverting to a totally public persona, can shift the emphasis and enter the public sphere in a committed, private-transcending way.[24]

---

[21] Ackerman, 1984, 1050

[22] Kahn, 1989, 20

[23] Ackerman, 1984, 1039, 1032-3

[24] Ackerman's debt to the earlier constitutional theorist Alexander Meiklejohn is evident here. The transcendance of the private persona is reminiscent of Meiklejohn's urgent appeal to abandon the excessive individualism of American life in favour of a higher public rationality. If people stopped thinking like 'farmers, trade-unionists, employers, etc, and become more of citizens devoted to the common welfare,' wrote Meiklejohn (1960, 74) the plan of self-government enshrined in the Constituion would be accomplished.

'While established Constitutional Law did not always resolve America's deepest crises, *it has always provided us with the language and the process within which our political identities could be confronted, debated and defined-* both during the periods of normal politics and on those occasion when Americans found themselves called, once again, to undertake a serious effort to redefine and reaffirm their sense of national purpose.'[25]

The effort is undertaken 'in sustained debate and struggle' through 'suspending self-interest' (that motivates lower-track politics)[26] and instead 'expressing deliberative judgements upon the rights of citizens and the permanent interests of the community.' Ackerman's two-track model accounts for that possibility and views the higher rank of politics as instituting a specific form of interaction, a specific forum of community.

SUNSTEIN AND MICHELMAN: 'EMPATHY' IN 'LAW'S REPUBLIC'

Since Ackerman's influential beginnings, new voices have enriched the tradition of civic republicanism. In the context of American constitutional theory, the most important theorists to engage in the debate and renew the tradition have been Cass Sunstein and Frank Michelman. Like Ackerman, these writers suggest constitutional law as the forum that will elevate politics from a bargaining process to a process of self-government and self-determination. But unlike Ackerman, whose republicanism invites and relies on popular mobilisation, Michelman and Sunstein propose elitist institutional solutions. It is because of this premise they share that I discuss them together, while ensuring that the distinctive features of each theory come across as such.

---

[25] Ackerman, 1984, 1072

[26] For Ackerman (and the republicans in general) it is vital to distinguish politics that are motivated by self-interest and politics of suspended self-interest, or the individual's and community's permanent interests. But many have argued that these dichotomies are descriptively implausible and normatively suspect. Pope (1990, 347-51) brings the example of the black workers' boycott in *NAACP v Clairborne Hardware* Co (393 So.2d 1290, 1295-97 (Miss. 1980), reversed 458 U.S. 886 (1982)). The case concerned the boycott of white merchants after a petition by of a Mississippi local union had petitioned the county government, urging them to provide equal treatment for blacks, and were rejected.) These demands - later to be viewed as political and fundamental - were initially seen as narrow, self-interested and factional.

Deliberation, Distance and Empathy

Michelman begins his most important contribution to civic republicanism - *Law's Republic* - with a footnoted definition of political freedom. Political freedom, he says, means the 'achievement of personal freedom through the institutionalized social power that regulates social conflicts.'[27] In the mode of a manifesto that characterises much of the argument in this work, Michelman declares law the sufficient and necessary condition of freedom. To assume otherwise is to fall into the classic liberal mistake of thinking negative freedom as co-extensive with freedom. Michelman declares the value of positive freedom as the appropriately political one.[28] He defines politics as the community's dialogical engagement over the terms of common life, and with the Constitution hosting the dialogue, he reserves the term 'citizenship' for 'freedom as activity'.[29] This is an argument that has many stages and we will need to discuss them in some detail.

Neither Michelman, nor Sunstein contribute much that is novel to republicanism's critique of pluralism. Michelman attributes to the (liberal) pluralist the misconception of assuming that negative freedom[30] is exhaustive of freedom as such and of treating the protection of this negative freedom as the organising principle of politics. Michelman's 'pluralist' is Ackerman's 'leveller', and the latter's distinction between 'constitutional' and 'normal' politics is replaced by Michelman by a similar one, that between 'republican' and 'pluralist' politics. The 'pluralist' view is set up as presupposing primary interests of individuals as pre-political, and politics as a secondary, instrumental medium for protecting or advancing those 'exogenous' interests. Sunstein also argues against the view that politics is about the competition of 'private preferences' or 'naked interests'[31] in the political marketplace. Republican politics calls for a commitment to deliberation, not bargaining. Unlike Ackerman, however, Sunstein refrains from renouncing liberalism; in fact, Sunstein's stance towards liberalism remains a matter of heated debate.[32]

---

[27] Michelman, 1988, n.2

[28] An argument similar to Crick's (1971)

[29] 'Citizenship stands for freedom as activity: the constant re-determination by the people for themselves of the terms on which they live together.' (Michelman, 1988, 1518)

[30] For the origin of the distinction positive/negative freedom, see Berlin (1969)

[31] Sunstein, 1986

[32] Sunstein argues against the liberal/rebublican dichotomy, in favour of his own 'liberal republicanism.' (1988, 1566-71) Because the republican revival, he claims, draws on a tradition that is both liberal and republican. 'In their emphasis on the possibility of forming public policy through deliberation, on political equality, on citizenship, ... republicanism and liberalism are at one.' (1988, 1567-8) And while the 'most collectivist forms' of republicanism contradict 'the most atomistic versions of liberalism ... [r]epublican thought, understood in a

The pluralists, for Michelman, are guilty of divorcing law from politics under the false assumption that 'law must, once enacted, immediately abscond from politics to higher ground. It must become an autonomous force against politics, a force elaborated through its own non-political modes of reason by its own non-political judicial organ.'[33] Sunstein, too, stresses that interest-group pluralism understands politics solely as the extension of market behaviour and principles into the public-political realm. Whereas interest-group pluralism treats politics as a mechanism of 'aggregating citizen preferences' and the constitution as the framework within which pre-political wants, needs and ideas could be negotiated, republicans 'treat politics as above all deliberative.'[34]

By departing thus from the 'pluralist' world-view Michelman and Sunstein can begin to counter-pose their own republican project that understands freedom as positive and thus as political. 'Another name for positive freedom is self-government,' says Michelman. 'Freedom can be both negative - the liberal freedom as absence of coercion and "positive"- action and self-direction according to reasons, but reasons that one gives to oneself.'[35] These reasons are not a-historical; they are drawn from common resource pools, from commonalities of meaning, where reasons become intelligible because they are informed by common narratives. The argument seeks its foundation on communitarian ground. 'Every person is thoroughly conditioned by a shared social context that helps constitute that person's identity ... each community is a community of individuals whose own identities are inseparable from their social involvements.'[36] The vision expressed is one of emphasising 'openness to "otherness" as a way toward recognition not only of the other but also of oneself.'[37]

---

certain way, is a prominent aspect of the liberal tradition.' (1988, 1569). Many have criticised Sunstein for conceding too much to liberalism. Sunstein explains he is 'too fearful of public power,' (1988, 1551) and 'not hostile to the protection of individual or group autonomy from state control.' (1988, 1569) Consequently he sets up criteria for when perspectives of 'losers' in the political process should have been taken into account. This he presents as a protection of the condition of the deliberative process, but for communitarians and radical republicans it smacks too much of inaliable rights and liberal 'loser' talk. As Sullivan says, '[a]ny criteria [about when perspectives of losers should be taken into account] will turn out to look suspiciously like rights emanating from "above" or "outside" politics - just what the republican deliberative norm was meant to avoid.' (1988)

[33] Michelman, 1988 1509. Note the inclusiveness of the categor 'pluralist' : depending on where the emphasis falls it applies to theorists as diverse as Hobbes, laissez-faire liberals and individualists of all kinds, libertarians, mainstream constitutional lawyers, fundamental rights theorists, etc.
[34] Sunstein, 1988, 1540, 1548
[35] Michelman, 1986, 25
[36] ibid., 32
[37] ibid., 33

Openness to otherness and the process of recognition require dialogue. Michelman and Sunstein share a concept of positive freedom grounded in dialogue; a dialogue that is both universal in its conditions and particular to the community. It is indeed politics understood as dialogue, the deliberative practice of a community, that make freedom and self-determination possible.

The situated nature of this dialogue - situated in time and in a community - lends a new (or maybe the only possible) reading to positive freedom. 'All pre-determinations of human essence are rejected,'[38] and with them all essentialist claims of 'natural', primary interests. The social construction of meaning precedes, contains and circumscribes the possibility itself of practical reason and thus the possibility of positive freedom as 'action and self-direction according to reasons.' The process of normative deliberation is one within which we 'recognize, reflect, define ... one another as we ourselves are reciprocally recognized, reflected, defined ...'[39] Positive freedom is possible only in situ and 'implies a social process of normative deliberation, based in commonality.'[40]

What the republicans need to ensure at this stage is that the dialogue will not degenerate into the pluralists' process of bargaining over self-interest. As in Ackerman, their republican dialogue needs to transcend ordinary bargaining and accommodate that extra-ordinary moment of transient association. Both Michelman and Sunstein need to insert criteria as to what counts as normative deliberation that can sustain republican politics - sustain 'the characteristically republican belief in deliberative democracy.'[41] They argue that 'political actors must justify their choices by appealing to a broader public good.'[42] Deliberative practice requires participants to reflect critically on their preferences and to alter those preferences if this is made necessary by the deliberative process that brings 'new information and different perspectives' to bear directly on one's choices.[43] 'Critical reflection' of this kind requires *distance*. While Michelman and Sunstein are at one in their commitment to critical deliberation (as they were in arguing against the pluralists), their precise prescriptions as to how this distance from one's own preferences is to be achieved vary.

Michelman calls his 'distance' principle 'practical reason' and undertakes to explain what it involves very much on Habermas's lines. Practical reason

---

[38] ibid., 31

[39] ibid., 33

[40] ibid., 31 To make his claim for the situated nature of meaning, practical reason and identity, Michelman draws on a vast variety of resourses. His references include Sandel, Taylor, Rorty, Pitkin, MacIntyre, Arendt, Cover and Habermas.

[41] Sunstein, 1988, 1563

[42] ibid.,1544

[43] ibid.

facilitates the 'recovery of practical knowledge, situated judgement, dialogue, and civic friendship.'[44] Practical reason, in the way Michelman positions it as the centrepiece of republican deliberation, alludes to Habermas's concept of *practical*, emancipatory reason, that involves self-reflection and an intersubjectivity of communication. Habermas distinguishes this form of reason from *technical* rationality that involves instrumentality, i.e. means-ends rationality.[45]

Michelman's debt to Habermas is not confined to the use of the distinction practical/technical reason. The notions of dialogue and consensus that underpin his republican project of deliberative politics, draw heavily on Habermas's account of communicative action. In particular it is from Habermas's ideal speech situation, that Michelman seems to draw his own criteria for 'normative interchange'.[46] Note the similarity here: Michelman's prescriptive criteria are that the interchange be (i) mutually intelligible, (ii) potentially critical and (iii) free from a priori privileged status; Habermas's that (i) a claim to intelligibility is precondition of all communication, (iii) 'only those are admitted [to the ideal speech situation] who have *equal* opportunity to participate,' [and Michelman's 'privileged status' would fall here under the category of impermissible 'external constraint' upon discourse,] and (ii) the ideal speech situation designates an 'equal opportunity ... to *problematise, justify or refute claims to truth.*'[47]

When it comes to suggesting criteria for filtering out self-interest from the deliberative process, Sunstein is more daring than Michelman. His argument is long and detailed here but it boils down to two major principles that will serve as safeguards of deliberation. The first is what he calls *'political empathy'*, a key concept of the republican political universe.[48] This 'embodies the requirement that political actors attempt to assume the position of those who disagree.' A second related requirement is that citizens during the deliberative process should set aside their own perspective and 'think from the point of view of everybody.'[49]

The prescriptive point in all this is that the individualistic perspective must be abandoned. Deliberation requires laws to be 'supported by argument

---

[44] Michelman, 1986, 25
[45] See generally Habermas, 1971, pp308ff
[46] Michelman, 1986, 32-33
[47] All references to Alexy, (1989, pp 108, 120, my emphases.) I am suggesting only that these similarities are indicative and nothing like a strict one-to-one mapping of criteria.
[48] Sunstein, 1988, Also Minow (1987), Winter (1991, 1002): 'Ultimately we must come to see it is our similar embodiment and shared social situatedness that jointly provide the common grounds upon which the work of empathy can - and must - be done.'
[49] Sunstein, 1988, 1569

and reason'[50] and private interest cannot be a sufficient basis for deliberation. Such private perspectives are cancelled out when one adopts the empathetic stance. But Sunstein ascribes to empathy an even more important task than that. It is not enough to agree to disagree; instead empathy is assumed to lead sooner or later to a convergence of opinion, a substantive consensus, and this convergence, Sunstein assumes, will only fail to be achieved if - and there will thus be political losers only if - the deliberative process itself, guided by empathy and the interchangeability of perspective, breaks down.

To summarise the argument up to this point: Civic republican dialogue under the requirements of 'distance' is about reaching a consensus on the question *of the common good*. The result of their dialogue is a conception of the common good, an agreement upon what is right for the community, in its specific circumstances of here and now. No-one is coerced into adopting this social vision for the future. In that the dialogue tends to nurture rather than to diminish *diversity*. The republicans are eager to stress that they do not intend to strait-jacket diversity with some 'old' solidaristic republican concept of the common good. Instead the republicans respect and celebrate diversity and invite all perspectives on questions of social value to engage in republican deliberation. Even so, there still remains open for the republicans the question of the apparent incompatibility of diversity and a good that is common.[51] How does the heterogeneity of perspective converge around common conclusions about the good? Moreover, the assumption that there will be a convergence of perspective in the end, let alone one guaranteeing a 'correct solution'[52] appears a statement of faith, an *a priori* in any case. I will contest these assumptions in my critique of republicanism. In the meantime let us reiterate the civic republican prescription for politics as this vision of a political dialogue, in pursuit of the common good, under conditions of distance from self-interest, that encourages diversity, is

---

[50] ibid., 1544

[51] The republican ideal of the pursuit of a *common good* is one of the most contentious aspects of the theory. Republicans argue that the articulation of a common good is compatible with the nurturance of social plurality (Michelman, 1988, 1533). But this claim to the best of both worlds has been condemned as implausible. Sullivan writes: '[R]epublican dialogue appears unworkable ... [Because members of different groups] conceive of the good differently depending on their different histories, experiences, needs, and attributes. Such fractures on perspective will mar agreement on an overarching common good.' (1989, 1718)

[52] Republicans claim that the deliberative process can settle 'normative disputes with sustantively right answers ...[or] uniquely correct outcomes' (Sunstein, 1988, 1541, 1555) This assertion has been often and seriously questioned (eg Powell (1989)) The criticisms, however, I think, fail to recognise the proximity of the republican argument to Habermas' (see thesis [3] below); where similarly, conditions for uncoerced dialogue are put forward as, optimally, conditions of *truth* of normative (as well as factual) statements.

historically specific, and in the very process of involving all in a discussion about all, substantiates community.

Institutional deliberative politics

So far the republican theories discussed offer little other than a version of mainstream communitarian theory that has integrated certain insights from discourse theory. At the threshold of institutionalisation the republicans are called upon to make their substantive contribution. So far they have talked about the acquisition of self-identity through social involvement; they have designated dialogue - or deliberative practice - in the community as the appropriate social involvement, an involvement that defines politics. Their contribution must be *to carry these insights onto legal institutional ground* and to explain how their political-theoretical claims can be translated into constitutional theory. Sunstein acknowledges this task when he undertakes, on behalf of republicanism, 'to design political institutions that promote discussion and debate among the citizenry.'[53] The challenge that the republicans need to meet is to carry the deliberative practice they profess across the institutional threshold without compromising it in the process.

As in the case of Habermas, they declare unanimously that constitutional law provides this possibility. Citizenship, the institutional category, is to be understood, say the republicans, in the context of deliberative commonality as 'direct, equal participation in the determination of common affairs.' According to the civic republican 'view of the human condition, self-cognition and ensuing self-legislation must be socially situated; norms must be formed through public dialogue and expressed as public law.'[54] Citizenship is about exposure to the national debate, self-identification, self-reflection, and self-revision thereof. Self-government and community fuse in the constitutive constitutional moment, to the extent that 'positive liberty is hardly conceivable without citizenship.'[55] In all, republicanism professes political emancipation through law; and in this lies *the crux of the containment thesis*.

To substantiate these claims, Michelman and Sunstein, like Ackerman before them, address the 'counter-majoritarian' paradox. It is the 'pluralist' misapprehension, they claim, that is accountable for the paradox that has plagued constitutional theory. They claim that the misapprehension stems from arbitrarily allocating law and politics to different fields. It consists in seeking a transcendental justification for law in justice, reason, nature,

---

[53] Sunstein, 1988, 1549
[54] Michelman, 1986, 27
[55] Michelman, 1988, 1503

morality, good sense, e.t.c., rather than viewing it as an intrinsic feature of self-government, the medium through which communities express, argue and revise their normative commitments. It is in this context that the paradox of constitutionalism - 'the problematical relationship between self-rule and law-rule'[56]- is answered. In the constitution Michelman and Sunstein discover the resources that enable the community's ongoing revision and the paradox is collapsed as law-rule becomes self-rule and the constitution becomes 'both law and ours.'

In their understanding of the counter-majoritarian difficulty and the collapse of law-rule into self-rule the republicans are very much at one. Both Michelman and Sunstein show ultimate confidence in the law as expression and 'home' of the community's politics. But while they agree on the possibility and logic of this convergence, at the threshold of institutionalisation - of translating the communal into institutional dialogue - they disagree about where, in constitutional politics, to locate the dialogue. Each of them puts forward a different view as to what legal forum is the most conducive to the republican project. I will explore both their suggestions in turn, with greater emphasis on Michelman's whose theory here will necessitate a first brief detour into Dworkin's legal theory.

Sunstein's institutional suggestion

The institutional solution that Sunstein offers is to locate deliberative politics in the legislative body - but a legislature made up of virtuous legislators. Legislative decisions, in Sunstein's scheme, are made following principled dialogue and deliberation. Legislative deliberation is taken up along republican lines. The cue that Sunstein takes from the federalists of early American history is that republicanism requires that 'representatives ... have the time and temperament to engage in a form of collective reasoning ... The representatives of the people would be free to engage in the process of discussion and debate from which the common good would emerge.'[57] Sunstein treats the motivations of legislators as the critical issue underpinning the possibility of republican politics. Consequently he argues that the constitution provides a number of filters ('institutional arrangements and doctrinal shifts') to inhibit what Sunstein terms 'naked preferences' from entering the process of collective reasoning.

Sunstein offers a number of institutional arrangements that I will only give a summary account of. In his earlier work which deals with the question

---
[56] Michelman, 1988, 1500
[57] Sunstein, 1985, 140

of 'naked preferences', he offers institutional safeguards for representatives' insulation and release from their constituents' and lobbyists' pressure, since unreflective representation of popular will would, according to Sunstein, allow self-interest to erode the republican dialogue in Congress. What underlies Sunstein's position is a willingness to distance the representatives from the represented, something which would increase, Sunstein believes, the representatives' predisposition toward public-regarding deliberation.[58] Another suggestion he puts forward is the endorsement of proportional representation to allow greater diversity in parliaments.[59] Sunstein's suggestions are numerous and extend to the level of detailed legal specification: from campaign finance regulation to provisions about devolution and local autonomy. One of his most important suggestions is relevant to the role he envisages for the Supreme Court. He suggests that judicial review of legislation should be strengthened. This would provide the incentive for legislators to abstain from the pursuit of 'naked interests' and engage in 'principled' deliberation. Judicial review is there to remind the legislature of its commitment to civic virtue. In this context the role of the Court is instrumental. It is not, as it will be in Michelman, the bearer of republican politics; its role is, instead to police republican politics within the legislature. Because, in the end,

'[i]n American government and in all well-functioning constitutional democracies, the real forum of high principle is politics, not the judiciary - and the most fundamental democratic principles are developed democratically, not in courtrooms.'[60]

---

[58] On a very experimental note, it would be interesting to compare Sunstein's with Hayek's criteria on how distanced or dis-interested legislative deliberation could be achieved (Hayek, 1979). Hayek's basic scheme is to distinguish governing from law-making; the first is delegated to the competition of political parties, 'government assemblies', which are 'quasi-commercial corporations competing for citizens,' (1979, pp132-3) a situation similar to the one Sunstein deplores in (1986). The second task, law-making, is entrusted to the 'legislative assembly', an assembly that Hayek prescribes be 'composed of independent public figures, mature individuals, free from considerations of personal or group interest.' (1979, 116) His 'nomothetae' operate in a climate that is very different from interest-group politics, are assured tenure and do not depend on party support. The similarity is only apparent of course and the differences of motivation and ideological background between Sunstein and Hayek are deep. Despite this, would it worry Sunstein that Hayek puts forward his "detachment" proposal under the label of 'dethroning politics'? For an excellent critical retelling of Hayek's suggestions see Bellamy (n.d.).
[59] Sunstein, 1988, 1588ff
[60] Sunstein, 1996, 7

Michelman's institutional suggestion

Michelman's suggestion of an institutional outlet for deliberation is very different from Sunstein's, and while it shares in the latter's elitism, it in fact owes much of its inspiration to Ackerman's theory. Yet even from Ackerman Michelman effects a double departure on two substantive points. While acknowledging Ackerman's as the 'most deeply popularist and genuinely republican [project]... now going'[61] (i) he abandons the criterion of popular mobilisation because 'actual episodes of such constitutional politics - of republican popular mobilization - have been and must probably forever be rare'[62] and (ii) he is not happy with the way Ackerman understands the role of the Court. In what concerns the latter, he criticises Ackerman for making judicial alteration of constitutional law dependant on judicial acknowledgement of prior popular ('constitutional') mobilisation. Without the intervening event of popular upheaval, a Court that claims to be truly republican has no legitimate reason to depart from prior constitutional understandings. In this Michelman sees a lurking danger of authoritarian Constitutional jurisprudence, an approach he deplores in *Bowers*.[63]

'In Ackerman's theory, the judiciary is cast as the agent of our constitutional past ... [which implies] that it cannot also be a spontaneous agent of our future ... the judiciary's role in the process of constitutional change can only be benedictory, never prophetic.'[64]

Michelman does not want the potential of the Court depleted; he attempts to disengage judicial doctrine from the community's actual transformative politics. The Court should not be confined to prior jurisgenerative episodes, as it is in Ackerman, but should be able to take upon itself the instigation of a constitutional moment. The Court becomes, in Michelman's theory, the very bearer of constitutional moments of republican politics; it becomes the vessel of the deliberative process, of the community's dialogue. 'The role we attribute to the Supreme Court,' he says, 'is that of representing to us the possibility of practical reason.'[65] This surprising claim that substitutes participation for representation while maintaining the republican ideal of political engagement draws for support on Dworkin's legal theory. It allows Michelman to build a theory of virtual transformative politics, and to make

---

[61] Michelman, 1988, 1520
[62] ibid., 1522
[63] 478 US 186 (1986). The US Supreme Court upheld the State of Georgia's ban on homosexual sodomy between consenting adults in private.
[64] Michelman, 1988, p1521
[65] Michelman, 1986, 24

the Judge the narrator on behalf of the community. How, precisely, does Michelman do it? How does he turn 'Law's Empire' into 'Law's Republic'?

In concluding his 'Traces of Self-Government' (1986), Michelman gives us a first indication:

'Dworkin's narrative-constructive model of legal interpretation is part of an account of political self-government through which socially situated individuals realize moral freedom or personal integrity.'[66]

Michelman undertakes to defend Dworkin's theory of Integrity by focusing on a question he too most urgently needs to answer. Dworkin maintains that '"integrity" asks the good citizen to interpret the common scheme of justice to which they [he and the judge] are both committed.'[67] But if the question is addressed to the citizen, why is the judge doing the answering? It seems a vindication of the moral freedom of judges rather than of citizens.

It is not hard to see why Michelman asks this specific question. He is accountable for a similar displacement of communal/political self-government from the citizen to the Court. Dworkin projects a theory of adjudication onto the citizenry and claims for it, as we will see, that it 'fuses citizens' moral and political lives.'[68] Michelman develops a theory of political self-government and entrusts it to the Court. These arguments exhibit an obvious symmetry. Both claim that the displacement (from citizen to judge and vice versa) is a legitimate one.

In the following section on Dworkin, we will discuss how Dworkin establishes that his theory of integrity as guiding ideal for legal reasoning is of constitutive value for the community itself. Michelman maintains that the answer to the puzzle why it has value for the community must finally lie 'in virtual representation.' 'Integrity's value to the community is representational: the judge represents integrity - self government - to the community, not of it.'[69]

Michelman endorses 'virtual representation' but he qualifies it first. What is most notably wrong with Dworkin's ideal judge, Hercules, is that he 'is a loner ... His narrative constructions are monologues ... He has no encounters ... He meets no otherness ... What is lacking is dialogue.'[70] But the US Supreme Court has nine members and can provide the possibility of dialogue. Dworkin has disregarded this plurality. 'We ought to consider

---

[66] ibid., 69
[67] Dworkin, 1986, 189
[68] ibid.
[69] Michelman, 1986, 76
[70] ibid.

what this plurality is "for".' It is here that virtual representation resides. As Dworkin 'envisions' him, 'the judge represents by his own self-government our missing self-government, by his own practical reason our missing dialogue ... Could that be what we value?' As we reach the end of the argument we are assured that 'there is a message here for the politics of law;' the dialectic stands complete: 'dialogue in support of judicial practical reason, as an aspect of judicial self-government, in the interest of our freedom.'[71]

Michelman recruits Dworkin's help in order to establish these interconnections that only together uphold the republican thesis. He recruits Dworkin's help particularly to justify his recourse to the Court as the political institution capable of carrying republican engagement. However crucially important all this is for the republican containment thesis, one is tempted to stop here and query the meaning of Michelman's qualification 'that carries plurality and dialogue into the Supreme Court.' Surely this qualification of the Court as dialogic blurs rather that clarifies the picture. If the communitarians make a case for dialogue it is because they want to stress that the individuals' embeddedness in community comes about through social involvement; and the dialogue is a means of involvement. But a dialogue between Appelate Court Judges is as external to community and self-identity as Judges' monologues are. We are not after all interested in the involvement or embeddedness of the judges in their setting. What is decisive for the argument is popular/communal participation in the dialogue, not the mere existence of a dialogue. Without participation, Michelman has not escaped the externality of that dialogue and the consequent need to justify the legitimacy of the authority of the Court's decision. *No communitarian correction can redeem that externality.* Only direct participation in the deliberative process would make the outcome - the decision - self-legitimating.[72]

---

[71] ibid., 77

[72] Let us ask with Michelman what the dialogue is 'for' and see how Drucilla Cornell, and Seyla Benhabib, two of Michelman's favourite writers, answer the question (Respectively in 1988, at 1220-24 and 1985, at 348) Cornell explains personal identity and freedom via law as grounded in interpersonal 'dialogic reciprocity'. Reciprocity is 'for' identity then, presumably not the judge's. Benhabib's recourse to dialogue is in order to reveal and substantiate plurality, where by plurality she means 'that our embodied identity and the narrative history that constitutes our selfhood ... is only revealed in community of interaction with others.' This 'revelation' addresses and concerns ('is for') the individual in community, not the judge. I do not want to labour the point further except to say that dialogue only has the identity-generating effect if it reveals to the participating members the narrative they share; the dialogue must be located in the community that is providing the narrative, not the community that is providing the official interpretation. In Michelman's later writings, the externality of the judicial dialogue is removed through the notion that *our* dialogue is 'of course' conveyed to *their* dialogue (see below). This argument creates new absurdities but evades the one above. In any

I will pick up this point again later, in the '10th thesis against republicanism.' For now let us return to the exposition of Michelman central thesis: how is the judicial office adequate an institutional vessel to carry the full weight of the republican project? Michelman reverses the terms of the traditional (counter-majoritarian) dilemma by claiming that the judge is no longer there to hinder political will but to assist in maintaining what he calls 'the jurisgenerative' political engagement. The judicial role consists in initially guarding the conditions for an uncoerced dialogic process.[73] But more importantly: judicial review is the corollary of the deliberative nature of republicanism. It no longer makes sense to succumb to the 'Thayerite objection,' the fear that judicial review may 'dwarf the political capacity of the people and to deaden its sense of political responsibility.' Dworkin allows Michelman to justify turning jurisgenerative popular politics into jurisgenerative judicial politics. He can then claim jurisgenerative politics to be a permanent feature of our political society, a permanent form our political engagement assumes in a way that 'spreads Ackerman's rare and far between constitutional moments over continuous political time.'[74] The second reason for locating republican politics in the judiciary is precautionary; '[t]he Court helps protect the Republican State - that is, the citizens politically engaged - from lapsing into a politics of self-denial. It challenges the people's self-enclosing tendency to assume their own moral completion as they are now and thus to deny to themselves the plurality on which their capacity for transformative self-renewal depends.'[75]

The Critique of Elitism and the Retreat from the Institutional Dialogue

Sunstein's and Michelman's projects attracted a critique that Ackerman's did not. They have both been criticised for elitism, because they both delegate the deliberative practice underpinning republicanism to elite institutions. The problem arises because both Sunstein and Michelman remove republican politics from the participants themselves. In the words of one commentator,

---

case, Dworkin steers clear of all this. One can pass over Michelman's criticisms here, because Dworkin defines clearly what his presuppositions for 'best' interpretations are, and it being 'dialogical' plays no part in it being 'best'.

[73] As Paul Craig has explained, the role that Michelman reserves for the court in the republican dialogue is first of all 'to establish the conditions for the process of dialogue. This process can only operate where certain prescriptive social and procedural conditions exist which serve to prevent any such dialogue from being coercive and a violation of one's identity.' (1990, 353)

[74] Michelman, 1988, 1525

[75] ibid., 1533

'[Michelman] reflects a retreat from the collective self-direction that has been the hallmark of republican thought; [Sunstein] a circuitous way of achieving it.'[76] What motivates republicanism is the question of how to re-animate and maintain participatory politics. The elitist solution may be an interesting answer to the 'institutional' question but the institutional question was intended as instrumental to the vision of participatory politics. The institutional solution thus appears to abandon what it was meant as a solution to. Because the debate among the two theorists re-enacts a debate between elites both claiming the republican mantle in the name of, but in the absence of, participation

Can the republican vision survive this distrust of grassroot participation? Michelman distrusts popular mobilisation enough to be willing to turn actual self-government into virtual self-government. Sunstein's willingness to distance representatives from represented is also suspect in a way that brings out a paradox. Because if the distancing stems from a distrust in the public then this republican distrust can be read as compromising participatory democracy itself. If civic virtue is to guide political debate why is the public assumed not to possess it?

There are several arguments along these lines, some convincing, but one, I think, decisive. The elitist solutions erode a crucial connection in the republican thesis. What underpins the thesis and holds it together is the identity-generating effect of the individual's involvement in the communal, political dialogue. Republicanism relies on dialogical engagement, in which, individual and community, speaker and discourse, come about simultaneously. It is in participation that the individual's political identity as member of a commonality is moulded, and it is this connection that makes the republican argument self-validating too. Elitist solutions sever the participatory element, the necessary social involvement. Without it, the republicans have lost their communitarian backing and find themselves in the very odd position of having put forward the strong position about the internal connection of law and community and yet falling foul of the much weaker and familiar objection which asks why should a process that is at a distance from the citizen be able to claim legitimate authority over the citizen.

The republicans see this but their response appears to hover uneasily between institutional solutions and populist, participatory ones in a way that cancels them both out. This is remarkable and intriguing; they appear to have moved beyond the state-centred republicanism they had so forcefully advocated, to one whose contours embraces 'social life at large.'[77] The new republicans now seek traces of republican self-government in local

---

[76] Brest (1988)
[77] Michelman, 1988, 1531

communities, unions, religious congregations and other intermediate groups[78] to the extent that, eventually, social controversy as such becomes synonymous to republican debate. So is the republicans' latest suggestion for dealing with the legal-institutional threshold to do away with it altogether?

Sunstein is quite explicit about it: '[c]itizenship,' he says, 'understood in republican fashion, does not occur solely through official organs.' Additionally, private associations can 'serve as official outlets' for 'deliberation,' 'community' and 'civic virtue'. Sunstein puts forward the appealing suggestion to 'multiply the points of access to government' and to 'generate institutions that will produce deliberation among those differently situated.'[79]

Michelman's work takes a similar sharp turn as he opts for a 'non-state notion of republican citizenship.' He includes 'voluntary organisations', 'clubs' and 'street-life' as fora of republican debate. Citizenship now becomes synonymous to 'dialogic engagement' and spreads 'to all arenas of potentially transformative dialogue.' He is worried that 'the formal channels of electoral and legislative politics ... cannot possibly provide much direct experience of such engagement.' Michelman is no longer advancing a theory of constitutional law then, or is he? He assures his reader that he is, since 'understandings that are contested and shaped in the daily encounters and transactions of civil society at large are *of course* conveyed to our representative arenas.'[80]

I will submit the republican position to critique in the chapters to follow, so I will confine myself here to a few first comments regarding this retreat from the legal institutional dialogue.[81] I want to argue against the retreat because I think it makes the republican argument self-defeating. And I intend to level a critique against a theory seen in its best light, not one that has cancelled *itself* out.

The innovative suggestion that the republicans professed to supply was about how 'our' dialogue could become 'legal' dialogue and still appear as ours and not external, securing autonomy and not heteronomy. The republicans, that is, professed to carry the deliberative practice onto institutional ground and establish that the legal/constitutional forum could contain it. Through the 'elitist' solution the republicans lost sight of the

---

[78] ibid. Also Sunstein, 1988, 1578

[79] Sunstein, 1988, 1573, 1585-89. For similar suggestions see Sandel, 1988, 20

[80] Michelman, 1988, 1531, my emph.

[81] Even Kahn, one of the most perceptive critics of republicanism, limits his criticism to Michelman's earlier work, while acknowledging that that more recently Michelman has 'moved away from the Court-centred perspective on the discursive community ... to argue for a non-state centred notion of republican citizenship.' (1989, p28, fn120)

potential participants in the deliberation. In attempting to restore that through the participatory/ 'social-life-at-large' type argument, they lose sight of institutionalisation, the specific nature and limitations of the institutional form. That prevents the interchangeability of communal and legal discourse as put forward by Michelman. In Michelman's argument the legal discourse is assimilated into people's ongoing normative speaking, like a radical version of Ehlrich's 'living law'. Our dialogue, he says, is always-already - 'of course' - the law. By collapsing law into the 'people's on-going normative contention,' and making law synonymous to dialogue in spontaneous contexts and unofficial fora, the republicans have comfortably evaded the institutional question; Michelman has buried it by presupposing it in that 'of course.' [82]

I believe that this latest retreat from the previous elitist solutions lets the project down, because *republicanism depends on the articulation of the deliberative with the institutional.* The latest retreat is an evasion, not an argument, and I will thus ignore it to the extent that it does not show republicanism in its best light. Republicanism is a theory about how law can contain politics and thus needs to be true to both the legal/institutional and the deliberative/political. There are ways of reconciling this tension, maybe, as opposed to defining it out, and republicanism needs to be judged on the merits of its attempt to do just that. That is why I will take the elitist solutions - the suggestions about containment - as the true republican solutions and now look at how, particularly in Michelman's case, republicanism finds its most precious ally in Ronald Dworkin.

---

[82] Citizenship only makes sense when it is conceived as our imput into the official processes, even simply as designating that relationship of individual to the state. Any other use of the term that removes its intimacy with the law shifts the coordinates unrecognisably. Are we meant to agree with Abrams' comments on Michelman, that 'acts or judgements that emerge from this [informal] process of recollection are regarded as law, regardless of the formal source from which they emanate.'[?] (1987, p1593) Or are we simply to concede that our informal dialogue crosses the line into law's expert, exclusive and official discourse without any loss of meaning, without compromise?

CHAPTER FIVE

DWORKIN AND THE LAW AS FORUM OF PRINCIPLE

'We live in and by the law. It makes us what we are. We are subjects of law's empire, liegemen to its methods and ideals, bound in spirit while we debate what we must therefore do ...
[Law] is a fraternal attitude, an expression of how we are united in community ... That is anyway what the law is for us: for the people we want to be and the community we aim to have.'
(Dworkin)

To classify Dworkin as a republican flies in the face of much conventional labelling, notably the division that wants interpretivists opposing republicans.[1] I will say nothing about the division because I believe it misleading, but will treat Dworkin as both interpretivist and republican because, it is my claim, his major work *Law's Empire* relies on law's interpretative nature to provide a powerful statement of the containment thesis. This work not only sets community at the heart of a theory of law, but also uses law as a lever for politics and the self-determination of community. I will take Dworkin up on his suggestions; the interpretative one, that the nature of law can only be understood in the practice of a community; and the republican one, about how the community substantiates itself through arguing legal questions in the interpretative way, and how this thorough involvement in legal argument allows communal self-government through law.

Initially I will outline Dworkin's interpretative thesis - the relevance of community to the practice of interpretation - and his prescription for 'integrity' as the guiding ideal behind the interpretative undertaking. This, I will argue is the point at which the interpretative thesis meets the republican thesis around a commitment to containment. As a consequence of this meeting, I will argue in the next section, the interpretative thesis isn't interpretative enough. The analysis of *Law's Empire* in this first part of the book is merely an exposition of Dworkin's version of the containment thesis, and I will reserve the critique, as I do for the republicans, for Part II. Provisionally only, what motivates this defence of the 'interpretative thesis' against Dworkin himself is the concern that Dworkin's imperialist theory of law undermines the interpretative, reflexive, ultimately political nature of community.

---

[1] Kahn, 1989, 43 and Feldman, 1992, passim.

The Interpretive Thesis

Interpretation of a practice, says Dworkin, such as that of law, is only possible in the community in which it occurs. Contrary to what theorists arguing 'semantically' assume there is no object - law - that is identifiable outside what the community holds as its practice of law. This shift he suggests from the 'semantic' plain-fact view to the interpretative view brings community to bear directly on the very possibility of a practice being meaningful. The meaning of the law, as is the case with every practice and concept, inheres in usage and is therefore can only be retrieved from within a shared context, a shared form of life.

With the 'interpretative' move to context, Dworkin shifts the understanding of the nature of law from text to practice, from settled fact to ongoing revision. Law is now an interpretative concept, its nature that of a practice situated in community and understood through interpretation. In every sense community makes law possible.

This last point cannot be stressed enough. Community underlies Dworkin's theory of law in more than one way. To begin with, Dworkin places himself in the hermeneutical tradition in claiming that an understanding of a social practice requires turning to the meaning it has for participants.[2] Interpretation of law is based on practice, requiring even from the social scientist to take up the participant's viewpoint[3] even if this participation is only 'virtual'.[4] The internal/participant's point of view is the central methodological assumption. Firstly, in order simply to understand the meaning of law one must participate in the community and in this sense the internal point of view becomes constitutive of legal practice itself.[5]

---

[2] There is an ambivalence in LE about where 'the point of a practice' is to be sought. Should we assume with Postema (1987) that the point of a practice exists as the shared understanding of participants, or should we take Dworkin up on his word that a practice is 'an entity distinct from [people]' (1986, 50) and has little to do with group consciousness? S C Smith (1990, 263) explains this confusion in Dworkin's account of the internal point of view, the latter carried at both the 'subjective' level of participants' minds and the 'social' level of the autonomous discourse. Smith pushes the independence between practice and practicing individuals 'further than Dworkin ever has,' by proposing a reading of 'practice' in Luhmann's systems-theoretical terms. An insightful argument this, but one that would disarticulate law's connection with politics and self-determination in community, a connection that Dworkin vitally needs to uphold.

[3] Dworkin, 1986, 55

[4] ibid., 442

[5] As Postema has resumed it: 'Law is a social practice. Participants of the social practices act from an understanding of their actions as appropriate to the practice and this understanding is constitutive of the practice.' (1987, 286). Dworkin says: 'This book takes up the internal, participant's point of view; it tries to capture the argumentative nature of our legal practice by

Secondly, Dworkin understands community not only as condition but also as object of interpretation. We identify community in terms of practices that we share. In interpreting law our efforts are directed to one such instance of community. The dialectic is intimate: Community in the sense of shared context of meaningfulness is precondition of what can be said about practices that in their totality yield community. There is finally a third sense in which community is significant in Dworkin's theory. Through recourse to the concept of integrity, community becomes, ultimately, the objective of interpretation, to the extent that interpreting law with integrity becomes 'constitutive of political community.'[6]

How is it, more specifically, that community informs the interpretative undertaking? For the interpretative attitude to take hold, Dworkin says, borrowing again from the hermeneutical tradition, it must be the case that 'people try to impose meaning on the institution - to see it in its best light - and then to restructure it in the light of that meaning.'[7] Institutions and practices embody purposes open to interpretation. The purpose is not to be imputed at will by the interpreter. To interpret is 'to apply an intention,'[8] and to impute purpose to the practice means for Dworkin, who cites Gadamer here,[9] to read the practice in its best possible light, i.e. in the light of what would most fully realise its implied purpose. This is a 'structural requirement', performed on objective ground; not, that is, by imposing upon the practice outside moral or personal purposes, but by retrieving purpose from within the practice, as it is intelligible to the people participating in the common form of life, the community.

To shed light on the intricacy of the process, Dworkin draws out three stages of interpretation. It would be wrong to see these stages as a temporal sequence; rather, the separation into stages should be seen as an analytic device, patterning out a process of understanding in its simultaneity.

At the 'pre-interpretative' stage 'rules and standards taken to provide the tentative content of the practice are identified ... Some kind of interpretation is necessary even at this stage. Social rules do not carry identifying labels... The classifications it yields are given in day-to-day reflection and argument.'[10] In a sense the pre-interpretive level furnishes the assumptions that people share when they share a cultural background. It is the inventory of common understandings, the ambit of possibilities of what a practice may

---

joining the practice and struggling with the issues of soundness and truth participants face.' (1986, 14)

[6] Dworkin, 1986, 211
[7] ibid., 47
[8] ibid., 56
[9] ibid., 58-9
[10] ibid., 65-6

require, and in that sense it is a condition rather than a phase because it locates the practice in the context we share of its possible meanings.

It is worth stressing here that at the pre-interpretive stage a level of understanding is established that is specific to the community. 'We share a pre-interpretive sense of the rough boundaries of the practice on which our imagination must be trained.'[11] This shared context of understanding, this field of possibility for the imagination is particular to the community in the specific circumstances of its here and now. Historicity and contingency reside here and Dworkin's theory is not vulnerable to the argument that has haunted liberals, the charge that their individual is not situated in community or in history.

The second stage, the 'interpretive' stage hosts a debate about the meaning and the purpose of the practice, or 'why a practice of [any] shape is worth pursuing.'[12] Interpretation is always justification says Dworkin, the imputation of justificatory principle or purpose, but a principle or purpose that is already embodied in the past record of the practice, retrieved not posited. It is in this tension between 'fit' and justification, that interpretation becomes possible. Competing interpretations are different rationalisations of the history of the practice competing on the terrain of 'fit'.[13] This tension and competition also exhibit interpretation's essentially conflictual nature; interpretation is the site that hosts conflict in the community by bringing together contrasting understandings laden with value judgement.

The 'post-interpretive' stage, finally, is the reformist moment of all interpretation. Again it is not to be understood as a temporally separate moment of reform of an already existing object - 'interpreted' law. Rather it involves a conceptual shift - a shift in the understanding of the practice - that occurs as the justification shifts the 'fit'. Interpretation is always, even at this stage, interpretation of the practice 'in its best light' not a change of the practice.

INTEGRITY: THE RIGHT ANSWER

Having established the interpretative character of all social practices, Dworkin lays out three directions that legal interpretation may take, or rather, three distinct priorities that may guide the interpretative undertaking; he calls them 'integrity', 'pragmatism' and 'conventionalism'.

---

[11] ibid., 75
[12] ibid., 66
[13] On this see Fish's argument (1982) that if we rightly take 'fit' to be interpretative it can no longer provide the testing ground for the competition of justifications, for as 'best fit' it is itself absorbed in the justification.

At its most simple formulation, 'integrity' would read something like 'treat like cases alike.' But integrity does not mean consistency pure and simple. Rather it means consistency in principle with past decisions which requires retrieving that principle in precedent. We can understand integrity better by looking at the alternatives: conventionalism and pragmatism. The conventionalist ties law to the outcomes of conventions and compromises reached in the process of political bargaining.[14] So long as decisions respect the rules of the game, conform to the designated, binding procedures and are products of genuine negotiation and compromise, the conventionalist will treat them as law. This view is compatible with inconsistent schemes of justice running through the legal history; principle may be differentially applied across the board.[15] The pragmatist's recourse to principles, on the other hand, only serves his/her own pursuit of an ideal. There is no commitment to working out common schemes of principle embodied in the law; simply principles are imputed strategically in order for 'judges [and lay participants] to make whatever decisions seem best for the community's future.'[16]

Like Integrity, conventionalism and pragmatism provide interpretations of law on the basis of imputation of purpose or principle. However '[i]ntegrity demands that the public standards of the community be both made and seen, so far as this is possible, to express a single, coherent scheme of justice and fairness in the right relation.'[17] Although every decision about what the law is can be debated as to what the principle to be read into text and precedent ought to be, integrity, unlike pragmatism, does not leave the question open, but provides a guiding ideal that will yield the answer. It insists that the operative principle should fit the most coherent scheme of justice that can be envisaged for the past history of legal decisions. Integrity demands that the rationalising principle of the decision at hand be part of a pattern that coheres as a whole.

Dworkin will not deny that people hold to distinct conceptions of what justice, fairness and due process mean and require in each case. Integrity does not privilege any of these conceptions on the basis of substantive criteria. Rather, it is a second-order value that attaches to first order values of

---

[14] Dworkin, 1986, 115

[15] A 'bare' rulebook community would opt for the conventionalist type of law. A conventionalist theory of law would attach the legitimacy of law or political obligation towards the law to the necessity of having publicly ascertainable rules for coordinating behaviour. Note the proximity of the conventionalist's 'checkerboard' legislation with the republicans' description of the legislative outcomes of 'ordinary politics', that also consist of compromises and coalitions in the political marketplace. (See also Hunt, 1991, 39)

[16] Dworkin, 1986, 95

[17] ibid., 219, my emph.

justice and fairness. It requires simply that the community does not alternate in its interpretation of law between conceptions of justice. Integrity demands that the community act in a consistent manner in applying the conception of justice, fairness, e.t.c. Through the notion of integrity Dworkin can construct a concept that is true to demands of interpretation and community. Interpreting a set of social practices under the demands of integrity sustains the unity of community.

By putting forward the argument for integrity, Dworkin has already made a strong case for the obligation to obey the law. The obligation to obey the law has usually been associated with the argument that there must be publicly ascertainable standards of behaviour that alone can make communal co-existence possible. Alternatively it has been associated with the law's inherent goodness, with the danger of anarchy that may result from disobedience, etc. The multitude of arguments in this vein impose external reasons for conformity. In Dworkin, like in the civic republicans, political obligation acquires an internal premise. Interpreting law with integrity gives the practice the coherence necessary to sustain the community. Then the obligation to obey the law is a requirement towards a practice that sustains community. The intimacy of the connection between law and community (that Law-as-Integrity is constitutive of community) allows Dworkin to explain away the externality of traditional theories about obligation to obey the law, and instead allows him to reconceive that obligation as one towards one's community.

INTEGRITY, COHERENCE, NARRATIVE

To bring the connection between law's interpretation and law's coherence forcefully home, Dworkin uses the metaphor of a collective novel in which judges assume the roles of the consecutive co-authors. The interpretation of law resembles the writing of a novel, where each of the writers must add their own chapter to an on-going story.[18] In adding his/her chapter the author must both ensure it reads coherently as a whole, as well as being the best in its genre. The author will add his/her chapter to a story s/he reconstructs as coherent.

On the question of the identity of the author, Dworkin establishes a direct link between community and adjudication. The role that Dworkin reserves

---

[18] Dan-Cohen puts it this way: 'that we should be wary of a fable that likens the operation of the judicial system to the composition of a novel. It is quite a strange novel that has as its dramatic punchline the execution of some of its intended readers. And this prospect, while no doubt concentrating the readers' minds, may put a strain on their interpretive skills that is quite unfamiliar in literary circles.' (1989, 1676)

for the judge is the task of applying 'law as integrity.' The judge is to act as representative of the community in making sure that the law is applied with Integrity. His decision will reconstruct the diversity of past episodes into one coherent whole that reconstructs the practice in its best light. In creating this role for the judge, Dworkin allows the community to be represented in the recollection of its history.

In writing his/her own chapter as a new contribution to a continuing story, the author reconstructs the novel as a meaningful whole; in the same way the judge, through his decision, reconstructs the practice as a meaningful whole, thus sustaining the unity of community by giving coherence to the understanding of its practices.

Note the proximity of Dworkin's notion of the chain novel to the concept of the *narrative*.[19] Narratives organise past events, diverse experience into coherent, singular stories. They order diversity and make sense of diversity by ordering it into a pattern of coherence. This pattern can be projected into the future to formulate predictions on the basis of what coheres now. For the narrative this projection is its litmus test. It will be revised or supplemented on the basis of what it cannot rationalise into its pattern of coherence.

Like chain novels, narratives are stories that we make up as we go along. They too make sense of the past by reading it through a rationalising pattern. They too compete with other narratives in telling the best, most coherent story of past diversity. They too reconstruct history into a story that best explains the present instance. They have justificatory power too because, like chain novels, they explain by justifying the inclusion of the present instance into this rather than that story. Like chain-novels, finally, they are revised in the light of every new instance that they must include, and this revision (if it is not going to be a breakdown), involves internal shifts of emphases so that the deviant instances may be accommodated and the rationalising pattern can in each new case be seen to cohere. In fact I have very little doubt that Dworkin was thinking of narratives when he was writing about chain novels.

In the end, underlying the coherence thesis is an argument about a communal narrative. If the law is interpreted 'as integrity' it yields coherence and with it a coherent narrative; by providing the narrative, it fulfils the interpretative condition for the existence of community. The rest is a story about the sustenance, in law, of communities' struggle over meaning and self-determination.

---

[19] The concept of the narrative is, of course, a favourite of the structuralists in the 60s. For an early, structuralist account, see Barthes (1977). I employ it here in the way MacIntyre does in (1981, passim and ps 204ff). Also Benhabib, 1987, 349: 'At any point in time, we are one whose identity is constituted by a tale. This tale is never complete; the past is always reformulated and renarrated in the light of the present and in anticipation of a future.'

DWORKIN REPUBLICAN

There are striking similarities between Dworkin and the republicans in how they envisage the relationship of law to politics.[20] It is particularly Michelman's debt to Dworkin that is the most notable. The analogy between their arguments Dworkin's is more intimate than even the excessive reliance on the Supreme Court suggests. In a sense, their theories are mirror images, motivated only by different questions. Michelman's is an argument from the point of view of politics, validating the Constitution as an ongoing instantiation of popular self-creation and therefore of political freedom. Dworkin's is a theory of political legitimacy based on self-creation, as the community pulls itself into self-understanding and substantiates its freedom with every new act of legal interpretation. In order to substantiate this claim about self-creation, both rely heavily on political community. In Dworkin, law-as-integrity constitutes the community, integrity is its constitutive commitment. Michelman's jurisgenerative politics also describe the moment of the community coming into being through law. Both theories locate the possibility of community squarely on adjudication.

In view of this, like Michelman, Dworkin needs to answer the question about why the community's self-constituting endeavour is delegated to the judge. It is true of course that Dworkin invites lay participants to the legal business of arguing the content of the chain novel's new chapter; integrity addresses the interpretative question to 'the good citizen.' In the end however it is the judge who will be the author on behalf of the community, it is Hercules who is entrusted with the articulation of the narrative. There lies a problem here, in the connection between vicarious authorship and the coming about of community that I will argue in the following chapters. Only briefly here, I find that any concept of 'virtual' authorship, such as that introduced by Dworkin, and adopted by Michelman as 'virtual participation', breaks down the intimate dialectic of community and narrative, their

---

[20] A difference between Ackerman and Dworkin is worth noting here. While for both the judge looking backwards retrieves and articulates the narrative that informs present identity-moulding legal decisions, what Dworkin describes as a task fit for Hercules, for Ackerman describes as a potentially oppressing activity that he attributes to the 'traditional professional narrative' (1991, ps 42-4, 62). The task is that of reading past constitutional history as a coherent whole. Such a coherence imposing reading would stemroller over Ackerman's constitutional moments as disruptions of the narrative and would thus 'unduly minimize [the community's] creativity.' Constitutional moments need to be preserved as breaking points with past history and as initiating future chain novels. Ackerman's would best be read as a three-chapter chain novel, coherence playing an important part in legal interpretation within but in no case beyond the time-span between two consecutive constitutional moments.

simultaneity and reciprocal inter-dependence. The argument applies to Michelman and Sunstein as it does to Dworkin. Without traces of participation we can hardly talk of authorship and justifiably the terms introduced by them are virtual participation and virtual authorship. Representation through the officials - whether delegates or judges - breaks the simultaneity of community and narrative. This abstraction makes the argument hollow. Virtual authorship runs very close to unreal authorship and virtual participation very close to non-participation, and these abstractions at such crucial junctions may be fatal for a community's effort to pull itself together into self-understanding.

To conclude: like the other republicans, Dworkin leaves behind the community's understanding of its politics in the name of constitutional politics that, as will become evident in the eleven theses against republicanism that follow, impose institutional assumptions and legal *a prioris* at those junctions where, in the name of politics, things ought to be understood and decided reflexively. This adherence to the legal containment of politics despite all that is imposed and all that is silenced is what makes Dworkin a republican.

CHAPTER SIX

THE CONTAINMENT THESIS

The more consistently the legal systems are worked out the greater their capacity to absorb whatever essentially defies absorption.
(Adorno)

Republican theory claims nothing less than that the constitution provides the possibility of politics and the substantiation of community. The legal-institutional connection is the significant one: what characterises the republican thesis is *the centrality of law both to politics and to the moulding of community*.

This is an argument that has had several steps. Implicit in the republican thesis is the communitarian argument about embeddedness in the community, not only in the social construction of the self, but also in the argument about discursive particularity: although citizenship is a universal category the dialogue into which it facilitates entry is specific to the historical community. It is in the very process of participation in the deliberative process - which becomes an end in itself - that perspectives engage with one another and conceptions of a good that is common are worked out. The deliberative practice that the republicans claim the Constitution provides a 'home' for, substantiates community between people who invest in a dialogue that matters to them deeply. But what of those, one might ask, that do not feel at home in the [legally] interpreted world?[1]

I will take issue with this question in Parts II and III. In the meantime it is vital to clarify, in summary form now, how the republicans establish that the Constitution comes to underpin the community's politics. The answer that the republicans give is that the constitution ***contains*** the deliberative practice of a community, the dialogue of all about all.

A double articulation is in evidence in the above. Firstly that of law and politics, because by participating in the dialogic-deliberative practice, citizens engage in politics. During the communicative exchange principles to guide public life are hammered out. Secondly that of law and community, because the participation in the public realm in turn feeds back in a way which 'interpellates' the individual as a political actor. The entry into the public sphere through citizenship - the legally backed capacity to partake in the political dialogue - mediates the assumption of political identity. Citizenship holds up the mirror for each participant to make sense of his/her

---

[1] The allusion is to Rilke:
'... daß wir nicht sehr verlaschlich zu Haus sind
in der gedeuteten Welt' (Duineser Elegien, 1)

identity within the community. As Michelman puts it, republican politics is about the intrinsic value of citizenship because 'the self is constituted by, or comes to know itself through, such engagement.'[2]

According to the containment thesis, then, law substantiates popular sovereignty by lending it constitutional forms and procedures as vehicles of political deliberation. But what is the nature of the vehicle and how, more precisely does it effect the containment? There are two essential presuppositions here. Were either of the two to be compromised, the containment thesis would not hold. These are the requirements:

(i) that the law will 'pick up' all voices in the political arena, and not be prejudicial or deaf to some of them.
(ii) that the law will pick up those voices such as they are, and will not re-align or transform them in the process. The law must accommodate without distorting, otherwise it could hardly be claimed a vessel for the community's dialogue.

Martha Minow, a favourite republican ally, says of the first requirement:

'Seeking unusual perspectives enables justices to avail themselves of the partial superiority of other people's views and to reach for what is unfamiliar and perhaps suppressed under the dominant ways of seeing ... Dialogue in courtroom arguments can stretch the minds of listeners ... [and] inventive approaches can *bring the voices of those who are not present* before the court ... The introduction of additional voices may enable adversary dialogue to expand beyond a stylized either/or mode, prompting new and creative insights.'[3]

One of the two fundamental conditions for the containment thesis is that the deliberative process that the republicans advocate is open to and attuned to voices from across society. Michelman stresses that voices that carry innovative potential into settled understanding, and that are likely to stimulate the social dialogue, are particularly those which 'enter the conversation - or, as we sometimes feel, seek to disrupt it - from its margins.' The capacity for 'dialogic self-modulation' depends on the inclusion of these voices, that alone allows 'the process of self- [and communal-] revision under social-dialogic stimulation.' He says that most of the country's 'normatively consequential dialogue' is carried out in informal settings, not formal channels of politics. Most areas of social life are 'arenas of potentially transformative dialogue,' or 'arenas of citizenship ... as it

---

[2] Michelman, 1988, 1503
[3] Minow, 1987, 88-9

encompasses ... distinct and audible voices in public and social life at large.' Michelman will not doubt for a moment that the voices that carry

'understandings that are contested and shaped ... in civil society at large are of course conveyed to our representative arenas ... So the suggestion is that the pursuit of political freedom through law depends on "our" constant reach for **inclusion of the other**, of the hitherto excluded- which in practice means **bringing to legal-doctrinal presence** the hitherto absent voices of emergently self-conscious social groups.'[4]

On the second requirement:

As participants in public life we can claim to be self-determining only insofar as we ourselves are able to revise and alter the terms of social life; insofar, that is, as no external constraints hinder our self-revisionary powers. Nor, of course, can these constraints be built into the institutions themselves. Should the institutional vessel carry its own limitations of vision into the community's self-revisionary process, then the republican argument would not make sense. If self-revision of a community is to be carried out through law, then the significant pre-condition must be that the law's own logic does not inhibit the possibilities for change. Otherwise there would be only limited self-government, its possibilities hedged in by, and dependant upon law. In order to avoid this pitfall, the republicans must ensure that their project does not stumble on the very institution they employ to effect it. They must treat law as malleable, as open to reflexivity, as capable of self-revision. This explains their (too often under-rated) debt to Critical Legal Studies. Michelman's work in particular, is full of references to and allusions to Roberto Unger. Unger allows Michelman to make the claim that law's institutional logic does not hinder freedom - of self-revision and thus of self-determination. The solution he offers is immanent critique. Law can be rationalised to meet specific, even competing, political objectives. It is a supple, malleable, 'infinitely plastic' means that can be made to express alternative social visions.

'The legal form of plurality is indeterminacy,' writes Michelman, and Unger's imprint could not be clearer. 'Legal indeterminacy is the pre-condition of the dialogic, critical-transformative dimension of our legal practice variously known as immanent critique, internal development, deviationist doctrine, social criticism and recollective imagination.'[5] This argument is vital to the republican endeavour to account for political

---

[4] Michelman, 1988, 1529

[5] ibid., 1528-9 We noted above that Michelman sees this process as unproblematical. Michelman collapses law into politics, into the 'people's on-going normative contention', and makes law synonymous with dialogue in spontaneous contexts and unofficial fora. In his argument the legal discourse is likened to people's ongoing normative speaking.

plurality through law. If the law is indeterminate it can harbour, in legal argumentation, a competition of views. Therefore the law should not be conceived of as sealed off from and immune to political challenge. Legal indeterminacy becomes the space that discloses political options. Immanent critique becomes the mode of political contestation and action. The scope of possible indeterminacies accounts for the scope of political plurality; law can accommodate, as indeterminacy,[6] every political challenge to settled patterns and so it contains in this way the potential for communal self-revision. In the republican argument, law discloses and circumscribes political space.

Like Unger, the republicans deny that law should be kept at bay from genuine 'controversy over the basic terms of social life.' Instead law should be seen as an intrinsic feature of self-government, the medium through which communities express, argue and revise their normative commitments. To see this is to understand the self-revisionary potential of law itself.[7] To ignore this is to fall for the false necessity of its inherent constraints; this is a myth expounded by the dominant formalisms and must be resisted. Against formalism Unger, and with him the republicans, will argue that our legal institutions have the in-built capacity for reflexive criticism and transformative capacity. Michelman (and to a lesser extent Sunstein) rely on Unger's account of legal politics to back their own collapse of politics into law.[8]

There are severely question-begging assumptions in both requirements (i) and (ii). I will only briefly mention them at this stage of the exposition and undertake a fuller critique in the part II. Briefly, this thesis presupposes a *congruence* that cannot be guaranteed at the outset. The presupposed congruence is that between official and unofficial processes,[9] between the

---

[6] Cf. Postema here: 'The principled politics of constitutional rights makes possible the continual re-articulation of a community's public conception of morality. The indeterminacy and lack of closure of this form of public justification is, in this instance, not a defect, but a virtue.' (1989, 127)

[7] Michelman alludes to this when he claims that 'an order or practice may retain its identity while undergoing transformation through a process of reflexive criticism.' (1988, footnote2)

[8] But this does not mean, as the republicans would have it, that law can accommodate political plurality as such. It merely means that law is not immune to its political environment. It is open to political challenge that feeds into it as indeterminacy. But this CLS 'law-as-politics' formula is not interchangeable with the republican 'politics-as-law'. For more on this see chapter fourteen.

[9] This kind of interplay between formal processes and informal networks of public deliberation is also characteristic of Habermas's account of the Public Sphere, and is specifically elaborated in (1992). In that article, Habermas stresses the necessity for a political process to be open to and sensitive to the influx of issues and value orientations from its informal environment of public debate at large. Only such an interplay ensures communicative pluralism. In other writings he sees some potential in the role of the New Social Movements and their

formal democratic process and informal networks of public deliberation. Let us see more specifically what this means.

Civil society consists of a wealth of groupings and collectivities and thus allows an infinite number of points of entry into public space. Many such groups generate communal attachments that do not correlate with the republican discursive model of civil association in the public sphere. Because all too often group attachments inhibit democratic character formation.[10] And all too often not only is the congruence not guaranteed but the 'voice' of such groups is in fact meaningful **as** incongruent. Incorporating them into the democratic process would then do away with what is crucially significant to them: their opposition to the democratic community, ethos and language. I am conscious that in this form the argument is still far too vague and I will attempt in parts II and III to state it more forcibly and at greater depth by utilising the concepts of systems theory. Suffice it for the moment to note the possibility of a deep incongruity between formal and informal deliberation. An example may prove helpful here.

In *Law's Empire* Dworkin claims that a 'true' community must meet four conditions: 1) the relationship within the community is special, it does not hold towards people outside the community; 2) the relationship is 'established directly from each member to each other;' 3) each member has a concern for the well-being of everybody else in the group; 4) the concern must be equal towards all.[11] Only when these conditions are met can we speak of 'true community.' This argument relies on a projection of congruence. Because Dworkin's postulation of equality conditions for true communities are inserted in place of the various communities' own understandings of equality, and more importantly their own understanding of the connection between equality and their existence as communities. There are communities that are avowedly anti-democratic in their organisation and that does not compromise their nature as communities since they are nevertheless unitary in their outlook, cohesive, permeated by an attitude they understand to be fraternal. In a similar vein, the republicans set up the conditions of 'true' political dialogue and claim that it will bring about community, often in spite of communities' own rather different understandings of their politics.

The privileged status that republicans claim for their 'communal deliberation' may well be postulated for a community in spite of the

---

involvement in 'Grenzenkonflikten' (boundary conflicts) (1987a, pp390ff, and for an overview White, 1988, 123-7) that in this case could be conceived, without much distortion I think, as the boundary between official and unofficial process.

[10] See Rosenblum, 1994, 73. Neither can the republicans guarantee at the outset that this involvement will be identity-generating.

[11] Dworkin, 1986, 199-200

community. If the community consists of self-interested individuals then their communal deliberation will be genuinely - and that is truly to the community - a bargain of interests. The republicans must either rely on a dialogue that is genuinely the community's (and generates identity through individual involvement) and thus run the risk that it may just be self-interested, racist, sexist, alienating e.t.c., or they must give up the claim to account for *that* community's dialogue and prescribe a framework for their preferred dialogue, that is civic, virtuous and 'dis-interested'. They cannot have the best of both without facing the paradox of a dialogue that is at once communal and community-excluding in having its conditions established in spite of the community whose dialogue it is. Either the republicans will have to postulate a congruence - in which case the (anti-democratic) association will be colonised by the democratic-republican ethic, or they will have to concede the non-congruence in which case it is hard to imagine how the republican project will get off the ground. I will return to this point several times and from many different angles and having recruited the help of systems-theory. My aim will be to uncover the republican readiness to abandon the interpretative premise which would require them to retrieve rather than impose community understandings.

This impossible dilemma facing the republicans is reflected in a deep inconsistency in their argumentative strategies. All too often, there lingers in the republican argument a tendency to abandon 'what the law contains as politics' in favour of 'what the law constitutes as politics.' Republicanism suggests an 'empowerment' of politics that all too often becomes a form of 're-constitution'.

Take, for example, Ackerman's question: 'What does the Constitution constitute?' He says:

'While established Constitutional Law did not always resolve America's deepest crises, it has always provided us with the language and the process within which our political identities could be confronted, debated and defined- both during the periods of normal politics and on those occasions when Americans found themselves called, once again, to undertake a serious effort to redefine and reaffirm their sense of national purpose.'[12]

Preuss renews this argument in the context of the drafting of the new Constitution for a United Germany:

'The classic division between the state on the one side and the individual on the other is extended and completed into a triad. In this draft there is additionally what the Americans call civil society. These are the social groupings and associations , the

---

[12] Ackerman, 1984, 1039

civil rights movements, the public interest groups that have never previously been represented in a constitution ... We have given civil society a constitutional, legal reality.'[13]

The question the republicans need to address before they themselves undermine their project in the very act of setting it up, is the following: *how true to Civil Society is the 'new constitutional reality' that they are 'giving it'?*

Why is this self-undermining? Let me summarise the republican self-defeating argument, and attempt to rescue at this stage, through a terminological query: I have problems with the use of the term *'constitutes'* because it suggests that the constitution 'depicts' associations and persons as something other than their own self-perception. This process of constitution inhibits the possibility of allowing these voices to be heard as their owners intend them to be; the voices enter the legal screen always-already colonised. The inclusion of the hitherto excluded is thus effected on the includer's terms - the excluded has not pierced the terms of inclusion. In all this there lingers an ambivalence that underpins a dilemma. If the constitutional rules are **constitutive** of a practice, then voices which exist in civil society at large need to be re-conceived (re-constituted) in order to be integrated in terms of the constitutive practice in question. Whereas this reconstitution maybe useful in integrating otherwise 'egotistical, self-interested individuals ... and associations of such individuals,' it is doubtful how far it will carry the quest for self-determination of such individuals and associations. If the communal dialogue is to be uncoerced it cannot re-cast or constitute anew the participants' self-understandings. The republicans cannot have it both ways: they have to side with one of the mutually exclusive options of colonisation or containment. Either the institutional dialogue will pick up existing voices or it will constitute them. It cannot do both at once.

Rather than dealing with republicanism as a strategy of colonisation I will deal with it, more charitably, as a case of containment. I believe this reads the project in its best light. To read it otherwise, i.e. to read 'constitute' as 'colonise', would make republicanism self-defeating, because a

---

[13] In an interview in the *Tageszeitung* of 7/4/90, quoted in Scott and Caygill (1995) [13] A parallel argument forms the main thrust of Alan Scott's and Howard Caygill's analysis of the draft of the new German Constitution. (1995) Their analysis suggests elements of the strategy of containment. According to them, the draft constitution, amongst its major innovations, proposes (I quote selectively): (i) "... constituting associations of civil society which at the same time have participatory rights, (ii) offers and guarantees a space for free societal formation for social movements, that carry cultural and value innovation and (quoting Melucci 1989) function as a social laboratory, (iii) "an attempt to constitute responsible, republican and social citizens ..."

constitutionalism that addresses Civil Society needs to be true to Civil Society, its diversity and authenticity. It cannot, without creating a paradox, profess to address it as something other than it is, as already colonised by means of the medium that was meant to merely 'carry' it onto institutional ground. That is why I opt for the term 'contain' rather than 'constitute'. In the case of containment, republicanism will appear as the endeavour to accommodate without distorting people's and associations' - individual and collective - self-understandings, by making room for them in newly instituted legal categories. If the republican project is to mean anything at all, it needs to be seen as a suggestion of *the constitutional containment of politics*.

In this context let me settle a possible ambiguity regarding my own use of the term containment. I use the term not to connote restriction but instead to denote undistorted accommodation. In this way, and in accordance with the point I just made, I attempt to read republicanism in the best light, that of its aspiration to make law the vessel of political deliberation.

The present chapter has aimed at an exposition of the republican project culminating in the **'containment thesis'**, which I take to be the crux of republicanism. Although I have hinted at the critique I intend to advance, my pre-occupation here has been to explore the inter-connections that make containment possible. Republicanism suggests an immediate constitutive link between politics, community and the law. Community is substantiated in political dialogue, and the constitution hosts the dialogue. The republicans claim, in effect, that law upholds the deep self-interpretation of political community. Then law, as Michelman puts it, can be claimed to be the institutional manifestation of the political community's existence and identity as such.[14] Legal personality, 'citizenship as activity' is a name for our political involvement, covers our contribution to the communal dialogue; on the basis of the republican endorsement of the communitarian link, citizenship then informs the sense of political identity of the situated self. By putting forward these inter-relationships, republicanism invites us to reconceive all that is political as legal. The aim of my thesis is to resist this legal imperialism, the false necessity of this assimilation of the political to the legal. There is both a descriptive and a prescriptive side to my argument.

As to the *prescriptive* side: I argue for an anarchy of political commitment that I will pursue under the heading of 'reflexive politics'. The claim is that political freedom presupposes the possibility to contest everything politically. Political freedom ultimately lies in the freedom to contest the meaning of political conflict, action and collective or communal identity.

---

[14] Michelman, 1988, 1514

Political identity thus only contingently overlaps or identifies with citizenship and to assume an identity between the two as necessary or self-evident is to abandon reflexive politics. My prescriptive argument (advanced in part III) is against imposing this cost upon politics.

As to the descriptive side: I will argue that the republicans falsely claim that law can serve as the vessel for the political recollection of the national community. In a series of arguments throughout part II I will identify a number of weaknesses in the republican argument and attempt to show that the republicans can only sustain their grand synthesis of community, law and politics by inserting illegitimate assumptions, illegitimate to their own central commitment to containment. I will attempt to show the falsity - more precisely the false necessity[15] - of the republican subsumptions of political conflict, political identity and political action under legal categories. In each case the republicans can only make their point, I will argue, at the expense of a political-reflexive question that they must conceal, and an *a priori* (therefore an anti-political argument) that they must insert in its place. In many ways my project is an exercise in teasing out meta-political assumptions, an exercise undertaken in the name of (reflexive) politics. The aim is to show that there is contingency where the republicans assume necessity or naturalness, a political question where a meta-political one obscures it - whether in Ackerman's dualist meta-structure of politics, Sunstein's prescription of empathy, Michelman's recourse to an always-already common normative 'fund', or Dworkin's meta-political prescriptions for political equality and methodological backing of the interpretative undertaking. They all culminate in one all-inclusive claim, a claim that my thesis attempts to disprove. The all-inclusive republican claim is that the law can serve as an (adequate) register of political meaning.[16]

---

[15] What begins as a false necessity turns into a falsity. The false necessity of assuming that a group's self-understanding is informed by the law becomes a falsity, when that self-understanding is assumed for the citizenry, that, as a matter of fact, includes groups whose self-understanding is not informed by the law. In any case the disjunction falsity and false necessity is an important one and gives my own position a more moderate tone. I am not claiming, that is, that law can never be a vehicle to political action or give expression to social conflict in a way that mediates the assumption of political identity in community. That would be manifestly an exaggeration. But law can perform this function, that republicans attribute to it anyway, only so long as political actors find it an adequate description of their conflicts and their own self-understandings. The weakness of the republican claim is in assuming -the false necessity- that it always does.

[16] My descriptive argument against the republicans is that this claim is founded on arbitrary assumptions. My prescriptive argument in favour of reflexive politics is to resist viewing this claim as a meta-political question.

PART II

Political Conflict Under Legal Categories: A systems-theoretical critique of Republican Constitutionalism

EXCURSUS

LUHMANN'S SYSTEMS THEORY: AN INTRODUCTION

To answer the republicans I am going to rely on Niklas Luhmann's version of systems theory, his theory of 'autopoiesis'. Generally, throughout the book, I will avoid any strict exposition-application schema, but will attempt instead to explain those aspects of the theory that are relevant to the argument as I develop it. The enterprise is weighted with a heavy burden of abstraction as we move from Luhmann's most abstract epistemological premises to more concrete applications. In the process I will attempt to set up an inventory of key notions for future use: the concept of the system, the key analytical distinction between operations and observations, the notions of complexity and contingency, coding and programming, etc. Attempting such an exploration within the narrow confines of an introduction is burdensome but necessary; because Luhmann provides a unique re-thinking of the traditions he draws from. It is this novelty that makes it necessary to take a number of steps back and pick up the epistemological thread in the way that Luhmann does. Clearing the slates for such an undertaking is no easy task. I thus hasten to warn that the analysis of the nature of systemic observation and the meaning of meaning is heavily abstract and will be understood better in the light of the more concrete subsequent sections.

My reason for the recourse to systems theory is to elucidate how meaning comes about both legally and politically. That is why I pursue here this question over the genesis of meaning. But I must clarify that in talking about meaningfulness I have already limited this discussion to meaning-related systems. Suffice it to point out that in his typology of systems[1] Luhmann distinguishes living systems, psychic systems and social systems, not all of which are meaning-related. The former were in fact the systems for which the term 'autopoiesis' was coined by biologists Maturana and Varela, in order to describe the self-reproduction of organic life.[2] Luhmann transfers their insight to Sociology, significantly not as a metaphor.[3] Social systems are autopoietic in as real a sense as living systems are: they too produce their own elements from their own elements, the difference being that their elements are not cells but, as we shall see in the next section, communications. To the extent that communications occur in the real world,

---

[1] Luhmann, 1984, 15ff, and 1986c, 173ff
[2] Varela (1981, 14-24) and Zolo (1992, 67) protest against the 'uprooting' of the theory from Biology.
[3] As Rottleutner claims in 1987, 97

the autopoiesis of social systems is an empirically verifiable fact about the world.

The autopoiesis of a social system is thus the self-reproduction of communications. *Self*-reproduction because communications of a system, like the legal system, the political system, e.t.c., are specific to the system alone and their meaning cannot transcend its radically closed world. We will return to explore why we should assume such absolute a closure when we look at the nature of observation. With observation made possible by a system yet decisively contained within it, there are some significant points to be made about how the system handles internal reference and external reference, reference to itself and to its environment; this of course is central to our discussion of how law 'observes' politics. Before that however, still in an attempt to elucidate the complex ideas involved here, let us draw an analytical distinction between observation and operation. It is not an exaggeration to say that observation and operation are the two 'worlds' that meet in autopoietic theory.

OPERATIONS

Autopoiesis means self-reproduction and is consequently defined at the level of operations: operations whereby elements reproduce elements of the system.[4] It is because the system exists as the linking up of operations that Luhmann sees as the most important question relating to the concept of society the question: 'which is the operation that produces the system of society and, we must add, produces it from its products, that is, reproduces it?'[5] He says:

'My proposal is that we make the concept of communication the basis and thereby switch sociological theory from the concept of action to the concept of system. This enables us to present the social system as an operatively closed system consisting only of its own operations, reproduced by communications from communications.'[6]

Thus Luhmann identifies communication as the operation that reproduces the social system and designates society, the most comprehensive social system of all, as *the totality of communications*. By positing communication as the

---

[4] An element, like a particle or a cell, is un-decomposable into a more elementary form, at least for the system itself.
[5] Luhmann, 1992b, 71
[6] ibid.

element,[7] Luhmann proposes something much more precise than the social category 'relations'[8] and side-steps the problems associated with employing individuals,[9] conflict/co-operation[10] and most significantly action,[11] as departures for sociological inquiry.

The *shift* of sociological inquiry *from action to communication*, a shift that marks Luhmann's decisive break from Parsons, is treated by Luhmann himself as a 'conceptual revolution.'[12] Society is for Luhmann the totality of communications, not of individuals or groups, nor of their relations, nor of their actions. Unlike Habermas for whom communication is a way of acting, Luhmann conceives of acting as a way of communicating; this reversal brings far richer possibilities into sociological inquiry and circumvents some fundamental problems of action theory. While sociology, as theory of action, has always been theory of meaningful action and thus the element of communication/meaning is already central, it is nonetheless anchored in a fundamental way to what we could call a certain *'ontology of doing'*; Luhmann's revolutionary suggestion in this context is to leave the latter behind altogether. Why? Firstly because it circumvents the difficulty of distinguishing the elementary action unit itself[13] - the individuation of the event as Davidson would put it[14] -, since we can only circumscribe what 'part' of the action we are talking about on the basis of criteria outside the action. Instead systems-theory suggests that what 'part' of the action does the communicating is up to the system, and at this point the possibilities are endless. Secondly because it circumvents the problem that action is not necessarily social, which has made it necessary for sociologists (e.g. Weber) to impose criteria upon actions as to what counts as their *social meaning*. Thirdly because it redresses the problem of treating in the framework of action the active decision to *abstain from action*; maintaining one's silence

---

[7] Because, naturally, 'in dynamic systems - which consist of their operations - operations and elements become indistinguishable.' (Luhmann, 1985a, 100)

[8] Luhmann, 1992b, 73

[9] Meaning must be defined 'without reference to the subject since the latter, as a meaningfully constituted identity, already pre-supposes meaning.' (Luhmann, 1971, 28)

[10] See following chapter

[11] 'Without a system there would be neither meaning, nor experience, nor action.' (Luhmann,1971, 29)

[12] Luhmann,1986c, 177-8

[13] Gouldner has criticised Parsons for this: 'A specification of the elements of social action is no more attainable by formal definition alone than are the attributes of "life" which the biologist regards as the "subject matter" of his discipline. Znaniecki, almost alone among the systematic theorists who have raised the question, has stressed that the characteristics of social action cannot be taken as a priori data but are also to be inductively sought and empirically validated.' (Gouldner, 1973, 178)

[14] Davidson, 1980, 163, and passim

in the courtroom, to use an important example we will return to, can be fruitfully thematised in the context of communication rather than action. Finally it redresses the problem that the focus on action screens off an essential social aspect of action, i.e. the *impact* of the action, that is something - how else could it be? - outside the action (someone is talked to) but not outside the communication that always involves communicators. These are not mere problems that are avoided in the shift from action to communication, but are in fact *brought back into sociology as questions that enrich sociological inquiry.*

How does Luhmann define the elementary unit, the single communication? A communication is not an action involving a spatial transference of meaning, or whatever; nor is it a meeting of consciousnesses; nor is it a function. A communication is a synthesis of three components: ***information, utterance*** ('Mitteilung' - sometimes translated as utterance, others as communicative act) and ***understanding*** (which may also be mis-understanding).[15] Conceiving communication as distinguishable into the three components is crucial. Interlocutor A may stand back and ask why information x is communicated to him/her; his/her understanding of the communication may depend on distinguishing the two. Understanding of the communication thus may involve not the content of the information but why something was said here and now; it may involve the difficulties of understanding the information content; or whether the communicated will be accepted or rejected.[16] Every communication opens up a choice between its acceptance and its rejection. This bifurcation is essential to the system's existence in time. As dynamic the system exists only as new communications link onto previous ones, by taking up the yes- or no- option which a communication as an offer (or provocation) carries with it. The communication's incompleteness, as something always tending into the future, necessitates an answer. This is something that, possibly in spite of Luhmann,[17] I will attempt

---

[15] Luhmann borrows the distinction from Karl Buhler, a distinction also employed by Searle and Austin. (Luhmann, 1986c n.2, 1992b, p72)

[16] Luhmann, 1992b, 71ff, 1986c, 174ff

[17] Why 'in spite'? Let me attempt to answer this, but only very tentatively as yet. Because Luhmann says that 'the selection of further communication is either an acceptance or rejection of previous communication or a visible avoidance or adjournment of the issue.' (1986c, 176). I do not accept that the latter option is possible. The way Luhmann lays the cards, communication reproduces situations with a specified and enforced choice. The enforced choice is either a 'yes' or a 'no', and avoidance or adjournment is, at least likely, to be thematised as a 'no'. And this is because communication is always system specific, the options available are available through dispositive concepts (tertium non datur) and the choice of abstaining from both - abstaining from the choice itself, is something that the system cannot see (and cannot see that it cannot see). To make this point, however, anticipates a great deal of the discussion on observation etc, so at this stage I will refrain from saying any more.

to exploit in the argument that follows. Why 'incompleteness'? Because the communication is always unfinished, it is in anticipation of a response. The system exists not as an aggregate of communicative acts - the communicative act is a zero-point in time - but as a linkage of new communicative acts to those past. Between the two there is a sense in which meaning is pending, because without memory or anticipation there can be no meaning. It is through this linkage capacity - 'Anschlußfähigkeit' - that the system exists and its autopoiesis consists of this generation of new elements from existing ones.

Finally back the question of the designation of communication over action as the elementary unit. Communication allows a more fruitful departure for theorising the social than action does because communication includes action as the 'utterance' component of the communicative event. What were hitherto problems themselves acquire sociological value, as action itself is thematised and information value is drawn from it, the latter too being an elementary component of the element. Luhmann says:

'Sociality is not a special case of action; instead, action is constituted in social systems by means of communication and attribution as a reduction of complexity, as an indispensable self-simplification of the system.'[18]

Action is first possible and meaningful against a number of horizons of communication, each absorbing action into a specific template and casting it through system reference. *The ontology of doing is now displaced by a parallel processing of the meaning of action,* and with both what 'counts as' action and what action means determined system-specifically, action becomes an ***artifice***. From being the *a priori* starting point for sociology, it becomes a variable, relativised in a broader element of communication that makes its meaning dependent on the addressee (understanding) and the information value (information) that does not belong to the action (but to the system and to the World). We will return to all this in examining more closely questions of attribution of action.

To recapitulate: the operations of the social system are communications, understood as syntheses of information, communicative act and understanding. A social system is autopoietic in that it produces and reproduces its own elements, new communications from a network of existing communications. The system does not exist as the aggregate of its elements but as their succession: it exists as dynamic, in the continuing linkage of new communications to ones already communicated. Systemic

---

[18] Luhmann, 1984, 191

meaning is thus based on the instability of elements, their connectability, the opportunities they raise, the potentiality that is actualised in linkage.

But why do we need the concept of the system to address the question of meaning? A system exists as the succession of communications, communications communicate meaning, but still, why is the question of meaning not prior to or a condition of the operation of systems? To answer this Luhmann asks: what makes meaning possible?

SYSTEM AND MEANING

'We cannot escape the fact that the world we know is constructed in order (and thus in such a way as) to be able to see itself.
   This is indeed amazing.
   Not so much in view of what it sees ... but in respect of the fact that it can see at all.
   But in order to do so it must first cut itself up into at least one state which sees and at least one other state which is seen. In this severed and mutilated condition, whatever it sees is only partially itself. We may take it that the world undoubtedly is itself (i.e. is indistinct from itself), but, in any attempt to see itself as an object, it must, equally undoubtedly, act so as to make itself distinct from, and therefore false to, itself. In this condition it will always partially elude itself.'[19]

'All cognition ultimately consists in distinguishing,' says Luhmann, it consists in splitting the whole with a distinction, inflicting a severing which alone allows us to escape from the 'undoubted' but unhelpful 'the world is what it is.' The slants that can be drawn in the whole, the distinctions that can be inserted in the unmarked state are endless, and systems theory in its Luhmannian version is very much 'a theory of a *perpetuum mobile* of [such] difference-making' as W. T. Murphy put it recently.[20]

'Draw a distinction,' says Luhmann, employing the calculus of George Spencer Brown's 'under-rated' epistemology.[21] The whole as unmarked state allows no purchase into it. A whole needs at least one internal boundary if it is to be observed, and for this, we will have to sever the whole by drawing a distinction. The unity of the whole as 'unmarked state' is violated, something is indicated that leaves something out. Something is in that it is not the World. Every distinction indicates a state and establishes an observer that (has to confront the paradox that he) views one thing (the indicated state) as being two (the indicated and the non-indicated). But to establish the observer

---

[19] Luhmann, 1991a, 210, n13, quoting G S Brown
[20] Murphy, 1994, 14
[21] Spencer-Brown (1972)

requires: (i) that the distinction be drawn, (ii) that one side of the distinction be indicated (iii) that the distinction be re-introduced into the indicated side (re-entry).

Note that no observation can be established before the first distinction is drawn. It is not possible to envisage the unmarked state before the initial distinction is drawn. Only by severing the whole can we see it but then it is only in the terms in which we have severed it that we see it. It is in this sense that Luhmann says that the whole always necessarily eludes us. Because all knowledge of the whole is always-already partial knowledge, dependant on the distinction we employed to observe it that alone, through its form, allows us to see the unity that is the world; because only from the inside is the distinction between inside/outside perceivable. But with the distinction itself determining the shape of both self and other (indicated and non-indicated), the world that is over and above both is determined through the mark we inflict on it, thus dispersing the 'modern' myth of the transparency of the object of observation, or rather, the myth of the equivalence of an object and its representation.

Luhmann relies on this calculus to define what a system is. Every observation of the world is a severing of the world; an observation is an operation that draws a distinction in order to indicate one or the other side of this distinction. The recursive linking of these operations establishes a system as observer. And just as there is no purchase into the unmarked state before the mark, there is no account of the world that precedes the system. Systems come about as distinctions are drawn, indications made and 're-entries' effected. We need to understand the concept at that, the most abstract level: the distinctive feature of the system is that it differentiates itself out by establishing a boundary between internal and external, between what it is and what it is not, and conceives of the world as spanning them both.

The operation of distinction-indication-re-entry, compounded in time, makes it possible for a boundary to be established, a system to 'see' itself because, as the non-indicated side re-enters, it can see what in contra-distinction to itself the outside world is. Establishing the self as self requires distinguishing it from something else. In order to define itself the system needs to re-introduce its Other; this re-introduction takes the form of 're-entry'. The process resembles Lacan's 'mirror stage' in the development of the system; through re-entry the system can observe itself-in-an-environment. Only thus does 'emerge the distinction for the system between the environment which it sees confronting it, and the world to which it belongs,'[22] enabling both self-observation and observation of the

---

[22] Luhmann, 1975b, 347

environment. Then Luhmann can say that 'a system that re-introduces the system - environment difference into the system is capable of equating its boundaries with those of the world.'[23] Without the difference, the indication and the re-entry we would have no purchase point into the unity that is the world, no slant into the continuum, or, in Luhmann's words, no 'interruption of continuity in the spectrum of the possible, [i.e.] system formation.'[24] System boundaries have to be drawn, internal and external space designated, for anything to make any sense at all.[25]

Thus, and in opposition to the dominant paradigm in cybernetics, for Luhmann what gives a system its unity is not some externally verifiable relationship among its elements or elements and structures. A system is a unity that is meaningful as such in reference to a difference: the difference of system and environment.[26] It is this difference that first enables the system to build up a relation with the environment. Within a system one can observe the environment, reflect on it, talk about it and make decisions concerning it. Underpinning the relation is the unity of the distinction, the now observable world.

To recapitulate: observation is defined by Luhmann as the unity of an operation that makes a distinction in order to indicate one or the other side of this distinction. Luhmann inserts 'unity' in this definition to denote that observation does not equal indication but what underlies the indication and allows the indicated side to reflect in the non-indicated side (or in Luhmann's terms, the non-indicated to re-enter). Observing on the basis of this distinction means that the system presupposes the *unity* of the distinction but actualises it from the perspective of the system, the indicated side. Each side, system and environment, depends reciprocally on the other. Through the continuous linking of operations, the system creates a lasting differentiation to its environment, compounds a boundary to it and thus ensures its own continuation. And it is the environment that holds up the mirror in which the system can observe itself (self-observation) in that it is not the World.[27] This

---

[23] Luhmann, 1986a, 21

[24] Luhmann, 1975b, 345

[25] '[A system] must be able to observe [its] operations as the drawing of a boundary, as the fencing in of what belongs to it and the shutting out of what does not. It must be able to distinguish between self-reference and external reference. The intrinsic value of intrinsic values - this is what constitutes the system: the system as boundary, as a form with two sides, as a distinction of system and environment.' (Luhmann, 1991a, 224-5)

[26] Indicatively, Luhmann, 1986e, 11, also 1986f 155

[27] Let us take a more concrete example to see how this works. Luhmann repeatedly returns to the problems that surround the question 'what is society?' (When Luhmann talks of society - or the social system of 'world society' - he identifies it as the totality of communication, therefore limited by the boundaries of what is not communicable.) In the sociological

also entails that because an act of differentiation of systems that establishes specific system/horizon perspectives is required for observation, no account of 'truth' can transcend the system and neither archimedean point nor ultimate observer is possible - one that would ensure the transparency of the object of representation and one that cannot in turn be observed.

Finally, as we saw, meaning comes about when a system differentiates itself out of an environment and (through re-entry of the system/environment distinction) sees itself in an environment about which it may communicate (trivially, it is individuals who will communicate: utter, convey information and understand or mis-understand the systemic communication). This is to stress that a system's operation is tied to a system's observation.[28] The two are linked internally in a mutually enabling way. Operations are communications about system and environment, internal and external reference, therefore observation. Observation, on the other hand, equips communication with a reference in terms of which it can continue, link up, and thus allows the system to effect its operations, produce new elements from existing ones and continue its autopoiesis.

OBSERVATION

Observation: system-centric and system-specific

We have already established that observation requires a system, and we will see now (in this and the following sections) why observation is specific to a system, possible only from a system's point of view. In the case of social systems with which this analysis is more specifically concerned, the question

---

observation of society, sociology has all too often treated society as component of a distinction - society/State, society/individual - and thus caused the discipline to designate its object as the 'other' in a distinction it was meant to contain. Luhmann overcomes the problems because for him "re-entry" is an indispensable moment; the distinction between self and other "re-enters" the indicated side - here the system of society - present yet suspended. Then the definition of society presupposes the unity of the distinction between society and its environment, the latter including of course individuals as living or conscious systems. The environment is excluded to be included (as mirror). This, to put it crudely, means that the distinction "acknowledges" both its sides. George Spenser Brown calls the unity of the distinction, its "form". Borrowing from him, Luhmann designates a system - here Society itself - as the form of a distinction. In this context what does Sociology gain by opting for the notion of social autopoiesis? Through the notion of the form, Luhmann will claim that it gains no less than the possibility to designate its object in the first place.

[28] The mode of that connection is neither uncontroversial nor undertheorised. For an overview of the discussion, see Teuber, 1993a, ch.2. A distinction suggested by Roth (quoted in Teubner, 1993a) is one between 'hard' and 'soft' operations, reproduction and observation respectively. Varela distinguishes 'operative' and 'symbolic' operations (1981a). Luhmann's account of their coincidence is the one I am following the reasoning of above.

of observation turns on the question of meaning. The system makes the world meaningful (meaningfully observed) and the world is made meaningful only for the system. Let us look at these in turn.

The system makes the world meaningful. As we saw, the unobservable whole is severed through the drawing of a boundary, and with it a vantage point is inserted. The two sides are separated, the one indicated then through re-entry the environment reflected in the system. Observation is now first possible as system-specific observation; there could be no other 'pure' observation since observation is only possible because a system first actualises - furnishes - a perspective into an otherwise undifferentiated reality. Drawing the (social-)systemic boundary means that the hitherto meaningless unity that is the world now makes sense as a difference between the system (that observes) and the environment (that is observed). System differentiation is a first move in an uncharted - and otherwise unchartable - territory. No system, no meaning. Everything follows from this: the peculiar processing of meaning within the system, its 'constructivist' observation of reality, its own peculiar self-observation, the radical incommensurability of perspectives, the post-modern condition itself as any hierarchy between systems - or ultimate observers - is abolished. We will examine these propositions in due course, focusing on what this analysis chiefly relies on systems theory for: the system's handling of external reference, its handling of distinctions between internal and other-reference.

If meaning requires the system, meaning is also specific to the system. How is the systemic perspective furnished, the world made meaningful? The answer is: through guiding differences. Systems observe by introducing a guiding difference and by making the World relevant to this guiding difference. The guiding difference organises, permeates and 'over-determines' the network of differences, the set of further distinctions and demarcations that meaning requires. Semantic codes specify the differences which form the basis for something to be received as information. The World is, in the case of each system, submitted to the difference that, for that system, makes a difference. A pattern of difference lies at the basis of the system's observation of the environment.

On that basis the system builds up an awareness of the environment, submits it to observation, and renders it meaningful. As we saw this presupposes 're-entry' of the difference between system and environment in the system. The system can see itself and see its other, self-reference and hetero-reference.[29] The function of the guiding differences is that they

---

[29] Varela explains how every operation is accompanied by a self-indication of the operation. 'Every observation, as the application of a distinction, makes possible not only an indication of what is observed but also an indication of the observation itself. One therefore arrives at the possibility of saying 'I' with the application of any distinction ...The system constitutes itself by

'carry' or depict this difference of system and environment in the system. This is the subject of the section on 'Guiding Distinctions'.

The Reduction of Complexity

The world is infinitely complex, it admits of a variety of ways it can be talked about, it possesses many aspects and possibilities of its description. New perspectives relativise older ones, the false necessities of 'natural' descriptions are shaken as they do; every such new description reminds us of the World's complexity but also increases that complexity by adding to the possibilities of describing it. So every time that a new system draws a boundary and establishes a specific difference of system and environment it of course adds to the overall complexity but also, importantly reduces it to that specific difference of system and environment. This reduction of complexity is a reduction of the possible states and events to ones that can be envisaged by the system as determined through its specific means of making selections and establishing relevance. Not every societal communication, not every state of affairs that can be talked about, may become subject of each system's communication. More importantly competing categorisations, interpretations of events will not all find expression in the system's terms; each system will restrict the modes in which the world can be talked about by perceiving it in a categorically preformed way.[30] This is how reduction occurs: the complexity of the environment is met from within the system through specific capacities of resonance. The system creates 'order from noise' by drawing selectively on the surplus of possibilities - the domain of high complexity - potentially available in the environment. 'Noise' is what is not yet reduced. In the process of this selective depiction the system constructs the external world that it cannot conceive in its complexity. A system knows by simplifying, and then by choosing amongst, manipulating and combining these self-produced simplifications that stand in for that which is too complex for the system to conceive. Systems are agents of reduction only in terms of which the unbearable complexity of the world becomes meaningful. This reduction, adds Poggi, allows the system 'a simple hold upon possibly highly complex stretches of reality.'[31] As complexity in

---

drawing limits, distinguishing itself from the environment and thus indicating itself ... When it observes the objects of its environment, in the process of observation distinguishes and indicates itself as an observer - whatever the difference-scheme and the object are which determine the observation in each case.' (Luhmann, 1985b, 391) Every time that the system observes the environment it achieves at the very same time a self-observation, the possibility to say 'I'.

[30] Luhmann, 1986e, 12

[31] Poggi, 1979, px

the environment increases, the system adapts its own capacities for resonance by building up its own complexity.

Meaning is always system-specific says Luhmann. It depends on a reduction of complexity, a reduction in the scope of possibilities of all that may be communicated.[32] A system comes about as a specific, reductive, selective way of observing a complex world, with a surplus of possibilities, is established. When a system observes an environment, it observes it through a form of selection that has to do with the distinction that guides it. Put another way, in Husserl's terms perhaps, the world is a horizon; it is not yet meaningful except as a background against which certain possibilities are actualised. This is what Luhmann is saying too, except in the more precise terms of infinite complexity (horizon, the World) and reduced complexity (the system). Systems are thus islands of reduced complexity in a World of infinite complexity. That relationship between *actual and possible*, the system and the world (I use World here to include the unity of system and environment) is the form of the distinction; 'form' (in the systems-theoretical sense) because in the system possibilities become actualised *over against those that are not*. Significantly, complexity is not eliminated in the process but reduced. It needs to be preserved, like the horizon, not only to furnish further selections but more importantly to make present ones meaningful. The dimension of time is also of the essence here: every actualisation as selection transforms the system and forms the basis for future selections. It is the specific form of *selectivity-in-progress* that constitutes the identity of the system.

Society and sub-systems

Society, as we said earlier, is the sum total of communications. In Luhmann's words, 'society is the closed system of connectable communications, reproducing communication by communication.'[33] Its boundaries include all that is communicated and communicable. But a paradoxical situation arises. Whatever unity the formula 'all communication' makes apparent is in fact dispersed; for within society's ambit there develop a multitude of sub-systems, each developing a selective and exclusive mapping of the world. Where society cannot communicate with its environment, since it already consists of all that is communicable, between sub-systems there does

---

[32] 'Everything which can be predicated of systems - differentiation into parts, hierarchy building, boundary maintenance, differentiation between structure and process, selective modelling of environments, etc - may be functionally analysed as a reduction of complexity.' (Luhmann, 1969, 256, trans. Poggi, my emph.)

[33] Luhmann,1992c, 1419

develop a communication of sorts. Each system of the 'social' type, albeit of the family group interactions, organisations or differentiated along functional lines,[34] is a sub-system of society and each makes sense of the world in different, mutually overlapping, mutually undercutting ways. Sub-systems are not strung together in any pattern of co-ordination. Society's subsystems aren't patterned in a whole/part schema,[35] but instead each system repeats a system/environment distinction within society, distinguishing itself from society through that distinction. Every formation of a sub-system is nothing less than a new exposition of the unity of the whole social system from its perspective. And yet, every formation of a sub-system breaks that unity of the whole system into a specific difference of system and environment.[36]

How does this differentiating out of a sub-system occur? As we will be dealing extensively with functional sub-systems, i.e. systems that are differentiated-out of society on the basis of performing a unique function in society, it may be helpful to say a little about the principle of its differentiation. Luhmann writes:

'I propose to characterize modern society as a functionally differentiated social system. The evolution of this highly improbable social order required replacing stratification with functional differentiation as the main principle of forming subsystems within the overall system of society. In stratified societies the human individual was placed in only one subsystem. ... This is no longer possible in a society differentiated with respect to functions such as politics, economy, intimate relations, religion, sciences and education. Nobody can live in only one of these systems. But if the individual cannot live in "his" social system where else can he live? As homo viator .. ?'[37]

Functionally differentiated systems are not manned or 'lived in'.[38] They consist of sets of differentiated and specialised resources and activities each articulating with others and each contributing through its own operation to

---

[34] On the typology of social systems see Luhmann, 1975a. On Functional Differentiation see chapter nine.
[35] 'The unity of the world is not the unity of an assemblage ..., but rather the unavoidable, indestructible possibility of moving from one thing to another - not an aggregation, but rather a correlation of meaningful experience and action.' (Luhmann, 1975b, 411, n.48)
[36] Luhmann, 1986e, 107 ff
[37] Luhmann, 1986d, 318
[38] Elsewhere Luhmann says: 'As an individual man lives outside the functional systems. At the same time, each person must have access to each functional system, to the extent that a person cannot conduct his existence without addressing claims to societal functions.' (1990b, 27) On the position of the individual vis a vis functionally differentiated systems see Luhmann (1986d, esp 319 on the subject 'underlying' and supporting attributes) and Teubner (1989) on role-taking and the 'multiple self'.

the functioning of the whole.³⁹ 'All these subsystems develop their own partial rationality: their own partial options and demands, goals and means, functions and products.'⁴⁰ Partial rationalities do not combine in a comprehensive social rationality as such, however, and in one sense at least, the sum of the parts is more than the whole. No system is of primary importance to the functioning of the whole, none provides a 'summit' (as was the case in stratified societies) or a 'centre' for society. Finally, according to the principle of functional differentiation each sub-system performs a function that is unique: were that exclusivity to be compromised the principle of differentiation itself would give way.⁴¹

'[Sub-system] differentiation,' says Luhmann, 'reproduces the system in itself, multiplying specialized versions of the original system's identity by splitting it into a number of internal systems and affiliated environments.'⁴² Each sub-system draws an internal boundary to reflect the whole system (and in effect the whole system's environment too). Each sub-system thus replicates within the system the difference between system and environment.

---

³⁹ As Klaus Eder puts it concisely: 'The decisive innovation is the functional autonomy by which structural arrangements are equally and without external constraints able to accommodate the functional consequences of the modernising mechanisms. By separating and multiplying the fields in which the construction of modern society can take place, functional differentiation makes this accommodation possible.' (Eder, 1993, 91)

⁴⁰ Willke, 1985, 288

⁴¹ Does this make Luhmann a functionalist? I think not. There is a vastly significant distinction to be drawn between his functional analysis and functionalism with the conservative connotations the latter carries. Luhmann's theory is committed to the first but in no way to the second. His commitment to the first, ie functional analysis, stems from the impossibility of causal explanation in a world where privileged or ultimate observation is no longer possible. Among other reasons because causation requires a succession of cause and effect that cannot cross systems - systems cannot act causally on each other - because it cannot survive the systems' differing self-organisation of time. But Luhmann's theory is not functionalist. (Luhmann, 1984, pp83ff, Smith, 1991, pp334-5, King and Schutz, 1994, pp265-6). Briefly: functions are not given at the outset but emerge as systemic selections that could be otherwise; what as observers we could identify as functional to society's maintenance is merely one systemic account among others; there is no premise within the theory from which parts could co-ordinate in order to contribute to the maintenance or survival of the whole, not least because fit, compatibility or integration between subsystems are ruled out at the outset. Habermas, it could be said therefore, 'won' his famous early exchange with Luhmann with too easy a charge of functionalism: 'Behind the attempt to justify a reduction of the complexity of the world as the highest reference point of functionalism in the social sciences hides the unavowed commitment of the theory to ways of posing the questions which conform with the structure of domination, defending the existing state of affairs in order to keep it in existence. Thus the theory is reserved for technocratic use.' (quoted in Murphy, 1984, p619)

⁴² Luhmann, 1977, 231

(It is because functional sub-systems replicate what is already replicated, that Luhmann calls them 'second-order' autopoietic systems) [43]

On the basis of the distinction system/environment, every sub-system perceives society and other sub-systems as environment. This reflection is 'totalising' in the sense that each encoding makes sense of the whole of reality and claims exclusivity for that depiction.[44] The social is thus given a reality from every systemic perspective, and done so in incommensurable ways: subsystems do not join together into higher level systems - no ultimate (or meta-) observer will resolve their differences - nor can they be conceived of as instances of a totality. This leaves society in the situation of being the totality of communications yet its unity forever undermined by the irreconcilabity of subsystems which not only perceive reality in different ways but also perceive their differences in different ways. *Unitas multiplex*;[45] a society that is at once unity (all communication as distinct from life and consciousness) and multiplicity. And at the same time, in the current evolutionary phase of functional differentiation, a heterarchy; the multiplicity of descriptions of society cannot be co-ordinated hierarchically.[46] This is how Luhmann summarises all this and we will have to elaborate it closer, in what follows:

'Each system is universally competent and at the same time a system within the world, able to distinguish and observe and control itself. It is a self-referential system and thereby a totalizing system. It cannot avoid operating within a world of its own. Societies [social systems] constitute worlds. Observing themselves, that is communicating about themselves, societies cannot avoid using distinctions which differentiate the observing system from something else. Their communication observes itself within its world and describes the limitation of its own competence. Communication never becomes self-transcending. It can never operate outside its own boundaries. The boundaries themselves, however, are components of the system and cannot be taken as given by a pre-constituted world.'[47]

---

[43] All internal differentiation entails the drawing if internal boundaries and the creation of internal environments. see, e.g., Luhmann's discussion of the internal differentiation of the political system in 1990b, p21ff, where he describes the political system as differentiated internally into party politics, government and political public

[44] Luhmann, 1986e ch16

[45] Teubner , 1993, ch 7 , Luhmann, 1986e, 108. Also: 'The unity of society is the unity of the difference between system and environment and in functionally differentiated society this unity can only be given expression from the perspective of the subsystems which have emerged in the course of social evolution.' (Murphy, 1994, 6)

[46] See esp. Luhmann, 1986a, pp 16-7, 28

[47] Luhmann, 1986c, pp178-9

Guiding Distinctions

Since this analysis does not aim to be an exhaustive account of autopoiesis, but rather aims to set specific questions in the context of the theory, the move from the abstract to the concrete within the theory will be informed by the aims of the application. The emphasis on guiding distinctions may appear unjustified, given that not all systems are meaning-processing systems (living systems), not all meaning-processing systems are social systems (psychic systems), not all social systems are functional subsystems (e.g. interaction systems, organisations),[48] and not all functional subsystems employ binary coding as guiding distinction (e.g. the educational system). However, the function systems that will be central to our analysis - law and politics - structure their communication through a binary or two-valued code, that from the viewpoint of a specific function claims universal validity. This makes it important to look at such binary schemata in some depth.

At the very root of the matter, then, the possibility of cognition for the system, springs from difference-controlled observation. According to Luhmann, 'the formulation of the concept of difference makes it possible for events to appear as information and to leave traces behind within the system.'[49] In view of this the interesting question is : 'with the aid of what distinctions can a [social] system observe internal and external objects?'[50]

The importance of the code cannot be stressed enough. The differentiating-out of a system (the original term Ausdifferenzierung implies movement-out-of) occurs when one difference acquires primacy, marginalises and re-aligns other differences to it, and in a sense then first enables the new system's observations to 'crystallise' around it and the complexity of the world to be reduced to this difference.[51] The code underpins the reduction on which totalisation depends. Other distinctions, operative in other systems, are re-aligned to this central difference that renders all the variances and contrasts understandable (observable) because relevant to the difference that enables the system to view the world. All other differences are semantically subsumed under the primary difference (überformt) and permeated with new contingencies (the contingency space specific to the system.)

---

[48] 'Functional differentiation is certainly no precondition for autopoietic reproduction,' says Luhmann (1984, 406)

[49] Luhmann, 1990a, 108

[50] Luhmann, 1985b, 393. We must be careful here to distinguish among guiding differences between those that underlie the identity of the system and give it its unity and other more secondary ones, such as those that are operative in programming.

[51] Historically, e.g., the move from stratification to functional differentiation in the West reflected both the emergence of functional systems with functions acting as catalysts for such crystallisations of meanings. See generally Luhmann, (1990b)

Binary codes are simply a difference between a yes and a no, the difference between a positive and a negative value. This is a calculus that is given specific form by systems at the level of differentiated communications. To explain how the codes of functional sub-systems came about, Luhmann draws from Parsons' theory of symbolically generalised media.[52] These media are not exclusive to a system but exist within society at large and in a sense hold systems together from below.[53] But functional sub-systems each reserve a special use for a medium ('couples it strictly') as a code and uses it to direct all relevant communication. Science does this for the medium of truth, for example, encoding it as true/false, politics that of power, economy that of money, etc. What is it that gives each binary schema the power to inform a reading of reality? The value and counter-value of the code, unlike 'evaluative' values, have formal equivalence[54] for the system: designating something as legal or true is not a more likely or favoured choice for the legal and scientific system respectively, than deeming it illegal or false. The power of the code lies in that the very constitution of the identity of a system involves the play between positive value and negative value: the designation of every position is always identified in relation to (in the mirror of) its counter-position. 'Communication x is legal, y is true,' claim the lawyer and the scientist. How could things be different? They could be different in being illegal or false. The identity of x as legal involves situating it in the difference between legal/illegal. Only by reflecting it in the mirror of its negation does the identity of x as legal come about. The abstract initial discussion of how differentiation creates meaning becomes more obvious in the concrete case here.

This is how the identity of the system comes about: identity as tautology (legal is what is legal) is replaced by identity as difference (the law is the difference between legal and illegal). It may be true that this 'identity as difference' means very little before it can be shown how through the latter the system can relate to the World. But it is crucial to note that in whatever context the legal/illegal dichotomy may be used in communication, it will underpin, cause, raise, provide the identity of any information. This is what the theory's critics don't see when they criticise the theory's exaggerated reliance on the code.

This line of criticism maintains that it is a simplification to purport to exhaust what law is about by relying on the difference between legal and illegal. Rottleutner reminds us that law assumes a variety of forms,

---

[52] See generally Luhmann, 1976b
[53] Cf. Teubner's account of the materiality continuum
[54] Although they started off their semantic careers as *Präferenzcoden* or *idées directrices* [guiding ideals] 1986f, pp149-50

regulatory strategies, licenses, incentives, includes processes for reaching decisions, scientific expertise, e.t.c., that cannot all be fitted into the legal/illegal dichotomy.[55] Bankowski points to the Scottish 'not proven' as breaking up the necessary binarism of the code.[56] There are other criticisms to this effect. One way of confronting these criticisms is to show that they rely too heavily on coding at the expense of Luhmann's insistence on programming and other functional equivalents like values, secondary codes (like prohibited/forbidden, e.t.c.; we will return to this in the next chapter). More importantly however, the critics cannot see that the code gives a communication in law its very identity as legal, allowing in the first place any further state of information about incentives, strategies, e.t.c., to appear, and all this in an immediate way.[57] However legal information is to be processed, and the variety here is immense, it is first comes about as such through coding.

Coding generates information. Codes specify the differences on the basis of which something is received as information. Experience, action, facts are grasped through difference, by virtue of their being submitted to the guiding distinction; information is possible only in this situating, this channelling into a pattern of difference.[58] It is in the situating of a stimulus (noise) in the pattern of 'this rather than that' that codes can be understood as duplication rules. They duplicate the reality they observe. Reality acquires a dimension other than that of being normal. When exposed to the code difference, say the legal code, pure facticity becomes information. Actions become legal or illegal, events become legally relevant. How they are allocated to either value is itself not a matter for coding.[59] What duplication means is that the very

---

[55] Rottleutner, 1989b

[56] Bankowski, 1994.

[57] Murphy points this out too. 'That coding is the starting point for which the term system is both a shorthand and an indicator of entrenchment of the coding is easily overlooked ... by the critics of the theory.' (Murphy, 1994, 17)

[58] This 'structuralist' use of semantic difference must be incorporated into the overall theory before its contribution can be assessed, and that means incorporating it in the dimension of time, at the level of the communicative event. This is the subject of the next section, where we will explore the intimate link of information with expectation, and how the codes themselves are caught up in the process and respecified in the temporal dimension.

[59] The critics' warning against reducing the legal universe to the difference between legal and illegal can be rebutted on this ground too. The plurality of legal forms can be well accounted for without giving up the primacy of the code. On the contrary, only because of that primacy of coding, that establishes the contingency space, can structures be built up with such ease ('a move that would be difficult to a legal system oriented towards fundamental values.' (Smith S C, 1991, 329) As Luhmann writes in *Ecological Communication*: '[E]xtreme elasticity is purchased at the cost of the rigidity of "contextual" conditions. Everything appears as contingent. But the realisation of other possibilities is bound to specific system references.' (1986e, 109)

identity of x as legal involves its negation, i.e. its reflection in the counter-value (x is not not-legal). A statement about x can be made, the system activates a perspective by duplicating reality and making 'x is legal' meaningful because it could be the case that 'x is not legal.'[60] It is this duplication that determines in what sense things could be different. Reflecting in the counter-value enables observation, by setting an assertion against the background of another possibility (this rather than that). Pure fact now acquires the possibility to register, to be observed.

At the same time the duplication through the negative value opens up a contingency space: x could be legal or illegal. The negative value allows us to see how things could be different. In view of this everything is neither necessary nor impossible, therefore contingent.[61] This is a contingency that is bound by the bivalency of the code, it is a 'first-order contingency'; there are other levels too at which we encounter contingency and we must be careful to keep these distinct. There is contingency at a second level, bound by specific system references, and there is a further level of contingency that this thesis attempts to establish as the ground for reflexive politics: a (third) level of contingency that allows us to challenge what at the other levels appears *always already* determined: the existence of the framework of choice and the necessity of circumscribing the contingent within it.

Back to the code. The code is the system's guiding difference because, by employing it, the system can steer its operations and make meaningful the designation of something as legal. But this difference can only designate a 'contingency space' - something can be a or not-a - but, as we said, can tell us nothing about how positive and negative values are to be allocated. At the code level there is no commitment to either value. The code itself provides no means for breaking its own perfect symmetry. Neither of the code values can serve as criteria of their own selection. In order to relate to the world it has to break the symmetry of its code; it needs to 'asymmetricize'. Secondary codes (prohibition/ permission, conservative/ progressive), conditional and goal structures, values and functional equivalents, even reflexive structures, will perform this function. I will employ the term programming to cover all these; to cover programming stricto sensu (conditional and goal structures) as well as all its functional equivalents, i.e. equivalents from the point of view of allowing the system to asymmetricise. All these further distinctions that

---

[60] It is only under the condition of openness towards both the positive and the negative option that a social system can identify with a code. The code is the form with which the system distinguishes itself from the environment and organises its own operative closure. (1991a, 78)
[61] Luhmann, 1984, 156

come under 'programming' are aligned and correlated to the code difference.[62] Let us look at an example of how this works.

The code [Recht/Unrecht][63] introduces a distinction into an undifferentiated reality. How else to handle the world that is not a binary one except by reducing it through the binarism of the code in a way that makes it yield information? It is for this reason that reduction is an 'achievement'. Things are meaningful as relevant to the code difference; because the legal system observes 'itself and everything else in terms of legal/illegal and must make indications on the basis of that distinction.'[64] All communication that aligns itself to this distinction belongs to and constitutes the legal system. Out of the infinite possibilities of describing a person's action, for example, the legal system addresses what is relevant to deeming it legal or illegal. Further, the person's will is thematised as intention or motive because that is conducive to a legal characterisation of his/her action. The economic system may re-cast that expression of the will as economic-rational preference, the political system assess it in terms of support or disaffection to Government or Opposition. Each system restricts on its own terms the ambit of what is meaningful by filtering communication through system-relevance established by the code. Further distinctions (programming) build on the code: intended/not-intended, fault/strict liability, incitement/ free expression, occupational/ political demand, speech/ action. All the distinctions on the one hand draw on the system's reduction of the World to a single difference (legal/illegal), while at the same time building up the system's internal complexity, that allows it to 'see' more things, and cope more adequately with external reality.

In this sense the code enables the system to 'construct' its environment, to set itself in context; it enables it to observe environmental stimuli on the basis of the distinction and deal with them by each time indicating one side of the binary schema. The structural technique that makes this possible is a 'difference technique.'[65] The system introduces its own distinction and on

---

[62] Cf Rottleutner, 1989b, 792. See Smith S C, 1991, 329-31, for a response.

[63] Much has been made of the translation of the original Recht/Unrecht into English. A convincing alternative, I think, is lawful/unlawful.

[64] Luhmann, 1985b, 393

[65] Autopoietic theory is clearly structuralist here. For Saussure concepts 'sont purement différentiels, définis non pas positivement par leur contenu, mais negativement par leur rapports avec les autres termes du systeme. Leur plus exacte caracteristique est d'être ce que les autres ne sont pas' (1973, p162). As systems operationalise different distinction schemas, concepts, for Luhmann too, are not free-floating signifiers, but draw their meaning from the difference pattern that is in each case operative. To use one of his favourite examples, the concept of society means in each case something different, depending on whether the observation draws on the distinction society/state (eg a liberal observes) or society/individual (a sociologist observes) or society/nature (Rousseau observes), or society (Gesellschaft) / Gemeinschaft (a 'communitarian' observes). What side holds up the mirror for the indication of

that basis grasps states and events as information. The 'difference technique' is the device that the system employs to decipher complexity by enacting a system specific reduction which results in a system-centric representation of reality. It is thus that the distinction 'establishes a universe, sets up systemic boundaries, structures a discourse.'[66] Together coding and programming provide the cluster of differences through which the world is localised within the system. Primacy of course lies with the code that underlies the identity of the system and ultimately generates information; it does not determine, however 'which pieces of information are called for and which selection they trigger.'[67] Programming provides criteria for fixing the conditions for the suitability of selections. In science, for example, the requirement of suitability belongs to theory and method, on the basis of which the truth or falsity of scientific statements can be assessed. Structures themselves can be changed at the level of programming, as is ultimately the case with a paradigm shift in science, without the system thereby losing its identity, which depends on the coding. To move this to law: norms (programmes) provide the correctness of the allocation of legality and illegality (code), method (programme again) here consisting of rules of interpretation of norms; structural variations, in law, occur when norms are varied through new legislation or new constitutional interpretations.

To recapitulate: the identity of the system comes about at the level of the code. The system's identity as tautology (legal is what is legal) is replaced here by identity as difference (the law is the difference between legal and illegal). But the symmetry has to be broken because it is otherwise unproductive for the system. On the basis of programming (other differences) the system is allowed to steer its operations by allocating events to either side of the contrast-schema. Together coding and programming allows the system to see the world in a certain way (it can be legal or illegal, true or false), and to operationalise its mode of seeing. We do not need any more background information in order to make sense of those cryptic and controversial descriptions of systems as 'closed and open at the same time,' of the legal system, for example, as 'cognitively open because normatively closed.' It is the difference of coding and programming that makes possible the combination of closure and openness in the same system. These are flip-sides

---

its other makes all the difference; observation both depends and draws on that unity. Its 'meaning schema' (1986e, 122) is contained in the distinction it puts forward (early/late, useful/catastrophic, system/environment), thus bringing much richer meaning possibilities into play and then reducing them through selective designation. Observation is selective designation from a pool of richer possibilities; the bracketing of the non-indicated side holds the mirror for the indicated side.

[66] Grundmann, 1990, 33
[67] Luhmann, 1982, p107

of the same coin, internally linked, mutually supportive, reciprocally enabling: it is the very structural constraints that enable the system to relate to the environment. The system is cognitively open in terms of its means of closure. It is only because the code reduces options and maintains the system's closure around its code, that it allows a point of view into an otherwise undifferentiated reality and that information about that reality can build up meaningfully. The system's capacity for reaction to the environment, 'resonance', which is steered through programming, rests on the closed polarity of the code. The possibility that the environment registers at all is due to the code, and in that sense closure is a pre-condition for cognitive openness.

Finally, in this context, let me point *to a distinction between identity and unity*. The system acquires its identity through its characteristic means of reducing complexity, in the act, that is, of imposing sharp edges on the world that has none. But what over and above this reduction accounts for the system's unity? We need to look at the dimension of time here to understand unity, because the system as temporalised acquires its unity over time. Unity comes to the system through the temporal dimension. Notice Luhmann's oft-emphasised departure from structuralism:

'Structuralists have never been able to show how a structure can produce an event. At this point, the theory of autopoiesis offers a substantive advance. It is the network of events which reproduces itself, and structures are required for the reproduction of events by events.'[68]

Structuralism cannot but conceive of the event in its reflection in a fixed structure, as always a realisation of an existing matrix. In a sense post-structuralism redeems structuralism's inability to draw the structure/event distinction. This is what the dimension of time is doing in Luhmann's theory too, and that is why unity over time is a necessary complement to the identity of the system. If it can be said, albeit somehow crudely, that the identity of a communication as systemic instantiates the matrix in a structuralist way, the unity of the system accounts for why it is that codes are re-embedded and thus re-specified as the system evolves and why the system thus respecified is still the same one. It is in this sense also, I think, that Teubner's elaborate account of what degree of self-reference counts as autopoiesis should be read. The autopoiesis of the system is maintained only when self-reference as self-observation, self-description,

---

[68] Luhmann, 1986c, 174-5. We will see how structures as expectations perform this function in the chapter to follow.

self-organisation and finally hypercyclical linkage[69] makes it possible for the system to re-instate its unity as it changes in time, only on the basis of which is the new element still an element of the system, kept within the system's bounds.

---

[69] Teubner, 1993, ch.2

CHAPTER SEVEN

Law, Society and Conflict

I will locate my discussion of conflict and law in two prevalent contexts. The first is the broad context of the sociological discussion of the relationship of conflict and society. The second is the narrower one of the 'juridification' of conflict. I will engage in both debates, take cues from both, but also distance my position from both by re-working central assumptions from the point of view of systems-theory, or at least of my view of how systems theory makes best sense of both debates. Such a fundamental re-tracing of the inter-relationship between conflict, law and society aims to confront the deep and multi-faceted mis-understandings that underlie the republican suggestion for the legal containment of politics in the crucial area of political conflict.

The relationship between conflict and society has been sociologically elaborated in two basic ways, each informed by radically different orientations and concerns. For the one 'school', conflict is constitutive of society. Society *is* its conflictual reproduction. Typical of this orientation is Marxist theory. The second orientation, sociological functionalism, sees society not in terms of cleavage but of an equilibrium of inter-related functions. Conflict is understood in its performing certain functions in society. Taking the cue from Durkheim, this tradition has developed very elaborate and insightful analyses of the role of conflict in society, its various performances where what may initially appear as a problem is reversed as functional. My discussion of Touraine on the one hand and of Simmel and Coser on the other, addresses some of the work done in both traditions and, in one sense at least, attempts to bridge them. I will use the terms *'constitutive'* to refer to conflict in the first tradition, the term *'phenomenal'* for the second. Anticipating much of what is to come, it can be said that systems theory accommodates both positions by posing the question of conflict as one of observation; observation and expectation structures mediate the disparity and allow both positions, but not simultaneously. An observer at any one time can see either one or the other state of affairs: either a state of conflict co-terminous with society or one where conflict is a pathology that performs certain functions in society.

I will take up this discussion in chapter eight. In the meantime, in a rather counter-intuitive move, I want to briefly locate my position regarding the other of the questions, the juridification of conflict. The republicans claim that law can contain politics and a crucial aspect of this claim is that law can contain political conflict. Much of the literature on juridification, too, purports to be about that containment. My own position is quite different here. I do not accept that only a certain type of law - regulatory law - has the adverse effects tied with juridification. Instead my claim is that all political conflict in law, all conflict juridified, is conflict de-politicised. Is all conflict then political to begin with? Yes, implicitly.[1]

THE JURIDIFICATION OF CONFLICT

Juridification is a term meant to denote not merely the increasing legal sanctioning of communication and action but more crucially the process whereby the law defines for itself the realm of its application, selectively bringing it into existence. This is an insight as old as sociology itself, so that neither the idea nor the term itself can claim any great novelty; in fact by the time Habermas popularised the notion, it already had a long history, loaded with political significance. Juridification was a denunciatory term used by radical labour lawyers in Germany in the thirties to describe a certain 'petrification' of class conflict.[2] What Habermas did was to abstract the term from its origin in labour relations and to use it to designate what he describes as a legal impingement on the social domain, a process whereby a spontaneous social context comes under legal sway. This is the theory of juridification as the colonization of the lifeworld.[3] It is a complex argument to which very little reference is made in what follows as I find the category both over- and under-inclusive; my own reliance on the concept of juridification is from the systems-theoretical perspective and aims to illustrate the ways in which the law appropriates and depletes politics by legally differentiating out the area of what is significant *as* political.

I will focus the discussion of juridification on conflict and, initially, employ Teubner's account of the phenomenon to set my own discussion in context. This is not only because Teubner's introductory article in the *Juridification of Social Spheres*[4] is, despite its brevity, one of the most comprehensive accounts of the problem to date. But also because while locating my argument in the context of his mapping of the debates, I want to argue against him that the juridification of conflict *is* its de-politicisation. This is in fact the crux of the whole argument of part II against the republican thesis of the legal containment of conflict.

---

[1] My discussion of reflexivity in the last chapter is relevant to this assertion
[2] Fraenkel and Kirchheimer, in Teubner, 1987, 9
[3] Habermas, 1984, esp. vol.2, 113ff
[4] Teubner, 1987

Teubner clarifies at the outset that to explore juridification as a problem of law in general would be asking the concept to do too much work; rather juridification can be more fruitfully explored as a problem associated with a special type of law: regulatory law. This is the type of law instrumental to the implementation of Welfare State policy, and juridification becomes an umbrella term to cover questions of function, legitimacy, structure and success of this 'managerial' type of law.[5] Teubner sets aside the usual frameworks for explaining the problem and instead pursues the explanation as a question of 'structural coupling' between the political system, where regulatory strategies are hampered, the legal system, that is the former's means of implementing that policy, and the social field to be regulated, each with its own autonomous logic that defies direct manipulation. Problems of juridification then appear as failures to respect the boundaries and logics of the systems involved, a failure to see that what is really involved is in fact a co-evolution of autopoietic systems, only reciprocally stimulated, *not* causally related. It is all too easy to overstep boundaries on all sides in this delicate process. The result of such over-stepping is experienced as juridification.[6]

In Teubner's analysis, questions of the function, legitimacy, structure, e.t.c., of the law are explored in view of the law's failure to achieve the goals it was set to achieve. Thus juridification is a name for that failure. Teubner's account is motivated by the desire to address questions of regulatory failure (a motivating force behind much of his work). This is important because it makes much of Teubner's account un-interesting to an analysis that is not driven by a concern about regulatory failures. For me, it also points to the limits of Teubner's account in what concerns 'the expropriation of conflict', and the easy dismissal on his part of a question that I will argue is broader.

Teubner begins with an attempt to establish an adequate definition of the term 'juridification', not 'for terminological clarity,' 'but in order to create a working framework.' Conceptions of juridification, he says, 'always contain a theory of the conditions in which it is developed, an evaluation of its consequences and a strategy for dealing with it.'[7] I suggest that Teubner opts for the definition he does because he has a 'strategy for dealing with it.' On the basis of the strategy and before establishing his own preferred definition, he visits the options not taken.

The first option that identifies juridification as 'legal explosion', an inflation of laws, can be discarded for relying on a quantitative criterion that is of practically no use. Because where would the threshold of tolerable quantity be set and why? To answer those questions would be to engage

---

[5] Kamenka and Tay, 1975, 127ff, Unger, 1976, 58ff, Cotterrell, 1984, 171ff
[6] On the notion of the 'regulatory trilemma' see Teubner (1983) and (1987)
[7] Teubner (1987)

seriously with the problem of a definition, and 'inflation of norms' pure and simple allows no purchase into that. The second and third options are more promising. My own suggestion, as I will explain later, is for an understanding of juridification that includes both these categories but cuts across the way Teubner has defined them.

The second definition of juridification, that Teubner draws from legal sociology, is that of 'the expropriation of conflict.'[8] Juridification here becomes:

'a process in which human conflicts are, through formalization, torn out of their living context and distorted by being subjected to legal processes ... In this view juridification does not solve conflicts but alienates them. It mutilates the social conflict, reducing it to a legal case and thereby excludes the possibility of an adequate future-oriented, socially rewarding resolution.'[9]

Teubner also suggests that there exists a third definition of juridification that he distinguishes from the second. The focal element in this definition is de-politicisation. This definition, not adequately worked out in Teubner's article, pivots on a co-operation/conflict distinction with examples here drawn exclusively from the area of labour law. 'Juridification re-inforces co-operative trade union policies ... at the expense of "conflictive" trade union policy.' The reference seems to be exclusively to the old, original meaning of the term in the context of labour relations denoting the dilemma which presented itself as the legal institutionalisation of employment relations threatening to petrify class-conflictual action.

Having discarded the first quantitative approach to the problem as naïve, Teubner turns to the second and third accounts. What, he asks, is the problem with the accounts of juridification as expropriation and as de-politicisation? He identifies failures in these accounts of juridification by relying exclusively on the strategies proposed for dealing with the problem. He only 'find[s] these accounts of juridification wanting' in that he finds the strategies put forward wanting. In dealing with the first of these, the problems that he identifies are all to do with the 'alternatives to juridification' proposed by the exponents of informal justice. He rightly, I think, finds the strategy of informal justice only surrendering conflict to different power constellations. More broadly he finds the relevant school in

---

[8] Typically Christie's notion of 'conflicts as property' would fall under this category. He argues for an organization of social systems such that 'conflicts are both nurtured and made visible and also see it that professionals do not monopolise the handling of them.' (1977, 1) There does remain the question of course as to what the nature of the free-floating signifier 'conflict' is, and also whether Christie's idea is not self-defeating by relying on the legal notion of property to save conflict from law.

[9] Teubner, 1987, 9

legal sociology misguided in 'confining itself to the classical tasks of law (conflict regulation) and has only marginally concerned itself with the really explosive aspects of modern juridification (social regulation).'[10] Rather than focusing on 'the explosive effects of law that threatens entire social spheres,' this first, 'legal-sociological formulation of the question, harmlessly and almost provincially' locates the problem as one 'delivering up conflicts to the court system.' In the end juridification as expropriation of conflict is confined by Teubner to a 'judiciary-critical' definition which he is happy to dismiss as an account of a relatively insignificant part of the problem.

Having dealt with the first category, Teubner turns to juridification as depoliticisation, a problem he sees as 'limited to the labour union perspective and abstains from socio-structural explanations.' He also 'finds wanting' this 'political science perspective which sees juridification as restricting the room for manoeuvre of social movements and interest groups.' On this account juridification 'tends to depoliticise social conflicts by drastically limiting the labour unions' possibilities of militant action.'[11] Again, what Teubner seeks in his analysis of this approach is the 'implied counter-strategy' it suggests.

I will argue two things. The first is that the distinction between the second and third categories cannot be seriously maintained. The expropriation of conflict *is* its depoliticisation. The 'co-operative or conflictive strategy' dilemma is only a case (in Labour Law) of the dilemma present in all expropriation: of either 'buying into' the official discourse, in which case the original conflict disappears, or of not being heard at all. The second thing I will argue, in the sections to follow, is that expropriation as de-politicisation represents the crux of what is at stake in juridification: the re-enactment of conflict from law's point of view.

I suggest that Teubner's analysis ignores both these points because it is driven solely by the desire to rebut accounts of juridification on the basis that they do not suggest feasible or desirable counter-strategies. No doubt the way one sets up a problem pre-empts certain ways of dealing with it, but the set-up of a problem and its treatment are distinct questions. More importantly, in the process of dealing with the category of expropriation, Teubner gradually belittles it to a judiciary-critical account, important no doubt, but certainly not broad enough. But there is no reason for this confinement. It is only because he quietly allows the slip, that Teubner can

---

[10] What's the point of this contra-distinction, one may ask at this stage. Is the former not instrumental to, or even identical to, the latter? What Teubner has in mind, that makes sense of this dichotomy, is a distinction ultimately between the function of law - tied to but not identical with the former -, and law's performance, its instrumentalisation towards policy implementation.

[11] Teubner, 1987

then designate the central category of de-politicisation - that one naturally assumes is a central category of expropriation - as distinct. Why is it important to resist this distinction and instead assume that de-politicisation is an instance of expropriation? Because a conflict conceived as a political one, in class-conflictual terms typically, is *expropriated* when cast in law, in a significantly similar way that a 'vital' or 'spontaneous' conflict is expropriated when cast in law. In both cases, system-internal relevancies are projected to make sense of the conflict, which then resonates in law in an alienated way or, as I will argue soon, is re-enacted in a way that distorts and depletes it. If moreover, as I will explain, the political is reflexive and harbours as such a conflict over conflict, to juridify is indeed (not only to expropriate but also) to *de-politicise*.

Of course all this creates problems that Teubner's careful account evades; most importantly his analysis evades the difficult designation of the point at which a conflict is expropriated, 'mutilated', uprooted from its spontaneous setting, usurped. This is a difficult designation because conflicts are often first cast in law: law often prompts, furnishes and creates conflict.[12] To delineate an area of 'original' conflict that can be usurped involves very difficult questions about the socialisation of law and the socialisation of actors into law, questions of the law's relative weight in social discourse, e.t.c. Teubner's account steers clear of these problems but at a cost. I don't intend to go into these questions any further because the argument of this chapter does not depend on such a delineation. The argument merely assumes *ex hypothesi* that actors often enough entertain normative orientations underpinning conflictual positions that may be irrelevant or hostile to law. The term 'political' is reserved for the freedom to contest the terms in which conflict is cast, and sees in law this possibility withdrawn. In that sense law usurps politics by eradicating conflict over the terms of conflict, thus *expropriates* and **in the same move**, thus *depoliticises*.

---

[12] For an interesting account of how this happens see Festiner, Abel and Sarat, (1980). For my own account see chapter ten.

CHAPTER EIGHT

LAW AND THE DOUBLE CONTINGENCY OF CONFLICT

Before I deal with the question of conflict 'constitutive' and 'phenomenal' (and its relation to law) I need to discard an ideological use of the distinction that only tends to confuse the issues in order to set up easy targets. This ideological use of the distinction mis-identifies phenomenal conflict with equilibrium, consensus and conservatism, and constitutive conflict with change. Associated with this, there has been a deep divide in much sociological literature between perspectives furnished by such purportedly exclusive alternatives as conflict and consensus. Conflict theory and consensus theory are all too often seen as seeking their departure from, gaining their leverage from, and positing some kind of teleology to, mutually exclusive alternatives. This in turn has occasionally led to simplistic equations of consensus to social structure and conflict to social dynamics. Confrontations on that basis have not been rare. For example, Lewis Coser's analysis of the function of social conflict of upholding group structures has been criticised by conflict theorists as depleting the radical potential of conflict theory.[1] This dichotomisation simply confuses the issues. Conflict is as much inimical to social structures as it is intrinsic to them. Co-operation contains conflict as it does consensus.[2] Of course whether one approaches questions from the point of view of conflict or consensus pre-empts much of what one finds, yet it is simplistic to deny the value of either theory by imputing pre-destinations or pre-commitments (constancy/dynamics) to either.[3]

Systems theory, too, invites a reconciliation of the exclusive alternatives by making the stronger claim that it is in fact impossible to keep them apart (except temporarily, as a distinction that 'unfolds' a tautology - see earlier discussion on distinctions and observation). For, as Luhmann would say, is it not the case that conflict is always-already in co-operation as implicit

---

[1] See Rex (1961) and Coser's answer in (1965, 5 and passim)

[2] 'The more one thinks of it the more he will see that conflict and co-operation are not separable things, but phases of one process which always involves something of both.' (Coser, 1956, 18. Also Coser, 1965, pp11, 26.) See also Simmel: 'Contradiction and conflict not only precede unity but are operative in it at every moment of its existence.' (1955, 13)

[3] 'The kind of theory we have been suggesting is, by its very nature, a theory of social disruption and social change. Finally, something should therefore be said about the rather unexpected theory that conflict contributes to the stability of systems.' (Rex, 1981, 72)

regulative of its forms and conditions?[4] In any case, to make sense of conflict systems-theoretically we will have to take a few steps back from the distinction conflict/consensus and pick up the thread at the level of the most basic question of sociology: how is the social possible? (and hence also, how is meaningful social interaction possible at all?) This is the prior question to all other questions and the set-up of all sociological categories, including that of conflict at issue here. Before any pattern of social interaction can be designated and distinguished, be that co-operation or conflict, it is necessary to establish how social interaction is possible in the first place. This may seem an extreme question but it is less so in view of Luhmann's account of society's overwhelming complexity.[5] Since society is (the sum total of) communications then the most basic question for the theory of society becomes 'how is a communication possible?', or in the way that Luhmann breaks up the elementary communication, 'how is the *information* content of Ego's *utterance understood* by Alter'? The cue that Luhmann takes from Parsons is that the answer to this most basic of sociological questions should be approached as a problem of **Double Contingency**.[6]

My purpose in the present chapter is to deal with questions of political conflict and the law and attempt to demonstrate the impossibility of the containment of the former in the latter. I begin to explore the realm of conflict by taking this discussion back to the question of double contingency because before we can explore what conflict means we need to explore how expectations articulate to pattern out interaction in the first place, albeit conflictual or consensual. Thus the recourse back to the basic question allows us to follow Luhmann's re-mapping of the territory on which much of my rebuttal of republicanism depends.

Luhmann returns to Parsons to retrieve a solution to the 'unlikeliness' [unwahrscheinlichkeit][7] of social interaction. Since Parsons, and Hobbes before him, the question has been traced back to how patterns of social

---

[4] The question can of course be approached from the point of view of the 'reflexive value of negation'. We know what it means to trust because we know what distrust is, we love 'relexively' in the mirror of the lack of love: in a similar way co-operation draws from conflict: not only are they not mutually exclusive forms of interaction, but conflict is built into cooperation itelf as secret regulative, i.e. as reflexive negation.

[5] 'Wie ist soziale Ordnung möglich?' In Luhmann (1975c)

[6] An early comprehensive discussion of Double Contingency is contained in (1972). As this is Luhmann of the pre-autopoiesis turn, one must be careful in selecting what part of this work is consistent with his later writings. Indeed that discussion has been qualified later in (1984, ps 148-190) (Earlier in 1971, pp44ff, later, indicatively, 1990c). The following discussion draws, with caution, from both periods.

[7] Luhmann, 1984, 165

interdependence can build up with any constancy; Parsons suggested locating the query in the context of the potentially erosive situation of double contingency, the problem that is, of the potential unlikeliness that people's expectations will articulate to allow communication and interaction in the first place. As Luhmann puts it:

'The radicalisation of the problem of double contingency ... articulates the question "how is social order possible?" in a way that presents this possibility as above all improbable.'[8]

Interaction depends on social-cognitive concepts regarding Ego/Alter relations. Interaction requires that the social actor relate the meaningful sense of his/her action to that of others. Interaction implies that success or failure of a communicative offer oriented to Alter depends on what Alter expects. Otherwise there is no communication and neither side can orient their action in a way either can comprehend, to the other's expectations. In order to achieve this elementary interaction with Alter, Ego not only has to predict and take account of Alter's behaviour but also Alter's expectations of Ego's behaviour. This creates a double indeterminacy that has to be settled. Parsons uses 'contingency' in the sense of 'dependence' and the term 'double contingency' to designate the double dependence of Ego's action on both Alter's behaviour and on Alter's expectation of Ego's behaviour. Because Ego's perspective on Ego/Alter relationships must take on board (is contingent on) Alter's perspective, there exists in this inter-dependence two self/other cycles that need to be co-ordinated. The locus classicus in Parsons for describing this interdependence is the following:

'Since the outcome of Ego's action (e.g. success in the achievement of a goal) is contingent on Alter's reaction to what Ego does, Ego becomes oriented not only to Alter's probable overt behaviour, but also what Ego interprets to be Alter's expectations relative to Ego's behaviour since Ego expects that Alter's expectations will influence Alter's behaviour.'[9]

In order for people to inter-relate their behaviour, the complexity of this double indeterminacy has to be settled, says Parsons, through the mediation of norms. That is because norms serve to integrate mutual expectations of behaviour and stabilise a certain 'complementarity' of expectations.[10] Luhmann suggests that in putting forward this function for norms, Parsons is bringing together Weber and Durkheim at a higher level of abstraction: on

---

[8] Luhmann, 1984, 165
[9] Parsons, 1962, 105. Also for a more detailed account, Parsons and Shils, 1951, pp3-29
[10] ibid, pp15ff

the one hand, Weber's focus on the subjective meaning of social action, on the other hand, Durkheim's insistence on the objective social normative structures through which meaning is experienced.[11] Parsons offers an integrating pattern for the two in his account of the function of norms:

'[T]he double contingency implies the normative orientation of action ... If punishment or reward by alter is repeatedly manifested under certain conditions, this reaction acquires for ego the meaning of an appropriate consequence of ego's conformity with or deviation from the norms of a shared symbolic system. A shared symbolic system is a system of ways of orienting, plus those external symbols which control these ways of orienting, the system being so geared into the action systems of both ego and alter that the external symbol bring forth the same or a complementary pattern of orientation for both of them.'[12]

If Luhmann is to accept this, he will first attempt to clear up some Parsonian misunderstandings. The first is the one-sidedness of viewing the structure of social systems as consisting exclusively of normative expectations to the exclusion of other kinds of structures.[13] There is also a second problem that Parsons creates when he emphasises 'shared symbolic system' and, underlying it, sufficient value consensus.[14] Parsons' pre-commitment to normative integration overestimates the consensus that is structurally necessary, or that exists.[15] Luhmann argues that neither the possibility of such consensus nor (contra Habermas) the willingness of actors to reach it can be guaranteed at the outset. Assuming it on the basis of a shared cultural background, leads Parsons to over-estimate the integrative function of culture which he employs as a ready-for-use provision, a postulate that begs the crucial question of how it came to be.[16]

Luhmann returns to fill in these gaps by emphasising Parsons' failure to engage with the dimension of time. The postulate of culture needs to be re-thought as a process of repetition in actual social practice. In the extract quoted above, Luhmann tells us that Parsons should have put the emphasis on 'repeatedly' to denote the notion of time as constitutive of normative

---

[11] Luhmann, 1972, 17

[12] Quoted in Luhmann, 1984, 175. Cf Weick: 'A mutual equivalence structure can be built and sustained without people knowing the motives of another person, without people having to share goals, and it is not even necessary that people know the entire structure or know who their partners are. What is crucial in a mutual equivalence structure is mutual prediction, not mutual sharing.' (1979, 100)

[13] ... other structures which are then integrated into other component systems of the whole action system, a displacement that obscures the function of the normative in society - see also Luhmann, 1972, ch1, n.23

[14] Luhmann, 1984, 175

[15] Luhmann, 1975a, 73-74

[16] Luhmann, 1984, pp149ff

orientation. Double contingency is transformed into ordered interaction, to begin with, as a process that repeats itself, and also, significantly, as a process where self-referentiality is at play.

Parsons' formulation of the problem of double contingency allows Luhmann a departure into his own preoccupations with complexity and contingency. Having relied on Parsons to formulate the problem but disregarded his notorious over-reliance on the existing normative consensus, Luhmann puts forward his own response to the problem of double contingency. That which is required in order for people to inter-relate their behaviour is that the complexity of the double indeterminacy be **reduced**. There are a number of levels at which this might happen; for Luhmann a number of types of systems that may achieve it. The achievement is that of *fixing a context*. This context furnishes a background of shared expectations that will accommodate the reciprocal communicative offers. Interaction first becomes meaningful when the communicative offer is bound to a common context, a background of reciprocity, that alone allows it recognition. More precisely, Luhmann talks of a reduction of double contingency through a structuring into frameworks that have the form of **expectations of expectations**. The structuring first allows every single communication to surface as meaningful (therefore as communication), as the common ground where Ego meets Alter around a communication they both understand; where, that is, the *information*al intention *uttered* by Ego is *understood* by Alter. Recognition of Alter's intended meaning must be structurally facilitated or it will remain under-determined. What is understood as a communication depends on how the context accommodates the communicative offer, what Alter expects and what Ego expects Alter to expect, which in turn varies according to how the message is filtered into the specific framework of expectations of expectations. And it is in *time* that such contexts form, as recurrent schemes of processing messages, ways of doing things that consolidate through repetition, rather than, for example, Parsons' fast recourse to culture. Our previous discussion of the unity of the system is particularly important here. The system is dynamic, its unity compounded in time as structures produce events-as-communications that are tested, feed back and re-embed the structures, thus reproducing the system. In time, then, systems come about, as constraints that facilitate meaning. And this is no paradox: only constraints as reductions can allow intelligibility and interaction by *setting up a context*, and carving out *only a certain part of the totality* (of possible communication) *as expectable*. The expectability of expectations underlies all social interaction, but acquires specific forms through specific reductions that are particular to systems. The structural processing is effected through systems, the set-up of specific templates that impose specific reductions to the open contingency of (proto-) communication and make it structured and meaningful. What reductions structures impose has to do with what observation-schemas the system avails to make sense of reality, what thematisations, what programming it activates and the rest. A lot has been said, and will still be said, about how the *selectivity* mechanisms set up the system domain and how themes of communication develop, around which communicative offers may be organised. Taking it all back to double contingency allows Luhmann to establish that communication is only possible through reductions which are in turn premised on system selectivity. In his own words 'Kommunikation ist koordinierte Selektivität.'[17] It is of constitutive importance for communication that communicative offers crystallise in systems around 'selective alignments of meaning selections'[18] and thus ensure the possibility of successful communication.

Contexts can be fixed at a number of levels. Simple interactions between, say friends, lovers, colleagues, develop as contexts that allow reciprocal perspective-taking and thus expectations to articulate. Interactions in wider settings also develop elementary contexts that allow meaningful interchange. But the greatest constancy of the context of reciprocity is achieved at the level of second-order autopoiesis, in other words by functional systems like science, the economy, *law*. Law secures this constancy by narrowing the expectability of expectations, by abstracting from various 'irrelevant' contingencies of the pragmatic situation, by providing norms that involve sanctions should Alter not conform (and thus granting Ego the security of the expectation that Alter *will* conform), but most importantly for present purposes, by abstracting from the 'concrete' parties involved and the reciprocal perspective-taking that in turn would involve knowledge of Alter and the contingencies that entails. Instead the legal system generalises expectations through institutionalisation which here (in Luhmann's terms in the 'social dimension') means the introduction of the third position of the generalised co-expecting other,[19] who by definition, could have no knowledge of the concrete people involved, and could not partake in mutual perspective-taking. The law provides a constancy peculiar to it alone. This is due to the function law has in society of stabilising expectations, of controlling normativity, of guaranteeing that its expectations will not be discredited if disappointed, that Alter is bound by the legal norm and will bear the consequences if she defies it.[20] Legal institutionalisation constructs a

---

[17] ibid., 212

[18] ibid., 192

[19] *Normatively* co-expecting, which means that the third party's expectation will not be *discredited* should Alter not behave as expected, only *disappointed*.

[20] For a similar argument outwith the systems framework see Aubert (1983). One of the most penetrating analyses employing Luhmann's insights is Guenther's (1993).

context of expectations by reducing double contingency and at the same time renders this context independent of the indeterminacy that comes from concrete interactions: *it allows people to encounter each other as role-players, here, as legal actors.*

Retracing the problem of double contingency not only allows Luhmann to begin from what he construes as the most basic question of sociology, but also points a way out of traditional impasses sociologists have faced when tackling such fundamental questions. Let us take the example of role theory in sociology to trace some of the problems encountered with double contingency. Interacting actors, says Parsons, perform roles which are orientations 'organized about expectations in relation to a particular interaction context.'[21] But the interaction contexts are numerous. In standard role theory, multiple roles - as mediators between structure and agency - substitute for 'concrete others' in order to meet the functionally specific requirements of communication of modern industrial societies.[22] 'So far theories of role-taking,' says Max Miller, 'concentrate only on one side of double contingency. They have been interested in Ego's or Alter's abilities to take multiple roles or perspectives, and they have left open the question how this taking of multiple roles or perspectives can be co-ordinated between Ego and Alter.'[23] The problem Miller is identifying is that while the assumption of roles by individuals is extensively covered, the co-ordination of multiple roles - the problem of double contingency - is not, and theory has indeed faced great difficulties in addressing that question.

In my view, systems theory treats this problem of the co-ordination of multiple role-taking in a way that turns what is seen as a deficit in theory construction into a source of sociological insight. A system ascribes roles as descriptions of identity, it allocates roles as the points of attribution and address of Ego and Alter within the system; roles are Ego's and Alter's 'modes of entry' into the system. Roles are part of the system's selectivity mechanisms, an aspect of its reduction achievement, the means through which the system simplifies the unbearable complexity of the interaction of the 'concrete' Ego and Alter. Through its specific mode of reducing complexity, then, the system establishes the possibility of communication between Ego and Alter *as always-already role-players*. Motive, identity, implied reciprocities that stem from role, are always-already aligned system specifically. So what about co-ordination problems? The answer that systems theory has to offer is that the problem of co-ordination of multiple

---

[21] Parsons, 1951, 38-9
[22] Roles, stresses Dahrendorf are more than just patterns of human activity. The connection with expectations is crucial. Roles are 'expected modes of behaviour corresponding to social positions.' Dahrendorf, 1968, p35
[23] Miller, 1992, 10

roles is a real social problem due to the fact that systems do not articulate amongst themselves and also do not admit any meta-coordination or meta-metric. So what appear to Miller and others as problems of theory construction, are instead dealt with as real problems that result from the fact that systemic logics do not meet at any level. Luhmann's answer is that role-indeterminacy as context-indeterminacy becomes settled *by* the system but only *for* the system. Co-ordination is settled *by* the system because the system that is doing the reduction work is thereby fixing the contingency space within which the interlocutors' offers can be nothing but co-ordinated, as each takes up one of two exclusive alternatives, the yes- or no- option (see above, on operations and linkage).[24] But co-ordination is thus settled only *for* the system. In the absence of any hierarchy between systems or meta-level at which (role-taking) differences between systems could be settled, role-co-ordination remains forever open to competing contingencies, competing observations as to what Ego expects of Alter and what is expected of Ego to expect Alter to expect. [25]

We must at this stage identify the variety of stages or number of filters through which double contingency is handled by each system and crystallises around specific structures of expectations. It is a constitutive feature of all social systems that they provide for their self-structuring, in a self-referential way. But the level of self-reference varies depending on the complexity of the system. In simple interaction systems the selectivity achievement is low and develops on a kind of base level of self-referentiality (basale Selbstreferenz); central themes develop and communicative offers are made sense of on the basis of contributing or not to the theme. For example, one's communicative offer of raising one's hand in simple interaction systems may serve as a salute in one encounter, may signal approval in a debate, a bid in an auction, a request to speak in class. In more complex systems, including of course functional sub-systems like law, politics e.t.c., a second-order self-referentiality develops, which Luhmann calls '*Reflexivität*'.[26] It is here that one would speak of structures taking hold as expectations of expectations, providing for the meaningfulness of communicative offers. The

---

[24] Context-indeterminacy is thus also settled by the system self-referentially, as the system establishes itself as the arbitrer of the co-ordination problem
[25] Problems of alienation, role-strain etc therefore come about due to the synchronicity of multiple/competing systemic role ascriptions
[26] Luhmann, 1984, p601, pp610ff

selectivity achievement, in complex systems, is thus premised on a second level of self-referentiality. [27]

At the level of reflexivity, expectations can be integrated and maintained in social systems. 'Integrated' in that double contingency is 'disciplined' through a structure that delimits what expectations are compatible within the domain of the system. 'Maintained' because a provision for cases of disappointment 'is built into the system itself'[28] so that the non-fulfilment of Ego's expectation does not discredit the expectation but only disappoints it; Ego does not assume that he has not been understood but that he has been understood and rejected. The expectation is not dissolved but rather maintained or corrected in given ways. [29]

Double contingency, in Luhmann's words, constitutes 'die Grundlage für den Aufbau sozialer Ordnung und für die ihr entsprehende Erwartungsunsicherheit,'[30] - the very foundation for the most primary form of social order. A number of templates/systems absorbs the double uncertainty of expectations in specific ways. 'Double uncertainty' is replaced by 'single' uncertainty: social systems stabilise 'objectively' valid expectations. Only once we agree on what we disagree about can we meaningfully disagree. The absorption of uncertainty occurs at the initial agreement, which is (more accurately) the setting up of a context of disagreement. I am still uncertain whether you will agree or disagree but my uncertainty is premised on the absorption of a second-order uncertainty of what we will disagree about, an absorption that is the foundation of order. Concurrence or contrast, consensus and dissent acquire *a rational basis*, conflict becomes *optimally finite*.

There remain, of course, many templates that may accommodate the second-order absorption and consequently many contexts against which the terms of disagreement can be cast. The argument of this chapter is against the false necessity of seeing only one - law. [31]

---

[27] At a third level of self-referentiality, Luhmann identifies 'Reflexion' as the final controller of selectivity, setting further conditions for the integration of communications in complex systems. (1984, 610)

[28] Luhmann, 1971, 46

[29] It needs to be clarified that all this is at a level prior the the distinction normative/cognitive expectations that we will analyse in the next section.

[30] 'the foundation of social order and the corresponding uncertainty of expectations' (Luhmann, 1981, 99). See also 1992a, 94-5

[31] It is a bit early to identify the 'political' at this stage, before the absorption. This can only be explained at a later stage, after the limitations of the process of 'absorption' into different templates is illuminated.

Before I attempt to deploy this discussion of double contingency in a first thesis against republicanism, let me draw a number of *interim conclusions*:

1. Note a point already made earlier as to the existence of *structures* (expectations of expectations). Systems are fully temporalised and exist at the level of elements. Structures do not exist in the same way that elements do. As emergent properties of systemic reproduction they allow the production of new elements thus underpinning the unity of the system. Functionally speaking they allow for a matching of elements, they make it possible for new elements to link up (Anschlussfähigkeit). They provide a kind of memory that allows the recognition of a new element as one belonging to the system. This has been their function as reflexive expectations: as constraints on possible communicative offers, they have provided for a 'fit' with previous systemic communications and thus linkage-capacity. Their existence is however always complementary to the elements, only in terms of which the system exists.

2. Luhmann maintains that the existence of double contingency as a real problem is a productive factor for human interaction, because new systems, therefore new possibilities of communication, emerge to deal with it. And whereas double contingency underpins all social interaction, it is settled by each system for itself [32] and establishes the reality of each system at a distinct level. At this distinct level meaningful interaction is settled objectively along systemic lines and order is achieved that is specific to the system. For social systems where 'reflexivity' is at play this means that a level of reality is established, at which meaningful interaction is stabilised and maintained that is reducible neither to the persons involved, nor to their interaction system [below (3) and (4) respectively].

3. The settling of double contingency at the level of the social system is the emergence of a level of interaction where the contingency of the interplay of the actions of Ego and Alter is facilitated according to intentions determined and imputed system-specifically, self-referentially (again, of course, trivially, it is the individuals who have intentions). It is in this sense that the system displaces the *actor*: intentions are handled by the system. What does this mean exactly? It means that the system designates a specific contingency space for intention: Ego may either intend *a* or *not-a*, where *a* and *not-a* are mutually exclusive alternatives specific to the observation possibilities of the

---

[32] 'Autocatalytically' Luhmann will add: '[double contingency] ermoeglicht, ohne selbst verbraucht zu werden, den Aufbau von Strukturen auf einer neuen Ordnungsebene ... Dabei ist, deshalb kann man von Auto-katalyse sprechen, das Problem der doppelten Kontingenz selbst Bestandteil des Systems, das sich bildet.' (1984, 170)

system. Such imputation of intention cannot be defied by the actor; because defiance of the choice between *a* and ***not-a*** will register as intention to ***not-a***. Denunciation resonating in law as contempt (see thesis [6] below) is a case in point. This re-alignment of intention applies even to silence. The political actor may decide to defy the law or play along. Either way his/her behaviour will not discredit a legal expectation. Whatever a 'political' intention to remain silent, the silence will be thematised into law around specific contingencies; law settles the options of what silence means for itself. That is why *'the law thinks'*[33] in ways that are not reducible to actors' thoughts. It 'thinks' on behalf of the actor because it makes sense of what the actor does by reducing the contingency of the actor's intention in ways that are intelligible to the system; the reduction of double contingency through reflexivity is the system's way of doing just that: of absorbing contingency into specific templates and thus displacing the actor in making sense of intended meaning.

4. The self-reference of the settling of contingency in social systems also draws a line between social sub-system (e.g. law, economy, religion, politics) and *interaction* system. An interaction system is typically one organised around a theme and requires the presence of the interlocutors. There is far greater fluidity in how contingency is settled in interaction than there is for a social sub-system. The interaction system answers to limited structural constraints because what are absent are the more complex requirements a social sub-system has to meet. In the case of a social system, settling contingency needs to be effected with an eye to relating it to the system's own stability and continuation (through the more complex processes of reflexivity and reflection).

* Thesis [1] against Republicanism

There is much in the argument of this section already to allow a first tentative rebuttal of the republican argument, a rebuttal that will be further qualified as the argument develops.

As we have seen the problem of double contingency has been described as a problem of settling or reconciling *Ego's and Alter's differences regarding Ego/Alter differences*. This basic formula of double contingency involves *a second order (a)* and *a first order (b)* contingency. Potential incommunicability from double contingency gives way to meaningful interaction once contingency (a) has been reduced, and we explored how this

---

[33] Teubner, (1989)

reduction is effected in social systems through the double filter of 'reflexivity' and 'reflection'. But this reduction carries a cost and this is the important point against the republican argument. That meaningful interaction requires contingency (a) to be settled, means disciplining the difference over context. Yet if the republicans are going to make an argument about self-determination, they must allow freedom of choice over the context of disagreement. What does this mean ?

First let me point to some repercussions of the argument more generally for the possibility of communication. Among communication theorists, Habermas too ties the possibility (or meaning) of meaning to intersubjective communicative action. For him meaning is identical signification in reference to a reciprocal reflexivity of expectations on the part of actors engaged in a communicative exchange.[34] But the problem that double contingency brings into relief is this: how can the 'reflexivity of expectations' be maintained while allowing expectations to articulate in context? How is the reflexivity over context - the leaving open of contingency (a) - compatible with mutual recognition of validity claims that alone allows communication to proceed? The problem of double contingency is that this initial reflexivity needs to be reduced to make communication successful. In *Faktizität und Geltung*, Habermas indicates his preferred solution to the dilemma by elevating law into the centrepiece of societal deliberation. To the extent that he does thus turn to law to set the framework of rational discourse he does establish the possibility of meaningful argumentation in context, but at the cost of remaining reflexive over the contextual conditions. Legal argumentation as practical discourse is *always-already disciplined by* the contextual conditions, therefore no longer reflexive *about* them.

Since the civic republicans also treat law as the centrepiece of political deliberation - the containment thesis - they need to answer the above objection too. But my first thesis against them can be expressed in a much more concrete way. For this we will turn again to their aforementioned foundational commitment to **empathy**.

---

[34] And Habermas's critique of Luhmann is particularly harsh in this respect. He contends that, in Luhmann, language affords no solid basis upon which ego could meet with alter in a consensus about something. 'For communication, language is used - but this simply permits signs to be substituted for meaning ... Supra-subjective linguistic structures would entwine society and individual too tightly with one another. An intersubjectivity of mutual understanding among agents that is achieved via expressions with identical meanings and criticizable validity claims [has no place in Luhmann]. [Neither does] the commonality of any intersubjectively shared context of meaning and reference - that is to an explanation of communicative participation in a lifeworld that is represented in a linguistic world-view.' (Habermas, 1987, pp370ff)

Empathy is a key concept of the republican political universe.[35] As we saw, it receives its fullest elaboration in Sunstein's theory. For him political empathy 'embodies the requirement that political actors attempt to assume the position of those who disagree.' It combines with the related requirement that citizens during the deliberative process should set aside their own perspective and 'think from the point of view of everybody.'[36] Sunstein says: 'If the groups cannot actually be included in the deliberation they are to be evocatively included by legislators' and judges' empathy with their perspectives.'[37]

My argument against the republicans here is that empathy cannot survive double contingency. The impasse that double contingency throws up for empathy is what happens with contingency (a), the contingency over context. Empathy always-already presupposes a context which in turn assumes away contingency (a). Why? Because one can empathise with Alter only if one knows or at least expects Alter's expectation, just like the exercise of empathy presupposes that at least the parties to the disagreement agree about what they disagree about. The empathetic stance is impossible both outwith the complementarity of expectations and about it. Because to empathise *outwith* is to fail to empathise. And because does not to empathise *about* the complementarity open empathy to infinite regress? Empathy thus must assume the expectational framework into existence and thus do away with the contingency of that choice, and with it the potential disagreement over the contextual conditions of the disagreement (contingency (a)). Empathy cannot but assume the double contingency away. But to concede this and assume the complemantarity of expectations, i.e. to assume agreement over the disagreement given, is also fatal for empathy. Because as an *a priori*, it postulates rather than retrieves a commonality of the pattern of disagreement. In the process of thus pulling itself up by its own bootstraps empathy denies that empathy is about addressing Alter's true - not postulated - expectation and becomes its opposite: it turns from Alter-regarding to Alter-excluding.

The 'containment thesis' allows the republicans to pass over the difficult question and define away difference (a) by assuming that the political actors' difference over their differences is always-already settled. This is because they take on board law as obvious context. It is a legal blindspot that treats as unproblematic the point of view from which difference is seen. While the legal 'reduction achievement' indisputably facilitates, by ruling out potential incommunicability from contingency (a), the price it inflicts is a compromise of freedom and self-determination; freedom to resist legal understandings

---

[35] See also Minow, 1987, passim, Winter, 1991, 1002
[36] Sunstein, 1988, 1569
[37] In Sullivan, 1988, 1717

and self-determination on the basis of that freedom. Law provides one of many rival templates for the absorption of double contingency. To ignore alternative templates is a decision *a priori*. To reduce contingency (a) on the basis of that *a priori*, is to close off the reflexive question over the understanding of differences, which *is* the political one.

CHAPTER NINE

LEGAL EXPECTATIONS

There is, as we saw, a fundamental need to discipline the double contingency of social life in order to provide a basis for interaction; in this framework, Luhmann's is a description of how systems counter potential incommunicability. Systems are templates that absorb the double contingency of social life and thereby reduce complexity. This is no easy feat for the complexity is vast: double contingency is, in fact, a short-hand formula that stands in for a multi-dimensional overlap of contingencies. Social interaction may demand that one does not only expect expectations but expects expectations of expectations 'and all this with a plurality of thematics, in the face of a plurality of people and with continuously changing relevance from situation to situation.'[1] The dissections of these multiple possibilities are mapped by and stabilised by system-specific reductions. Each system organises the picture by turning, for itself, second-order into first-order contingency (contingencies (a) and (b), above). What is designated thus is a specific space for contingency that is a huge reduction in the scope of contingency of possible states. At the first-order level, the uncertainty remains. Something that is legal today may well be illegal tomorrow. But the space of that contingency is fixed through the reduction at the second-order level of what the uncertainty is about.

In the present section we will turn to the legal system to explore the system-specific reductions that law imposes on double contingency. In other words we will be exploring how the complexity of the social world is probed and deciphered through legal expectations.

In order to explore how double contingency is absorbed in law, we will have to turn to the function that law performs in society. Why? It is true that a vast number of systems make sense of social interaction by imposing reductions on double contingency and yet not all perform a function in society. Not all social systems are differentiated-out as functional sub-systems, not all acquire their identity in connection to a function they perform. As Luhmann stresses 'functional orientation is certainly not a requirement for self-referential reproduction.'[2] So while it is misleading to seek the logical and systematic conditions *per se* of autopoietic closure in functional differentiation, in systems that are differentiated-out as functional sub-systems, function underpins the self-reproduction of both identity and

---

[1] Luhmann, 1972, 28
[2] Luhmann, 1984, 406

unity. Because the important thing about the functional sub-systems of society is that they achieve their unity as systems *in view of their function*. At a second stage, after we have explored the connection of function to the formation of expectations and therefore to the autopoiesis of the system, we will turn to the intimate connection of the function of law with conflict.

THE FUNCTION OF LAW

We have already briefly visited the key notion of functional differentiation. For Luhmann social subsystems are differentiated out of the social system in terms of their performing a unique function. The function of every sub-system needs to be sought in reference to society, not other sub-systems (for the latter relationship Luhmann reserves the term 'performance'). According to the principle of functional differentiation, a social sub-system is, and can only be, differentiated out of the totality of social communication by performing a unique function. To compromise this uniqueness would undermine the differentiation principle. All the more so because in functional analysis, a function is understood as a problem area concerning alternatives. If the designation of the function is not itself water-tight and itself invites alternatives - functional equivalents - then the overlapping sets of alternatives at both levels would be devastating. Devastating because function serves as the principle of differentiation here and cannot as such be compromised without undermining the very existence of the system. Hence the one-to-one mapping of (sub-)system and function is essential. In Luhmann's words:

'The system performs a specific function which is not performed anywhere else in society. As a result it becomes possible for the system to treat everything else as environment ... The subsystems relate everything which they use as unity to their function and at the same time can assume that there is no equivalent for this in their environment ... The sub-system [creates its autopoiesis] by exclusive orientation to a function.'[3]

Let us pause to stress the intimacy of this connection: the system exists by drawing a boundary and isolating itself from all else, where the drawing of the boundary, in functional sub-systems, is oriented towards the function that the system performs for society in general. Luhmann says that the legal system is functionally differentiated in that its specific means of achieving closure and openness are informed by its function:

---

[3] Luhmann, 1988b, ps26-7

'There exists a connection between the principle of differentiation of the social system [functional differentiation] and the form in which subsystems in society differentiate themselves as self-referentially closed and as open to the environment. ... For the legal system this means the differentiation of a connection between normative closure and cognitive openness. Here that which serves as a contrafactual norm is, in the process of social evolution, increasingly pointed to the function of law.'[4]

This last point about normative closure points us in the direction of the function of law. Is law about generating 'normative' expectations? If it is, is that narrow enough as a designation of a unique function? Or should we define the function of the law in terms of social control, conflict resolution, co-ordinating behaviour, social regulation, discipline and punish, or even, why not, 'giving lawyers an income'? Which of these captures what is specific about the function of law and thus grounds the delineation of the legal and the non-legal?

This is a difficult question and it is an open one. Luhmann has an answer but he invites, 'like in an auction' he says, better offers.[5] It is quite obvious that all the above suggestions, while in themselves important suggestions, cannot do the job. For example, while the law is definitely about producing normative expectations - that is expectations that do not learn from disappointment - so does morality, as does social custom. But law 'claims a specific use of normativity for itself.'[6] Because in the case of custom, the normative expectation is *ad hoc*; in the case of both custom and morality there is no way of guaranteeing either the stability or change of the normative expectation as is the case in law, where there exist institutional/systemic guarantees for both norms' stability and change. In this way law guarantees a kind of second-order normativity, whereby normative expectations, abundant throughout society and operative in many systems, may be normatively expected. Law provides these internal systemic guarantees and thereby 'stabilizes normative expectations through regulating their temporal, material and social generalisation.'[7] Law guarantees reliability of normative expectations under recognisable, systemically stipulated, conditions.

So what is the function of the law according to Luhmann? As is often the case with Luhmann, the answer to this has been qualified throughout his writings. According to the early Luhmann of *'Die Funktion des Rechts'*[8] the function of law consists, merely, in the stabilisation of expectations, an

---

[4] ibid., 31
[5] Luhmann, 1992b, 79
[6] Luhmann, 1988b, 27
[7] Luhmann, 1993a, 91
[8] First appeared in 1974 and included in Luhmann (1981)

account echoed also in the *Rechtssoziologie*. Law's function is there described as the 'congruent (consistent across all dimensions) generalization of structures of expectation,'[9] since law, functionally understood, 'attains selective congruence and therefore forms a structure of social systems.'[10] With the autopoietic turn, with law no longer a structure of society, this account had to be qualified and enriched. Because, as we said, for there to be functional differentiation no two systems could be seen to perform the same function as would be the case if we did not narrow down the account of the legal function. The existence of functional equivalents would erode the premise of functional irreplaceableness, differentiation on the basis of that, and finally systemic closure in view of the function .[11]

Luhmann's suggestion for the function of law, is that it be viewed in conjunction with 'the exploitation of conflict perspectives for the formation and reproduction of congruently generalized behavioural expectations.'[12] Law achieves order by *'using the possibility [better: occasion] of conflict for a generalisation of expectations in temporal, social and substantive aspects,'*[13] a formulation also echoed in his recent *Das Recht der Gesellschaft.*[14]

For the remaining part of this section we will take issue with this formulation of the function of law: 'the exploitation of conflict perspectives for the formation and reproduction of congruently generalised behavioural expectations,' the generalisation, that is, 'of expectations in temporal, social and material[15] dimensions.' In a nutshell, if rather crudely, it could be said that the function of law is to discipline double contingency and achieve order by 'exploiting' conflict in order to stabilise expectations in particular sorts of ways (temporally, materially, socially). Having explored the function of law, and stressed that only by reference to its function can the legal system differentiate and distinguish itself from the environment, we will now turn to what it means for expectations to be generalised along the three dimensions and explore the role of conflict in (its structural coupling with) the legal system. I will reserve the connection with conflict for the end for reasons of

---

[9] Luhmann, 1972, 40ff, or pp24ff)

[10] ibid., 77

[11] For more detail see Luhmann, 1986b, 120 and Luhmann, 1993a 92

[12] Luhmann, 1988b, 27

[13] Luhmann, 1986b, 121

[14] In Luhmann, 1993a, ch. 3; deemed 'a slight variation' 1986b, n.24. Cf. Teubner's definition of 'the central function of law: using the occasion of conflict to create congruently generalized expectations.' (1992, 1459)

[15] Luhmann's term *Sach-dimension* has been translated variably as objective, substantive or material dimension. I will employ the last term.

exposition. For the time being suffice it to say that in order to 'generalise' expectations the law relies on (a legal perception of) conflict.

THE GENERALISATION OF EXPECTATIONS AS LEGAL

A generalisation is an abstraction. Expectations that stand in some 'measure of independence' apart from particulars to which they refer can be called generalised.[16] Of course one might say that generalisation is of the essence of expectations, that expectations exist as generalisations, as links between instances. Two concrete instances can only link up through an expectation that generalises certain of their features to establish their mutual relevance and thus allow their linking. Luhmann will add that there is a second level at which systems (reflexively) establish and entrench expectations of expectations. It is at this second level that double contingency is absorbed into functional sub-systems where - through 'Reflexivität' - expectations are generalised into more abstract types that can be held constant and then 'function as generative rules for individual expectations.'[17]

When one generalises one organises particulars into certain patterns, into encompassing categories. A generalisation tracks a distinction between member and class by designating amongst instances certain of their features as significant. In the process of that designation and in order to organise the generic category, a generalisation selects certain aspects of the instances as significant, keeps them constant, and only on the basis of what is selected and kept constant does it include each instance within its ambit as member of a class. As selectivity grids for particulars, generalisations are at once selective inclusions and selective exclusions. In this sense generalisations are 'selective suppressions' as Schauer put it recently,[18] but also importantly selective *actualisations*: they actualise as their instances aspects of the world that meet the properties they designate as relevant to their operation.

Put in this way a generalisation can be clearly seen as a system-specific abstraction. What features are isolated and kept constant are particular to each system. The selective organisational principles are many, and in fact a particular instance is at any one time simultaneously absorbed by a number of them (this explains the simultaneity of an infinite number of competing categorisations of events in the world.) But each time, each system actualises

---

[16] Luhmann, 1984, 445. 'Generalized expectations leave to a greater or lesser extent undetermined as to the content, what exactly is expected ... Through temporal, objective and social generalizations is uncertainty taken up and absorbed.'

[17] Luhmann, 1972, 64. Thus it is, at this second-order level, that in law one normatively expects normative expectations.

[18] Schauer, 1991, 21

the instance from the point of view of what it holds significant and builds into its generalisations. I must stress that I am consciously simplifying the picture at this stage of the exposition by implying that the instance has a common ontology amongst systems; it does not. My purpose however here is still to stress something more elementary. That it would be definitely wrong to see generalisations as penetrating through systems; they are specific to systems and run counter to generalisations within other systems.[19] That is why, contra Parsons, the reduction of double contingency does not rely on generalisations with a social base of the type 'culture', but on the specificity of systemic reductions.

Law uses conflict 'for the generalisation of expectations in temporal, social and substantive aspects.' Leaving aside the connection with conflict till later, what does it mean for expectations to be generalised - abstracted - in the three directions?

The temporal dimension

Law gives a kind of priority to the temporal dimension since legal expectations are primarily understood as a transference of normativity. The system is temporalised, as we have seen, and expectations 'carry' it through time in the following sense. The expectation will produce a legal claim to be tested; the claim will be fulfilled or disappointed and in that will furnish a new expectation of the legal position. Within this schematic account of evolution, there has occurred a transference of normativity between two points in time. The priority of the temporal dimension for law lies in the transference of this quality of meaning from element to element.[20] What 'transferring normativity' means has to do with how the system handles the disappointment of expectations.

Two types of expectation can be differentiated on the basis of how disappointments are handled: *normative and cognitive*. The nature of expectations as normative and cognitive is based on their different ways of 'learning'. 'Normativity means clinging to expectations despite disappointments.'[21] Cognitive expectations on the other hand 'learn' through disappointment. Cognitive expectations change and adapt in cases of disappointment whereas normative expectations do not. This of course is not absolute, as Luhmann points out;[22] normative expectations exceptionally learn, as when the law provides procedures for its own change or when the

---

[19] Smith, 1991, 333-4

[20] Luhmann, 1988b, 20

[21] Luhmann, 1972, 22

[22] ibid., 38

elasticity of legal structures prompts judge-made law. On the other hand cognitive expectations do not always learn, as when a disappointment is classified as an exception to the rule. Not every slight deviance from the expected results leads to a paradigm shift in science.

To prevent a misunderstanding that has caused some confusion: normativity has no transcendental status across society, there are no social expectations which are normative or cognitive *as such*. Rather these qualities have to do with how an expectation is processed within a system, whether the system maintains expectations despite disappointment or not. The system itself - the legal system in this case - will determine which disappointment it will learn from and which it will not; under what conditions it will vary normative expectations; and, of course, as pre-condition to these other questions, it will determine what counts as a disappointment, what events in its environment it reads as having the disappointing effect. This is all to say that no expectation is naturally normative or cognitive. Where an expectation begins; its content; what possibilities of variation it permits; what forces it into variation; how elastic it is; what disappoints it; are all questions that are determined by the system that projects or releases expectations for - what Luhmann would call - selective actualisation. In systems-theoretical terms we could say that the distinction normative/cognitive expectations that is to be found 'loosely coupled' all over society is taken up and processed by each system and 'strictly coupled' within it - imbued with system-specific thresholds of disappointment.

Legal expectations and their reproduction are seen as an ongoing process. Normativity - generalising expectations as disappointment-proof - is one way in which expectations are stabilised. 'In a way that no other system does, the law processes expectations that are capable of maintaining themselves in situations of conflict.'[23] It is one way in which complexity comes partially under control. And by 'combining normative and cognitive, learning and not learning dispositions'[24] the system will respond to noise from its environment through perceiving an instance as confirming an expectation, varying its own (expectational) structures to accommodate it, rejecting the stimulus, or ignoring it.

The social dimension

Until now the discussion of double contingency and stabilisation of expectation structures had only involved two parties, Ego and Alter.

---

[23] Luhmann, 1989, 140
[24] Luhmann, 1986b, 122

Luhmann reserves the term *institutionalisation* for the introduction of third parties.[25] For Luhmann, this gives the legal system its social dimension.

The most important consequence of the introduction of third parties is that it is through this institutionalisation *that the shift from the interactional to the social-systemic context is primarily effected.* [26] Law disciplines the double contingency of social life because it allows one to abstract one's expectation from the 'concrete' Alter. The personality of Alter ceases to determine the context of expectations and is substituted by Alter-as-role-player. Or, what amounts to the same thing, an expectation becomes legal in that it is assumed to be backed by the expected consensus of third parties who do not know the concrete Alter and so must rely only in his capacity as role-taker to form expectations. The introduction of third parties as normatively co-expecting means that the expectation context is now first abstracted from the concrete interactional setting and first cast through a system-specific referent. Institutionalisation thus abstracts into an impersonal context and allows specifically legal attributions that are removed from the person that expects or is expected to act.

An expectation is legal only if third parties normatively co-expect it. This is what is meant by the generalisation of expectations along the social dimension. For the expectation to be legal it must be backed by the expected consensus of third parties.[27] The social dimension of law makes such consensus constitutive of legal expectation. But at the same time the impersonal backdrop for institutionalising legal expectation makes any pragmatic conditions of consensus irrelevant. Third parties are removed from any concrete context and only in this is the expectation lifted from interactional contexts to the systemic context of law. Any actual consensus is irrelevant, and the power of institutionalisation depends on this irrelevance,

---

[25] Luhmann is not alone in claiming this. Outwith the vast anthropological literature on the function of third parties in dispute settlement, Aubert makes a powerful argument similar to Luhmann's here (1983, pp57-75). His central hupothesis is that 'the development of legal thought is a concomitant to the intervention of a third party... When a conflict is turned into a law suit ... the basic interaction changes from a dyad to a triad. Between these two transformations there exists a functional relationship.' (pp63, 69) Aubert traces the shifts in the parties' interests, needs, wishes, etc, that accompany the transformation. He concludes that "with the third party the norm of objectivity has been institutionalized." (71) He relates this to a most insightful distinction. He says: 'Irrespective of the qualifications and mode of recruitement of the third person, it may be asked why this conceptualization [of the relationship with the third party] should tend to be normative and not causal or functional.' Aubert ties his answer - although not in these words - to what he takes to be the emergent quality of the dispute as legal, which demands that the third party normatively co-expect (in his words take sides rather than "cure" the dispute which would mean looking at the causal not the normative).

[26] On the distinction between social and interaction systems, see chapter seven above

[27] Luhmann, 1972, 73

on removing the pragmatic conditions of any such consensus. The third co-expecting party has no concrete features, no social location. Law depends on the fact that the consensus is fictitious, abstracted from real social relevancies.

In this way law depends for its existence on a kind of 'a-social' social dimension. But how will law give *content* to expectations and make interaction possible because reducible to an expectational context? It will have to abstract from specific people's expectations of specific people and provide a plane where these expectations can latch on and be attributed to fictitious, but invariant from case to case, units. This is where the abstraction of the legal person becomes operative. The legal personality is such a point of attribution and address of the subject in law. Thus the introduction of the third party allows the system to abstract from what Ego expects Alter to expect in an interactional setting and to settle double contingency in a legally specific way. In order to complete the picture of how such disciplining of double contingency is effected in law, we will look into the third axis of generalisation, the material dimension.

The material dimension

In characteristic style Luhmann explains that 'the expectation of expectations is only possible through the mediation of a common world to which expectations are identically attached.'[28] Meaningful interaction is only possible on the basis of a commonality of events, visible action and symbols for the invisible. The infinite possibilities of envisaging events and deciphering them through symbols is reduced though system specific reductions that provide horizons of other possibilities against which selections can be tested. In the *Excursus* we discussed how a system observes through distinctions that set up system specific horizons, an idea that will be revisited in chapter twelve under the heading of *thematisation*. All that was (and will be) said at various stages regarding observation becomes operative here, contained in the material dimension, and operationalised in time by being integrated into expectations.[29] In the legal expectation, therefore, legal meaning comes about in the selective access to other possibilities. The world becomes meaningful as legally relevant, through the selectivity, the alignment to referents provided by law. That these possibilities of

---

[28] ibid., 62

[29] Indeed we are approaching the same questions but integrating them in the dimension of time. By focusing on how expectations carry the system in time, the nature of systems as temporalised comes to the fore. The material dimension of expectations is, in other words, where observation meets operation.

observation are self-stipulated and internally select the object of observation means that the system duplicates its map as object. More will be said on this in the reversal of 'brute and institutional' that I will attempt in chapter twelve on the re-enactment of conflict. Suffice it for now to point out that distinctions enable and condition the selective access to meaning.

The next question is, in Luhmann's words, 'at which level of abstraction the relatively invariant core of meaning formation is fixed by which the context of expectation is fixed.'[30] We will identify here roles, programmes and values.

We saw previously, in discussing the social dimension, that institutionalisation brought about a shift from the personal to the impersonal so that expectations could be associated with the *role* rather than the 'concrete' person. The system's 'self-description' of person as role (legal personality) indicates a first abstraction along the material axis. A more concrete and inflexible frame of expectations can be fixed to role, and stabilisation of expectations is facilitated in more ways than one. In the *Rechtssoziologie,* for example, Luhmann mentions the knock-on effect of 'stabilization through indifference': the fragmentation of Alter's self into roles prohibits a disappointment of one role from spilling over to discredit Alter in other roles, as would be the case with personal expectations, i.e. expectations we have of 'concrete' others.

Roles are not the only abstractions into which generalisations in the material dimension crystallise. There are also programmes, and values. *Programmes* fix expectations through rules, both goal-oriented and conditional. Again, correctness of behaviour is lifted from the personal context and fixed at the impersonal level, at which level rules ground the normativity of expectations of individual action through impersonal criteria of correctness that displace the personal reference. One can mention here, indicatively, how legal liability is fixed on objective grounds through objective indicators of *mens rea* that are removed from concrete personal capacities of predicting consequences and assessing correctness; or how responsibility is fixed (variably) in various areas of law: family law, tort law, e.t.c.

Values, the most abstract of abstractions along the material dimension, furnish rules of preference even if they do not specify the content of preferable action.[31] They also do not specify their own hierarchy for cases of clashes of values. In *Soziale Systeme*, Luhmann, writes that

---

[30] Luhmann, 1972, 65

[31] For the difference between programmes and values see Luhmann, 1984, pp432ff

'[v]alues are general, particularly symbolized rules of preference regarding states or events ... Actions can also be evaluated as friendly, right, polluting, as expressing solidarity, readiness to help, racial hatred ... But the fact that actions can be brought under the positive or negative description, the ascription of value tells us nothing about the rightness of the action.'[32]

This would require a ranking of values, that the enhancement of freedom, for example, is more important than that of peace, culture, profit, e.t.c. No ranking, no criteria of rightness. Luhmann argues thus that values are crude, poorly selective devices for reducing complexity, appropriate only to a 'pre-modern, old-European' phase of social development. The selectivity aspect brings us to a second point. The values that can be employed in critique or appraisal are tied to specific patterns of observation, the system-specific processing possibilities. What market economics may assess as catastrophic behaviour, may be all at once conducive for a centrally-run economy, politically dangerous, morally right, etc. Due to these various indeterminacies, values contribute very little to the stabilisation of expectations and the reduction of double contingency.

Roles, programmes and values are mutually dependent and determine each other reciprocally: rules determine hierarchies of values, roles are operationalised through rules or become points of attribution through rules and values, and rules depend on the existence of self-descriptions such as roles.[33] For example, in the case of the rule of law it is evident that the programme level becomes the level at which third values like certainty and formal equality - excluded at the two-valued code level - become accommodated. These 'third values' are ways to handle the choice of 'which code value?', since the code itself provides no 'top value', no means to furnish a choice. Again, revisability in the material dimension depends on the fact that some of the expectations remain constant as the structural backbone that allows the system to make sense of change. As the law evolves, roles, programmes and values shift and, what is more striking, their interplay and interdependence shifts. The rise, for example, of formal rationality and the uprooting of legal relations from their Gemeinshaft context, as well as the reversal of this evolutionary trend in the era of the Welfare State, is reflected in a mutually re-enforcing re-negotiation of *values* (certainty and justice), a shift in *programming* (a retreat of conditional and an expanse of goal programming) and a 're-materialisation' of *roles* (from the all-inclusive legal personality to more concrete *loci* of attribution of rights and duties.)

A more important interplay and reciprocal determination, however, is the one among the three dimensions of meaning, temporal, social and material.

---

[32] Luhmann, 1984, pp433ff, my trans.
[33] See Luhmann, 1972, pp70ff

This is of extreme importance for the arguments to be advanced later in the thesis. It goes without saying that the temporal dimension that determines the nature of the expectation as normative (disappointment-proof) relies for content on the material dimension and for backing on the social dimension. But there are subtler interplays. We already briefly examined the interplay between the social and material dimension in reference to the way that the shift from personal to impersonal contexts of expectation in the social dimension was mediated by the self-description 'role' of the material dimension. Another is an interplay between the material and the temporal: role is necessary for identifying the disappointment threshold of the normative expectation (temporal). I will bring the example of love and marriage to illustrate this, an example that will be often used and extensively analysed throughout the book. In law (marriage) as opposed to love, the spouse's expectation will turn normative at the point at which the law designates a disappointment, sanctions an attribution of wrong-doing and provides remedies for the frustrated expectation. On the other hand in love, as opposed to law, the disappointment threshold varies according to what the lover normatively expects of the concrete Alter - the beloved; this in turn turns on questions of what matters enough, what the expector is ready to concede, overlook or on the other hand be especially sensitive to, all of which can only be answered from within and uniquely about the specific relationship. No 'material' objective disappointment thresholds can be set in love, no co-expecting third parties. The normativity threshold is not set through impersonal standards but through interpersonal ones. Only where such disappointment thresholds are fixed through universal and thus impersonal standards can normative expectations be born, and voiced as appropriate to marriage; and in love the standards are not fixed but retrieved interpersonally. There are other aspects to this interplay of role and normativity. The very differentiation of cognitive and normative depends on whether we are approaching the loving relationship from law or from love. Love is oriented to getting to know the beloved, the world becomes relevant through the beloved. This points to an overwhelming priority of the cognitive and an overwhelming hesitation to switch to normative; i.e. one who loves is always willing to learn from disappointments by shifting expectations. On the contrary, role provides more or less fixed points for the switch from cognitive to normative.[34] This is all to say that the very character of an

---

[34] 'I need not inquire into your motives deeper, there are laws for spouses that act as you do!' Ego's expectation of Alter is not qualified in the light of Alter's action to expect something new next time, but is disappointed instead (normative not cognitive); the law designates what actions have this effect, and, although this will only be undersoot fully later, Ego reads in this not only a disappoinment of a right in law but one that re-enacts a disappointment of the love Ego had invested.

expectation as cognitive or normative depends on the material dimension for providing the 'switching point'.

In the process of effecting these reductions on double contingency, only a narrow section of the possible is fixed as expectable; expectations furnish narrow possibilities of observation of the environment. Through expectations an event is 'isolated, individualized, personalized and becomes a reference point for a processed explanation of disappointment.'[35] Expectations are generalised in law in ways that are specific to the legal system. They are abstracted in ways that run counter to generalising tendencies and directions within other systems. Expectational structures therefore cannot directly infiltrate or colonise other systems that acquire their identity and continuity through time by generalising expectations and forming structures on their own, different system-specific premises.[36] In each case the reductions through which this is possible will be peculiar to the system. The generalisation of expectations along temporal, social and material lines through the appropriate reductions allows the unmanageable complexity inherent in double contingency to give way to the possibility of (legal) communication; it maps out the world of legal meaning. But to effect these reductions and these generalisations the law has to rely on conflict, or more accurately, on the 'exploitation of conflict perspectives.' Without the reference to conflict there can be no legal operation. Only in relation to conflict can 'the formation of congruently generalised behavioural expectations' be achieved, that once 'systematised by juristic skill, comparisons of cases, by concepts and by doctrine, results, and is experienced as, law.'[37]

---

[35] Luhmann, 1972, 70
[36] No juridification due to colonising structures then, only due to excessive reliance on the legal system for political ends.
[37] Luhmann, 1988b, 27-8

CHAPTER TEN

THE RELATIONSHIP OF CONFLICT AND LAW

Having explored how expectations generalised in the three dimensions emerge as legal, we now need to establish the final leg of Luhmann's definition of the function of law: the connection with conflict. Note that it is this final connection with conflict that pivots my critique of republicanism, although the connection could not have been made in a way that brings out the weakness of the containment thesis, without the discussion of double contingency and the formation of legal expectations. The disciplining of double contingency that comes with the emergence of systemic expectations is important if one is to understand how social expectations change at the threshold of legal institutionalisation. And yet the function of law of stabilising expectations cannot yet be understood if one does not look at what gives law the *opportunity* to perform its function. It is here that one needs to look at conflict, and more specifically 'at the exploitation of conflict perspectives.' And also to keep a reversal in view: Luhmann is here not describing the function (in systems theory one would say 'performance') of law in situations of conflict - albeit their resolution or creation.[1] Instead Luhmann is describing *how conflict is functional for law*, in allowing it to draw its boundaries and perform its function in society. (Note that this

---

[1] Which is to answer the question: in what way is *law functional for conflict*? On the one hand, law is important to conflict in a number of ways. By drawing on a number of Luhmann's writings we may isolate three functions in this respect: law solves conflict, first enables conflict and prevents conflict. Law solves conflict by setting up 'distinct contexts of interaction which specialise in handling disputes and conflicts.' (1985a, 84) Law prevents conflict by establishing conflict-proof expectations to be maintained in cases of dispute (1986a, 149) One is motivated to avoid conflict if the outcome is already known. Law is also productive for conflict in many ways. It provides additional possibilities for seeking out and withstanding conflict. This latter is evident in cases where without law conflict would be impossible because one is weaker, in a minority, or finds oneself in a morally reprehensible position. In these cases law supports behaviour which otherwise could not be sustained. Law secures freedom, including freedom of conflict and freedom of socially undesirable behaviour by backing with legal securities what outwith law may be deemed unreasonable or immoral conflicts. Law's function in creating conflict is emphasised in *Soziale Systeme*: 'Law is not only a means of solving social conflicts, but in the first place, and most important, a means of creating social conflict: a prop for presumptions, demands and rejections even in cases where resistance is expected' (1984, 451) For law's role in multiplying conflict opportunities, see Luhmann, 1984 ps 518, 535 and Freund (1974). There is a whole other "grey" area of conflict creation, prevention and solution which could be designated as existing 'in the shadow of the law.' The severity of the solomonic lose-or-win principle gives rise to an area of negotiation set up under the threat of recourse to the law. For an overview of the large literature on this in the sociology of law, see Cotterrell (1984)

connection is absent in Parsons' work. While Parsons' stresses the importance of boundary-maintaining mechanisms for social systems, he reduces conflict to 'dysfunctional strain' and fails to stress the connection of conflict to system maintenance.)[2]

In the influential essay *'Konflikt und Recht'* in the *Ausdifferenzierung des Rechts*, Luhmann explores the complex interdependence of conflict, law and the stabilisation of expectations. A theory of law needs to be able to rely on a theory of conflict, he concludes,[3] in order to elucidate the complex process of relating and counterpoising stability and instability that will lead law to form congruently generalised behavioural expectations. But let us take things more gradually.

Conflict is productive for law in a very important way.[4] Conflict provides the legal system with an occasion of openness to the environment. It is in litigating conflict that the law perceives the social environment and it is in communicating about conflict that law links operations to previous operations and exists as a system. The expectations it employs to make sense of reality refer to conflict. It is in reference to conflict that law generalises expectations and thus evolves as a system, fulfils its function in society and acquires its unity and identity.

Instability, says Luhmann, is inherent in any system, because a system is dynamic, temporalised, it exists in time. Its resonance capacity, its ability to react to a changing environment, to adapt and co-evolve, relies on instability. To achieve closure in the first place it needs openness (it is after all a [closed] system in relation to [openness] an environment). Autopoiesis does not mean 'autistic' self-determination but co-evolution. The absence of a high degree of 'coupling' with the environment would lead the system to reduced relevance to - and reduced 'fit' with - the environment and finally to stagnation. In order to retain its dynamic nature it must remain sensitive to environmental stimuli which requires it to remain sufficiently open to pressure, sufficiently unstable.

In view of this, instability, stresses Luhmann, must not be defined in a way that erodes the distinction between constancy and change. The

---

[2] Parsons and Shils, 1951, 108, and Parsons, 1951, 482

[3] Luhmann, 1981, 112

[4] There are other, secondary, ways in which conflict is productive for law: it provides the pressure to come to a decision, the continuation of operations, the system's evolution. Also, as we saw conflict tends to expand to new themes. The expanded conflict, not limited to the initial situation that triggered it, offers the chance to refer mutual behaviour to the conflict and from such thematic openness the law profits by developing wide applicability, juridifying social life. Law furnishes criteria for similarity of conflicts as it defines and develops comparison points that acquire a weight of their own. Independently of what sparked off the conflict, law provides for abstracting from the specific features of the case into conflictual patterns of general applicability / validity, etc.

distinctions stability/instability and constancy/change are separate and should not be confused. In particular instability must not be equated with change; in a counter-intuitive manner Luhmann draws a tight connection between instability and constancy, since the latter is 'only possible in complex systems through a sufficient degree of instability.'[5] Dynamic, temporalised, autopoietic systems rely on that instability. It is of their essence that they are endogenously restless. Later, in *Ecological Communication*, Luhmann will write: 'The structural improbability [of autopoietic systems] can be released easily [principle of variation]. Striking an equilibrium means that the system makes instability its principle of stability.'[6] To avoid entropy the system must be able to control instability. To strike the balance, instability must assume the form of uncertainty of expectations, the fulfilment or disappointment of which will be processed by the system. Through expectations the system opens towards the environment in controllable ways, and while the environment becomes all the more complex and unpredictable, the system builds up its own complexity to meet that unpredictability. It ascertains its own constancy in meeting that environmental complexity and not being threatened by it. We have already mentioned one of Luhmann's examples of this 'co-evolution' relating to how the law of contract has become more complex in order to respond to the increasing complexity of economic transactions. Luhmann gives examples from politics and economics too.[7] And yet there is no guarantee, says Luhmann, that instabilities will be sufficiently absorbed, determined and reproduced by the system. Drawing the link between instability and constancy more closely than ever, Luhmann introduces conflict in this context, and designates the function of conflict as the establishment, for the system, of a stable relationship to its own instabilities.

What Luhmann is essentially saying when he assigns to conflicts the function of stabilising systems is that it is in occasions of conflict that expectations are tested and reproduced and varied to meet the requirements of an ever more complex environment. Conflict provides the occasion of openness to the environment, and it is by exploiting such occasions ('exploiting conflict perspectives') that expectations are 'congruently generalised' as legal. It is in these terms that conflict completes the picture and that the interweaving of ('die Zusammenhang von') double contingency - complexity - instability - uncertainty of expectations - conflict and law is portrayed by Luhmann.

While it is in the above terms that Luhmann sees the interdependence of all the components of the definition of the function of law, we are in danger

---

[5] Luhmann, 1981, 95
[6] Luhmann, 1986e, 119
[7] Luhmann, 1981, 96

here of passing over one of the most valuable insights of the theory. It lies in the precise meaning of the term *'exploiting'*, and requires us to take a step back to look at *conflict* in its own right.

We have seen how the complexity that results from double contingency is dealt with through reductions that are peculiar to systems. Each system offers a way of managing the complexity by deploying specific contingencies, specific forms of expectation-uncertainty. A conflict is one such system. That is to say that *conflicts are themselves systems in their own right* and extraordinarily stable ones at that. They manage complexity and relieve expectation-uncertainty in so far as Ego assumes Alter as enemy and uses this assumption as a certain principle for the establishment of expectations. From this Ego derives certainty; uncertain expectations are replaced by problematical but stable ones. The fundamental problem of double contingency - what to expect of expectations - is crystallised as a confrontation. 'We can speak of conflict,' says Luhmann, 'whenever one participant in an interaction refuses to accept the choices or selections of another and communicates this refusal.'[8] As conflict takes over the interaction a new basis for action is furnished.

An interaction system within which a conflict was triggered, cannot easily accommodate it. Whatever interactional expectations or communication themes formed the context of the interaction quickly give way to the conflict. Simple interaction systems can either avoid conflict or become conflicts. It is in this sense that Luhmann describes conflicts as 'parasites' that take over the interaction system that generated them.[9]

In colonising the interaction from which it sprang, the conflict-system tends towards an overwhelming development of the *social* dimension at the expense of the *material* one. This means that the opposition Ego/Enemy absorbs and redefines the thematic of the interaction. Everything becomes relevant to the vantage point of the opposition; relevancy is built on what may harm Alter and benefit Ego.[10] This re-orientation allows the conflict a tight constellation. Details of Alter's behaviour that would normally be overlooked or go unnoticed suddenly become worthy of interpretation. The temporal dimension is also subsumed under the social one: the future becomes threatening and compels action. So conflict, like all interaction systems, has its own rules and follows its own logic, a self-reproducing, autopoietic one in fact,[11] as conflict 'devours increasingly new resources,

---

[8] Luhmann, 1975a, 82
[9] ibid., 83
[10] Luhmann describes them as highly redundant orders in this sense 1985b, pp404ff
[11] Luhmann did not in fact make this point as this is still prior to his *'autopoietic turn'*. He talks instead of social structure, and, in language reminiscent of the *Rechtssoziologie*, claims

usurps time and contacts,' includes increasingly 'new themes and new persons,'[12] and finally aligns the world to it.

Can a conflict's means of reducing double contingency and thus of building certainty of expectations in instability, be directly appropriated by the law? Does the legal system, in other words, profit from the stability of expectations as they crystallise in conflict? The answer is no. *Systems do not 'meet', they do not share reductions, they do not release instability or relieve uncertainty in common ways.* In sanctioning conflict, in providing it with a legal-institutional site, the law inserts a measure of instability in the expectations that had become certain through conflict. Law *exploits* conflict perspectives, it does not take them up as such. In the *social* dimension, through institutionalisation, the law will insert third parties that will engage in the conflict (normatively co-expect). But while, in effect, a measure of objectivity is imbued, on the other hand uncertainty is re-introduced as Ego no longer has to reckon exclusively with the enemy but also with the interfering third party and has to deal also with the latter's presumed orientation to the new situation. In the *material* dimension too, the certainty that was achieved in conflict is eroded as law 'thematises' conflict and appends issues of conflict on legal conditionals. We have explored all this in the previous chapter on the formation of expectations, and we will revisit it again in the critique of republicanism, so I will not expand here, except to say that the stake that divided the parts and crystallised in conflict, is now re-imbued by the law with instabilities that cut across much of what had become stable. So while conflict, through its polar structure, had infused instability with a measure of security of expectations, this certainty is now broken up anew and permeated with uncertainty again through law, with *its* introduction of third parties to the conflictual opposition and the legal thematisation of the issues. This newly introduced uncertainty, says Luhmann, runs counter to the thematic and strategic openness of conflict. Law filters this openness by inserting the differences that, in law, make a difference.

In all: the ***appropriation of conflict by the law*** introduces an entirely new situation. The conflict that gave law its occasion is left behind. A new array of possibilities appear in law, in this '"externalization" of conflict in the direction of third parties'[13] and the thematic reshuffling. To put it in terms Luhmann would use: the regulative principle behind the legal conflictual

---

that "[i]f it is true that conflicts absorb expectation uncertainty and therefore social instability .., one can accept that social evolution produces and requires conflicts in order to transform expectation structures, to generalize them and to equip them with sufficient flexibility.' (1981, 105)

[12] ibid., 100

[13] ibid., 110

reality cuts across the boundaries of the interaction system which occasioned it. In law, uncertainty is increased through the interference of the third party but decreased in other directions, as for example through and the breaking up of the conflictual complex into issues that can be objectively described and thus controlled in legal terms. The picture of how conflict is domesticated by law is not exhausted in institutionalisation and 'issue control'. Conflict is further conditioned by the legal restriction of legitimate means (e.g. the restriction of violence). Another selection from the vastness of conflict lies in the filtering out of trifling conflicts;[14] not every disagreement is litigable or worth litigating. In all, the production and reduction of complexity in the directions outlined are specific to the legal system and together map out the conflict as it is relevant to the law.[15] This is what it means then, for law to exploit conflict towards the production of congruently generalised expectations. The expectations produced by the law hinge upon the pattern of conflict but recast it through increasing and decreasing uncertainty, to produce specifically legal expectations and filter conflict through them.

This is the backbone of Luhmann's treatment of conflict. We have traced it all back to the basic sociological problem of double contingency. Departing from there we saw how the contingency is reduced in law to form and furnish legal expectations that allow interaction and communication in law - legal meaning. Then, turning to conflict, we saw how double contingency is reduced in the interaction system of conflict; we saw how the conflict re-aligns everything to the conflictual pattern and imbues contingency with certainty on that basis. Finally we explored the relation of law to conflict and concluded that conflict provides law with its occasion of openness but that the conflictual reality is re-worked in law.

Having drawn those inter-relationships as Luhmann describes them, we will turn to the relationship between legal and political - or what I will describe in the final chapter as 'reflexive' - conflict. Drawing insights from the theoretical framework I will complement an argument I have already begun against the civic republicans [thesis 1] with a series of further arguments [theses 2-11]. My main point throughout is that law depoliticises conflict, where to politicise conflict would be to allow a conflict over conflict. In each of the arguments to follow, I will argue that rather than empowering politics, the republicans, by 'containing' politics in law, replace questions over which

---

[14] ibid., 103
[15] In Teubner's words: 'Social conflicts trigger processes in law which formulate legally specific conflicts of expectations ... social conflicts are not merely translated into legal terminology; they are reconstructed as autonomous legal conflicts within the legal system.' (1993a, 58) Also Teubner (1992)

there is conflict with legal *a prioris*. In this they impoverish the 'reflexive' potential that inheres in conflict; they impoverish rather than contain or empower that which is political. I will advance the critique under four headings, depending on whether the republicans' 'depoliticisation' of the question relies on a prior 'conflation', 're-enactment', 'severing' or 'normalisation' of conflict.

CHAPTER ELEVEN

CONFLICTS CONFLATED

Peace is nothing more than a change in the form of conflict
(Weber)

We began the chapter with a distinction between conflicts constitutive and phenomenal, and to pursue my argument against the republican containment of conflict I will correlate that distinction to a system-theoretical one between conflict-system and conflict-occasion. We saw that conflict both constitutes a system in its own right as well as provides the legal system with an occasion of openness to the environment. Whether we are discussing expectations from the point of view of conflict or of law determines what we find differently. In the system of conflict expectation-uncertainty is relevant to the interactional context and contingencies are cast in a way that runs counter to the way the contingency of expectations is cast in law, where the conflict becomes the system's 'occasion of openness' to the environment. Specifying the context will lead to totally different answers to what is uncertain, what contingent, and how expectations embody both. Furthermore, keeping the system-referents (contexts) distinct will help us explore what is wrong with a theory such as republicanism, that collapses them into one.

The world can be observed by both systems, but the observer cannot assume both perspectives simultaneously. While this is all consistent with Luhmann's theory, Luhmann himself unfortunately appears to occasionally conflate the perspectives, which not only makes his position - at least in *'Konflikt und Recht'*- inconsistent, but more importantly submerges one of his theory's most promising heuristic devices for deciphering conflict. The conflation lingers in a number of points. Most noticeably it lingers in his offhand dismissal of an argument advanced, among others, by March and Simon. 'We assume,' they write, 'that when conflict is perceived, motivation to reduce conflict is generated. This assumption that conflict represents a disequilibrium in the system is implicit in all treatments of the phenomenon.'[1] Now March and Simon confine this assumption to Organisation Theory, as relevant to organisation systems, but others have broadened it to cover social systems too. Lewis Coser, for example, in his influential work in the sociology of conflict, insists that one is 'sensitized to

---

[1] March and Simon, 1958, 115

the fact that wherever there is conflict or disruption there will be social forces that press toward the establishment of some new kind of equilibrium.'[2]

What is common to these positions - March and Simon's in organisation theory, Coser's in social theory - is that they perceive conflict as a disequilibrium that automatically generates a reaction. Luhmann dismisses this self-healing process and attributes it to a misunderstanding of conflict. Conflict, he says, once generated does not subside; instead as parasite it takes over the interaction system that generated it, then totalises its image of the world as a universe of conflict. But surely we need to insert the distinction here that we have been discussing. Luhmann's dismissal of the self-healing process may be correct for the conflict-system, where conflict rather than instigating a return to order instead makes reality - action, expectations of behaviour, time - conflictual. However, March, Simon and Coser have described the function of the conflict-occasion quite accurately. Neither the organisational nor the social system, (more importantly the latter type that concerns us here,) 'give in' and neither are 'taken over' by conflict. Instead each manipulates it - exploits conflict perspectives - to gear its own self-reproduction. The essence of 'conflict as occasion' is that, by allowing the legal system to release and control its instability, it leads it back to restabilisation and order.

A number of arguments against the republicans follow. They are relevant to the conflation I identified. I will explore, in other words, through the systems-theoretical distinction of the two referents, some fundamental weaknesses of the republican argument: the failure to draw distinctions where distinctions are called for, and the impoverishment of possible conflict through a fast and easy recourse to law.

* Thesis [2] against Republicanism

The distinction between the two system referents allows us to formulate this second argument against the republican containment thesis as follows: *the law addresses conflict as system but contains it as occasion.* Republicans see conflict as an occasion of openness for law and have no time for conflict as a

---

[2] Coser, 1967, 10. See also his 1962, 172 in this respect. Importantly this in itself does not elevate the idea of equilibrium to normative grounds, in assuming that disequilibria are 'deviances' that threaten legitimate order. This is a move typically associated with certain types of sociological functionalism. Coser is careful to distance his analysis from such a pitfall and in a much earlier essay (Coser, (1950)) attacks Parsons for his 'ideological' use of functionalism.

system in its own right. In the process, I will argue, they lose sight of the possibility of reflexive politics.

The conflation of conflicts, inherent in the very meaning of 'containment', comes across most clearly in Dworkin's theory. In his theory law provides a kind of 'meta-narrative' that will accommodate without distortion the conflict of normative commitments. His own preferred way of putting this is that law lifts conflict 'from the battleground of politics to the forum of principle.'[3] *The legal position becomes the conflictual position par excellence*; in *Law's Empire* law is the argumentative practice of a community, the practice that hosts its conflicts. Dworkin completes the conflation as he forces social actors in situations of conflict into positions of participants in legal conflict, by methodologically assigning them insiders' positions, and thus assimilating their understandings of conflict to legal accounts.[4]

Inherent in Dworkin's thesis, as in the very meaning of 'containment', is a certain conflation of conflicts - of conflict as functional to the legal system and of conflict as system in its own right - or, in other words, a collapse of the distinction between 'constitutive' and 'phenomenal' conflict (see above). What is precisely the meaning of this assimilation of conflict-system into conflict-occasion? The decision to focus on the latter referent cloaks a decision (methodological or ideological) *to adopt the legal system's perspective to the exclusion of conflict's own perspective*. The asking price for the use of the tools of observation of one system (in this case law) is the acceptance of the exclusionary effect this choice has on other perspectives. This effect comes most dramatically into relief as the observation of conflict in law is effected to the exclusion of a different conflict perspective in which law itself has a specific place in the set-up of the conflictual domain.

The existence of a blindspot is in evidence here: the law can only thematise conflict at the expense of being itself thematised in conflict. The law cannot in one operation observe the distinction it is using to distinguish. It cannot observe conflict through distinctions and at the same time observe those distinctions it is operationalising.

What these systems-theoretical conclusions mean for the republican containment thesis is that in taking to law to provide the perspective they lose sight of the perspective that is specific to conflict itself. The most serious effect of this is that they thus lose sight of the position of law in conflict, by assuming that law is always-already the natural setting of conflict. Let me put this more concisely then: the republican containment thesis extends an invitation to read conflict in the community as a conflict

---

[3] Dworkin, 1985, 71

[4] Christodoulidis, 1994, pp11-13. Also, more generally Postema, (1987)

around positions in law. There is a political question that needs to be rescued from this imperialism: it is the question over the *staging of the conflict*. In republican theory, law is always-already the stage that will host conflict over normative understandings. What disappears as contested in this 'always-already' is the conflict over the mode of staging the conflict. This is the effect of the conflation of the two systems. The recourse to law as providing the perspective allows a designation of the staging or forum of conflict such that over it there can be no conflict.

As we saw in our discussion of the formation of legal expectations, in law conflict is staged through categories that pre-ordain its form and content, demarcate the problems and pre-empt what can be said about them. At the same time other demarcations of the problem and its object are prevented. To put it briefly, in the legal system conflict is necessarily aligned to legal co-ordinates where concepts of rights, liberties, legal notions of harm and legal analogies, legal tests and legal presumptions first make sense of it. Who can allege to have suffered harm, who counts as injured, why and when, as well as what enters the balance and what tilts the balance, to what side, all depend on a multitude of legal descriptions and conditional attributions (programming) that create the necessary relevancies and legal evaluations; in a word all that is experienced as law. All these relevancies allow for conflict selectively, they impose reductions on possible conflict. What remains outside the sphere of legal relevance, outwith the area of legal contingencies, appears as natural, obvious, given, inert to conflict. But further: in the process of submitting the conflict to these legal categorisations, what one party in conflict may see as depicted, the other may see as distorted. Then the opponent's action of taking the conflict to law and thus attempting to legitimate this distortion becomes a strategic move in the situation of conflict, an ideological move aiming to conceal what the conflict is really about. My point is that by taking law as the neutral forum for conflict, one loses sight of the position of law itself within the grander framework of conflict. Unacceptably to a theory that purports to account for political conflict and 'addresses itself to politics in the broadest sense,' the unquestioned recourse to law imposes a selective screening of what actors and communities assume to be politically at stake.

Therefore: the unquestioned prominence of law as neutral container of conflict, in republican theory, steamrolls over a plurality of political options at the level of staging the conflict and has serious repercussions on the grand scheme to account for community through law. If it is the case, as Dworkin and the republicans maintain, that community is substantiated in engaging in interpretative questions, then, in the area of conflict this means that the question over the staging of conflict needs to be an interpretative one too. This would be achieved if conflict over the staging of conflict were absorbed into conflict itself, if it were left interpretative, left to the community and *its* understanding of *its* conflict. But in the containment thesis the interpretative question over conflict is strait-jacketed by an a priori commitment to legal conflict. This privileging is arbitrary and not interpretative.[5]

In many ways, the question over the staging of the conflict is the reflexive-political question. The reliance on conflict as the system-referent was meant to make obvious this dimension: the conflict over conflict captures the reflexive moment. In the conflict-system the question over its staging is absorbed into conflict itself. Defining terms, stake and form becomes a question over which there is conflict. And that is why the distinction of the two system referents, conflict and law, is a good way of setting up the notions that need to be kept apart - reflexive conflict and conflict in law - and which civic republicanism is guilty of merging and thus submerging the possibility of reflexive political conflict.

There is a possible objection to this. As Luhmann stresses, conflict arises only around something about which there is no conflict.[6] The complexity of possible patterns of conflict must be reduced to determinable complexity if conflict is to be meaningful. Teubner renews this warning when he talks about turning infinite to finite conflict.[7] What all this means is that contradictions that give rise to conflict arise around structured contingencies; in the same way that what appears as natural, obvious, given, is inert to conflict, so the indeterminable complexity of overlapping mappings of conflict must be reduced to make sense of conflict in a mutually comprehensible way. Law provides those contingencies in reduction from possible states of conflict and there is surely a gain in reducing that complexity (in very similar way as there is a gain from the play of all exclusionary reasons - see part III). My more urgent concern however is with a loss. Because once reduced around specific legal patterns, what was challengeable in the initial conflict becomes naturalised and given, if only in order to make the specifically legal contingencies possible. Legal

---

[5] And thus exhibits features of what Freund has described and dismissed as 'legal utopia' (utopie juridique). 'J'entends par utopie le procédé qui consiste a extrapoler une relation sociale, dans ce cas la relation juridique, et a en faire la relation idéale de la solution des problèmes sociaux par méconnaissance de la pesanteur des relations politiques, économiques et autres. Il s'agit donc du procédé qui privilegie une relation dans l'infinité des relations existantes.' (1974, 49) In the context of deep social conflicts that questions the form of society in the light of models of 'utopies de la contre-société', it would be to mis-construe their stake, were one to 'méconnai[tre] la contestation du droit comme tel" and to ignore that "le droit lui-meme ... devient objet de litige.' (1974, 47-8).

[6] Luhmann, 1971

[7] Teubner, 1993a, p17 For the origin and meaning of the terms see Coser, below.

contingencies are hedged in by reductions on all sides, reductions of possible conflict. Where there was challenge and grounds for change, there is in legal reduction the givenness of the world in law. The exclusionary language of law bars access to the reflexivity of conflict. My argument against the republicans is that in celebrating the specific legal reduction of conflict they cannot see the impoverishment of possible contingencies. Normative commitments shape around a diversity of contestable premises. It is the acknowledgement of this wealth of contingencies of conflict that the republicans need to take into account, rather than relegating to legal contingencies alone the constitutive function of driving communities to shape around normative commitments. The republicans cannot have the best of both worlds: reduced conflict *and* community substantiated in conflict.

* Thesis [3] against Republicanism

I will put forward an argument that straddles both the one that precedes it and, if the focus is shifted, the one to follow it. It concerns a latent almost natural pull towards *consensus*, present in the republicans' accounts of conflict. The question that I want to address to the republicans is this: Why should one assume conflict to have a latent, in-built tendency to resolve itself?[8] And yet without this assumption, however, the containment thesis does not hold.

Unlike Habermas, neither Dworkin nor the civic republicans address the question of consensus directly, though, I will argue, they too make the question-begging assumptions, only by virtue of which can they salvage the containment thesis. Appropriately enough though, to the defence of the necessary orientation of conflict towards consensus - come sociologists of conflict of the Frankfurt camp. Max Miller subdivides social conflicts into three classes:[9] the first class contains those conflicts where 'participants don't even agree upon what their conflict is all about.' This is the case of infinite conflict that Teubner too mentions in passing and that both borrow from Simmel and Coser. In such cases 'social communication is powerless, the persons involved may as well stop talking ... because they could not reach a joint definition of their conflict.'[10] With infinite conflict out of the way, Miller can concentrate on the remaining two types. Finite conflict generates

---

[8] Luhmann says: 'It is false to impute to communications an inherent, quasi-teleological tendency to consensus. If that were the case, everything would already have been over long ago and the world as silent as it once was.' (1992b, 72)

[9] Miller, 1992, p11ff

[10] ibid.

what Miller calls 'co-ordinated dissent',[11] a kind of compromised Habermasian consensus that retains most of the elements of rational structures of discourse. A 'co-ordinated dissent' involves a joint identification of the points of controversy. 'If the persons involved also succeed in transforming the co-ordinated dissent into final consent we have an example of the third class of social conflict.'[12] (Why this final consent is still a conflict, I do not know).

All this is not yet particularly interesting until Miller advances an important claim:

'Once a co-ordinated dissent has been reached the persons involved will have an interest in transforming it into final consent - after all, the primary action goal of the complex verbal action "discourse" or "collective argumentation" is to find a jointly accepted answer to a jointly identified controversial situation.'[13]

This is why 'co-ordinated dissent' is so important. Because it serves the 'primary action goal' of human communicative action. And this is where law becomes so important too - in ensuring that 'co-ordinated dissent' may come about. Reducing infinite conflict to finite conflict is an achievement of law and in that law exhibits that vital 'integrative power of available structures of social co-operation.'[14] None of this is in fact very far from Luhmann's own account of the reduction achievement of law that facilitates the constellation of disagreement around specific contingencies. On the basis of the previous argument from the collapse of the levels or systems, one might ask Miller: reduction achievement, yes, but at what cost for reflexive politics?

Let me explain my objection here by drawing on this discussion of conflict finite and infinite - and the importance of the former for communicative action - to address two arguments to the republicans:

(i) how can they justify the *pre-commitment to finite* - i.e. resolvable - conflict?

(ii) Why is *finite conflict indispensable to community* and thus a 'primary action goal' whereas infinite conflict inimical to community?

(i) Through an argument that merely reproduces its presuppositions, the republicans can establish that conflict is finite because they hold the containment thesis. A community's conflict is assumed always resolvable because it is contained in law and law can - and has to - reach decisions. Such imposition of the decisionist model on conflict, that alone turns it finite,

---

[11] A notion that is central to his other work, see, for example, Miller, 1994
[12] Miller, 1992, 9
[13] This precommitment is typical of the work of Habermas. See also Miller 1987
[14] Miller, 1992, 10

is quite obviously question-begging; there exists in the republican argument a vicious circularity. They want to establish that a community's politics can be contained and indeed empowered by the law and they do it by first imputing legal assumptions to that politics. That they remain oblivious to this imputation can only be explained on the basis of how steeped in law the republican leading assumptions are. For example they always pitch their community at the level of citizenry; however divided that citizenry, the division is assumed internal (see thesis [5] below). Or, there is always a 'pre-interpretive plateau' of legal proto-understandings (in Dworkin) or a 'jurisgenerative fund' (in Michelman) and legal argument is the process of retrieving something that is already there (see thesis [4]). My argument here is that they can only get away with these question-begging assumptions because containment conflates the systems, collapses the referents. Only because conflict is already presupposed as contained - treated as an occasion - can the law's assumption about finitude be super-imposed on political conflict and *consensus assumed the implicit telos of conflict*; these in-built presuppositions alone in turn - and totally circularly - allow the republicans to deduce that politics can in fact be contained in law in a way that better resolves the conflicts and thus allows people a greater proximity in community.

(ii) Making no effort to hide his suspicions about consensus theorists, Horowitz wrote in the 60s:

'Consensus theorists starting from the metaphysical need for consensus as universal, can talk only about absolute or relative consensus, complete or partial integration but never about conflict as a means of expressing genuine social needs and aspirations.'[15]

For Miller, for example, consensus is unquestionably the primary goal of communicative/social action and at least the *possibility* of consensus - as 'co-ordinated dissent' - needs to be established. This is the premise from which the republicans also depart. Conflict is entertained in the community as 'co-ordinated dissent', as divergent yet optimally resolvable confrontations. But why this *a priori* commitment to finite (as opposed to infinite) conflict? Interaction is perfectly possible in the face of conflict, it is possible even *as* conflict. Conflict mediates the assumption of identities through which individuals enter public space (and thus also community). It allows people to see what public life is about and the lack of 'co-ordination' underpins the freedom to make sense of the social in mutually cross-cutting and

---

[15] Horowitz, 1962, 183

under-cutting ways.[16] None of this is detrimental to community, to people coming together under meaningful group self-descriptions. So why give up infinite conflict for the possibility of consensus *in the name of* community? I suggest it is because of the conflation of conflicts. In the republicans' argument, conflict is always-already treated as 'occasion'. By abandoning the possibility that conflict itself (as system) may shed perspective on the world, its community-generating power can no longer be sustained. Infinite conflict is assumed incompatible with community precisely because the republicans have no time for the community-generating effect that conflict itself has. The legal perspective that takes over brings with it its own form of conflict - finite - and its own community: the citizenry. The form of conflict that would have allowed it otherwise has been defined out, collapsed and conflated. The containment thesis can now contain a conflict that is always-already finite. The rest follows unproblematically.

Co-ordinated dissent around conflicting legal positions is a theoretical device through which a pattern of resolvable conflict is superimposed on a group that shares a location;[17] with both the matching of the positions of conflict and the possibility of consensus already patterned out in law, a community is artificially pulled up around a conflict that is always-already internal to it. By assuming the community engaged in argumentative practice around a finite legal conflict, the drive to consensus is assumed for the community that employs law as the medium to settle its internal conflicts. Miller's 'interest to transform [dissent] into final consent'[18] is really the decisionist interest of law, as is Dworkin's assumption that common normative understandings will settle again in the new post-interpretive phase, as is Michelman's conviction that new common principles will be hammered out over which, for some time at least, there will be no conflict. At the junction of law and community, optimal consensus - or finite conflict - is assumed necessary for both. In the name of what, then, this reified parcelling of the political? The community or the law? [19]

---

[16] A correlation here of finite/infinite conflict to Coser's distinction between realistic/nonrealistic conflict (1956, 46-50) would not be unhelpful. Particularly if we resist identifying the function of nonrealistic conflict with the harmless 'tension release' (49), the distinction could give an insight into why it is the conflict itself, not its resolution, not consensus that is so important to identity and community.

[17] See my argument about "trivial" community in (Christodoulidis, 1994, pp9-10)

[18] Miller, 1992, 12

[19] The conflation has effects not only in the direction of imputing features of law onto conflict but also drawing from conflict features and imputing them to law, even where the law cannot possibly accommodate them. Minow, for example writes: 'Dialogue in courtroom arguments can stretch the minds of listeners ... [and] inventive approaches can bring the voices of those who are not present before the court ... The introduction of additional voices may enable adversary dialogue to expand beyond a stylized either/or mode, prompting new and creative

* Thesis [4] against Republicanism

Republicanism is an invitation to read conflict in the community as legal argumentative practice. It is the conflation of the separate systems that allows the collapse and imposes the blindspot on the containment thesis. My argument is that the fact that a conflict can be described in legal terms does not mean that a community necessarily employs the legal account as the one that does justice to *its* understanding of *its* conflict. To assume that it does is to insert an *a priori* where there is an interpretative question and thus to impoverish the community's politics by removing that question from contestation. Let us see how two of the theorists effect this screening off of the interpretative political question.

As Dworkin develops his argument for the connection between integrity, community and the interpretation of practices, he initially uses law as one instance of an interpretative practice, and there are many others that exhibit the same link to community. As the argument develops however, he uses law at the expense of any other instance for the function of the 'recollection' of community through its practices. The point where the transition from law-as-an-instance to law-as-the-paradigm is effected is not obvious since Dworkin oscillates with ease between 'political integrity' and 'law as

---

insights.' (1987, 88-9) This argument of Minow's in favour of 'multi-polar litigation' and against the necessity of circumscribing legal argumentation to two voices flatly pitted against each other defies what is in essence the reduction-achievement of legal argumentation. Legal argumentation is about reducing Minow's multi-polar perspective through legal relevancies. Legal argument is, to paraphrase Simmel, about dissolving such divergent dualisms. Then meaningful argument can come about because through its reductions the legal discourse resolves potential complexity and enables voices to be pitted against each other in meaningful confrontation. The legal decision cannot evade a resolution in an either/or mode. To 'salvage the power of seemingly antagonistic views'(what function does the moderating 'seemingly' perform here I am not clear) Minow recalls the old story of the rabbi who listens to the claims of both adversaries and replies to both that they are right. To his wife who reminds him that this is not possible he also concedes that she is right. It is a strange coincidence that Luhmann resorts to the same story to claim the opposite. That the judge does not have the luxury to avoid an either/or choice. (Luhmann, 1988c) Another way of putting this is that the existence of conlict and law's processing of (what it perceives as) conflict only coincide contingently (see also thesis [5]). As Freund put it, 'C'est parce que le droit appartient aux conditions du conflit, soit qu'il forme l'objet du litige, soit qu'il le nourisse, qu'il peut aussi en être la solution.' (1974, 52) Where there is contingency, the republicans assume necessity. But to complicate things even further, even fully institutionalised conflicts like the ones that Freund too, here, has in mind, i.e. 'those whose end-points can be specified and recognised by the contenders' (Coser 1956, 12, 40), only transforms infinite to finite conflict to the advantage of community (in fact only bears on the question of community) on the assumption that it was communal conflict to begin with. In that the transformation is a necessary but not sufficient condition for the existence of community.

integrity', the overall and the particular. But it is arbitrary that Dworkin chooses the legal chain novel as the means for recollecting his society's history; the law's story is *only one among many narratives and to employ it as the definitive one steamrollers over questions that should be interpretative*. Dworkin yields community by presupposing it. Michelman is also guilty of this slippage. He writes:

'The legal form of plurality is indeterminacy. Legal indeterminacy is the pre-condition of the dialogic, critical-transformative dimension of our legal practice variously known as immanent critique, internal development, deviationist doctrine, social criticism and recollective imagination.'[20]

In presenting this as a simple sequence, Michelman like Dworkin, has inserted the legal *a priori*. For him legal indeterminacy becomes the space that discloses political options. Immanent critique becomes the mode of political contestation and action. The scope of possible indeterminacies accounts for the scope of political plurality; law can accommodate, as indeterminacy, every political challenge to settled patterns and circumscribes in this way the potential for communal self-revision. In the republican argument law circumscribes political space, and that is the crux of containment.

What the republicans are silent about in all this, is why we should consider law as the primary vessel of our engagement in dialogue or conflict with others over the terms of social life.[21] They simply assume we do that in law, and since law harbours and voices our conflicts, it generates community and 'fuses moral and political lives'[22] even among people who find law oppressive or irrelevant to their normative commitments. The point is that narratives that inform normative commitments, conflictual positions and identities are cast in as diverse forms as there have been communities in history. But for the republicans communities reach self-understanding through law and this leads surely, if indirectly, to a deep identification of the political actor with the citizen, as the law's history is the past narrative of our collective political identity - law our collective repository of value and justice commitments. Identity is immersed in an overwhelming legal narrative. This side-steps all the intermediate loci where commitment takes shape, conflict is consolidated and identity is formed, and I use 'intermediate' with no connotation of hierarchy under the State. This locus may be, among others, the religious community, the ghetto, the closed

---

[20] Michelman, 1988, 1528-9
[21] This echoes Lawrence Tribe's implausible claim that we are all constantly engaged in 'constitutional choices.' (1985, vii)
[22] Dworkin, 1986, 189

secular community, the racial or national minority movement, the new social movement, the party or the revolution. Each creates a normative cosmos and casts identity and 'otherness' in diverse and incompatible ways. Each avails an alternative template to the same social complex, making sense of conflicts in different ways, applying them to different rationalising patterns, employing different terminologies to describe them and different causal relationships to explain them. This is an argument about normative anarchy, of narratives that cast conflicts and communities in varied and incompatible ways, none of which is definitive at the level of the citizenry.

The republicans proceed on the assumption that law is constitutive of the 'texture' of our communities, the means through which our communities are instituted and within them commitment and conflict perceived and voiced.[23] Sometimes this is so, sometimes not. But by building their theory on that premise, the republicans again impose that assumption rather than retrieving it, again concealing an interpretative question with an *a priori*, again containing the political question that defies containment and thus, again, silencing the reflexive political question.

Before ending this section, I would like to point to some linkages between the argument about the 'conflation of conflicts' and those that follow. The distinction of two system referents will be central to the discussion of 're-enactment' that follows. Re-enactment relies on accounting for the first of these systems (conflict) in terms of expectations projected from within the second (law). In discussing the first of these systems, Luhmann told us that conflict is a system that builds (and stabilises) world relevancy around the reduction to its polar pattern. The system of law exploits conflict but it does not take on board the certainty that results from this reduction. Conflict provides law with an occasion of openness. But the conflict is only picked up by the legal sensors as already re-aligned to legal-systemic co-ordinates that break down (reduce) issues in ways that are legally processable. The uncertainty introduced thus works all the way back to recast the conflict as is relevant to law.

The distinction of the two system referents will also be central to the discussion of the 'severing' of conflict as well as its 'normalisation'. The severing occurs as issues that divide the parties in conflict and the identity of those parties are removed by one system (the law) from their embeddedness in another (conflict). Normalisation, on the other hand, results from

---

[23] Note another absurd consequence: under this identification of law and community to raise the question of the obligation to obey the law would be to raise the question of one's commitment to the community's existence as such. The invitation to conceive communal obligation as legal can be refuted also, following a suggestion by Dan-Cohen (1989), by employing Goffman's concepts of role-taking and role-distancing.

integrating conflict into structures that have already imposed reductions on possible conflict. Normalisation is the process of re-alignment of what has meaning in one system to already existing frameworks of meaning in another. Thus our future discussion bears on the present one of the designation of system-referents.

CHAPTER TWELVE

CONFLICT RE-ENACTED

If, on the one hand, the law is the site of class struggle, its ideology, on the other hand, must make it unaware of the ground on which it is in action. The juridical expression of the relation between law and the political in this way necessarily implies the dialectic of this contradiction.
(Edelman)

The argument about re-enactment is the argument about how hetero-reference, i.e. (law's) reference to the (political) environment, builds on the back of the system's own self-reference. *The legal containment of conflict, I will argue, is the story of its re-enactment.* Both with and against Luhmann and Teubner I will argue that: (a) legal roles, programmes and values are not merely translations of political into legal conflict but are the co-ordinates around which political conflicts are re-enacted as autonomous legal conflicts within the system; (b) 'political interests' act more often than not as law's surrogate environment of politics. Much of this chapter centres on political speech; theses [6] and [7] focus the broader discussion of the re-enactment of conflict on political speech, develop and deepen it. Regarding political speech it will be argued that the political utterance never enters the legal screen but all reference to it is instead mediated through a legal distinction that makes the meaning of the political utterance dependent on law. Law's reference to politics, its hetero-reference, is based on self-reference, on the projection of a legal distinction that makes sense of politics. Law thus imposes upon politics the realm of relevance - in carving out the ontological space of the action it takes as political - and the mode of relevance - the sense in which something is 'politically' relevant.

Let us see more gradually how the law re-enacts conflict. The system builds hetero-reference - its understanding of political conflict - on the back of its own conception of conflict - self-reference. In order to deal with political conflict the legal system uses a number of concepts, and distinctions around those concepts, that make it possible for law to observe social conflict. What the law in effect does is to project certain criteria and delimit a realm of relevant conflict according to these criteria. What is delimited through these criteria is a projection, yet it is taken in law as conflict itself, pure and simple. Teubner puts forward the notion of re-enactment of conflict very concisely:

'[T]he resolution of conflicts through law can be construed as legal self-regulation operating strictly within the system itself. The legal system detects the presence of conflict in its social environment with its internal sensors (roles, concepts, doctrines).

It then reconstrues these conflicts in its own terms as conflicts of expectations, processing them through norms, procedures and doctrines. ... All this takes place exclusively within the limits of legal communication as defined by the law itself.'[1]

The description provided by Teubner is extremely close to Luhmann's account that we examined in chapter ten. Teubner's 'law reconstrues conflict' is Luhmann's 'law re-imbues conflict with system-specific instabilities.' Teubner's simplifying formula 'sensors' in which he includes 'roles, concepts, e.t.c.,' is a short hand formula for Luhmann's more complex account of how law generalises expectations in temporal, social and material dimensions. We will explore, by repeating to some extent what has gone before, the notion of the re-enactment of political conflict in law.

Before that, a minor objection to Teubner's formulation. The problem I will identify may, of course, be due to the brevity of Teubner's exposition here. In any case, as we saw, what signals a conflict in law may not constitute a conflict in a different context (system) and alternatively what is a conflict in a different system may not register in law as conflict. Therefore it is a mistake to assume that law always picks up or is stimulated by something that is already conflict in the environment. Already existing, full-fledged, social conflict is not a requirement for a stimulus to register as conflict in law.

Luhmann is more careful on this point. He says, on the one hand, that social conflict does not always stimulate a legal response. For example trifling conflicts are not reckoned with in law: not everything is worth litigating. On the other hand, and this is the point I am making against Teubner, he says that law facilitates conflict, in that for example, it first allows conflict that would otherwise have been impossible, by propping up assumptions for conflictual positions (see chapter ten). Law may thus do two things not accounted for in Teubner's passage. On the one hand it may deny social conflict by not picking it up and thus defining it out of (legal) existence. On the other it may first create conflict where there was none in its environment. That is why Teubner's account captures only part of the story.

Notwithstanding this minor objection, the notion of re-enactment comes across strong and clear in Teubner's extract. The crux of re-enactment is that when 'social conflict' is picked up it is reproduced as a conflict of expectations in which the 'sensors' are operative in determining *the **when** and **how** of the **disappointment*** that gave rise to conflict.

What does the term 'sensors' in Teubner's text signify exactly? Teubner calls roles, concepts, e.t.c. 'sensors' because their function is to be attuned to and 'pick up' social conflict. They perform their function by picking up social

---
[1] Teubner, 1993a, 99

conflict *as relevant* to the law. This brings us to the crux of the matter. Information about the environment, including the environment of social conflict, can only be acquired by the system through affirmation or disappointment of what we could call *a projection of possible states*; expectations carry these hypotheses and test them. What is thus produced is a mapping of the (inaccessible to the system) environment of social conflict. The reason it has been mapped out 'as relevant' to the law is because what was operationalised in the first place - furnishing the expectations - were *specific sensitivities, vulnerable* in specific ways. That is why Teubner calls them the system's 'sensors' that serve to scan the environment. We will look at how disappointment thresholds are set up, making normative expectations 'sensitive to' and 'vulnerable to' specific environmental stimuli.

We will approach this argument by explaining away two important misunderstadings about re-enactment that must be resisted:
(i) The first is to view it as a *fictional* reproduction of real social conflict. Autopoietic systems are (empirically) real systems and the conflict they harbour and give expression to is in no way fictional.
(ii) The second misunderstanding relates to their nature as institutional representations of a 'brute' reality outwith them.

The first of these points is vividly illustrated in the misguided attack that one of the most prominent exponents of the empirical sociology of law, Hubert Rottleutner, levels on systems theory.[2] Either Luhmann is describing empirical, real systems, he says, or he is describing analytical forms, calculi. Either way he is wrong. If he is doing the latter, then his theoretical exercise ('autopoetry' Rottleutner calls it) is hardly relevant to sociology. If he purports to be doing the former then he is contradicting himself. Because then he must acknowledge that 'constitutive role of legal norms for the majority of social relationships'[3] in which case law is constituting reality in a way that cuts across the supposed complete autonomy/closure of social systems that are deemed to each constitute their own reality.

The idea of law's constitutive role in society is convincing but undercuts nothing of what Luhmann has to say. The law employs its guiding distinctions to guide its operations and on the basis of those distinctions thematises reality in system-specific ways. Law constitutes reality but it constitutes reality for itself- for the world of legal communications and communicators. It totalises its description of the world and makes sense of everything through its totalising, guiding distinction (codes, secondary and

---

[2] Rottleutner, 1989b
[3] ibid., 282

primary, and programming). 'This is specific because of the way the difference divides the world up, but not at all partial in the sense of dividing up only part of the world,' as Sean Smith points out.[4] The reason Rottleutner cannot make sense of how legal categories can at the same time be constitutive of reality and not cut across other subsystem accounts of the world, is because he is relying on some version of 'ontological realism.'[5] His is a world where legal categorisations exist at the expense of other system mappings. But he does not understand Luhmann's more profound account of the existence of temporalised systems.

Conflict within and outside the legal system, thematised in interaction, in religion, in the family, in law, or in politics - to name but a few rival thematisations - all exist simultaneously, where the (same) communication that communicates the conflict is absorbed into rival linkings by each system. (An example that will be used later is that of a Northern Irish district councillor's refusal to repudiate Sinn Fein which is at the same time a political statement in politics and a non-political-because-terrorist statement in law that in fact disqualifies him from political office.) Meaning is actualised in the world from a multitude of perspectives and these rival worlds of meaning exist simultaneously, (which may explain why an observer only sees one at a time.) 'The same is different' according to Glanville,[6] the visible sign absorbed in systems that clash around it and couple through it.[7] We will have to look closely at system organisation of time, notions of 'synchronicity' and 'structural coupling' to make full sense of this, but, in any case, we must do away with any ideas of causality transcending systems. This may explain why Rottleutner, the empirical scientist, has a problem with it. What motivates people to accept one linking and refuse to accept another has to do with questions of (legal) socialisation, or in more systems technical terms, 'symbolic media' that attract people to certain mappings of the world, sometimes with such force as to vest what is perceived with a sense of self-evidence. Whatever the motivation may depend on, and however strong it may be, law is never constitutive of reality tout court, but only of yet another systemic perspective on reality, an additional possibility of making things meaningful.

So much for the 'reality' of systemic constructions, but what about the second misunderstanding? The idea of re-enactment as explained above is a reversal of the usual way of understanding the relationship between 'worlds I and II,' i.e. respectively the world of raw, brute facts and the institutional

---

[4] Smith S C, 1991, 334

[5] For a defence (of even the pre-autopoiesis *Rechtssoziologie*) along these lines see Smith, 333-4

[6] Glanville (1981)

[7] On this see Teubner (1992)

mapping of that world. Contrary to the view that draws on MacCormick and Weinberger's seminal work,[8] systems theory (indisputably amongst others here) suggests that what is conceivable as brute fact only comes about as a projection from the institutional world. One goes into the world to look for the brute/natural datum 'political conflict'. What one encounters as natural fact depends on what one has set off to look for, on the basis of what assumptions the search is initiated. These assumptions are institutional. It is thus misleading to assume that the same ontologically existent conflict gives rise to rival mappings in the institutional worlds on the basis of some kind of institutional 'distortions' brought about by the peculiarities of institutional logics. Institutional projections precede 'natural' conflict in every sense, 'individuating the event' as Davidson would put it, delimiting its contours. And yet law perceives a conflict as 'naturally' occurring and purports to fix sanctions and conditionals upon that which exists as a matter of fact, independently of law. In thesis [6] this reversal will be further developed.

Now neither Luhmann nor Teubner explicitly reverse the worlds in this sense but I think it only follows from their accounts. It is only a small step from hetero-reference, as an 'unfolding' of self-reference, to the reversal I pointed to. In the case of conflict, the system does not simply re-align previous conflict but first carves it out as such - abstracts and isolates a section of its environment as 'brute' conflict.[9] For example Teubner says that '[s]ocial conflicts are not merely "translated" into legal terminology; they are reconstructed as autonomous legal conflicts within the legal system.'[10] This does not necessarily imply the point I made but can nonetheless accommodate the strong reading of re-enactment I suggest. This reading is in line with the constructivist premises of the theory in general. It holds that the purchase into reality, into the natural, is provided by the system. In neither Teubner's nor Luhmann's account is social conflict taken on board as such. This means that there is no 'real' but only constructed hetero-reference. In Teubner social conflict is 'reconstructed'; in Luhmann law does not take on board social conflict either, it 'exploits conflict perspectives,' and 'generalises' them in system-specific ways. In both cases they are generalised 'as conflicts of expectations.' What can be disappointed, and at what threshold, have to do with what assumptions furnish those expectations. Such vulnerabilities and disappointments are all institutionally projected. These are all the institutional assumptions that carve out a realm of

---

[8] MacCormick & Weinberger (1968)

[9] This further step in re-enactment helps us get around those inconsistencies and minor objections to Teubner's formulation of the presupposition of some form of social conflict that triggers legal conflict. It also bridges the two categories in Luhmann of conflict re-worked and conflict first propped up (see also Luhmann (1989)).

[10] Teubner, 1993a, ch 3

interaction as 'natural' conflict. When, therefore, the communication of a refusal (Widerspruch) becomes a conflict has to do with what can be taken a refusal of what. All these stimulants are set by a system. That's why they are identified as 'sensors' in Teubner's text. To give an example: the fact that law establishes a duty of care between spouses and gives that duty specific content also establishes the threshold and occasion of the disappointment. Levels of aspiration and feelings of disappointment are relative to institutionalised expectations. The transgression of a duty as stipulated by law may go unnoticed in love where care may be given a very different content and disappointment threshold. Or love may set a much higher level of care so that disappointments that do not register in law disappoint expectations in love. Similarly with other interaction systems, each with its specificity of setting conflict thresholds. Teubner calls roles 'sensors' because they identify conflict thresholds and they do so in system-specific ways, as the 'roles' (system-descriptions of identity) of spouse and lover indicated in this example.

Luhmann explains the re-enactment of conflict as its being re-imbued with instabilities. Conflict is re-cast along all three dimensions. In the social dimension the Ego-Alter confrontation is mediated by the positing of the co-expecting third. We explored previously how this institutionalisation of the conflict abstracts it from its social basis. We will pick up that argument again in the following chapter. For the remaining part of this one, we will explore more systematically and in some detail how the re-enactment of conflict affects the stake of the conflict.

The notion that the political conflict is re-enacted means that what appears as the stake of the conflict is legally projected. Not in a simple, superficial way as would be the case with legal distortions of actual positions. Rather the duplication works all the way down. The conflict is first set up around a stake that is a stake in law. The stake is then projected into the realm of politics; what conflict is read there as environmental ('sensed') depends on what was projected in the first place. It is thus that hetero-reference becomes an unfolding of self-reference. The legal system effects specific projections into the political realm and reads stakes and contestation of those stakes when it senses specific environmental reactions to its projections. Again, what is contested and when has to do with what is projected. What the legal system avails as disappointment sensors are the ones Luhmann describes as pertaining to the material dimension of the system: roles, programmes and values.

Expectations from *role* allow stakes to appear around which conflictual positions emerge. Roles are the first type of sensors that set thresholds of disappointment around specific stakes. Roles, that is, orient the allocation of importance to specific issues, furnish certain expectations pertaining to identity, that, when contradicted, create conflict. Here is an example: where adultery constitutes a reason for divorce in law, the marital status itself is endangered by the adulterous spouse. Where refusal to consummate marriage is repeatedly communicated from one spouse, a disappointment from role is perceived that may lead to a set-up of a conflictual situation in law. The law steps in to protect an 'interest' in sex, or less crudely perhaps, an interest in fulfilling the role of sexual partner institutionalised in marriage, and now disappointed. The disappointed spouse may seek remedy in the termination of marriage in the first case, its annulment in the second. Significantly for the notion of re-enactment, it is a disappointment from love that the law perceives here, a disappointment from the 'brute' world of love not the 'institutional' one of marriage. The disappointment that is generated from legal role is projected into love, *as if* it were a disappointment of love that was at stake. The legal expectation re-enacts an expectation from love here, it makes sense of the referred on the basis of the referrer oblivious to the fact that both are institutional creations. I will take up this example and explore it more fully in part III and, for present purposes, suggest a politically more relevant one - rights and interests - below. But the love/marriage example still brings out the point I am arguing: that conflicts are perceived on the basis of projections of disappointments that stem from assumptions that furnish legal concepts, in this case roles.

The same can be said of programmes and values, only in terms of disappointments of which, can a conflict resonate at all in law. We have discussed the meaning of the terms in chapter nine. **Programmes**, like roles, serve as selectivity mechanisms. They serve the selective processing of information from the environment, they determine the terms in which the environment is perceived as relevant to the system and therefore also select conflict from the environment as is relevant to law. System selectivity depends on programming. Luhmann identifies two types of programming in the legal system, conditional and goal-oriented programmes.[11] In a conditional programme a condition is stipulated and kept invariant so that whenever that condition is seen to be fulfilled, the effects that append are activated and the system thus responds in the stipulated way. This is the form of programming most typical to law, the 'if p then q' formula. In a goal-programme on the other hand, the system selects a response as desirable, sets it up as invariant and uses it as a rule for selecting causes that can bring it about. This is a formula increasingly apposite to the interventionist type of law. Luhmann adds that

---

[11] Luhmann, 1986a and 1967, ps110-113

'these two fundamental types of program are jointly exhaustive. But they can be combined in numerous ways and embedded in each other, so that it is often difficult to assign concrete programs to the one type or to the other.'[12]

Programmes select and activate *values*, the final, most abstract 'sensor'. Programmes assimilate values, select and take some on board while neutralising others. The goal-oriented programme, for example, fixes a value as the invariant rule for selecting causes that will fulfil it; it becomes, so to speak, a cause for selecting causes. But values are at play in conditional programming too, as is the case of the value of the rule of law underpinning the 'if, then' formula. Of course this does not in any way mean that the conflict of social values is taken on board in law. The assimilation of values into programmes means that in the case of goal-programming, the law will perceive the conflict in a way that it may gear it towards a resolution that may further the goal, and in the case of a conditional program, the law will isolate as relevant that component of conflict that can activate the 'if p then q' sentence and will build its account of conflict as a confrontation in view of that sentence. As always, to paraphrase Luhmann, only a small portion of possible conflict is thus fixed in law as expectable.

The relevant point of all this for our analysis of social and legal conflict is that all these are selectivity mechanisms that transform (re-enact) social conflict into legally relevant, or legally resolvable, conflict. These are more than 'filters'; the closed system that has no access to reality projects hypotheses that allow that environment to resonate inside the system. Only via these projections into the social environment does conflict acquire legally meaningful form. Re-enactment means that these issues about which there is conflict, are assumed in law to have divided the parties naturally, as a matter of brute fact.

I will give an example of the re-enactment of conflict that is central to a discussion of the relationship of law and politics. I will introduce the term *thematisation* here, which is an important aspect of re-enactment - of how hetero-reference builds on the back of self-reference. That the conflict is thematised means that it is worked into the law through legal concepts. In the example to follow, *'interests'* is the concept that law reserves for what clashes in political conflict. Law treats interests as exogenous to its analysis, as pertaining to politics proper. Law itself purports to come into a world of already clashing interests. It gives people rights and thus a way out of the 'battleground' of politics (Dworkin) and the irresolvable clash of pure interest (Sunstein). Interests are mediated through rights; in this way law's hetero-reference to a political clash of interests, is transcribed, purportedly

---

[12] Luhmann, 1967, 111

without any significant distortion, into a clash of rights that is possible to process in law. But the point is that *interests are as much concepts of the legal system as rights are.* Interests carry into politics claims that are processable in law. They are the names for what has resonated in law as politics.

A very short account of the interdependence of rights and interests is contained in Luhmann's *'Interesse und Interessenjurisprudenz'* (1990).[13] In its reference to its political environment, law perceives politics as encompassing 'the constant conceptualisation of the protection of interests in [terms of a] search for common grounds and grounds of comparison,' and on the other side, its own (legal) 'constant questioning of [legal] concepts and conceptual constructions [rights, balancing formulas] in the direction of interests that are affected by them.'[14] It is thus that Luhmann describes how reference to political interests is mediated by law in a way that is constitutive of the law's picture of politics; law's account of politics is only an unfolding of its own self-reference. Interests are politics re-enacted, the re-enactment completed in the natural assumption that the *lingua franca* of law gives expression to political interests that exist as a matter of fact.

* Thesis [5] against Republicanism

To see more precisely how 'interests and [legal] concepts organise other-reference and self-reference for the legal system'[15] it would be worth looking at a specific political conflict and its re-enactment in law, in terms of a clash of rights 'carrying' political interests. I suggest focusing the discussion on a specific problem that engages both law and (feminist) politics.

There are many sides to and expressions of the dissatisfaction of women with the way the claims and demands of the feminist movement(s) are processed in law, or, more appropriately in the present context, to the way feminist claims carry in legal argument. Some strands of feminism, usually grouped under the umbrella term 'liberal feminism,'[16] define the problem as one of the application of the law. Were 'like cases treated alike' the inequality and oppression suffered by women would be substantially lifted. Biased application of the law is attributed to sexist motives and attitudes of individual decision-makers. This is a case of legal inertia or contingent

---

[13] Cf. Teubner's analysis of "interest analysis" (1989, 747) for some similar, if more confined, formulations.
[14] Luhmann, 1990d, 10, my thans.
[15] ibid., 11
[16] Brown, 1993, pp152ff

prejudice, and there are, at least aspirationally, ways of redressing this discrimination that can be brought about institutionally. In effect, this 'liberal' feminist understanding of oppression does not pose unsurpassable problems to the republican containment thesis.

But there is a second, more radical, understanding that does. On this account, the law structurally inhibits the feminist case from surfacing and prevents the claim from being heard. Although much can be made of the 'hidden content' of the law, I am primarily talking here about the inhibitions inherent in the 'form' of the law.[17] Catherine MacKinnon, for example, treats the form of law as the reflection of male power. She argues that it is part of the feminist project to reject the 'objective' and the 'neutral' as these are the very projections of male power that objectify women.[18] 'When law is most ruthlessly neutral,' writes MacKinnon, 'it will be most male; when it is most sex blind it will be most blind to the standard that is being applied.' And then: '[a]bstract rights will authorise the male experience of the world.'[19] Carol Gilligan too, suggests that the moral code, transcribed in law as general rights and neutrality, reflects men's values and can therefore not accommodate women's concerns. 'This form of critique,' summarises Beverley Brown, 'finds the very ideals of neutrality and objectivity unacceptably indifferent to the concrete specifics of lived reality.'[20]

I will use the example of *pornography* not to show the more general point that politically conflictual positions are distorted in law, but the more difficult point that what is perceived in law as the political positions in conflict is re-enacted from the point of view of law.

Politically speaking, we can identify a number of divisions in the stance that feminism takes towards pornography.[21] While the denunciation of discrimination informs or accompanies most of the formulations of the argument against pornography, some more radical versions of the argument are worth particular mention. Broadly speaking, we can identify three: (i) the argument that likens pornography to violence and represents it 'on a continuum with rape and child abuse ... [Pornography] reflects and reinforces the reality of male power at its most coercive.'[22] (ii) the argument that 'centres on the axis of discrimination and the mechanisms of inequality.' The emphasis here is on the function of legitimation through belief systems, that legitimate ascribing to women only one social role, that of sexual objects, an ascription that carries through social life and spreads outside sexual

---

[17] ibid, pp163-4
[18] Smart, 1986, 121
[19] MacKinnon, 1983, pp644, 658
[20] Brown, 1993, 164
[21] My discussion here draws heavily on Brown (1990)
[22] ibid., 137

relations.[23] Finally (iii) 'pornography as representation' feminists argue that pornography 'objectifies' women:

'[i]t constructs woman as object of an objectifying, consuming, fragmenting gaze ... This position of the woman identified with the to-be-looked-at quality of pornographic images underlies important processes of identification and vulnerability.'[24]

Law takes the plurality of stances and the maze of the underlying political values and levels them down to incorporate them under its own central distinction, that of legal/illegal. The law is after all, to paraphrase Simmel, about resolving divergent dualisms: that is its reduction achievement. Either pornography is illegal or it is not. Then, to use Luhmann's terminology, the law complements that guiding distinction - coding - with programming. If pornography is illegal, it is because the harm it creates - where what counts as harm is determined through legal criteria - outweighs legal reasons for protecting pornography. If it is lawful it is because the harm in censoring pornography outweighs the reasons for protection from the harm it might cause the alleged injured side. Who counts as injured, why and when, as well as what enters the balance and what tilts the balance, to what side, can include a multitude of legal descriptions (the definition of pornographic), conditional attributions that create the necessary relevancies and legal evaluations, hierarchies of norms (for example, constitutional guarantees of freedom of speech against legislative prohibitions of harm) and criteria, e.t.c., in a word all that we experience as law. There is no doubt a lot of room for manoeuvre in all this and critical scholars (including feminist CLS) are surely right to identify transformative potential within law, shifting priorities and relevancies, upsetting legally settled meaning (see chapter 14). Whatever the possibilities of immanent critique, however, they do not relax the rigidity of the guiding reduction that, in an enabling way, makes possible all subsequent flexibility. One would have to look to the dependence of programming on coding; I will not repeat that argument here about the ultimate reduction that underpins the discourse of law. What it means in this context is this: that ultimately either pornography is illegal or it is not.

---

[23] 'This is what pornography means ... It institutionalizes the sexuality of male supremacy, fusing the eroticization of dominance and submission with the social construction of male and female. ... pornography is the harm of male supremacy made difficult to see because of its pervasiveness, potency, and principally, because of its succeed in making the world a pornographic place.' (MacKinnon, 1992, 461)

[24] Brown, 1990, 138. Also: 'Those aspects of pornography's recognisability so often regretted on aesthetic grounds, far from being gratuitous, are essential to it; it is the way in which the organization and disorganisation of bodies operates as a short cut to desire which constitutes "objectification".' (Brown ,1985)

All that's well, but what does it tell us about the *re-enactment* of political conflict? The question turns on the political interests that the law 'sees' associated with the raising of the question of pornography. For the law, one abstains from raising the claim because one is politically motivated by the interest to uphold the freedom of speech. In contrast, the political motive behind raising the claim is the interest to prevent the harm. Both of these are political interests in a broad sense, political motives that the law picks up as motivating the conflict around pornography. That is a hetero-reference based on self-reference. The clash of interests in politics is the legal postulate of the clash of rights in law. This was the point repeatedly stressed by Luhmann: 'what occurs in both directions is internal structural workings of internal operations and not a pressure of interests originating in the social environment.' The 'semantics of "interests" makes the legal system sensitive to stimulation and thus sets in motion the system's own explorations,' activating in the system a process of turning noise into order and the rest. Throughout this process 'the interests that the legal system processes are its own constructions, [and] these constructions make explicit the irritation from the environment.' But 'in the construction of interests a considerable reduction of environmental complexity has already been effected,' because 'the boundaries of the system excludes all that cannot be expressed in this language of concepts and interests.'[25] To negotiate conflict through negotiating rights, is to allow a vast area of conflict, and an infinite area of potential conflict, to be defined away.

How does this apply, more specifically, to pornography? What is here the broad area of political conflict that has been defined away during the legal processing of the issue? It is this. If feminists denounce pornography as violence (above, i), the question in law becomes the force of the causal connection between the two. There is a silencing here. Law seeks a political interest to refer to, but the political interest it finds is so weakly captured in law, it practically collapses: it becomes that of seeking to redress the serious crimes of violence and exploitation of the young and other vulnerable categories. The question in law is how forceful a causal connection can be established between pornography and the protection of vulnerable categories.[26] The political perspective that gets lost is the denunciation of the male-power context that frames, informs and re-inforces these instances of

---

[25] Luhmann, 1990d, 11

[26] "The requirement that demostrable connections be shown urges that pornography have its effects in a very literal way ..." and concentrates only on the most extreme material that may have such a literal hamful effect. "The classic dilemma around pornography is thus a balancing of extreme harms of doubtful direct connection with pornography against the harms censorship offers ... But this anxious irresolution is not the essence of feminism's problem with pornography." (Brown, 1985, 12)

coercion and violence. Gender-based violence becomes in law violence *simpliciter*, and as such furnishes a claim that is only too weak, or needs to rely on analogy (with harm to other vulnerable categories like children.) No political denunciation of gender-informed practices can be accounted for in law, because the gender-neutral category of citizenship screens off the discrimination. But even if harm were to be proven, the law still needs to put the claim to the test and balance it against the freedom of the press, that of speech, that 'to indulge tastes and pursuits.' The feminists denounce oppression and find themselves, in law, opposing basic constitutional principles instead.

In what concerns the second strand: here feminists denounce pornography as discrimination, and the law sees this denunciation as motivated by an *interest* not to be discriminated against. The re-enactment here is in form and in content. In form because the claim is couched in terms of an interest, by definition therefore *balanceable* against others. In content, because the concept, at this second stage of legal self-reference, acquires its meaning from, and grounding in, *formal equality* before the law. Upholding legal/formal equality is postulated, by the law, as the political reason for taking pornography to court. The political (I always mean reflexive-political) cost of this processing is the withdrawal of the possibility:

(i) to defend the priority of non-discrimination over the balancing itself. In law this priority disappears and anti-discrimination becomes a competitor in the balance of freedoms that the law hosts. But the political claim that needs to be discerned and kept out of the balancing act, is that non-discrimination is not one among many freedoms but a necessary condition of how freedoms should be understood in the first place, as well as what it means to balance freedoms fairly;

(ii) to contest what constitutes discrimination, beyond the confines of formal equality.

Neither of these political claims make sense in law. For law, politically speaking there is an 'interest in not being discriminated against.' This interest stands in for, re-enacts, and exhausts whatever the feminist may conceive as the political stake of discrimination.

Finally, the strand of the argument that denounces pornography as objectifying women is also silenced in law. In the eyes of the law, if these feminists do not raise the harm principle it is because they value freedom of expression too highly. The law cannot see the political motivation for not taking to law: that law does not offer the categories for redressing the objectifying effect or the overall cultural reproduction of meaning that is at issue. This assumed endorsement of a basic constitutional principle extends to cover even a polemical stance towards law. The claim that the masculine fragmenting gaze that objectifies women in pornography is the one that gazes at them in law too, can only resonate in law as its reversal, as endorsement. From the point of view of politics, these are paradigm cases of non-engagement and travesty, and from the point of view of sociological observation, cases of what Brown elsewhere calls 'a contradiction in the most basic terms of social analysis.'[27]

I have gone to some length in the example of pornography to show how the law re-aligns political voices in the public realm by re-casting claims about facets of oppression into claims about political interests that, when resonating at all (in the case of pornography-as-representation they didn't), resonate as something alien to what was politically intended. To put this claim against the republicans concisely: *what is re-enacted is not contained*. If the republicans are putting forward a theory about how political conflict can be contained in law, and thus allow law to accommodate people's entry into public space by accommodating their conflicts, *then people's conflicts need to be depicted not re-enacted*.[28]

There is a possible counter-argument here; that not all conflict is re-enacted. After all, as we saw, law often first props up assumptions that furnish conflictual positions. Also, to the extent that people are socialised through law to a significant extent, they may come to perceive legal conflicts as expressing genuine feelings and aspirations. To that extent, genuinely, there maybe no re-enactment.[29] But there remains a problem for republicans because their claim is a strong one. They cannot afford to distinguish between conflicts depicted and conflicts re-enacted; they cannot afford to acknowledge *at all* the category of re-enacted conflict. Were they to concede such a distinction, they would need to justify something impossible: that re-enacted conflicts too express genuine political engagement. In the absence of such a possibility the republican position is untenable. While it may be true that some people and groups, sometimes, perceive their conflicts as already institutionalised, already legal, the assumption cannot be universalised except at the cost of carrying a blindspot. And if it is not universalisable, it cannot uphold the republican position.

I would like to stress, once again, a valuable insight we have gained from systems theory regarding the aforementioned blindspot. The re-enactment is

---

[27] Brown, 1990, 142

[28] The logic of re-enactment covers here also Ackerman's notion of a constitutional crisis that precedes his constitutional moments. This would be an argument about the legal-institutional reception of the political crisis. How does a crisis present itself to law? Law, in view of its re-enacting political 'noise' cannot serve as a register of political crisis. It can only re-act to what it re-enacts as crisis in its environment. The political crisis does not feed into law, the law feeds off what it feeds itself as crisis.

[29] 'C'est parce que le droit appartient aux conditions du conflit, soit qu'il forme l'objet du litige, soit qu'il le nourisse, qu'il peut aussi en être la solution.' (Freund, 1974, 52)

always latent. The conflict perceived in law is a conflict that the law perceives as really occurring; it is a conflict that the law assumes has divided the parties as a matter of brute fact. *Law is innocent of its blindspot.* It cannot see that the conflict it sees is an enacted environment that acts as surrogate. It cannot see that what it takes to be 'brute' conflict is always-already institutionalised conflict; it cannot see its re-enactment of conflict. The ideological, mystifying, moment is the republican moment, where law is mobilised, in view of its innocence, to perform a task it cannot accomplish - contain all conflict - and is celebrated, by the republicans, as having accomplished it.

* Thesis [6] against Republicanism

In the first chapter of the thesis we analysed how, in republican constitutionalism, citizen praxis underpins political sovereignty. The argument about citizenship in a democracy advanced there is an argument about this sovereignty of citizenship. Sovereignty means self-government and freedom of speech underpins it in this sense: the speech of the individual citizen is the input into the formation of public opinion that drives self-government. The status of citizenship is realised in this contribution. Citizenship is not a pre-condition of the freedom to speak. Nor is freedom of speech merely one among many rights of equal weight. The right to speak, as input into the collective self-determination is the vessel of citizenship; only in that process is citizenship realised. The intimate connection between speech and citizenship is essential if the argument about citizenship is to be understood properly: speech is the mode of existence of the citizen; free speech makes him/her sovereign. Freedom of speech is integral to rather than a result or a condition of democracy; it defines the democratic conception of politics.[30]

Let me here introduce a specific perspective from which to talk about political speech; not its importance, nor its nature, but its limits: *sedition*. The analysis to follow will centre on seditious speech, the utterance that the law forbids as subversive to the constitutional order. The critical question is: why is any instance of speech that purports to political self-determination not protected under the law on the basis of the sovereignty of citizenship? Or

---

[30]See generally Ackerman (1980). Tassopoulos, (1993, intro), for an account of the role of the protection of speech in constitutional continuity and change. Also Kalven: 'If my puzzle as to the First Amendment is not a true puzzle, it can only be for the congenial reason that free speech is so close to the heart of democratic organization that if we do not have an appropriate theory for our law here, we feel we really do not understand the society in which we live.' (Kalven, 1966, 45)

better: if Freedom of Speech bears that constitutive relationship with sovereignty - the citizen is sovereign in that his speech is free - then we cannot curtail the freedom of political speech and still claim sovereignty for the citizen. Or can we?

'Yes' is the counter-intuitive answer, and on the basis of this question and this answer, we will explore the legal meaning of political praxis. The formulation I will put forward is paradoxical and the theoretical approach I suggest does not explain away the paradox but treats it as real (in the same way that Marxists talk of real contradictions). This is how the paradox of citizen sovereignty reads: the restrictions that sedition carries into freedom of speech do not compromise the sovereignty of citizenship but uphold it, because they are suffered not by the citizen but by the political actor in the name of citizenship. This paradoxical formulation belies the serious intent of addressing the sovereignty of citizenship where it matters most and where it is most sensitive and revealing. It tells us that the limitation to speech that sedition threatens or imposes, as the case may be, does not hedge in sovereignty but substantiates it within an institutional system of public opinion structured around the legal co-ordinates of identity (citizenship) and action (rights). The law against sedition, that is, disqualifies a certain category of speech from politics by addressing the question of political speech in a very specific way. It imposes, it will be argued with the help of the theory of autopoiesis, a discourse-specific reading of political sovereignty and in the process submerges an interpretative, reflexive, therefore political (see part III of the book), understanding of political sovereignty and the kind of praxis that makes it possible. Sedition illustrates the logic and mechanism of how law displaces politics and projects its own perception of politics in its place.

The importance of speech to citizenship and the public sphere make this paradox of shielding democracy from sedition in the name of sovereignty the litmus test for republican theory. The analysis here will be so extensive and detailed because the republican containment of political speech is pivotal to the project; my aim in this sixth thesis is to turn their organising principle against them.

In a much quoted, controversial article written in the early 1970s, Robert Bork expounds what has since been held as the minority position in First Amendment (freedom of speech) constitutional doctrine. Bork sides not with the much celebrated dissenting opinions of the Smith Act cases[31] but rather

---

[31] The Smith Act of 1940 made it unlawful to 'knowingly or willfully advocate, abet, advise or teach' the duty of violent overthrow of the government. This initiated the Smith Act prosecutions in the 50s against members of the Communist Party who were charged with

with the forgotten majorities of those cases. In order to confront the opinion of Justice Brandeis in *Whitney*,[32] he says of subversive speech:

'Speech advocating forcible overthrow of the government is not [political speech] ... *It is not political speech because it violates constitutional truths about processes* [crit. 2] and because it is not aimed at a new definition of political truth by a legislative majority [crit. 3]. Violent overthrow of government *breaks the premises of our system concerning the ways in which truth is defined, and yet those premises are the only reasons for protecting political speech.* It follows that there is no constitutional reason for protecting speech advocating forcible overthrow ... [In instances of suppression of subversive speech, what] was struck at [was] speech not aimed at the discovery and spread of political truth but aimed rather at destroying the premises of our political system and *the means by which we define political truth.*'[33]

His argument can be summarised as follows:
(1) we define political truth by means of constitutional processes (most importantly constitutional protection of speech). Political truth is thus contained within the constitutional framework
(2) revolutionary speech is directed against the constitutional framework
(3) therefore, revolutionary speech is directed against political truth
(4) therefore, revolutionary speech is not political.
(5) the only reason for protecting speech is that it leads to political truth (equally, because it is political)
(6) therefore there is no reason to protect revolutionary speech.

Statements (5) and (6) do not necessarily follow from (1)-(4). We can, that is, hold (1)-(4) as valid and still abstain from (5) and (6) because we support additional reasons for protecting speech (because, for example, we value toleration). Bork urges that seditious speech be prosecuted. This is a prescriptive point and as such need not concern us here. In fact confident constitutional regimes rarely have recourse to anti-sedition legislation. What interests us is not whether the sedition charge ought to be pressed. What interests us is the logic (1-4) underlying it: *the law against sedition is directed against speech directed against politics.*

Revolutionary speech violates 'constitutional truths about processes' which are identified in turn with the 'premises of our political system'. The term 'processes' is used to make the connection with truth, as instrumental to

---

conspiracy, and the enactment of more than 300 laws aimed at subversive activities by the federal states. (see Gellhorn, 1952, 358). Famous treatments of the Smith Act in Court include *Dennis v US* 341 US 494 (1951), *Yates v US* 354 US 298 (1957), *Scales v US* 367 US 203 (1961)
[32] *Whitney v California* 274, US, 357 (1927)
[33] Bork, 1971, pp31, 32 (*my emphases*)

it, as rendering it. Without undoing Bork's argument, one could substitute 'process' for 'paradigm'[34] to do justice to the comprehensive model of politics that is inscribed in constitutions and to which Bork, too, is alluding. A political paradigm provides answers to three interrelated questions : (a) What are the *stakes* of conflict and/or the issues of action; (b) Who are the *actors* and what is their mode of becoming collective actors; (c) What are the procedures, occasions, sites and *institutional forms* of action through which conflict is carried out.

The contention is, and I think this is Bork's contention too, that the Constitution provides specific answers to each of these questions and thus sets up the constitutional paradigm for politics. Bork's 'processes' then circumscribe possible action within this framework, and it is here that political action in institutional form is geared to (articulating) political truth. It is also, only naturally then, on this basis that speech will be assessed as contributing to politics or not. Attempting to dismantle the constitutional system means attempting to abolish the processes we have for reaching political truth - processes which are determined by and contained in constitutional rules.

Laws against sedition sanction that containment. The question of sedition throws the problematic into relief, because it is through laws against it that certain utterances are banished from the accepted parameters of *political* discourse. The question that motivates this analysis is: *If political action is action contained in and prescribed by constitutional processes how is the politics of those who defy or oppose those processes to be expressed?*

Sedition, as I employ it here, covers the category of offences where what is punishable is the subversion of the constitutional political process, and where this subversion is carried out by rhetorical means. Both premises are inscribed in the *actus reus* of all the offences that will come under the category of sedition. Sedition in my use becomes a functional term that gathers together commonalities existing in various jurisdictions, with focal and penumbral cases, where subversion may be explicit or implicit, more or less dangerous, its intention direct or indirect. As is obvious from the broad scope of instances chosen, across jurisdictions and over a large period of time, the point is not to labour the details of individual legal provisions, but to provide paradigm cases where, under constitutions that entrench popular sovereignty, speech is prosecuted for being subversive to the polity. The choice of broad framework is also meant to support the magnitude of the claim; these are conclusions that are meant to hold for constitutionalism as

---

[34] The term 'political paradigm' that I borrow and redefine from both Raschke (1980) and Offe (1985) has the advantage of providing a comprehensive model of what politics is about.

such (liberal and republican) and not the oppressive practice of one specific legislature or judiciary.

Instances of 'sedition' share two defining features:

(i) the offence is of a rhetorical nature - i.e. it pertains to speech, discourse, the propagation of ideas,

(ii) the offence being punished is the attempt to disrupt the constitutionally sanctioned political process.

Speech is excluded from protection if it endangers or is aimed at endangering, if it offends or aims to offend, the political system as laid out and sanctioned by the Constitution. The precise aim of sedition laws is to remove the conflict in a way that leaves the political process intact, when the conflict is alleged to have arisen at the level of the rules of the game. The rationale behind the criminalisation of utterances is the disruption of the political life of the society at the level of respect for the rules of the political process. Notice how what is prohibited is a form of behaviour - speech - that is generally permitted [35] particularly in the public domain where it occupies a 'preferred position.'[36] Notice also, in certain instances (below a, b, c), how the *prima facie* permitted form of behaviour - speech - only becomes an offence as the locus of liability is placed one step back, from the feared action to the encouragement of the action, the latter a behaviour that does not in itself offend or otherwise harm.

The main point, however, is that the criterion for deciding whether a political act falls under the category of permitted speech or of seditious offence, is whether it is conducive to or subversive of the institutional setting of the political process. Is the act aligned with the formal requirements of the institutional structure of the public sphere and does it, thus, channel conflict through the stipulated ways, or is it subversive of the structure itself, carrying a threat of de-stabilisation to the constitutionally sanctioned political process?

As was mentioned above, this focus is carried in two categories of offences, both of a rhetorical nature. We will explore in turn, both i) where the offensive behaviour is an incitement to subversion of the constitutional system, an invitation to further undertaking of action (predominantly

---

[35] 'The fact that political speech is by definition speech that is directed to other people by giving them the possibility of choice and agreement, becomes in the cases of conspiracy to advocate subversion, the primary harm to the state and the very justification of the crime, the reason that is offered to establish its constitutionality.' (Tassopoulos, 1993, 182)

[36] First encountered in the famous fourth footnote by Chief Justics Stone to *US v Carolene Products Ltd* 304 US 144; see also *Jones v Opelika*, 316 U S 584 at 600; see further Nowak and Rotunda (1991) at 941-2. See also Barendt, 1985, 146

violence) and (ii) where the offensive behaviour itself constitutes and exhausts the feared subversion.[37]

i) Incitement to subvert
The common law offence of sedition in England

It is surprisingly hard to pin down the precise *actus reus* of the common law offence, as it is 'necessarily somewhat vague and general.'[38] In his *Digest of the Criminal Law*, Fitzjames Stephen provided the following wide definition:

'A seditious intention is an intention to bring into hatred or contempt, or to excite disaffection against the person of her Majesty ... or the government and constitution of the United kingdom, ... or to excite Her Majesty's subjects to attempt otherwise than by lawful means the alteration of any matter in Church or State by law established.'[39]

Brazier comments that this could 'encompass any forceful criticism of the existing structure of authority within the state.'[40] The words of an Irish judge in 1868 reflect and confirm the breadth of this definition: '[sedition] is a comprehensive term and it embraces all those practices ... which are calculated to disturb the tranquillity of the State ... and subvert the government and the laws.'[41] While relying on Stephen's definition, Justice Cave attempted to narrow it down slightly, in his direction to the jury, in *Burns*. In this leading case, the judge identified the nature of the offence as

---

[37] There is at the outset, a possible objection: sedition laws occupy only a marginal role in constitutional practice today and do not warrant the significance I am attributing them. I am not persuaded by this objection. Even when sedition itself has been supplanted by legislation that fulfils an equivalent function on public order grounds (see below), sedition laws come into their own when governmental authority and the legal system itself are challenged. In times of internal crisis, often through the enactment of emergency legislation, the freedom-sedition balance will weigh on the authoritarian leg. If on the other hand, during 'confident' constitutional regimes, sedition "is hardly ever taken down from the armoury in which it hangs," the fact supports rather than undermines the argument I will make connecting sedition to the system's self-maintenance.

[38] Cave J in *R v Burns*, (1886) 16 Cox CC 355, 2 TLR 510. 'Brownlie notes that the most detailed modern analysis of sedition was made (in 1951) by the Canadian Supreme Court, one of whose members commented that "as is frequently mentioned in the authorities, probably no crime has been left in such vagueness of definition."' (Townsend, 1993, p117)

[39] Fitzjames Steven, 56, art.93; 8th ed, art 114

[40] de Smith, 1985, 470

[41] Quoted in Williams, 1967, p197

two-fold, '[that] of speaking seditious words, and the other offence is the publication of a seditious libel.'[42]

'The common law of sedition,' write Bailey et al., 'sets the bounds for general political discourse.'[43] In similar terms, Barendt writes that 'the common law still draws a distinction between the expression of political opinion and the advocacy or incitement of violent political action.'[44] We should not consider it decisive that 'sedition is hardly ever taken down from the armoury in which it hangs,' as the judge remarked in *Aldred*.[45] 'In time of crisis an uncertain executive might resort to it again, as it has done in modern times in areas of British colonial rule.'[46] In any case the argument I am putting forward depends on deciphering the logic behind the designation of the offence and does not depend on its frequency. It is significant for example that although there have been no reported decisions on sedition in Ireland since 1922, the Irish Constitution preserves the offence of seditious libel in the very article that guarantees citizens' freedom of expression.[47]

Subversive Advocacy

'The frequent use of the charge of sedition in the eighteenth and early nineteenth centuries in England,' writes Barendt, 'has been contrasted probably too starkly with the intellectual climate that led to the drafting of the First Amendment.'[48] The question of subversive advocacy, i.e. the incitement to violence as a means of effecting political change, has been a consistent pre-occupation of American constitutional courts, and it would not be an exaggeration to say that few other single legal issues have generated in US jurisprudence such wealth of theory to solve them. The long and fierce debate centres on whether the damage inflicted through the censorship of subversive political statements ought to be seen as a contradiction of democratic founding principles.[49] The debate turns on the inclusion or not of

---

[42] (1866) 16 Cox C. C. 333. In this case the defendant was acquitted after having made an inflammatory speech in Trafalgar Square, calling for support for the plight of unemployed workers in London.

[43] Bailey et al., 1991, 291

[44] Barendt, 1985, passim. and 155

[45] *R v Aldred* [1909] 22 Cox C. C. 1

[46] Brownlie, 1990, 239

[47] Art. 40.6 of the Constitution of Eire. Barendt (1985, p154) calls this co-existence 'paradoxical', echoing the ('real') paradoxical articulation I hinted at earlier.

[48] Barendt, 1985, 153

[49] For an overview of the debate see Baker (1989). For an overview of the history of the debate in the American Supreme Court and the succession of 'tests' devised, see Greenawalt (1989). For comparative studies see e.g. Barendt (1985), Tassopoulos (1993). For an analytical philosophical approach to the problem, see Schauer (1982). In his very interesting work,

'revolutionary' or 'subversive' speech under the protection afforded by the principle of free speech. If that principle underpins political sovereignty, by protecting a sovereign citizenry's right to be heard, does the silencing of any political statement, albeit subversive, not fundamentally undermine democratic politics? Or conversely, should we not accept that the subversive effect on democracy is itself too intolerable, so that censorship becomes necessary in the name of democratic politics?

Recently in American jurisprudence the question of the constitutionality of the prohibition of 'subversive advocacy' has made a spectacular re-appearance with the flag-burning cases.[50] But it has had a long history involving the contested constitutionality of the curtailment of 'fighting words', 'criminal conspiracy', 'criminal syndicalism', and other political activity that was seen to have an intolerable subversive effect on the polity. These debates over the censorship of political statements are in fact very complex ones, involving a number of mutually cross-cutting and under-cutting distinctions. One important focus is whether or not political speech should be afforded privileged protection. This debate is complicated by the disagreement as to what counts as political speech. The various readings of the justification of the principle - among others truth, democracy, toleration, utility - have unwittingly served to relativise positions further. The rather easy - because blanket - 'absolute protection' position has led to occasionally uncomfortable conclusions regarding, for instance, commercial speech and pornography. I cannot hope to even begin to address that debate here, although other parts of this chapter are full of references to it. Suffice it here to point out that the offences that come under the umbrella term 'subversive advocacy' share the seditious element: they are all directed against action that endangers or aims at endangering the constitutional political process.[51]

The US and the UK legal systems are not alone amongst those of democratic liberal states to sanction subversive advocacy. Seditious offences

---

Greenawalt, in a thoughtful attempt to avoid the impasse, suggests a distinction drawn from linguistic philosophy, namely that between (prima facie) subversive statements that carry locutionary and those that carry illocutionary force.

[50] On symbolic speech more generally see Ely, 1975, 1482. Protection of symbolic speech was recognised in principle as early as 1931 in *Stromberg v California* 283 US 359. Later in *US v O'Brien* 391 US 367. Recently considered in the context of nude dancing as entertainment *Barnes v Glen Theater Inc.* 115 L: Ed 2d 504 (1991)

[51] There is not enough space to trace the same dilemma in other jurisdictions. Indicatively only, in Germany, the Federal Constitutional Ct declared the Communist (and neo-Nazi) party unconstitutional under article 21(2) of the Grundgesetz. (2 BVerfGE 1 (1952); 5 BVerGE 85 (1956). See also, decision as to whether the propagation of Marxism is protected as "research and teaching" (5 BVerfGE 85, 141-6 (1956). In Greece, the Constitution of 1952 similarly outlawed the Communist Party.

against the state and the 'free democratic order' abound in a number of other Western jurisdictions. At the height of the terrorist threat in West Germany, for example, the government introduced a number of amendments to the criminal law, including the anti-Constitutional Advocacy Act of 1976. Section 88a of the Penal Code provided that offences 'against the Constitution' could be punished with imprisonment for up to three years. The seditious element was designated here as 'capable of encouraging the willingness of other persons to commit offences against the existence or safety of the FRG.'[52] The legislation was not seen as contradicting the Constitution which requires fidelity to the free democratic order and thus arguably excludes forms of militant democracy and direct action. Section 88a was finally repealed in 1981, but other parts of the Penal code designating offences 'Endangering the Democratic Rule of Law' (Title III), and punishing the defamation of the federation (90, 90a, 90b) in conjunction with provisions against criminal association (sections 129, 129a) may be used to punish sedition.

Support for Terrorism

The offences relevant to our discussion of sedition are those that pertain to the propagation of ideas that law forbids on the basis that they are subversive. The following is only an indicative selection from the mass of relevant provisions of both the Northern Ireland (Emergency Provisions) Act of 1991 and the Prevention of Terrorism (Temporary Provisions) Act of 1989. Three categories will be outlined as indicative.

The first is the expression of support for terrorism. Since 1974,[53] terrorism has consistently been defined as 'the use of violence for political ends.'[54] Amongst the organisations concerned in, promoting or encouraging terrorism in the UK, the 'most dangerous' are 'proscribed'. While under all the Acts since 1974 the Secretary of State reserves the power to add other organisations to the list, it is only the IRA and the INLA that have been proscribed to date.[55] How is the - for our purposes seditious - expression of sympathy designated? According to section 28 (on 'Proscribed Organisations') it is an offence (a) to belong or profess to belong to a

---

[52] Quoted in Finn, 1991, 211.

[53] Prevention of Terrorism Act 1974, s.9(1), 1989, s.20(1)

[54] For difficulties or objections to this definition, see Finnie, 1990, 2. On the self-contradictory nature of the definition, see Christodoulidis and Veitch, 1994, 463.

[55] The provision has proved a regulatory failure of the first order. On the one hand because to 'de-proscribe' an organisation - such as the INLA which arguably is no longer one of the 'most dangerous' - would be a propaganda coup to it. On the other hand, to proscribe another, quite apart from the publicity that would cause, would be ineffective given the ease and frequency with which organizations change their names. See Finnie, 1990, 5

proscribed organisation, (b) to solicit or invite support for a proscribed organisation[56] (d) to arrange or assist in the arrangement or management of, or address, any meeting of three or more persons (whether or not it is a meeting to which the public are admitted) knowing that the meeting (i) is to support a proscribed organisation or (ii) is to be addressed by a person belonging or professing to belong to such an organisation. Note that not only speakers but knowing listeners to the seditious utterances are held liable under the Act. Note also that the breadth of activity designated seditious is extended beyond speech to embrace also symbolic communication. Section 29 of the Act, under the heading '[d]isplay of support in public for a proscribed organisation', punishes any person who in a public place (a) wears any item or dress; or (b) wears, carries or displays any article in such a way or in such circumstances as to arouse reasonable apprehension that he is a member or supporter of a proscribed organisation.

Another example of the law against sedition in the field of anti-terrorist legislation concerns a disqualification from political office. Section 3(1) of the Elected Authorities (Northern Ireland) Act 1989(3) declares that 'a person is not validly nominated as a candidate at a local election unless his consent to nomination includes a declaration in the form set out in Part I of Schedule 2 to this Act.' That form is as follows:

'I declare that, if elected, I will not by word or deed express support for or approval of (a) any organisation that is for the time being a proscribed organisation...; or (b) acts of terrorism (that is to say, violence for political ends) connected with the affairs of Northern Ireland.'

If the candidate is elected having signed the declaration, he or she may be deemed to have breached the terms of that declaration if, at any time whilst a member of the local council, he or she expresses such support or approval either at a public meeting or in circumstances such that they know or could be reasonably expected to know that such support or approval is likely to become known to the public (s.6(1)). A public meeting includes (s.6(5)) any meeting in a public place, any meeting which the public is permitted to attend whether on payment or not, and any meeting of a local council.

What all three categories of offence - the common law offence of sedition, subversive advocacy and the censorship of statements in support of terrorism - share is that they proscribe seditious behaviour in the way we have been employing the term here. That is, all three categories describe behaviour pertaining to speech, discourse, the propagation of ideas. In all three, the

---

[56] The 1989 Act's lengthy special provisions on 'financial assistance', (Part III) extends its scope outwith the organisations proscribed in the Act.

action struck at is the subversion of the constitutional political order. The two categories of offences to which we now turn are again both 'rhetorical' and subversive, but they aim to subvert something more limited than - if vital to - the polity itself: they are subversive attacks on the judiciary.

ii) Contempt of Court
'Scandalising the Court'

'"Scandalising the Court" is a convenient way of describing a publication which, although it does not relate to any specific case either past or pending or any specific judge, is a scurrilous attack on the judiciary as a whole, which is calculated to undermine the authority of the courts and public confidence in the administration of justice.' [57]

The elements of the *actus reus* of the common law offence are as follows. The bodies protected are only Courts of Justice properly so called, both superior (predominantly cases have been about superior courts) and inferior. [58] It is of paramount importance that the attack is directed at the judge *qua* judge, at the judicial office itself and not the personal reputation of the judge. This general limitation is well established in decisions[59] and in doctrine.[60] The *degree of harm* required to constitute 'scandalising' sets a low threshold to the offence: that of creating a real, albeit small, risk of prejudice to the administration of justice.[61] But the requirement of 'substantial risk' of the Contempt of Court Act has been interpreted restrictively,[62] and in effect any undermining of public confidence in the administration of justice can fairly be described as a serious impediment to justice. The *offending conduct* is the publication of material that either constitutes 'scurrilous abuse' or imputes a political motive and thus challenges or compromises the assumed impartiality of the judicial office.

I choose to focus on scandalising because it is here that the seditious elements are most pronounced:

1. The offensive instance alleges a political motive behind the judicial decision.

---

[57] Lord Diplock in *Chokolingo v AG of Trinidad and Tobago* [1981] All ER 244, 248, PC
[58] *Re Borowski* [1971] 19 DLR (3rd) 537 (man QB) where the offended judge was a magistrate.
[59] Miller C J, 1989, 368
[60] Goodhart, 1935, 898: 'Scandalising the court means any hostile criticism of the judge as judge; any personal attack upon him, unconnected with the office he holds, is dealt with under the ordinary rules of slander and libel.'
[61] *A-G v Times* [1974] AC 273, 307, [1973] 3 All ER 54). Also Walker , 1985, 359, 362
[62] See Miller C J, 1989, pp155, 369

2. The offence is attributed to the judicial office, not the personality of the judge but to a functional unit itself and thus, as every judge and commentator has stressed, to the system of law itself.

3. The mens rea in scandalising through imputation of political motive includes a requirement of 'ulterior' intent. The mischief must be aimed at shaking confidence in the administration of justice and is therefore that of sedition. The intention to subvert the legal system rather than incidentally subverting it, is inscribed into the offence of scandalising the Court in a way that it is not in direct contempt. *The confrontation between scandaliser and judge is total and pre-meditated.*

4. It is significant that scandalising the Court is not tied to a case *sub judice.* It is aimed at justice as a continuing process. This quality of the attack further stresses its character as an attack on the administration of justice as such, as subversive to the legal system itself rather to the decision in a specific case.[63]

Direct Contempt of Court

I will limit this discussion then to direct confrontations in Court that carry an overtly political denunciation of the system. With the cases *sub judice,* contempt here is mainly dealt with at the level of rules of criminal procedure, in the form of refusals to all petitions, withdrawal of the right to speak, expulsion from the proceedings, penal custody, e.t.c. Such examples of *political confrontation in law* were at their most dramatic during the trials of

---

[63] The English case of *Wilkinson*, concerning a communist agitator, came before a Divisional Court in 1932 and sentences of imprisonment of up to nine months were imposed upon persons responsible for publishing *The Daily Worker.* At issue was the imputation of political bias to the judges of a previous case. The passage in question read as follows:
"Rigby Swift, the judge who sentenced Comrade Thomas, was the bewigged puppet and former Tory M.P. chosen to put Communist leaders away in 1926. The defending councel, able as he was, could not do much in the face of the strong class bias of the judge." Lord Hewart, C.J., said that the offender had committed contempt by scandalising the court because the comments had the effect of bringing the judge into contempt - a "gross and outrageous contempt" at that - and lowering his authority (*R v Wilkinson* (1939))
See also the Canadian case of *R v. Murphy* ([1969] 4 DLR (3rd) 289), or the French case of *Schroedt* (Gaz. de Palais, 1963 (2), 350), in which charges were brought against the political journal *Voix Ouvriere* for an article published there against the judicial decision of the "Conseil de prud'hommes de Montbeliard" of December 20, 1962. That decision upheld the termination by the Peugeot administration of the employment contracts of the workers' delegates who were held responsible for the insurrection in the Peugeot plant during November 1961. Under the title "Justice de classe", the article attacked this "parodie de justice". The article continues: "Les motifs du jugement ne tiennent pas debout ... C'est se moquer de la classe ouvriere - comme au temps des despotes et des rois, on juge et frappe ceux qui ont le courage de s'opposer aux patrons, au regime ... la justice est bien celle du patronat."

terrorists in the days of urban guerrilla warfare that succeeded the big social upheavals of the late 60s and early 70s. The crack-down on the Red Brigades in Italy and the Baader-Meinhof group in Germany provide some of the most spectacular examples. The examples to follow are from the trial of some of the protagonists of the latter, the 'first generation' of the Red Army Faction, a trial that began on 21/5/75 and culminated in the suicide of Meinhof, and later the deaths 'compatible with suicide' (official expert release to the press on 18/10/77) of Baader, Ensslin and Raspe.

(5/8/75, 23rd day of the Baader-Meinhof trial)[64]
Baader: "What Federal Prosecutor General Buback is doing is by exact definition terrorism, state terrorism. And so the terrorist Buback ... "
Judge Prinzing: "Herr Baader I am withdrawing your permission to speak. If you are trying to accuse the Federal Prosecutor General of pursuing a course of state terrorism, that goes beyond what we ..." (Here Baader wanted to say something but his microphone was switched off.)
Meinhof: "Terrorism operates amidst the fear of the masses. The city guerrilla movement, on the other hand, carries fear to the machinery of the state."
Judge: "I cannot accept you giving reasons which have no relevance to the case."

Ensslin: "As you've demonstrated, you're a judge under whose auspices two out of five prisoners have been killed ... "
Judge: "First and last warning."
Ensslin: " ... and if one of the remaining three now speaks out against the state machine that you sit here to represent, and as whose representative you sadistically act, you interrupt and refuse to allow him to speak ... "
Judge: "You are not entitled to raise objections on the grounds of persistent insulting language."

Baader: "I find it hard to say anything at all here. It is my view that we ought not to talk to you or about you any more. Action is called for to deal with the antagonism of the state machine towards humanity, as it actually presents itself in ..."
Judge: "You were not permitted to speak to make a declaration."
Baader: "You want to stop me speaking?"
Judge: " If you are not about to make a petition, then I can't allow you to speak."
Baader: "We are not on that plane any more. We are not on the plane of petitions made to this court, this rat-heap."
Judge: "You are now forbidden to go on speaking for insulting the court."

30/7/75 (Submitted in a petition to challenge the Court's jurisdiction,)
Meinhof: "This is the first political trial in the FRG since 1945. The Federal prosecutor's Office and this Court are not intelligent enough to see that the object of their destructive means is also a victim. All that the Federal Prosecutor and the court see is an enemy they want to defeat. This also shows the difference in the definition of

---

[64] All extracts of the Baader-Meinhof trial from Aust (1987)

our struggle. We are able to see, in a Fascist, the product of his circumstances and the state machine. We ourselves do not need fanaticism; the Federal prosecutor and the court are the fanatics. They have never come to understand the content of the arguments put forward by Andreas [Baader] and the rest of us. They are merely observing the formalities."

Possibly the most substantive dimension of what the radicals were saying lies in their conception of themselves and the 'state machine' as warring sides. This underlying idea emerges implicitly and explicitly in the statements of Baader, Meinhof and Monhaupt (and in many others before and since). Similarities can be drawn with the trials of other radicals, where the confrontation took the form of ridicule.[65] Underlying the stance of the accused was a firm refusal to acknowledge the court as the agent of justice and the legal discourse as a forum where the confrontation could be resolved.

The prime problem with this aspect of the confrontation as war or as ridicule, is that it goes unacknowledged in law.[66] These 'total' confrontations go unobserved by the judges. In systems-theoretical terms they do not resonate in law, they trigger no response in the legal system, no environmental stimulus to be picked up by the legal sensors. The sensors, instead, break down the confrontational context by picking up stimuli like contempt. Notice how the activists' declarations of 'war' remain irrelevant to law. This irrelevancy, as a case of silencing, will be dealt with as a case of what Jean-François Lyotard calls the '*différend*'.

But first, to establish what precisely is the meaning of the exchange between activist and judge. What is repeated in each case is a common pattern of non-engagement, of an impossible dialogue. In each case political activist and judge are talking past each other along one basic line: it involves an incompatibility between different definitions of politics. The political activist says 'you are exercising class justice' and the judge is responding 'this is a contemptuous statement.' In this exchange the political statement of the revolutionary is rendered invisible. What causes the 'invisibility' is that a statement that opposes the system can never be understood by the

---

[65] See, e.g. the trial of the 'Chicago Seven', Hoffman (1970). Conspiracy charges were brought against seven anti-war activists for conspiring to cross state lines to commit a riot. The seven defendants were apparently selected to 'represent the varying components of what has been called the new left.' (Dorsen and Friedman, 1973, 81). The writers draw out a typology of political trials and classify modes of behaviour therein and the understandings that were conveyed.

[66] Cf Bankowski and Mungham, 1976, ch5. I am not making the claim here that the confrontation was not played out in law, merely that it could not be resolved. The activists may have well intended their utterances to have been deemed contemptuous as part of a political strategy. This is not something I am disputing: what I am describing is why their utterances could not be heard *in* law.

system; law will incorporate its negation by including it as an illegal act, a contempt.

From the point of view of law, there can be little doubt that the revolutionary's statement is just that - a seditious contempt. The notion of independent justice underpins constitutionalism and lends to it a legitimating basis. Courts are agents of justice above politics and also courts are the guarantors of the political process itself primarily by securing that political action in the form of rights is not inhibited. What brings courts into disrepute, in our case the allusion that they are implicated in power, erodes these assumptions and is clearly seditious. To attack courts as class instruments is as subversive as is advocating forcible overthrow of the constitutional order. The activists' statements were seditious, the courts' logic was not flawed. My argument, therefore, is not an argument about the verdict; it is an argument - and I will employ systems theory to substantiate it - about the re-enactment of what was at stake, and the silencing and the terror that accompanied it.

In order to deal with the seditious utterance, the law applies a distinction. It asks: can this utterance be protected as an exercise of citizenship (sovereignty) or is it seditious? By virtue of employing that distinction, the law enacts fictively the universe of politics it must refer to. In this enacted universe of politics, the activist who is punished as subversive by the law has been punished as subversive to politics itself, i.e. is punished in the name of politics. Having recast the universe of politics from within, the law then loses sight of what is significantly political in the act of denouncing judges as the instruments of oppression in a class society. This act of political faith is invisible to the dilemma that divides the universe of action into permitted-political and forbidden-seditious action.

With the help of systems theory we will look at how the distinctions operate in perpetuating law' self-reference. The line between permitted and forbidden speech that licenses speech to enter into the political debate is the very presupposition of seeking political truth. In sedition, the criterion of what is so licensed is brought to bear on the question of respect to the law. That is how the law sets up and circumscribes the possibility of politics; and it is at that point that sedition meets autopoiesis.

The present thesis aims to explore a certain 'invisibility' of the political utterance deemed seditious by law. We saw at the level of doctrine a suggestion as to why the 'revolutionary' utterance should be excluded from law's definition of 'political truth'. What systems theory does is to give this exclusion an epistemological grounding. I want to suggest - and I will qualify this - that the variety of legal options in the definition and treatment of sedition is in an important sense only superficial. There is a threshold beyond which law cannot accept speech as political. At this threshold the legal demarcation of what counts as political speech is closed off self-referentially. In a nutshell, this is how the exclusion is accounted for systems-theoretically: it is through coding and programming that the environment of politics is legally re-enacted in law's own image in a way that occludes what is specifically political about the seditious claim. Exploring in depth the self-referential logic of the re-enactment of political speech will explain (i) why the law has to refer beyond itself to a projection of politics (unfold its self-reference) by its very nature as a system-in-an-environment and (ii) demonstrate that the legal system never in fact engages with politics but is always talking about itself when it talks about politics. But with the question of what is political speech removed from politics - and thus ceasing to be reflexive as I define it - politics is silenced. The silencing does not depend on whether the seditious speech act is punished or not. The political claim is always-already silenced in being perceived by law through the category of sedition.[67]

Law provides the co-ordinates of reference. As we have seen, for law to operate at all, the basic tautology of 'legal is what is legal' must be 'interrupted' or 'unfolded'. As the 'unfolding' takes place, law becomes the difference between what is legal and illegal (coding) and the way of handling that difference (programming) in reference to an environment.

What is designated legal and what illegal as speech in the case of sedition? The exercise of the freedom of speech is protected activity, therefore legal, except where the intention is to subvert the constitutional order, where it becomes illegal. The distinction, henceforth free/seditious speech for brevity, covers both coding and programming. The stimulus to be picked up in the political environment (the referred - politics) will be allocated (by the referrer - law) to one of the values of the code; the precise allocation will be decided through programming. What will be the mode of this allocation? Indicatively here constitutional provisions regarding the limits of freedom of speech, constitutional tests and criteria developed by the judiciary, doctrinal classifications, even legal-theoretical writings concerning the value of free speech (notably in civilian jurisdictions), all may inform this allocation. Coding determines, programming informs the mapping of any possible environment selectively, by placing specific 'sensors' that pick up specific stimuli that can be communicated about. 'Referrers' are the legal concepts that serve as sensors. A great deal can be (and has been) said about

---

[67] To locate the invisibility at this fundamental level means that the emasculation of the revolutionary utterance is present even in the most liberal of interpretations of the principle of freedom of speech. On the basis of the theory of Autopoiesis, the function of the treatment of revolutionary speech in the evolution of the law will be more accurately assessed and distanced from the republican myth of the 'creative tension' between politics and law.

legal programming, that under the aforementioned guises gears the allocation of the event detected in the environment to the one or the other of the values of the code. Programmes can be and are perpetually varied. What remains stable, the rigid base underpinning that incessant movement, is the closed duality of the code. It is within this duality that the space for contingency is enclosed, i.e. the sense in which things could be different is hereby delimited. The legal/illegal code has this triple function: a) it delimits the ambit of possibility: things can ultimately be only legal or illegal, protected or seditious; b) a specific instance is legal in that it is not illegal, protected in that it is not seditious, the two structurally articulated; and c) everything, with no 'ontological' limit, can be forced into this ambit of relevance (or remain invisible): codes are totalising constructions.[68] Why? Because every time that the legal system uses the distinction freedom of speech/sedition to observe the environment of political action, by virtue of employing this very distinction, it universalises its claim to totality and purports to exhaust the scope of possible political action. Of course there are other distinctions that befit political action. But all political action can *also* be aligned on the axis seditious/non-seditious and hence the distinction's claim to totality (c). And as for claims (a) and (b): an instance x is either seditious or not, *tertium non datur*. Caught in the specific cluster of the exclusive alternatives *a* and *not-a*, the identity of the instance can only be asserted in the mirror of its negation, (each is what the other is not) that brackets out and suspends latent what it is not.[69] Autopoietic observation is clearly structuralist here, the identity of a concept identified, in Saussure's words, 'purement differentiel.'[70] It is through this pair that the legal system places possibilities within the environment and reads what it finds there as a selection from within: x is the non-negated variant.

Both coding and programming are operative in how the political element will be designated. Coding is significant in that the political utterance can only be either the exercise of a right or a seditious offence. The alternatives are mutually exclusive: it cannot be both but it must be one or the other. At the same time it is one in that it is not the other: it is the exercise of a right in that it is not seditious. The specific structural articulation of the distinction works to entrap the radical utterance also at the level of programming. Sedition is programmed in law as the offence where the intention is designated as the subversion of the constitutional process. That free speech and sedition are coded together in the distinction, brings the exercise of the

---

[68] Indicatively, Luhmann, 1986e, 38
[69] See non-indicated value as 'Reflexionswert' in Luhmann, 1986f, 148, and on the function of negation generally, Luhmann (1971)
[70] For explicit recourse to structuralism see above.

right to reflect on the counter-value, structurally drawing on the negation to depict the essence/nature of the right.

Having explored first the law-'referrer' we now turn to the distinction itself between referrer and referred because it is here that the law pulls itself into political context (by its own bootstraps as it were) and reconstructs in its own image the universe of politics as context it finds itself in.

Confronted with the denunciation of judges as class enemies, the expression of sympathy to terrorism or the appeal to overthrow the constitutional order, the law asks the following question: should this utterance be protected under the freedom of speech principle as the exercise of a political right or is it seditious? The political utterance is picked up as relevant to law through the distinction free speech/sedition. In that structural articulation, law brings the existence of the institutional process to bear on the possibility of political truth.[71] Why? Because law reflects its criterion of what counts as political activity (political rights) in the mirror of negating activity that subverts the constitutional process. In the process the possibility of politics becomes negated sedition, 'negated' subversion of the institutional process. The political questions whether judges are instruments of class justice, whether terrorism is political, whether political action can and should be directed against the State and its law, are *reduced* by the law to a question whether this question contributes to the constitutional political process, a question that the law of course solves for itself, as a question of contempt, scandalising, criminal advocacy, disqualification from the district council, etc. The question of what is politics - and what it means for the political actor to be free and sovereign - is asked in law through an internal distinction that makes sedition - as negated other - the significant criterion in the definition of what it means to act politically. The law is simply drawing internal distinctions, always talking about itself when it is talking about politics. But by employing these distinctions to make sense of the political environment, the law brings itself to bear on the very constitution of the political context it purports to 'find' itself in. By drawing on self-produced distinctions that it attributes to the environment, it sets up a political context and itself-in-context. This is the context in which law 'finds' itself. It is in this sense that the system finds itself in an environment of politics that it has re-enacted, drawn its own boundary to reflect. Law's re-enactment of the concept of political action is premised upon a specific rationality of politics that relies on legally projected means, limits and possibilities. Law is always already there, 'earlier' than political sovereignty. And it is only a natural consequence of this setting itself in context that the positive side of our distinction free speech/sedition becomes the sign of politics as such and that

---

[71] Note how Bork's defence of the system's political truth finds here a necessary internal premise.

sedition now becomes observed as the breaking off point of political action itself. The radical hypothesis that political actors are politically emasculated as right-holders cannot be voiced within a system that circumscribes the political within the exercise of rights. It is the blindspot of the distinction. By operating that distinction and by virtue of its blindspot, the law prescribes the context within which it is to be recognised as guarantor and watchman.

So what of Republicanism's celebration of free speech? What of those political utterances that Michelman especially appeals to law to protect, particularly when 'we feel they want to disrupt [law] from the margins?' and that Sunstein entrusts to the empathetic judge. The answer is that the judge cannot empathise with and then protect something he cannot see. Michelman's appeal becomes an appeal to listen to the seditious claim; but the seditious claim is not the political one, it the re-enacted-as-political legal one. The political utterance cannot enter the legal screen save as disruptive - seditious.[72] The initial radical question is duplicated fictively in this reduction, turned into something that it is not, and in effect not contained but silenced.

Until this point we have discussed a certain silencing of the political utterance in its re-enactment as seditious. I want to finish by suggesting that the law against sedition is in fact the site of a ***double silencing***. Not only is the seditious statement silenced as re-enacted but the means of challenging that initial silencing are withdrawn in law. The law's silencing of politics remains unchallengeable, the activists' counter-claims impossible to register, the actors themselves invisible. I borrow from Lyotard and use his terms ***différend*** to refer to the fact of unchallengeability, ***terror*** to characterise the silencing and its cover-up.[73] This is how Lyotard summarises his central concept:

'As distinguished from litigation, a ***différend*** would be a case of conflict between (at least) two parties, that cannot be equitably resolved for lack of a rule of judgement applicable to both arguments. One side's legitimacy does not imply the other's lack of

---

[72] Meinhof: 'This is the first political trial in the FRG since 1945. The Federal prosecutor's Office and this Court are not intelligent enough to see that the object of their destructive means is also a victim. All that the Federal Prosecutor and the court see is an enemy they want to defeat. This also shows the difference in the definition of our struggle. We are able to see, in a Fascist, the product of his circumstances and the state machine. We ourselves do not need fanaticism; the Federal prosecutor and the court are the fanatics. They have never come to understand the content of the arguments put forward by Andreas [Baader] and the rest of us. They are merely observing the formalities.' (Submitted in a petition to challenge the Court, 30/7/75]

[73] Lyotard, 1988, passim, 1984, 46, respectively

legitimacy. However, applying a single rule of judgement to both in order to settle their differend as if it were merely a *litigation*, would **wrong** (at least) one of them (and both of them if none admits the rule). A *damage* [dommage] results from an injury which is inflicted upon the rules of a genre of discourse but which is reparable according to those rules. A wrong results from the fact that the rules of the genre of discourse by which one judges are not those of the judged genre or genres of discourse.'[74]

Let us repeat then, here, the logic of the re-enactment of the political utterance that we took in the previous section to be the (first) silencing that the law imposes on subversive political speech. Any one of the seditious utterances we discussed will do: the 'scandalising' or contemptuous 'judges are instruments of class oppression', the sympathiser's expression of sympathy with terrorism, the activist's incitement to the crowd to overthrow the Constitution. I will not repeat the referrer/referred argument, I will merely point to the equivocality that is suppressed by each system. For activist and judge alike the utterance links up to specific possibilities of meaning. But what for the first is a political statement, for the second undermines politics. That is because, as we saw, the law here operates on the basis of the distinction that is a contrast. The distinction political/subversive that is operative in the actus reus of the offences we have discussed, allows an utterance to be designated as political in that it is not subversive. That is because, as we have said, distinctions themselves are blindspots. Not only can the system not see what it cannot see, but it also cannot see that it cannot see this. In our case it cannot see that an utterance may be both political and subversive because it can only see on the basis of a distinction that contra-distinguishes the two.[75]

The différend is set up in that incompatibility of (genre- or) system-perspectives into what counts as political. For the sympathiser, the utterance is politics; for the judge, it subverts politics. The activist treats the utterance as an instance of establishing political reality through struggle; the judge sees it as undermining the very possibility of political reality. For the radical, the utterance is a political denunciation of a system of domination; for the judge it undermines the (guarantor in the last instance of the) political process itself. But note also how second-order différends build on this initial incompatibility of perspective, and how the différend then perpetuates itself ad infinitum: how do we settle the first-order différend? the activist: through struggle against the judicial definition of political reality; the judge: through

---

[74] Lyotard, 1988, xii
[75] In Lyotard this analysis would be less straightforward. It would have to rely on what linkings law seduces the 'subversive' sentence into, and how on that basis the 'genre' of law sets up an incompatible 'universe' to rival linkings within a different genre.

dialogue in terms dictated by political reality as constitutional democratic process. It is particularly here, in the build-up of différends, that the double silencing is in evidence.

This dispute is unsettlable except in terms of one or the other of the systems. No neutral tribunal can be set up to arbitrate the claims. It is now that we move into the domain of *terror*. The law does not stop at this incommunicability. It introduces both claims to litigation - as if they were litigable - and on the basis of an application of criteria of law, (of one of the systems) decides a winner and a loser. The law operates a strict win-or-lose principle according to the force of the better legal argument. In the tribunal of law the activist is, legally speaking, the one with the inadequate claim and is therefore legitimately silenced. Of course, one could argue this is exactly what the law was intended to achieve, to censor the subversive utterance. But the point is not quite so simple. The terror comes about at a second stage: what the law cannot account for is that the activist has not simply lost but that s/he has suffered a damage which s/he *cannot prove*: in that, s/he has suffered a *wrong*:

'This is what a wrong [tort] would be: a damage [dommage] accompanied by the loss of the means to prove the damage. This is the case if the victim is deprived of ... the freedom to make his ideas public, or simply of the right to testify to the damage, or still more simply if the testifying phrase is itself deprived of authority ... In all these cases, to the privation constituted by the damage there is added the impossibility of bringing it to the knowledge of others, and notably to the knowledge of the tribunal.'[76]

Why are the activist's means of proving the damage withdrawn? Because those means would be the statement: 'but my statement is political; to censor it is anti-political, it is against politics'; such a claim is non-negotiable in law, it is rebutted in law as non-political.[77] What is withdrawn is the status of that statement as negotiable, the privation therefore of the means to allege or prove a damage. Such a claim can never be heard in litigation. The paradox of the non-engagement is enhanced by the fact that the activist's political utterance is rebutted by the law in the name of politics.

Law's terror lies in effecting a silencing that goes unacknowledged by it. The law can legitimate its move (censorship) because it cannot account for

---

[76] Lyotard, 1988, 7

[77] Let us take again the 'sympathetic' statement of the type: 'we proclaim the right of the proscribed organisation to be heard' or, 'the terrorists are making a political statement here which the Council should at least consider,' or even most extremely 'we espouse the cause of the IRA.' To this, the law answers: 'Your statement is for terrorism, therefore not political' (or, what amounts to the same, 'not appropriate to this forum.') The double silencing consists in this: what the law cannot acknowledge as political is the claim that terrorism is politics.

the wrong it inflicts. The wrong comes about when a différend is violated. But the law cannot acknowledge the wrong because it can only see the confrontation of the claims as litigation. That is its blindspot. Claims enter the legal forum - they are 'referred' to - as always-already litigable, always already thematised, their ontology given as a matter of brute fact, their equivocality suppressed. Coded to sedition's political/subversive distinction, the defence of the subversive statement as *both subversive and political* - and therefore negotiable - faces the impossible task of making the system aware of the différend - of its blindspot. The existence of the différend does not register in law, as is always the case when the arbitration between claims of different systems (genres) is submitted to the tribunal of the one system (genre). In litigating the différend, law censors the speech while establishing its own innocence.[78]

Law's *innocence* depends on not needing to account for this move from différend to litigation: it depends on not seeing that it is doing this; it depends on the blindspot. We saw how the blindspot is inevitable for law because the law first submits the utterance to scrutiny under the distinction subversive/political, filtering entry into the realm of the latter of only what is not the former. This blindspot underpins law's innocence in a strong sense. For the system this innocence is in-built. The legal system, like every system, can only see on the basis of a blindspot. It makes sense of politics through its means of arbitration, by submitting politics to differences. Turning différends into litigations is the only natural way for the system to make sense of the world, the conversion of différend to litigation is indeed the reduction of complexity that first allows observation of an environment of competing political claims. Law can only be innocent of this move from différend to litigation and therefore of the wrong it imposes on the political utterance.

The dilemma that the law presents to the activist is 'be litigable (enter litigation) or disappear.' Of course this is an apparent dilemma about an *impossible dissensus*. The différend has already disappeared in entering litigation. The dissensus that underpins the différend is confronted with the dilemma: either accept the language of the tribunal in which case the différend vanishes - the claim against the system has to be processed as a claim (couched in terms that the system can accept) of the system - or do not register in law at all. Either way there is no dissensus. This is system terrorism. The original claim has been re-enacted, hijacked into becoming a legal claim in the broad sense, a legally processable claim, that is, a claim that can be heard, a claim to which the legal system can respond - and in which case the claim becomes something other than it was - or, it will be

---

[78] Litigation means taking as arbitration rules the rules of one system/genre and therefore ignoring that the differend depends on the existence of another genre/system.

eliminated. All that remains is for the discourse to be imposed, the tribunal to be set up. The question that remains to be answered is who has the power to litigate the meaning of the sentence.[79] I suggest that we treat this as a 'wrong' inflicted upon the political activist: it withdraws the language in which to state his/her claim.

But the Republicans advocate that theirs is a theory about the containment of politics in law. They purport to a dialogue that accommodates all voices. Even as only a test case, sedition shows up a non-containment of the 'disruptive' voice, which is structural and cannot be healed by 'empathy'. Containment is purchased at the cost of the infliction of a wrong, a différend that cannot surface. My argument against republican containment is that not only does it concede to the imposition of this invisibility of politics but also with law always allegedly containing every dissensus, it legitimates and celebrates the silencing as empowerment. Why? For the republicans law is the medium wherein all statements are negotiated and negotiable. Law is a form of practical discourse and as such, aspirationally, an ideal speech situation where the meeting of validity claims works discourse pure of coercion. In the argument about law's self-referential casting of politics we saw that the political utterance is re-enacted as seditious, not contained, but colonised. The political claim behind sedition ceases to be heard. The radicals' speech is fully compromised. Now, at the site of the second silencing the means to prove the coercion are in turn withdrawn. Not only is the curtailment of speech effected in law (as re-enactment) but the possibility of challenging the curtailment rendered non-negotiable. Republicanism 'addresses itself to politics in the broadest sense' by, ironically, containing only law's surrogate for politics and secures the containment by effacing all the posts where the containment may be challenged. Containment, I will argue more fully in the final chapter, cannot be exclusionary.

At the extreme opposite of ideology, the essence of the reflexive thesis is that it allows différends to surface. My argument for reflexive politics is a suggestion as to how the imposition of forced choice and the exclusion of dissensus may be resisted in politics. As opposed to institutional dialogue that is litigation, reflexive action is agon. Political praxis is not contained in the institutional setting of citizenship and equally it is not about that institutional setting - it is neither exercise of or contempt of a right. This would be the trap of litigation. I will have a lot more to say about this, but provisionally the reflexive thesis understands political action as action that embraces the différend and respects the contingency of its own

---

[79] 'The question is,' said Alice, 'whether you can make words mean different things.'
'The question is,' said Humpty Dumpty, 'which is to be master - that's all.'

setting-in-context; action as agon brings the criterion of what is political to bear on this respect of its contingency.

CHAPTER THIRTEEN

Conflict Severed

Because collective action questions the system's structural logic it is destined to reproduce itself beyond the forms of mediation that can interpret it.
(Melucci)

If the failure to draw the necessary distinctions between the two system referents conflated conflicts, republicanism is also guilty of ignoring the severing of conflict that this entails. The crux of this is that there occurs a severing of the connection between the broader conflict and what appears as the object of litigation. How the meaning of conflict changes as a consequence will be explored, in turn, along two dimensions, 'material' and 'social'.

The Material Dimension

When we discussed conflict as a system in its own right, we saw a certain dominance of the social dimension - the perception of Alter as enemy - in the sense that it sets up both the temporal dimension - time would work to the advantage or disadvantage of the enemy - and the material one - in the sense that reality became confrontational, situations acquired meaning as relevant to the conflict. From the point of view of the legal system, however, neither the temporal nor the material dimension of the conflict are in any similar way subordinated to the social dimension. The social dimension ceases, in law, to dictate the terms; in the material dimension, that will concern us first, the identity of Alter-as-enemy ceases to be the pivotal point for the casting of a conflictual reality. The identity of Alter is neutralised as litigant, remains meaningful only as a point of allocation and address of rights and duties. Broadly speaking, law introduces a new emphasis on the material dimension, an exclusive focus on the matter that divides the parts.

That the material dimension is rescued from its submersion under the social one does not mean that law treats the theme of the conflict as such. We have already explored one aspect of the 'appropriation' of conflict by the law in terms of its re-enactment. Law re-enacts conflict by perceiving through sensors it makes available, and in this re-casts conflict in its own image. The emphasis in this section shifts: what is important here is that the ties between the parts and the whole of the conflict are severed in law's dis-embedding from the theme of the conflict of a specific (legal) issue. The emphasis this time is not on the re-enacting but on the *severing*. The difference is not always plain to see, but depends on the legal breaking up of a political conflict, of disarticulating connections that are constitutive of political conflict. Let me clarify this by discerning and discussing two instances of severing under the seventh thesis against the republicans.

* Thesis [7] against Republicanism

In the first instance, the theme of conflict is appropriated by the law in so far as it is fragmented, decomposed, 'factorised' or 'fractionated'[1] into simple issues to which concrete (legal) solutions may be provided.[2] When a conflict is 'fractionated', the 'complex' dispute is dismantled into partial questions. In the material dimension of legal conflict, the theme of the conflict is fragmented into issues and *the totality that conflict claimed for itself is compartmentalised*. While the observing system 'fractionates' by inflicting divisions on the subject matter that are relevant to how it can process the problem, the accompanying notion of 'factorising' connotes that the breaking up is into components that are constitutive of the conflict at hand. On the one hand, lines of division are drawn that depend on what the law can process as issues; on the other hand, the parts are assumed at the same time parts of a more inclusive whole and yet processable separately. The law can depict, conceptualise and process the parts: the break-up is effected in a way that is relevant to the system. Taking a suggestion from Luhmann,[3] the break-up is effected by positing functionally specific differences upon the whole. Fractionating thus means assuming the whole by depicting conflict-components in ways that are relevant to the observing legal system. The discussion is quite technical, and the technicalities are not all necessary for my argument here. 'Factorising' denotes that there remains in the legal observation of conflict a severing, a *compartmentalisation* of the whole into parts that *stand in for* the conflict. Where workers contest models of managerial organisation in the name of the democratic control of the workplace (the whole), the law perceives a conflict with the employers expressed as legal or illegal occupational demands (the parts). Where the workers proclaim solidarity in industrial action, the law sees 'sympathetic' strikes (and 'secondary' picketing), action whose aim is not to forward occupational demands and which is thus illegal because overtly political.[4] The severing in both cases is the breaking up of the comprehensive

---

[1] According to the formulation of Fischer, 1964 . Luhmann relies on this in his account of conflict in 1981, 110

[2] ibid.

[3] Luhmann (1984)

[4] On the relevant UK legislation see Davies & Freedland, 1984, pp,798, 805-13

categories 'democratic control of the workplace' and 'solidarity', that inform the workers' political conflict, in terms of the legal 'occupational/political claims' distinction. Why is this a severing? Because the insertion of the occupational/political legal distinction defines the two as mutually exclusive. The distinction is the blindspot that prevents the legal system from seeing that what is occupational may also be political. More accurately, the insertion of the distinction that divides the whole into differentially distinguished parts, is the (analytically, not temporarily distinct) moment that accompanies the severing, which occurs as the 'occupational' is abstracted out of the broader 'political' context. The worker's perception of the conflict is mutilated into the occupational (lawful) and the political (unlawful) components, and their interdependence is severed as the former component is abstracted from (and defined in opposition to) the broader latter.

There is a related aspect to the severing and this time it turns on *symbolic* conflict. Let us turn to pornography once again to understand how this severing is effected.

As we said, the severing in the material dimension is the decomposition of a theme into issues. The point that needs to be highlighted here is the difference that it makes to view pornography as an *issue* and to view pornography as an exemplary *instance* of a much greater stake. To see pornography in the first limited sense as an issue in itself, engaging questions of freedom of speech and harm, violence, e.t.c., is to be dealing at the level where the greater theme has already dispersed and the constitutive links between the instance and the whole are already severed. In systems-theoretical terms it means seeing the conflict-as-occasion at the expense of the conflict-as-system. It is only if we resist the legal reading, the substitution or conflation, that we may appreciate how pornography becomes the name of the greater stake in the larger complex gender-power conflict, in the clash with patriarchy itself. And this involves understanding pornography in its symbolic dimensions. In the politics of the symbolic pornography becomes exemplary of a greater conflict. Because, as Brown says,

'[p]ornography speaks the culture of sexism in its exemplary form. Pornography is thus the issue representative of the whole of patriarchy ... A political world that cannot see pornography as the most outward and visible sign of a patriarchal culture ... has made itself intentionally deaf and blind to the obvious.'[5]

The emphasis on the symbolic function of pornography is evident throughout the spectrum of feminisms; MacKinnon, for example, writes:

---

[5] Brown, 1990, pp134-5

CHAPTER THIRTEEN

'[t]he critique of pornography is to feminism what its defence is to male supremacy. Central to the institutionalisation of male dominance.' Then 'tolerance to pornography is an index of the society we live in.'[6]

Gusfield's notion of a 'symbolic crusade' illustrates an instance of political conflict in the domain of the symbolic.[7] The notion is useful for both the social dimension of the conflict to be analysed below and the material dimension here. For the social dimension the notion is useful, as we shall see, because it is relevant to the group's description of itself.[8] In the material dimension the notion is useful because it denotes that the issues in a certain sense 'stand in' for the conflict, turn it into a test case and perform the function of 'emblem or metaphor, a genre of iconography that stands to the social order as a whole and represents its collective values.'[9]

The symbolic achieves a specific link between the particular and the total conflict. It provides the reason why the total is instantiated in the particular. The problem with an argument such as the republican, that relies on law to address political conflict, is that the symbolic connection is invisible to law. In the realm where conflict sheds perspective on the world it thematises the instance; then 'total' conflict can be played out in small arenas, symbolically. But with the severing inflicted by law on the totality of conflict, the legal issue contains and exhausts what is at stake; the legal issue is no longer seen as indexical to much greater questions and stakes of conflict. And with that connection severed, the possibility of symbolic politics - a vital aspect of our political engagement - is withdrawn too.

Systems theory allows us to articulate this severing of the symbolic in law, and what I suggested here is but one possibility.[10] Two distinct systems at once at play 'structurally couple' around pornography. In one of them - the legal system - the conflict is necessarily aligned to legal co-ordinates where concepts of rights, liberties, legal notions of harm and legal analogies, legal tests and legal presumptions first make sense of the conflict. In the other - the system of conflict - where reality is ordered as conflictual, there is room for the symbolic. Here, conflict first sheds perspective on the world and as specific issues are absorbed into the conflictual pattern they are thematised as instances of the greater conflict, acquire meaning in the light of the greater stake, yet are *symbolically* played out in small arenas around smaller questions.

---

[6] Quoted in Brown, 1990, 139
[7] Gusfield, 1963
[8] Notwithstanding the affinity of this politics, in the case Gusfield describes, with specifically conservative concerns for the maintainance of group status.
[9] Brown, 1990, 147
[10] For another see Smith S C , 1991, 329-331

Not only the invisibility of the symbolic, but also a certain distortion is at issue here. In the mirror of pornography the law reads a conflictual pattern about rights, and appended on them, claims of harm. What for law is a mirror of representation for the conflict-system is a mirror of distortion. The distortion itself then generates demands for political action. Even the opponent's action of taking pornography to law and thus attempting to legitimate this distortion becomes, since everything is absorbed into the pattern of totalising conflict, a strategic move in the situation of conflict, an ideological move aiming to conceal what the conflict is really about.

The political costs of the severing spill over from the material to the social dimension too. Because the legal abstraction from the identities of the parties-in-conflict carries through to the legal assumptions that furnish the legal tests. Who can be harmed and how? The formal category of the legal person blocks in law the visibility of the specific political vulnerabilities of women's social positions. Where there is no category to accommodate harm as degradation of women-objects of pornographic imagery, that in turn underlies identification of women's positions, no claim of harm can resonate. This is a restatement of the masculinity-as-form argument.[11] Here legal abstraction is viewed as rendering the conflictual position unintelligible as such. The severing is structural and in effect, ingenious as the attempts may have been to draw the legal analogy between pornography and sexual violence,[12] the reliance on the legal medium of legal personality to provide formal comparators and furnish analogies and presumptions, undercuts not only much of the specificity and urgency of the claim, but also the nature of the conflict as such.

To re-iterate: The silencing of symbolic politics is one part of the impoverishment of possible politics that comes with the 'severing' in the material dimension. The fragmentation of total conflict into particular conflicts is another. In the former case, as in the pornography example, the law severs the connection that would allow the particular conflict to be played out symbolically, as an index of the greater one. In the latter case, as in the workers' conflicts example, the severing withdraws the possibility to articulate the overall political stake that disappears in the legal processing of the conflicts. In this the law silences the claim for the democratic control of the workplace and therefore the self-determination of the workers' productive life, as well as any notion of class solidarity. In severing the connections between total and particular conflict, the law disarticulates connections that are vital and constitutive of political understandings. This means that certain

---

[11] Brown, 1993, 164
[12] Brown, 1990, 142

political understandings and claims do not 'carry' into law. Most significantly, and unacceptably to a theory that celebrates the legal containment of political conflict and 'addresses itself to politics in the broadest sense,' the severing imposes a selective screening of what actors and communities assume to be politically at stake

THE SOCIAL DIMENSION

Where the conflict claims totality no more, where conflict no longer equates its boundaries with those of the world, the source on which the individual draws to make sense of his/her identity changes and with it possible perceptions of what is at stake also change. To turn to the social dimension of conflict is to focus on the intimacy between stake and enemy that is eroded in the legal processing of political conflict.

I want to now focus this discussion on possibly the most crucial area of the republican argument concerning the ideal of community. The severing of conflict, that I claim occurs when we take our conflicts to law, is best illuminated when we look at the question of ***collective identity***. The hallmark of the republican thesis is the empowerment of community. If the severing along the social dimension can be conclusively argued as a case against the containment of collective identity in law, then the republican attempt to account for (let alone empower) community through law fails even aspirationally.

I will take the category ***social movement*** as an example of a category of association whose collective identity cannot be given a 'legal reality', since, I will argue, the law severs the movement's perception of conflict, which alone would establish such an identity. I will explore this argument by relying on two major theorists of social movements, Alain Touraine and, only briefly, Alberto Melucci. I will then complement their argument about the connection of conflict and identity, with the arguments of Georg Simmel and Lewis Coser.

By exploring the nature and action of social movements today, I will attempt to show that what singles out movements as such is the challenge they present to the capacity of the institutional sphere to deal with the kind of politics they advance. The movement can only be understood as advancing a political discourse that cannot generate organisational forms to act within institutional politics without becoming something other than itself. It creates a rupture in that system, revealing the incompatibility of legal form and the politics it informs and understands. In this sense, law does not contain the movement, it denies the movement.

Touraine and Melucci: Identity and 'constitutive' conflict

Touraine insists that New Social Movements struggle primarily to re-assert collective identity, whether that takes the form of 'defensive' withdrawal into collective identity or that of the creation of societal counter-models. The insistence on collective identity is not accidental, particularly in the French context. The 'political' is (and has traditionally been in France) related to a certain 'quality of association.' In that sense, a movement represents a very distinct moment of intersubjectivity, marked out by a distinct level of integration, sociality and imagination in the pursuit of politics. It is what the French, in more inspired days, called 'la verité du movement'; what Sartre refers to when he defines the group by its undertaking and by the constant movement of exclusion and integration which tends to turn it into 'pure praxis';[13] and it is that undertaking that Willener claimed was re-situated as both form and content of politics in the events of May.[14]

The central theme in Touraine's sociology of action is an image of society which produces itself through the conflicting action of class actors struggling over the control of 'historicity'. Conflict is situated at the heart of society so that society is seen as its own conflictual self-production. 'At the core of the society lie the social struggles in which what is at stake is society's self-production.'[15] Rather than viewing conflict as a 'phenomenal' (see above), a pathology when order and interdependence within the functional whole break down, rather than viewing conflict, that is, as occurring at the boundaries of society, Touraine chooses to situate it at the heart of society. Social movements are the central collective actors[16] involved in class-conflictual action.[17]

---

[13] Sartre, 1976, pp256ff

[14] Willener, 1970, passim and 281-98. Willener argues that at the period of upheaval the emergent (instituant) had only the most tenuous links with the established (institué). Of the two elements that Melucci identifies as characterising the ideology of the movement, the first is 'the negation of the gap between expectations and reality. The birth of a movement is marked by "moments of madness" when all things seem possible ... Ideology thus overcomes the inadequacy of action.' (1992, 133)

[15] Touraine, 1981, 30

[16] Touraine's theory invites critique at least as to the definition of social movement it advances. Touraine reserves the term Social movement for too broad a category of action since he uses it to cover the whole field of conflictual collective action.

[17] The theory is susceptible to criticism on the identification of the action of social movements with class struggle. The class nature of social movements is at least questionable. For example the student struggles of the 60s and 70s did not in themselves embody class struggles but rather assumed the role of catalyst through worker-student contacts and alliances intended to

Touraine provides an analytical concept of a social movement as 'the organized collective behaviour of a class actor struggling against his class adversary for the social control of historicity in a concrete community.'[18] The components identified here are: the actor (and the sense s/he makes of his/her identity), the adversary, the social field and the stake. Indeed, for Touraine, 'the social movement [presents itself] as the combination of a principle of identity, a principle of opposition, and a principle of totality.'[19] Identity (I) as the answer to the question : 'what self-understanding underpins "our" struggle?'; opposition (O) as the adversary to be identified within the field of reference, against whom to wage the struggle; finally the stake of the struggle, which for Touraine is 'totality' (T), the control of historicity. [20]

The three components do not in themselves suffice to describe a social movement if they are not conceived of *as interdependent*. The interdependence (I-O-T) must be *'total'*. Only together do the components constitute the field of reference against which context each of them in turn draws for meaning. If we conceive of the relation I-T (that between actor and stake) without (O), then what we are describing is not the stake of a struggle, a conflict, but a society as a single actor striving for an objective that can be described e.g. as progress or modernisation.[21] The linkage O-T on the other hand is what reveals the aspect of domination in society, in the sense that the actor (I) is excluded from the definition and the pursuit of the stakes which become determinable by (O). At a more fundamental level, (I) only becomes (I) in contesting (O) over (T), and that holds true of the other components as well. The connections are numerous, as are the conclusions that can be drawn from these connections. Touraine provides such a detailed

---

mobilise the 'true' class actors. Melucci has challenged this aspect of his teacher's work (1989, 80)

[18] Touraine, 1981, 77

[19] ibid., 81

[20] Although the latter may seem to overstate the case for social movements, it remains crucially important to be able to identify what constitutes a stake adequate to uphold a social movement. This must be more comprehensive than the partial demands advanced at various stages of the conflict. It is a matter of distinguishing (middle range) strategic aims from the stake itself. To give an example, the middle-range targets of the student struggles of the late 60s in France and 70s in Germany, were the authoritarian way universities were run, the lack of student representation in the decision-making bodies, the prospect of unemployment, etc. It would be a mistake to identify these as the stakes of the movement. The student movement also and explicitly challenged the social utilisation of knowledge in the way the normative structures of their society supported it, and in that sense even advanced a counter-model for society. What is in doubt is whether we can call this the new site of class conflict in the way Touraine does, but what is not in doubt is that the stakes of a struggle, if it is to uphold a movement, must be identified at the more comprehensive level.

[21] The point has been elaborated by Melucci (1982)

exposition,[22] making sure that it comes across clearly that, '[a] social movement can never be defined by an objective ... It is nothing but the ensemble made up of the three components, an unstable ensemble, never fully coherent...,'[23] but nonetheless always presupposing that interdependence.

The crux of the matter is that the total interdependence (the integration of the three components in the three dimensions) is what forms the political context, within which movements and their struggles make sense. Withdrawing from this context, the social relation within which they are situated, leaves the struggles politically under-determined. When it comes to making sense of the movement this withdrawal from the context is potentially destructive. The insights that this lends to the legal/political problematic are valuable: within the categories of legal discourse (i) the actors are not defined in their class conflictual relationship (I-O), (ii) their field of struggle and the stake is defined independently of them (T-I, T-O). *By abstracting from that interdependence (I-O-T)*, the interdependence that stems from the situation of the parameters in conflict, *law severs the political basis of the movement.*

If this contention is true it provides a solid base for proving the claim advanced here: that legal discourse submits the political self-understanding that the group has of its identity to such abstraction that it annihilates it. The question we are seeking to answer is how actors conceive of themselves, of their identity. It is trivially true that a pre-condition for collective action is the possibility of identifying with the other members of the group, the self-reflexive capacity that allows actors to say 'we'. That in turn means that the movement must constitute a field of reference wherein identity is conceived.[24] On the basis of Touraine's sociology that field can be described

---

[22] Touraine, 1981, ch.5, and 1977, pp310-25

[23] Touraine, 1981, 84

[24] Cf Teubner, 1989, 729, for the mode of that emergence in self-reference. Teubner describes how the capacity for collective action emerges when organised collectivities produce actions and then organised action feeds back to produce collective identity. See also his 1988a, 137-8: "It is ... communication on its own identity and capacity for action that constitutes the corporate actor or collectivity as a mere semantic artifact, as a linguistically condensed perception of group identity. It is only to the extent that such a corporate actor becomes institutionalized, ie that organizational actions are actually oriented round this self-description, that the corporate actor takes on social reality." (137-8) This indeed appears to me correct and insightful. But there is an ambivalence in Teubner's paper that makes his argument occasionally baffling and does not live up to his own presupposition of the radically constructivist nature if the legal person. The ambivalence is relevant to his demarcating the "social substration of the legal person". Teubner here spends a lot of time trying to find an adequate description of the social reality underlying the legal person, and, having discarded both individuals and groups as such, names it as a communicative process on which, and this is important, the legal reality superimposes itself and reworks to the extent that the two are no

as a tightly integrated I-O-T; within it the common identity is articulated through identification with the stakes of the conflict. Collective identity is conceived here as emergent property of collective action. There are neither fixed identities nor determined ascribed memberships prior to their generation in 'totalised' conflict. But in contrast to this focused commonality, the law's projection of the universal category legal subject/citizen screens off the forcefield where identity is shaped, by defining out the significant Other: the opponent. The category provides no purchase into partiality[25] and opposition, where partiality is what underpins the actor's political identity. By disarticulating this frame of reference, severing the connection with conflict, the legal discourse renders the movement invisible to itself (and to others) and its political praxis meaningless.

Alberto Melucci, a student of Touraine's, has extended and enriched this analysis by focusing it on the cultural and symbolic reproduction of collective action. He stresses that

'The very idea of a social conflict implies the opposition of two actors struggling for the same resources, symbolic or material. The adversaries share the same field but they interpret it in opposite ways... They identify themselves with the whole field while denying any role to the opponent.'[26]

---

longer "identical" (138) in any possible sense. But in what sense is the social substration a communicative process in its own right at all? I think it cannot be. Because the communication underlying the law - albeit organisational or interactional - and "strictly coupled" by it into the law's own idiom, has its own boundaries around its own topics and own self-descriptions. If that is so, the social substration of the legal person is thus not co-terminous with the legal person, and if it is not, it cannot be a substration. The law's selectivity is constitutive of its "substration"; the law enacts into being its own "surrogate" environment - including its social "substration" through its own editing. It is thus impossible for the observer to demarcate an area of communication to serve as substratum that precedes what area of social communication the legal institution itself selects as constituting its substratum. The law is always already there before its social substratum. My objection to Teubner then is that in this paper he too goes down the same line of inquiry as the theories he rejects, and that he rejects the theories on the basis that they have found something wrong not that they have gone about looking for it in the wrong way. His methodology here concedes too much and undermines the crux of his substantive argument.

[25] As Sullivan writes in her defence of partiality, '[i]ntermediate organizations not only facilitate individual self-definition and expression but also keep the state from replicating itself by nurturing deviance, diversity and dissent. These functions depend on subgroups' private status - on their detachment and distance from the all-inclusive State.' (Sullivan, 1988, 1721)

[26] Melucci, 1992, 137. Melucci explains the interdependence in similar terms to Touraine (note the proximity of the following exposition with Touraine): 'The meaning of collective action, which is to be found in the system of relations of which the actor is a part, is identified with the particular point of view of the individual actor: the field of social relationships, which is always made up of a network of tensions and oppositions, is restructured according to the

The point here is the one that Touraine suggested before: that individuals within the movement 'construct' their action in ways that are incompatible to outsiders' understandings and in the process appropriate the relational field of conflict (they 'reify' it according to Melucci). To append meta-political categories to such understandings of action, conflict and identity, and to fix the conflict through categories alien to the parties involved, cancels out the understanding that the movement has of its identity and action.

But more importantly, Melucci discusses the New Social Movements in a way that raises the central question of whether there are forms of conflict that are being directed against the logic of complex systems. He designates not only solidarity and engagement in conflict as definitional elements of a social movement, but designates as a necessary feature that 'a social movement breaks the limits of compatibility of a system.'[27] The system Melucci has in mind is the one the republicans have in mind too: the legally constituted political system of participation. What defines a movement is a conception of its opposition to a system. The 'expressive politics' in which it engages as a continuous source of identity consolidation, is an exercise in defying the dominant codes of participation, the institutional forms of politics. Contrary to what republicans assume, the movement draws for self-understanding from its very resistance to the containment of its identity in law.[28]

Simmel and Coser: Identity and 'phenomenal' conflict

While Touraine and Melucci elaborated the mode in which conflict, that is 'constitutive' of society, constitutes social and political identities, Simmel, and following him Coser, focus on the 'phenomenal' performance of conflicts in the maintenance and consolidation of identity. And as opposed to the former's focus on class conflict, the latter extends the

---

position occupied by the actor ... The adversary is seen as only having a negative relationship to the totality: the adversary is in fact the very obstacle that prevents general needs from being satisfied, or general goals from being attained ... It is, then, always possible to identify in the ideology of a social movement a definition of the social actor who is mobilized, of the adversary against whom the movement must struggle, and of the collective objectives of the struggle.' (1992, 132)

[27] Melucci, 1989, 29. Melucci provides abundant empirical evidence of such forms of collective identity- generation through expressive activities in (1989)

[28] Eder writes: 'Theories of social movements assume that the self-description of the collective actor as a social movement places him beyond the institutional framework.' (1993, 60) But cf. Turner here, who argues that social movements are "*inevitably [!] movements about the rights of citizenship.*' (1986, 92)

collective-identity-moulding function of social conflict to gender conflict, inter-generational conflict, national and ethnic conflict, e.t.c.

In his influential study on conflict, Simmel has placed particular emphasis on the connection between conflict and collective identity. His central thesis is that 'conflict is a form of socialisation.' The analysis is undertaken on two axes, in-group and out-group conflict. Regarding the former, Simmel maintains that in the absence of conflict, groups would be devoid of process and structure: the existence of conflict is not necessarily disruptive to the unity of a group but may in fact be instrumental to strengthening group solidarity and identity. About out-group conflict Simmel says:

'Conflict heightens the concentration of an existing unit, radically eliminating all elements which might blur the distinctness of its boundaries against the enemy; ... The unifying power of the principle of conflict nowhere emerges more strongly than when it manages to carve a temporal or contextual area out of competitive or hostile relationships.'[29]

Taking the cue from Simmel, Coser provides a systematic account of the *Functions of Social Conflict*. Coser built on Simmel's idea that social conflict is organic and intrinsic to social structure and more specifically that it fulfils a number of determinate functions in groups and interpersonal relations. In what interests us most directly, Coser undertook to establish that 'conflict serves to establish and maintain the identity and boundary lines of societies and groups,' and that, 'conflict with other groups contributes to the establishment and re-affirmation of the identity of the group and maintains its boundaries against the surrounding social world.'[30] He pursues these matters under the eloquent groupings: 'Group-Binding Functions of Conflict', 'Group-Preserving Functions of Conflict', 'In-Group Conflict and Group Structure', 'Conflict with Out-group and Group Structure', 'Conflict-The Unifier', e.t.c.

Coser's is a complex analysis that apart from the central in-group/out-group distinction engages various others; he attempts links with social psychology by stressing throughout the distinction between an engagement of 'total personality' and 'segmental' engagement through roles; he analyses the balance between the multiplicity and the intensity of conflict; he also brings an innovation to Simmel with a distinction between realistic and non-realistic conflict. We will not go into all this now except to note that the general thrust of the work is toward proving the 'various conditions under which social conflict may contribute to the maintenance, adjustment or

---

[29] Simmel, 1954, pp98-101
[30] Coser, 1956, 38

adaptation of social relationships and social structures,'[31] predominantly group cohesion and group identity.

Simmel and Coser both argue the 'phenomenal' connection between conflict and collective social identity. They stress the facilitative, constructive side of conflict: in conflict are identities formed and consolidated, through conflict is entry into public space effected in a way that attracts commitment and allows solidarity in consolidating oppositions. Because in Simmel's telling phrase: '[c]onflict is designed to resolve divergent dualisms; it is a way of achieving some kind of unity.'[32] 'Once groups and associations have been formed through conflict with other groups, such conflict will serve to maintain boundary lines between the group and the surrounding social environment.'[33] In this context Coser develops an argument that is of utmost relevance to the republican theory. He says:

'Conflict may serve to remove dissociating elements in a relationship and re-establish unity. Insofar as conflict is the resolution of tension between antagonists it has stabilizing functions and becomes an integrating component in the relationship. However not all conflicts are positively functional for the relationship, but only those which concern goals, values or interests that do not contradict basic assumptions upon which the relationship is founded.'[34]

This difference allows Coser to draw a distinction, following Simpson and MacIver between 'communal and non-communal conflicts':

'Non-communal conflict results when there is no community of ends between the parties to the conflict ... Non communal conflict is seen as disruptive and dissociating. Communal conflict, that is based on a common acceptance of basic ends, is, on the contrary, integrative. When men settle their differences on the basis of unity, communal conflict will ensue.'[35]

Marxism expounds the typical case of non-communal conflict. We will re-visit the republicans' containment thesis now to see how in order to argue for containment they always-already dispose of the dangerous non-communal type of conflict, and follow up this argument with a number of related arguments about collective identity, some more general, some more particular, drawing from the severing of conflict as I have explained it here.

---

[31] ibid., 151
[32] Quoted in Coser, 1965, 1
[33] Coser, 1956, 155
[34] ibid., 80
[35] Coser discusses their argument in 1956, 75ff

Thesis [8] against Republicanism

It is the republican theory of community that will come under scrutiny here.[36] Many theories claim an integrative function for law and there is many valid and sophisticated arguments to this effect.[37] But without nuances and qualifications, it is simply wrong to claim as the republicans do, that law binds people and creates a sense of community amongst them. Coser's aforementioned distinction inserts one such elementary qualification. Employing it here, I suggest that the republican argument relies upon the *assumption that conflict is always-already of the communal type*. In that, the idea of the 'basic cleavage' that underlies non-communal conflict, is already conveniently disposed of. Then, of course, by definition, people's engaging in conflict will bring them closer together because there isn't a basic cleavage in the first place that could drive them further apart. Having presupposed that the conflict was of the communal type anyway, having therefore begged the 'reflexive' question, the argument about the consolidation of community can be made straightforwardly. For the republicans, any cleavage, however deep, can always be bridged. I will rely on their concrete treatment of some historical examples to show how the republicans establish their preferred type of conflict by begging the question (or at least defining away the reflexive one).

There are three moments in American Constitutional history that no constitutional theory has been willing to ignore, let alone one like civic republicanism that advances a re-interpretation of American political identity. The first is the enfranchisement of Black Americans. The second is the re-interpretation of equality in *Brown v. Board of Education*.[38] The third is the Civil Rights movement that - and this is problematical for the republicans[39] - *post*-dated *Brown*. The civil rights movement found its

---

[36] Note that I am not for a moment suggesting any blanket formula for community, a name that has been given to as diverse groupings as those which share, among others, a paradigm (Kuhn), a nomos (Cover), a culture, or a world-view (Goodman). My argument pivots on the 'sharing' and allows the 'what' to be designated reflexively by those whose sharing of it appears significant and adequate to their sense of togetherness.

[37] Virally, e.g., describes law as a force of collective integration in 1960, 210ff. For an overview of theories and debates on the integrative function of law see Cotterrell, 1984, 73-103

[38] 347 U.S. 383 (1954)

[39] It is problematical for the republicans in that the period of popular mobilisation did not, as they would have it, feed the new understanding of equality into law. And Ackerman needs to rely on a previous constitutional moment to justify the reasoning in the case, not the civil rights moment that had not yet occurred.

constitutional expression in the Warren Court 'revolution' of the 1960s in a series of path-breaking decisions.

Ackerman,[40] Dworkin[41] and Michelman deal extensively with all or some of the above, but it is Michelman's analysis of them that is the most revealing in the context of this argument about conflict, communal and not.

To argue the republican interpretation of the historical events, Michelman elaborates his own vision of the republican project which, as we have already seen and discussed earlier, he calls 'jurisgenerative politics'.[42] He writes:

> 'Jurisgenerative political debate among a plurality of self-governing subjects involves the contested "re-collection" of a fund of public normative references conceived as narratives, analogies ... Upon that fund those subjects draw for identity and by the same token, for moral and political freedom. That fund is the matrix of their identity "as" a people or political community, that is, as individuals in effectively persuasive, dialogic relation with each other, and it is also the medium of their political freedom, that is, of their translation of past into future through the dialogic exercise of recollective imagination. The republican idea of political jurisgenesis thus presupposes that such a fund of normatively effective material - publicly cognizable, persuasively recollectible and contestable - is always already available ... [The normative efficiency of the fund] depends on a context that is everyone's - of the past that is constitutively present in and for every self as language, culture, worldview and political memory.'[43]

Jurisgenerative politics argues Michelman should not be understood as requiring a pre-existing consensus. All that is required is the existence of a fund that consists of various narratives, normative commitments, e.t.c. By drawing on the fund, people are able to enter the dialogic relationship. And

---

[40] For Ackerman only the first of the moments, the 'Reconstruction', is a full-blown constitutional one. The second is a compelling synthesis of the Reconstruction moment with the New Deal moment of activist government (1991, pp140-1). It is thus a prime example of what Ackerman calls 'intergenerational synthesis' by the Court. The third moment is a minor constitutional one because it does not fulfill all the necessary criteria Ackerman identifies. The civil rights movement is more or less a late expression of the New Deal constitutional moment. What matters for present purposes however is that there exists in Ackerman's account an intimate feedback, a dialectic, between legal understanding and direct political popular mobilisation. And that the political voices calling for inclusion and equality carried into law and forced a revision of fundamental legal understandings.

[41] 1986, 387ff

[42] 'Jurisgeneration' for Cover is the process of giving birth to meaning within community but the community he is talking about is bound to a normative universe (a nomos) that is discrete, insular and specific. Cover makes this point over and over again. 'The nomos that I have described requires no state.' (11) His community is not a part of but an alternative to the state. (Cover, 1983) For more on Cover, see chapter sixteen.

[43] Michelman, 1988, 1513-4

as long as the dialogue respects some minimum requirements,[44] as long as the point is to persuade each other rather than to coerce, it will generate community in the strong sense of it being identity-generating.

On the basis of these thoughts, Michelman advances his republican interpretation of the favourite historical examples. About the civil rights movement he declares: Black Americans used *their* own 'partial citizenship' and effected a self-revision of *our* communal standing; they drew from the common normative resource pool - the 'fund' - to pursue a politics that lead to a self-revised position.

'So the suggestion is that the pursuit of political freedom through law depends on "our" constant reach for inclusion of the other, of the hitherto excluded- which in practice means bringing to legal-doctrinal presence the hitherto absent voices of emergently self-conscious social groups.'[45]

But there is a problem here for Michelman. Does the legal redefinition of equality in the celebrated *Brown* case, the Warren Court extension of political and civil rights to Black Americans, or even, ultimately, the great constitutional moment of their inclusion in the citizenry through the extension of equal political status (universal citizenship), create community where there was none? Michelman will, at least, concede that initially 'they [Black Americans] had an oppositional understanding of their situation and its relation to our (and increasingly their) Constitution.'[46] He does accept, then, that at the start there was no community, just a stark confrontation of narratives, of two positions that only generated community within and not between them. The one was a narrative of oppression, of enmity, and of the promise of emancipation through struggle. The other, in so far as it wasn't split into further, even more partial, patterns, was one of privilege and achievement, of a sense of ownership of the land, but also of insecurity and fear.[47] There is a problem here, and its solution depends on how seriously Michelman takes his own presuppositions. If, as he admits, communities

---

[44] For the connection of Michelman's theory with Habermas's see part I
[45] Michelman, 1988, 1529
[46] ibid.
[47] 'Fear of the Negro ... is a means of keeping the status system intact, of rallying all members of the white group around its standards.' Because if the Negro is seen as dangerous, 'those in the white group who befriend him can be effectively characterized as "renegades" endangering the very existence of the white group.' (Coser, 1954, p109). For the facets of fear and the function in maintaining the white group's identity, see indicatively, Mydral (1944). Tannenbaum describes it thus: 'The South gives indications of being afraid of the Negro. I do not mean physical fear. It is not a matter of cowardice or bravery; it is something deeper and more fundamental. It is fear of losing grip upon the world.' (Tannenbaum, 1924, pp 8-9)

draw from oppositional and mutually exclusive narratives, surely they have very little, if anything, in common to recollect from the fund.

That Americans at the time of the Reconstruction - both Blacks and Whites - 'shared a political memory, world view [e.t.c.]' is simply wrong in the face of starkly oppositional narratives; surely Michelman is not employing here the notion of a shared memory to describe the experience of both master and slave of their 'common' history? If, on the other hand, Michelman is making the smaller point that the 'fund' is an all inclusive category that includes potentially all those proto-understandings that will later furnish normative positions in such stark confrontation as the ones he is dealing with here, then the point is so small as to become trivial; because in 'sharing' the fund - the precondition of community - the communities in conflict share nothing in any recognisable sense of sharing. This is as true for the republican 'fund' as it is true for Dworkin's 'pre-interpretive' plateau, their arguments strikingly similar here.

So much for sharing the fund. But further: to the extent that the black movement was successful in each of the mentioned moments, does it follow that this led to integration into communal identity? Why ever would it? Why would superimposing the status of equal citizenship on a genuine diversity of identities, needs and expectations fulfil the quest for community? In fact could not the converse be argued? That the success of the movement rather than creating a community actually divided one, in that a substantial minority of white segregationists found themselves pushed out of a community of new sensibilities?[48] Theirs would be a story of the birth of a new narrative that explains past common history of the white community in a new way, probably by explaining away the original unity. How do the republicans suggest dispensing with this possibility? Why should one assume that the end result of our dialogue will move us any closer to a shared community, the sharing of a narrative, rather than a breakdown of the communal? What makes the danger impossible?

---

[48] Historically there is abundant evidence of this danger. And the republicans can celebrate the Constitutional moment only at the expense of downplaying the often successful resistance 'within' the new community. Even the most widely celebrated republican moment of 'Reconstruction' is conceived as a birth of a new community only by downplaying the successful white Southern resistance to the practices of Reconstruction that profoundly altered not only the nature of the objectives of the 'Radical Republicans' (Ackerman's critical constitutional vanguard) but also the depth of implementation and ultimately the constitutional form of the ensuing era. (On this see Foner E (1988)). As Simon stresses, '[a]t a minimum the Redeemers must be seen as achieving a special status for the South as "a distinct society" within the new constitutional order of the Union ... The same forces that galvanized the Reconstruction Republicans also mobilized couter-revolutionary forces in both sections of the country that sought to find ways of channeling and eventually dissipating the Reconstruction effort.' (1992, 510, 512)

This is precisely the problem that Dworkin also faces. Even if we concede that national citizenries are in fact unified as communities through law at the expense of all that divides and differentiates them, Dworkin's argument, like the republicans', is still fallible. To argue as he does that a community in the process of self-revision (every act of interpretation is potentially an act of self-revision) will yield community, is to fix an outcome that ought to be contingent. There are many reasons why communal narratives break down and why the co-ordinates, around which the unity of identity takes form, are shifted. All this may turn a process of self-revision into a process of breakdown and disintegration of communities.[49]

Dworkin's community is not vulnerable to such real dangers because it is a postulate. Postulates don't suffer breakdowns. The continuity of Dworkin's community over time is guaranteed because the community is a projection of unity, its narrative the law and its communal identity the citizen as legal personality. The unity is built into the concepts and it is therefore not vulnerable to real danger. Dworkin is caught up in circularity: he is attempting to yield communities by presupposing them in the form of national citizenries. For him there is always, by definition, a further chapter to be written in the chain novel. Why does the community's self-revision never create a disruption substantive enough to destroy the narrative? The answer is because the narrative precedes the community; because in Dworkin's mind it is the narrative that counts and the community is simply postulated on the basis of that narrative's coherence.

To recapitulate: Michelman's community-moulding jurisgenerative politics, his deliberative dialogue, depends on a shared context, 'on a context that is everyone's,' and this context Michelman assures us, is 'always already available as shared language, shared world-view and political memory.' In juxtaposing language, world-view and political memory as functional equivalents, Michelman submerges the difference that makes the difference. Dworkin does the same when he passes all too easily from a plateau of intelligible argument to a plateau where people engage (already) as community in reasoning about the meaning of 'their' practices (Dworkin's methodological assignation of the internal/participant's viewpoint to all - actual or virtual - parties in conflict is crucial here).[50] Like Dworkin, Michelman has no problem in designating the American culture, worldview and memory as already a common fund. He thus sets himself the easy task of arguing that politics will bring to the surface as political/communal identity

---

[49] I owe this point to Maurice Glasman. It relates to the argument that McIntyre makes about 'epistemological crises' that come about when narratives can no longer rationalise the unexpected. (McIntyre, 1977).

[50] See Christodoulidis, 1994, 11-12

an identity that is already there. But why is the difficult question avoided? Why are the terms 'common' and 'fund' used for the very thing that separates Americans? Theirs can only be claimed a common fund because a community is postulated, a community mistakenly read into the simple sharing of a language and a location. With the community smuggled in, the republicans can reverse the very terms we use to describe our separateness. And it is then that those paradoxical catchphrases that the republicans are so fond of - as exhibiting a tension that they find constructive and insightful - reveal their true nature as oxymora: that republicanism 'invites recognition of how difference is our sameness,'[51] that 'our community [is one] of diversity,'[52] that 'difference is what we have in common,'[53] or that it was all a question of 'oppositional understandings of their situation in relation to our - and increasingly their - constitution.'[54] Is it not more likely that the political dialogue that the republicans envisage, is not that of one community coming to self-realisation but the cacophony (or in systems terms the 'noise') created by a number of distinct communities that partly overlap, partly confront and partly talk past each other?

The difference between conflict communal and not that I have relied on in this eighth thesis can be described more abstractly in the following terms: in conflict, the shaping of identity pre-supposes the existence of Alter-as-Enemy involved with Ego in a situation of conflict. According to the republican position, however, the shaping of identity takes place under conditions where conflict and the positions of Alter and Ego are instrumental to bringing them together in a community that then includes them both.[55] For the republicans the alignment around the stake of conflict is transitory; basic assumptions, basic understandings of which are always shared anyway as 'fund' or 'pre-interpretive' understandings, will in the end be shared again, qualified by having undergone the process of conflict. There always exists latent in the republican argument an overriding common interest to secure the 'common good' that in turn allows them to depict conflicts as always secondary or sectional, conflicts that are about how to bring the common good about. And Alter-as-enemy never remains for long the mirror for the assumption and maintenance of the identity of Ego.

---

[51] Michelman, 1986, 32

[52] Sherry, 1986, 615

[53] Michelman, 1986, 4

[54] ibid.

[55] In discussing the 'emancipatory activity of Black Americans,' Michelman asks: 'Does anybody doubt that the judicial agents of the challengers' accumulating citizenship drew on interpretive possibilities that the challengers' own activity was helping to create?' (1988, 1527)

My argument here is that we should resist the stipulation of conflict as always-already communal on the grounds that it imposes an *a priori* where there should be a reflexive question. How does the community understand the conflict? If one is professing to contain the politics of a community it is a question for the community to answer whether or not a conflict allows the community to consolidate its collective identity *in overcoming it or in preserving it*. Republicanism silences the reflexive-political question whether or not the conflict is in fact communal, and only thus clears the scene for the law to contain a conflict that is *a priori* postulated as such.

* Thesis [9] against Republicanism

In Touraine's sociology, the constitutive link between I - O and conflict over T is in broad outline very close to how the system of conflict 'orders' reality; in the social dimension the assumption of identity is effected through the confrontational pattern where the existence of the enemy is all important. In law, where the conflict can no longer claim totality, in Touraine's sense, or as system guarantee the conflictual ordering of reality, in Luhmann's, identity (as legal personality) retreats into a capacity to operationalise legal claims. Constitutive importance is relegated to the material dimension, i.e. to the question of the content of those claims.

We discussed above that the depiction of conflict in law involves a substantive shift from the social to the material dimension. The friend/foe opposition ceases to be in law the 'distinction directrice' and thus the key to deciphering conflict. Law introduces an exclusive focus on the issues that divide the parts, the parts themselves retreating to mere neutral 'points of allocation' of claims that may be operationalised in law concerning the issues at hand. This shift withdraws from conflict conflict's constitutive importance for political identity because it disassociates a community from its constitutive involvement in conflict, i.e. the drawing from conflict of its (the community's) standing, of its form and the strength of its binding. One's entry into public space is no longer effected conflictually, in solidarity to one group, in enmity to another, over a stake that can accommodate such total confrontations. Instead the instrumental role that law reserves for identity - instrumental to the material dimension - renders social-conflictual identity irrelevant. There is a crucial area of conflict that is defined away in creating this 'irrelevancy': we may designate it as the *politics of identity*.

In the conflict-system, questions of the definition of identity were absorbed into conflict itself. Conflict dictates what significant features underpin the self-understanding of the common 'we'-in-conflict, and more generally, under what capacity or in the name of what cause the political actor enters conflict. The important correlate is what one attributes as identity to Alter. In the example of the strike that was mentioned earlier, for the workers the politics of identity turn on the question of whether the opponent is designated as an employer, with whom we have entered a contractual relationship, or an owner of the means of production who appropriates our surplus production; whether the opponent is designated as a formally equal party to each employment agreement in which case the strikers are ganging up on him, or a member of a class to whom the workforce relates in class-conflictual terms. The freedom to designate these identities, to contest them, to be reflexive about them, is withdrawn in law where identities are either rigidly fixed (in essence invisible as mere operators of rights) or at least restricted to a limited pool of alternatives. The assumption of legal personality as presupposition of legal conflict withdraws the contestation of the identity of the enemy from the conflict itself; law makes identity a neutral container. The two aspects of conflict that are screened off in law are relevant (i) to the freedom to choose the description under which one enters the conflict (in the name of what one wages the struggle) and (ii) the correlate freedom to deny the identity of Alter, which includes the freedom to choose how to identify Alter. These are the two aspects of the politics of identity that do not resonate in law. And the republicans, by relying on law to voice politics, lose sight of how this important aspect of the political is legally annihilated.

There are numerous examples where the political is played out on the terrain of identity. Marxism provides the obvious example and both the rise and defeat of insurrectionary politics in the 60s is testimony of the importance of the politics of identity. Insurrection by the radical groups involved in the university uprisings was conceived as a means only, to serve as catalyst for the emergence of class consciousness and working-class solidarity. Such strategic use of conflict turned on the assumption that the State would not fail to rise to meet the challenge and in the process reveal its real nature as an instrument of class oppression; that would in turn trigger processes that would foster class-consciousness. Importantly for the present discussion, it was through law that this politics was defeated. It was defeated because in law the logic of this politics was screened off. Movements as a whole have no legal personality, no point of entry into the legal world. Entry can only be effected by disintegrating and defusing that which is constitutive of the movement - its collective nature - and the basis of its claim to legitimacy - the collective claim to which individual actions are only instrumental. But the law screens off all else and focuses directly on the latter by initiating selective prosecutions on individualistic grounds (how could *mens rea* apply to the group?) The legal system collapses the understanding behind collective action. It does not give voice to that which is essential to the politics of collectivities: the corporateness of the group that underlies its politics. It is no surprise then that an invitation to learn from the 'repeated lesson of many struggles' comes from Marxists; Piccioto for example, writes:

'Substantive gains are achieved through collective struggles building up class solidarity: the channelling of such struggles into the form of claims of bourgeois legal right breaks up that movement towards solidarity, through the operations of legal procedures which recognize only the individual subject ... Of course we have learned and must go on struggling to overcome this: in criminal prosecutions through collective defence strategies and solidarity groups, [etc] ... But these merely enable us to probe the limits of bourgeois law as a social form. To transcend those limits ... involves a determination to struggle within but also through and beyond those legal forms, or around and in spite of them.'[56]

Law offers a 'we' beyond politically constituted differences. When Sunstein prescribes that the judge ought to assume 'the point of view of everybody' he is prescribing the point of view of such a 'we'. Law '*stills*' identity in a way that allows political conflict to be played out around 'material' stakes neither affecting nor affected by the politics of identity. It is not that the law 'intends' this in any way, only that it cannot evade assumptions that are in-built in the system's most fundamental premises of observation, the self-descriptions it sets in motion to observe its environment. Outwith (and in spite of) this 'innocent' observation politics continues, and the party that takes the conflict to law may be seen by the opponent as performing a discursive manoeuvre aiming to obscure the identities of the parties, as performing, that is, an ideological/mystifying move. Taking to law is not an innocent move in that understanding of conflict. To this the republicans respond with innocence and the best intentions. But by assuming and propagating the naturalness and innocence of law's perception of collective identity, the republicans are conspiring to the silencing of politics in a way that transposes the ideological/mystifying moment from the level of practice to the level of theory.

---

[56] Piccioto, 1979, 171-2

Thesis [10] against Republicanism

The argument I will put forward here, in very brief form, is an argument about and against the *delegation of conflict*. Very explicitly in Michelman, Minow and Dworkin, implicitly in Ackerman, Sunstein and other republicans, the community's conflict is delegated to the judge to 'solve'. The problem here is one of the incompatibility of this delegation with the function that republicans, rightly, attribute to conflict: that of allowing people entry into public political space and consolidating a collective identity among its members. A community's engagement in conflict, albeit a heated competition of claims, a confrontation or a struggle, is constitutive of the community. Can such a necessary engagement be delegated without losing its essential quality *as* engagement?

At the one extreme, Dworkin (and following him Michelman) will unproblematically delegate the resolution of the community's conflicts to Hercules. The judge will undertake the task with Integrity and add his/her chapter to the on-going chain-novel, the community's narrative. The community's existence in time is sustained by the narrative of how its disagreements and conflicts have been resolved in law, a narrative authored by a judge or judges. There lies a problem here, in the connection between vicarious authorship and the coming about of community.

Communities and their narratives are in a dialectic relationship, so that the continuity of the community requires and informs an on-going narrative. This means more than that communities require a narrative. If we take communities, as Dworkin rightly does, to exist as communal imagination, as the bringing of meaning to practice, then they must exist through the narrative, they must exist in articulating their narrative.

The question is then: if community emerges in the authorship of the common narrative, can the community be replaced or represented in the very activity that constitutes it? I find that any concept of 'virtual' authorship here, such as that introduced by Dworkin, breaks the intimate dialectic of community and narrative, their simultaneity and reciprocal inter-dependence. Dworkin acknowledges this and is at great pains to establish that his is a theory that addresses the citizen and expects from the layman 'fidelity to a scheme of principle each citizen has a responsibility to identify, ultimately for himself, as his community's scheme.'[57] In the end, however, the task is entrusted to the judge as he has the resources to do it better, even if on behalf of the citizen.[58] My argument is that no single authorship, however

---

[57] Dworkin, 1986, 190

[58] This is not strikingly different from the old position in favour of common law that argues that judges express the mores of the community. On this see Lindsay Farmer's excellent (1993)

Herculean, can ever replace the community's authorship because it breaks the dialectic of community and narrative. I find this concept of virtual authorship deeply self-contradictory; an abstraction that removes any element of participation (and thus community in the literal sense) from the process. Virtual participation runs worryingly near non-participation and a theory that propounds it worryingly near ideology.

CHAPTER FOURTEEN

CONFLICT NORMALISED

Where theorists in earlier times were haunted by the fragility of order, [today theory] appears to suffer from a surfeit of order. And ultimately, of course, the heroic meta-theorist will suffer the fate; his agon will be routinized.
(Wolin)

The argument that follows is the most difficult one to level against the republicans, because it aims to confront the republicans' most inspired moment, their debt to Critical Legal Studies, particularly that to Roberto Unger. Unger's is a powerful version of the law-as-politics position, in so far as he vests in law the possibility of pursuing radical politics and of countering the 'false necessity' of the confinement of our political vision within rigid institutional assumptions. What puts him in the broad republican category here, is that he gives his politics legal leverage. Nothing, says Unger, compels us to reduce the political to the exclusive alternatives of 'tinkering' with the institutions or revolting against them.[1] This disjunction blinkers the very real possibility that the political may draw its inspiration from the institutions' - significantly here law's - own powerful imagination. Unger's work in legal and social theory is the constant endeavour to do just that, to tap that imagination. This argument has for some time now been expounded by the Critical Legal School that seeks to upset the legal system's tendency to assimilate the new to the old, its overwhelming of the innovative, its tendency to rationalise the incongruent into coherence, thus conspiring to the impoverishment of legal analysis through its foreclosure of broader conflict. In contrast, Critical Legal Analysis is geared to restoring 'deviations and contradictions as intellectual and political opportunities rather than threats.'[2] To resist the severing of legal analysis from broader conflicts, it will draw from the system itself to reveal suppressed possibilities by showing legal dogma to be incoherent, then playing up the 'dangerous supplements'. Where the law exhibits the overwhelming tendency to assimilate the 'deviant' case within already existing schemata of processing it, the critical scholar will emphasise alternative possibilities, new relevancies that upset settled patterns. There is a strong continuity in Unger's accounts of how this strategy of 'dis-entrenchment' and 're-construction' is envisaged, going back

---

[1] 'In this way we can break a little further from the tedious, degrading rhythm of history - with its long lulls of collective narcolepsy punctuated by violent revolutionary seizures.' (Unger, 1987b, 1)
[2] Unger, 1996, 9

to at least his CLS manifesto,[3] and variably described as 'deviationist doctrine',[4] 'negative capability',[5] and 'mapping and criticism'.[6] In each case, significantly, the same political logic of disruption draws from within the institution: as Unger put it in the Chorley lecture,[7] his Critical Legal Theory understands the institution as law but undertakes it as politics.

Undertaking law as politics and fusing the two in a constructive synthesis is, of course, the aspiration behind the republican 'containment thesis'. I want to argue that Unger, and with him the republicans, are wrong in the following crucial respect: while they are right to say that the system's inertia can be shaken from within, the endeavour cannot carry through to those constitutive assumptions that underlie the institutional identity as such. Following Luhmann we saw that there are certain constitutive reductions at play in law's picture of the world and to challenge those would not be to undertake law as politics but to do away with law altogether. To denote this form of unshakeable inertia I call it 'structural' and distinguish it from a second form, 'simple' inertia, that can indeed be successfully redressed. In effect, this is the dilemma that, I suggest, republicans have to face: either they concede the 'structural' type of inertia in which case they *can* exploit the transformative potential of the system to combat 'simple' inertia *but* within the limits dictated by the system, or they concede nothing, undertake law as politics, but then collapse the specific institutional achievement that is law, and the possibilities *it* offers.[8] And if law is thus collapsed into politics what remains of the heuristic value of the politics *of* law? I argue, counter-intuitively perhaps, that if law *does* harbour transformative opportunities *it is because* there are limits to law's institutional imagination that take the form of reductions which, at a deep level, cannot but remain in place. We cannot retain the opportunities if we do away with the reductions. And as a result law cannot but foreclose broader political conflict and, in the last instance, assimilate transformative opportunity to its own self-maintenance, assimilate the disruptive to its own controlled evolution and steamroller over reflexive politics in the process. This is the argument about the 'normalisation' of conflict and I will pursue it in a systems-theoretical way by taking the cue from Luhmann's argument about law as an 'immune system' of society.

---

[3] Unger (1983)
[4] Unger, ibid., pp15ff
[5] Unger, 1987b, pp 81, 156-7
[6] Unger, 1996, pp20ff
[7] Unger, ibid.
[8] I have argued this at some length in Christodoulidis (1996)

When Luhmann talks of 'immunisation of expectations' he is referring to the disciplining of Double Contingency.[9] Expectations allow uncertainty in specific, controlled ways and immunise the system towards other uncertainties it cannot control. The system reduces the complexity of possible contingencies: it allows for some, and re-produces itself by responding to them. By the same token it immunises itself against others, that are precluded because expectations are not attuned to them. A system modulates its reaction to its environment by changing expectations and controlling this change at the level of expectations of expectations. We have explored all this already and focused it already on law. We have already asked: how does the legal system stabilise system-specific contingencies and achieve an immunisation of expectations? We saw that this occurs along all three axes of meaning: in the *temporal* dimension expectations are immunised through normation, i.e. held to even when disappointed; in the *social* dimension, expectations are immunised from real dissensus through institutionalisation, through the assumption of a fictitious co-experiencing third party; finally, in the *material* dimension, expectations are immunised in relation to content. The contingency of what is at stake is reduced through fixing expectations to specific issues and contents through 'roles', 'programmes' and 'values'. In Luhmann's words:

'Generalization bridges the discontinuities ... Thus normation gives a lasting quality to an expectation despite the fact that it is disappointed from time to time. General consensus is assumed by institutionalization regardless of the fact that individuals do not agree. A unity of meaning and context are guaranteed by identification regardless of the material differences between expectations. Thus generalization achieves a symbolic immunization of expectations against other possibilities.'[10]

This immunisation from other possibilities is law's reduction achievement. It is the consistent theme of my argument throughout, but one that will be more fully articulated in the final part of the book, that this (immunisation or reduction) achievement, while facilitative in many ways, imposes a cost on reflexive politics. The immunisation that facilitates the crystallising of expectations works to the exclusion of other possible political conflict. We have explored the impoverishment of conflict, a conflict that was re-enacted, conflated and severed in law; normalisation, now, underpins in law *the deep affiliation of conflict to order*. This affiliation extends to include, as always, conflict that is radical and dangerous. And while immunisation through reduction and generalisation is a feature of all systems, Luhmann reserves for

---

[9] See above, chapter eight
[10] Luhmann, 1972, 74

the legal system the function of serving as society's 'immune system'.[11] As uniquely geared to the resolution of conflict,[12] law must:

'forestall society by producing its own insecurities and instabilities, and thus not be aloud to go "astray", not permitted to wander outside the problems that can be expected.'[13]

I think it is fruitful to tie the discussion of normalisation to the *evolution* of the legal system, in order to show how the evolutionary logic of the autopoietic legal system imposes exigencies on conflict that lead to its normalisation. A few words on the evolution of systems, therefore. A system's 'openness' to the world consists in its reading disappointment or fulfilment of the expectations it projects. Of course the system is neither static nor insensitive to change; to remain responsive to a changing world the system must also vary the expectations it projects. New legal possibilities need to be projected to respond to new situations. New expectations test new patterns of conflict around new issues, and their fulfilment or disappointment is fed back into the law as valid new premises for future decisions. The legal system thus varies its structures, re-constructs and alters them, and in the process 'learns' and *evolves*. It does this by providing legal answers to the conflictual expectations that face it requiring litigation. Conflict is necessary for law because it provides input to the reproductive process without which the system of law would stagnate. But in dealing with conflict, law only achieves a new return to order. It pushes back the threat of disorganisation by conceiving and resettling disturbed practice on the basis of uncontroverted practice.[14] Law conceives of conflicts as disturbances that must be overcome. The conflictual pattern is transitory;[15] a destabilisation that allows legal evolution through successive steps of return to order. The uncertainty of expectations that face law in a situation of social conflict is fruitful ground for internal innovation and simultaneously for the genesis of legal order.[16] The system overcomes the turbulence that it sees conflict as presenting it with, by resettling disturbed practice and sanctioning the re-settlement with

---

[11] Luhmann, 1984, 509

[12] See chapter ten, above

[13] Luhmann, 1984, 512

[14] On examples of this see Heller, 1988, 187 and n. 15

[15] On the transitory nature of conflict situations in law see also Broekman, 1989, 318

[16] The degree to which the system is open to learning is, of course as always, an internal matter. In Luhmann's terms this would be expressed in the following way: the system itself controls the balance of redundancy and variety. It is a distinction that bears on the system's readiness to vary its structures in the face of an evolving environment. Variety is about increasing responsiveness, redundancy about suppressing the element of surprise in the system.

permanence for the time being. For the legal system the conflictual pattern is a pathology in the healing of which law evolves.

Theorists of autopoiesis describe the process of evolution of a system in biological terms, as a process of variation, selection and stabilisation. This is a complex discussion, a much contested one, and I will only very briefly rehearse it here. Luhmann borrows the biological analogy[17] and generalises it to the evolution of all systems. Teubner provides the most articulate, I think, account of the logic of evolution of the legal system. The way he suggests that the law internalises these evolutionary functions is that 'norms take over the function of variation, institutional structures (particularly procedures) that of selection, and dogmatic[doctrinal]-conceptual structures that of retention.'[18]

Much of the internal theoretical debate turns on how to combine 'endogenous and exogenous evolution' in a way that does not compromise the closure of autopoietic systems. I will say nothing further on this because I see no immediate relevance to my argument about normalisation. My aim here is to employ the logic of evolution to address the republican logic of containment, to explore what exactly happens as the voices in political conflict cross the threshold of the legal system. How do (e.g. Michelman's) 'voices' in interactional (spontaneous) settings feed into the institutional arenas and how do political claims for change resonate in law, if at all, as an impulse for evolution, a pattern of variation? The more general political question I am seeking an answer to is: what is resistant to conflict and challenge and why the inertia. Is 'normalisation' an adequate description of what happens to political claims that inform positions of conflict as they enter the legal discourse?

Rather than treating the question of evolution at a general level, where the theory has to answer the charge of social Darwinism and the rest, we will draw a cross-section in the way Teubner does, and visit the evolutionary logic at the level of the individual episode. At this more localised site we will look at both evolution and normalisation, as specific political claims are confronted and negotiated in the *trial*.[19] Incidentally, this focus on the trial is

---

[17] On this see Teubner, 1993, pp51-5 and for the critique of systems theory as neo-Darwinist, see Rottleutner, 1988, 97

[18] Teubner, 1993, 51

[19] Cf. Luhmann on the nature of the trial: conditions concern 'the specification of the interaction system in preparation for a binding legal decision under previously established criteria instead of the general task or arbitration with consideration of all the relevant circumstances; the neutralisation of the judge's individual personality as factor in decision-making; the removal of the orientation to one's other roles for all involved parties ..., ignoring public reactions, particularly the colere publique ... ; and finally a separation between court and procedure... For their part such differentiations require complex societal

interesting for yet another reason. In both Michelman's and Dworkin's theories, the judge is accorded central significance in picking up the voices from the margins, as well as in substituting the community in settling its conflict for it. (above, thesis [10])

In order to explain how the law learns and evolves during the trial, Teubner borrows from Habermas's vocabulary of 'ontogenetic learning and phylogenetic development.'[20] He suggests that this is a useful framework for describing the complex interplay between the individual trial and the law's evolutionary mechanism. (Ontogenetic) learning occurs in the trial in which a specific solution is given to a clash of expectations. The problem is how this learning feeds into the dynamic of legal evolution and informs legal (phylogenetic) development. So while possibilities of variation are developed as new legal possibilities are tested at the level of the trial, the innovations only feed into law to inform its evolution through an interlocking of the two cycles that are distinct systems, one interactional (the trial), one functional (the law). The process of variation, retention, stabilisation is best captured in that interlocking.

What Teubner is attempting to explain here is how expectations, competing at the interactional level of the trial, feed into the legal system to re-shape its assumptions and vary the expectations it will henceforth project. It is the individual interaction that makes social experimentation possible, says Teubner.[21] 'Social experimentation' as variation allows new impulses to be felt in law. The trial is where the claims for change are articulated. In this sense the trial, itself an interaction system, is the **negotiating post** between the vast area of social demands and their sanctioning in law, i.e. their being vested the status of confirmed legal expectations. The innovation that Teubner's schema brings is that it is through this negotiating process that evolution makes sense and that, thus, evolution must be understood as involving the 'interlocking of two communicative cycles,' that of the trial and that of the legal system proper. The legal system's mechanism of retention (the legal decision) 'bequeaths what has been learnt in the process of interaction.' Stabilisation, the final step, involves the play, in law, of all those mechanisms that 'enable insights gained in one trial to ... become part of the memory of the law,' and thus

---

preconditions; for example those concerning contact mobility, degree of abstraction in the processing of experience, tolerance and indifference within social relations.' (1972, 134-5) See also 1993, ch.6

[20] Teubner, 1993a, pp59ff, but adjusts it to describe the relationship between a single interaction and society as a whole. What he retains from Habermas is the interface mechanism, the connecting process between the two.

[21] Also Heller: 'Litigation, when not simply a form of debt collection, is designed to upset legal practice, invoke the search for meaning in legal reason.' (1988, 186 n.13)

allow its autopoiesis when that memory furnishes new legal expectations to be tested, affirmed or disappointed in future legal episodes. Through the tripartite process, the insight gained in one trial, (a variation), is 'skimmed off as normative surplus,' to establish (through retention and stabilisation) a principle for future selection in law.

There is no real need to emphasise again that the two interlocking cycles do not occupy separate ontological space; it could in fact be claimed that the interlocking itself is an achievement of the two systems' organisation of time. The clash of expectations does not 'happen' in the trial at the expense of its 'happening' in law. The clash is at once an event in both the interaction system of the trial and the functional sub-system of law. Similarly the legal decision is simultaneously the moment that ends the interactional system (the trial) and the moment of selection in the legal system. (In the same way that a communication in any other interactional system may cross thresholds of legal relevance and become a legal communication without ever 'leaving' the interactional system. The simultaneity of the existence of systems around the single communication is one of the most central and fruitful insights that the theory of autopoiesis has to offer.) What permits the assignation of the clash to either system is the alignment to system co-ordinates that make sense of it.

There is, however, a problem with Teubner's formulation, a problem that makes a great deal of difference. The problem lies with his designation of the trial as the *locus of social experimentation*, this, of course, an assertion very convenient for the republican argument of law as centrepiece and forum of political debate. The problem with Teubner's formulation is that he *stresses one boundary when in fact there are two*. Teubner is surely right to discard any simple linear progress from the legal expectation in the trial to change in the legal system itself; there does exist a boundary in the complex logic of the interlocking of the two cycles, the interface of the two systems, that prevents any direct conclusion of a trial to be fed immediately into the legal system as valid premise. But there is another boundary too. It is the one that prevents social claims from entering trials as legal (variation) claims directly and at no cost. In the way that Teubner buries this additional boundary, the expectations that clash in the trial are at once both 'social' and legally processable. What is not true is that '[e]xpectations of the various subsystems coincide, complement, supplement each other and conflict with each other in the individual trial ...'[22] Instead, negotiation systems, like the trial, develop double boundaries to both systems whose expectations they mediate. Teubner stresses the subtle interplay at the trial/law boundary at the cost of losing sight that what resonates in the trial

---

[22]Teubner, 1993, 62

itself as social expectation has *already* met thresholds of legal relevance. For us, it is of paramount importance that we discern this initial boundary, because it is in the trial that conflictual political claims for innovation and change will enter negotiation, and the boundary comes to symbolise the limitations that the negotiating process itself inflicts upon the conflictual positions that it negotiates.

I have argued that there is a boundary, a submerged one, between political claim and what can possibly enter the trial as legally processable claim. My claim has been that, here too, the specific logic of interlocking of political discourse and legal trial imposes its own conditions and therefore, in a sense, a boundary. Why is this detrimental to 'containment'? Because the boundary filters what is conceivable as 'variation'; and this is turn is tied to evolutionary exigencies. In a nutshell, the evolution of a system is structural *variation*; and what can vary depends on what already exists. This has major consequences for radical political critique. It brings already existing structural assumptions into play as pre-conditions to all attempts to push for change. The only way in which a claim for change may register is if it manages to surprise projections of expectations. Following the principle that we can only see what we know how to look for, perception must be based upon an already existing pre-conception of what is to be seen or understood. For a challenge to register, that is, the system's memory has to be tapped.[23] Law controls the context against which informative surprises may be articulated. Change will only always come about as structural drift, a move away from already existing structural givens. This is where I suggest locating the system's *inertia*. While both Unger's and Luhmann's theories capture this powerfully, Unger, and with him the republicans, elide a distinction here that matters: a distinction that needs to be drawn between **simple** and **structural inertia**. It is a distinction that turns on the question of what can be meaningfully challenged within the ambit of the politics of law. It is my claim that we need to take full account of the selectivity of legal imagination and the 'structural' inertia that comes from the reductions that underlie that selectivity, if we are to make the 'politics of law' aware of the field in which they operate usefully.

The question of simple inertia from a systems-theoretical perspective is this: given law's function in society of stabilising expectations, and the values that consequently accompany its development (rule of law), it is only congruent that 'the surprising or anomalous event is grasped as concretely

---

[23] Cf Neisser, 1976, pp20ff. Neisser calls these pre-conceptions 'orienting schemata' and they orient the observer within the cmplexity and equivocality of the immediately available environment by constructing certain expectations about relevant information.

as possible, so that the required structural changes can be kept limited in scope and made to proceed along predictable lines.'[24] Does this mean that one can never take to law to challenge existing structures? No, it only means that:

'[a] special effort and special measures within the system are required if this normalisation tendency is to be changed into a tendency for existing structures to be questioned or problematised and information evaluated as a symptom of impeding crisis, as cost, as dysfunction in the prevailing order, or somehow or other looked at as a possible source of alternatives.'[25]

A 'special effort' is required because the system will always, initially at least, give a disciplining, non-random response to the random event.

Luhmann borrows from information theory the term *'redundancy'* to denote the system's tendency to reduce the element of surprise within it. Information is produced when the system is surprised in some way. On the other hand, a system is redundant 'in so far as it supports itself in processing information on what is already known ... Every repetition makes information superfluous which means, quite simply, redundant.'[26] The problem of law's 'simple' inertia is that the legal system is paramountly a redundant order. In processing information on the basis of what is already known it supports itself and self-referentially assimilates what is new to what already exists. Legal argumentation, says Luhmann, 'overwhelmingly reactivates known grounds.' Information becomes confirmed in subsequent operations, gradually becomes entrenched in self-descriptions, acquiring orientation value for new arguments and condensation value for the system.[27] Of course the assimilation cannot be complete. The system needs to react to a changing environment, and to this effect *'variety'* comes into play. Significantly the practice of distinguishing and overruling 'occasionally invents new [grounds] to achieve a position where the system can, on the basis of a little new information, fairly quickly work out what state it is in and what state it is moving towards.'[28] The reason why it requires 'a special effort' to shake the redundancy of the system and stretch its imagination is because the system tends to 'reduce its own surprise to a tolerable amount and allow information only as differences added in small numbers to the stream of reassurances.'[29]

---

[24] Luhmann, 1971, 33
[25] *ibid.*
[26] Luhmann, 1995, pp 285, 291
[27] On confirmation and condensation, see S.C.Smith (1995)
[28] Luhmann, 1995, 291
[29] *ibid*

In an extract that could easily have been written by Critical Legal Scholars had it not preceded them by a decade, Luhmann says:

'[s]uitable information ... must be specially produced, brought to light by uncovering some latent aspect of *existing order,* or retrieved from the existing decision-making process by incongruent questions.'[30]

Both central elements of CLS deviationist doctrine are here: the retrieval *in* law of the dangerous supplement; and the strategy of playing it up so that what is suppressed surfaces to subvert established patterns and entrenched principle in law. Unger's declaration of war in *Politics* against all institutional 'formative contexts' is very much the logic of deviationist doctrine writ large, a strategy re-activated in his recent prescriptions for 'mapping and criticism'.[31]

The project is no doubt both intriguing and promising. It is a remarkable feat of deviationist doctrine that it forces the system to thematise the ordinary as a possible source of alternatives - Luhmann's 'redundancy' and 'variety'. But it also points to the limitations of the project that are associated, it is my suggestion, with inertia of a second, 'structural' type. I draw on this for my eleventh and final argument against the republicans.

* Thesis [11] against Republicanism

My argument against all those who advocate that the interpretative nature of law, its discursive, 'plastic', 'jurisgenetic' and flexible character, its positioning as 'forum of principle' or privileged instance of practical discourse, e.t.c., make it the ideal container or vessel of politics is that they disregard law's 'structural' inertia and the deep normalising effect this has on conflict. If the Critical Legal Scholars, and with them the republicans, present an answer to the normalisation of conflict in law, the answer is confined to combating simple, not structural, inertia. In other words, their attempt is to feed deviant conflictual counter-theses into law in ways that will resonate in law. But this, in turn, has to rely on the system's *structural* flexibility to accommodate such strategic inputs. The strategy relies on an argumentation that must re-activate known grounds if it is to secure a surprise, let alone effects, within the system. It relies on creating what could be called an innovative - or, to use Maruyama's formulation, a

---

[30] Luhmann, 1971, 34
[31] Unger, 1996, 20

'goal-generating'[32] - dissatisfaction in the receiving system. Although this is a powerful weapon against 'simple' legal inertia, consider the flip-side: it in turn depends on a manipulation of a systemic reduction already in place, that one is therefore prepared to leave intact if only to allow the dissatisfaction to register. That is what Luhmann means when he says that '[e]volution works epigenetically,' and that 'only in this way can innovations that presuppose themselves arise.'[33] What makes this a compromise, and a debilitating one at that, is that a limitation is thus imposed on the levelling of challenges; because whatever challenge is to register in law, will only make a difference in the evolution of the system on the basis of its *alignment* to already existing reductions. Something is an informative surprise against a background of settled meaning. Challenges are dealt with by the (legal) system by being so interpreted as to accord with already existing or accepted meaning, always-already normalised, kept within the confines of what legal expectations can read as conceivable alternatives, always hedged in, always tamed. That is why in the legal system '[t]he unknown is assimilated to the known, the new to the old, the surprising to the familiar.'[34] This is the deep 'normalising' function of the law where contingencies have already been reduced in specific ways. The events that will set off information processing within the system must play on existing redundancies, must articulate with systemic reductions if they are to make an impact at all. The possibilities of radical political change are radically circumscribed by such structural necessity that, contra Unger, is not 'false'. Challenges *to* the structure can only be accommodated *by* the structure as demands to draw new internal distinctions and boundaries. And thus, as Heller put it,

'a self-referential system's evolutionary history is one of continual internal differentiation of newly organized patterns of information out of pre-existing states.'[35]

---

[32] Luhmann, 1971, 85. The problem that is being identified here is that of providing the strategically correct stimulus that may make the idiosyncratic system respond in the desirable way, desirable, that is, in terms also of how the social environment will receive the legal decision. We have learnt from Teubner how precarious the process of this '***structural coupling***' between diverse fields is, how easily it can go wrong, how easily the logics of the systems can be abridged, boundaries overstepped (regulatory trilemma) (See Teubner, 1983, 239). But Teubner's departure point is from problems of regulatory failure, whereas, for us, the question is different. It is about taking our conflict to law - conflict that arises from and informs spontaneous social contexts - and deciding whether or not we must pay the price that it be compromised, normalised.
[33] Luhmann, 1989, 147. In other words, it relies on 'bying into' the discourse one wishes to confront, to go back to that dilemma described by Mathiesen some twenty years ago in (1974)
[34] Luhmann, 1971, 33
[35] Heller, 1988, p 197

This assimilation of the extra-ordinary to the ordinary, of that which defies the context to that which qualifies it, places a wooden hand on the possibility to politicise and contest.

In the process of arguing against the republican containment thesis, I have focused this final argument on the republican's use, implicit or explicit, of the CLS strategy of 'immanent critique'. Admittedly the republican debt to Critical Legal doctrine is both tentative and often unacknowledged, and while the affinities of Michelman's or Sunstein's arguments with Unger's are many, Unger and Dworkin may justifiably appear as very strange bedfellows. In any case, the inclusion of Unger's argument here is not incidental or dependent on acknowledged debts or obvious affinities, but on the following two factors. Firstly that critical theory, when employed, strengthens the republican position and thus allows it to be seen in its best light. Secondly, that Unger's is itself a powerful version of the law-as-politics position, in so far as he vests in law the possibility to pursue radical politics and counter the 'false necessity' of the confinement of our political vision within rigid institutional assumptions. So, while not sharing much of the republican vocabulary, he too gives his politics legal leverage.

My argument has been the following. The republican/CLS position presents an argument to the effect that it is false (falsely necessary) to view conflict as normalised in and by law. But this, I have claimed, elides the distinction between inertias. My argument is that whatever the merits of the thesis against the first form of inertia, it stumbles on the second form because the deep-structural reductions of the legal system cannot be negotiated away.

Where the law exhibits the overwhelming tendency to assimilate conflict within already existing schemata of processing it, the critical scholar will emphasise alternative possibilities, new relevancies and upset settled patterns. This is an effort to confront the inertia of the system; as such it does not simply fail to address the second type of 'normalisation' that comes from the system's 'constitutive reductions'; rather, it relies on them. The revolutionary idiom that accompanies much immanent critique actually blinkers the very real limitations within which the critique is undertaken. It aspires to be both structure-dependant and structure-defying. It draws this quality from the 'spirit' of law as a 'structure-denying structure.'[36] To deny law this potential would be to adhere to a disempowering 'structural' or 'institutional fetishism.'[37]

My argument here is that structural reductions cannot be employed and defied at once. To see them and then to defy them as constraining involves

---

[36] ibid, 575
[37] Unger, 1996, 19

stepping onto a different level from where one can observe the observation. But at the first-order level at which the legal achievement is effective, where complexity is reduced, and where the world becomes legally observable, the reduction cannot but remain a blindspot: it cannot be at once effected and observed. Thus there can be no structure-defying structures; the institution cannot see its blindspot and shake it off.

And as a result the impossible dilemma facing republican containment remains: If the institutional imagination is stretched too far what is eroded is the institutional achievement of disciplining double contingency and the definition of expectations in context (and there can be no other definition.) It is a fine line that needs to be discerned between expanding the boundaries of institutional imagination and acknowledging and respecting the existence of those boundaries. It is a fine line but it makes a world of difference. By treating the disjunction as false, eroding institutionalisation itself and defying the system's constitutive reductions, the republican containment thesis ceases to be a theory about law by giving up what is distinctive of law. The legal achievement ceases to be recognisable as such and law merges with the world.

If on the other hand the institutional achievement is respected, some mileage can be gained out of its imagination - mainly by exploiting possibilities of internal differentiation - but there are things that cannot be done. A system that makes sense of the world by reducing possible states, cannot account for a challenge that defies those reductions, because it is those reductions that first make that challenge meaningful. And what would 'structure-defying' challenges look like, how would the structure itself accommodate their expression? The asking price for a politics *of* law is that the legal structure in the situations that it structures is not itself put to the test.

In all, in dealing with the normalisation of conflict, Unger and the republicans are at one in advocating both the containment thesis and attributing to law the reflexivity that would allow it to do the job of politics. Immanent critique, deviationist doctrine, negative capability, disentrenchment, critical legal politics, are all supposed to furnish a language for political conflict that is uncompromising, that is able to institutionalise solidarity, and institutionally back any political claim without compromising it by normalising it. My argument has been that while, in principle at least, Unger and the republicans can thus counter one source of normalisation, simple inertia, their endeavour is less powerful than they think when it comes to deep-seeded structural inertia. In dealing with the simple inertia of law, I think they are right. There *is* transformative potential in law, doctrine *can* be manipulated, and to that extent transformative conflict *can* be harboured in law. But all this is only possible at the cost of cashing in on the transformative leeways the system itself provides, and thus of taking on board its main structural givens, its reduction-achievements. Political contestation as such cannot be accommodated in legal indeterminacy, because what is indeterminate is fixed by concepts and assumptions that frame it as such, what is contestable is partly given, as are the in-roads of critique, the slants of the discourse. Inroads of critique map onto given or possible variation. To register as critique something must first register as information. The improbabilities are already institutional and selections will be made within dilemmas already in place. Law's resistance at some level is unavoidable. We cannot, that is, defy its very reductions - reductions in all dimensions social (questions of identity - legal personality - and institutionalisation - co-expecting third parties), temporal (the question of normativity of law) and material (the very existence of legal roles, programmes and values), without losing sight of what is legally meaningful. Challenging the variables of observation successfully would do away with the very reduction-achievement that is law. The distinction needs to be kept constantly in view, between what is inert and thus challengeable, and what is resistant structurally, as in involution, and unchallengeable. As with every system there is a facilitative/confining tension here, between what the law permits us to observe and what it is blind to. The CLS, and following them the republicans, are surely right to suggest that the facilitative/confining balance can be exploited in the direction of the former; immanent critique makes law more aware of what is latent within it and thus less confining. But to identify the facilitative with the reflexive itself, either cloaks the confining moment which makes republicanism ideological, or collapses law into politics, sacrifices the former to the latter by doing away with its reduction-achievement that requires the confining moment, and makes republicanism, as a theory about *law*, self-defeating.

PART III

Reflexive Politics

CHAPTER FIFTEEN

THE EXCLUSIONARY AND THE REFLEXIVE

The concept of an 'exclusionary reason' was introduced by Joseph Raz in his important early work *Practical Reason and Norms*.[1] Having set the concept of a reason for action at the centre of practical philosophy, Raz draws an important distinction between first and second order reasons for actions. First-order reasons are reasons to perform an act; they go into a balance where their relative weights are decided. Second-order reasons are reasons to act for a reason. They may be positive (such as is a reason to act on the basis of the weightiest first-order reason) or negative (a reason not to act for a reason). The latter Raz terms *exclusionary*. An exclusionary reason provides a reason for not acting on the basis of a reason. Moreover, as Bankowski explains drawing on both Raz and Atiyah[2] 'we treat this reason as conclusive because it is there, we do not need to inquire behind it.'[3]

An exclusionary reason stands in for the background arguments that justify it, and moreover prevents recourse to those arguments. If Ann, to take Raz's example,[4] has decided not to make financial decisions when she is fatigued, her regarding that as a reason for disregarding other reasons for action is what makes it exclusionary. A particular financial case is not weighed up on its merits against the fatigue (conflict of first- and second-order reasons); the balancing is simply cancelled.

It is not as arbitrary as it may seem at first, that Raz asserts as a general principle of practical reasoning that exclusionary reasons always prevail.[5] As Shiner put it, even a much less controversial principle like 'one ought, all things considered, always to act for an undefeated reason'[6] would have the same effect given Raz's set-up of competition and defeasability of reasons. Raz then claims that the concept of an exclusionary reason is vital in distinguishing rules from other non-rule reasons[7] and that the exclusionary

---

[1] First published in 1975, now 2nd ed, 1990. All references to this edition
[2] Atiyah, 1986.
[3] Raz, 1991, 103
[4] ibid., 38
[5] Raz, 1990, 40
[6] Shiner, 1992, 7
[7] Raz, 1990, 51

function is distinctive of, among others, roles,[8] legal rules[9] and legal systems.[10] In all of these, balancing of first-order reasons is blocked.

This 'blocking' effect is of great value, it is greatly *facilitative* for practical reasoning. It insulates our decision-making from always needing to take on board all the considerations that inform all reasons. There are obvious advantages to such 'blocking'. Most significantly we can thereby entrench and prioritise the reasons that we value most; by having backed them with the formal trumping effect of the exclusionary, our decision-making is greatly facilitated. In the case of law, for example, the exclusionary effect allows the decision to be made at the level of formal reasoning ('because the law says so'), rather than the substantive level ('the reasons behind the law saying so.')

There are gains but there are losses too. Having entrenched the reason for action at the exclusionary level how easy is it to dis-entrench and revise it? Whatever else has been said and written about exclusionary reasons, it is the question of *revisability* that is the most intriguing and difficult one, and certainly the one most crucial to the present discussion. As we said, the exclusionary function is to entrench certain reasons for action at a level where first-order reasons cannot defeat them. The exclusionary reason elevates certain reasons over and above competition and also significantly stands in for those reasons. By raising certain first-order reasons over and above competition, the competing reasons are outweighed by kind. By standing in for the reasons it entrenches, these too are displaced from the balance of reasons at the exclusionary level. What does this mean? It means crucially that unlike first order reasons, second-order reasons can never be in conflict with the first order reasons they either exclude or entrench. The balancing process itself is displaced. How would one go about (or even think about) revising the exclusionary reason? Certainly not by resurrecting first-order reasons. These, as we said are invisible at the exclusionary level, having either been excluded by kind or substituted (entrenched). Therefore, 'inquiring behind the exclusionary reason,' lifting the lid, as it were, to look at how the balance stands now, is not possible in a way that resurrects the initial (first-order) balance. Because, first, we would not know **when** to lift the lid. We can no longer see when a first-order reason increases its weight because the first order reasons cannot make their presence felt at the exclusionary level. But even conceding that, to assume that a first-order reason of increased weight now forces us to revise our exclusionary reason would be assuming that which the theory tells us is impossible. Because to

---

[8] ibid., 196
[9] ibid., 144
[10] ibid., 139

allow that competition, would turn the second-order reason into a first-order one and would thus cancel out the novelty and heuristic value of Raz's schema. Instead, revisability of exclusionary reasons is a process with a rationality of its own, which has nothing to do with the now displaced first-order balancings. If Ann decides to waive her exclusionary reason of fatigue before a trivial financial decision, it is not (nor could it be) that new convincing first-order reasons have shown up; instead it is a balance of different (second-order) reasons, at the second-order level, that decides that the exclusionary function is not worth sticking to. ('I can make trivial decisions even when I'm tired' is a second-order waiver. The impossible first-second order competition is of the type 'should I make favourable trivial investment x or am I too tired?')

To use an example that I will visit again soon at greater length, marriage provides an exclusionary entrenched repertoire of reasons for action. Atiyah uses the example to show that the reasons that inform certain patterns of interaction between lovers become entrenched by marriage into rules that inform the marital interaction. Substantive reasons for action are temporarily, says Atiyah, 'frozen' into formal rules that facilitate decision-making. But should these formal rules cease to mirror their underlying substantive reasons, they will be revised in the light of the latter. There is, for Atiyah, a dialectic between formal and substantive. We allow that the substantive reasons for a decision are subsumed under formal exclusionary ones; the latter will inform our decision-making only insofar as the substantive reasons entrenched at the formal level remain significant. Shauer seconds the value of that dialectic

'[i]nsofar as it is possible for an exclusionary reason to tell an agent to look just quickly, if possible, at the excluded first order reason to see if this is one of the cases in which the exclusion of that factor should be disregarded ...'[11]

Bankowski renews this line of accounting for the dialectic, with a recourse to Fuller's distinction between the moralities of 'duty' and 'aspiration'.[12] The legal rule fixes the substantive reason that is the site of aspiration at a certain formal minimum threshold of duty. But the substantive aspiration continues to inform the formal duty and will force it into revision (or new interpretations) should the aspiration no longer adequately underlie the duty. Of course, therefore, marriage provides rules for love. But in the absence of aspiration behind them those rules would be meaningless. No one has learnt how to love on the basis of rules, rules do not make love meaningful. And

---

[11] Schauer, 1991, 91
[12] Bankowski, 1991, passim, 1993, 49-51

should they cease to mirror the aspiration they will become an empty shell in need of revision.

This is my query and my objection then: how will the signal that revision is needed be received at the exclusionary level given that first-order reasons no longer resound at that level, by the very nature of a reason as exclusionary? Because, put simply, dealing at the formal level forbids recourse to the substantive level.[13] The formal-substantive dialectic is impossible. Raz stresses this again and again: valid exclusionary reasons defeat the first-order reasons within their exclusionary scope. But the defeat is not the upshot of their relative weighting:

'the strength of the exclusionary reason is not put to the test in [conflicts with first order reasons]; it prevails in virtue of being a reason of higher order.'[14]

What would have driven us to revise the exclusionary reason, on the accounts of Atiyah, Schauer and Bankowski, would be an upset of the balance of first-order reasons; powerful counter-reasons would outweigh the entrenched ones. But the exclusionary level remains immune to such upsets because counter-vailing first order reasons cannot challenge exclusionary ones. In that, exclusionary reasons displace the balancing process itself. Revisability has been cut off from the concerns that informed the entrenchment of a reason as exclusionary in the first place.

This impossibility of a competition between reasons of different orders is not a matter of definitional fiat. There can be little doubt that Raz has described quite precisely how exclusionary logic works by withdrawing rather than outweighing reasons. Unlike most of his critics I do not think that exclusionary reasons do not work; I rather think that they work too well. And that the flaws that critics attribute to the theory[15] as being unable to

---

[13] For an overview of some aspects of this interesting debate, see Edmundson (1993) Edmundson says: '[Exclusionary reasons] cannot therefore straightforwardly conflict with a first order reason to act' (337)

[14] Raz, 1990, 46

[15] Perry, for example writes: '[t]he two modes of reasons that Raz distinguishes can thus be regarded, in effect, as the two extremes of a continuum; at one end action is to be assessed on the basis of a balance of reasons in which no reason has been assigned anything other than ordinary weight, while at the other end action is to be assessed by a balance of reasons some of which have been assigned, on the basis of second order reasons, a non-ordinary weight of zero. Between these two extremes lies an indefinately large number of further possibilities, all of which are variations on the idea of a weighted balance of reasons.' (1987, 223) In this account, the specific nature of the exclusionary reason has disappeared, because Perry allows a reason to be assigned exclusionary function on the basis of substantive criteria. What this means is that there is always only a balance of substantive first order reasons amongst which certain of them, as weightier, displace others. This collapse of first- and second-order reasons

conceive of reasons on a continuum, are real problems of incommunicability and incommensurability of reasons in reality. For example: we resolve a moral dilemma and entrench our solution to the balancing at the formal exclusionary level as a legal rule. Let us take this exclusionary reason for action, this law, and inquire into its revisability. How do we decide that we need to go back to the first-order 'raw moral judgement'[16] waive its exclusionary function and re-think it in the light of first-order reasons? Typically because we perceive a regulatory failure. And how is such a failure perceived? Because at the formal level a signal is received that the legal rule is not performing. But is this really an indication that the outweighed moral reasons are suddenly important again? Or could it be that new reasons have arisen, some of them specifically legal in nature, tied to the function and performance of law, in a word formal rather than substantive countervailing reasons? Laws may need to be revised because judges cannot adjudicate them (the example of proportionality, recently), executives cannot adequately implement them or supervise their implementation. Laws need to be revised because they create new unforeseen pathologies and are revised to respond to these, and the revisions in turn may give rise to new pathologies and so on.[17] The argument that I oppose has to do with the alleged dialectic between formal and substantive; as I understand Raz's concept, formal reasons are not revised in the light of substantive reasons that they 'stand in' for and exclude, but other reasons that are formal too. Revisability is dictated by formal failures and in the direction that formal failures call for. At the individual level, too, how will I know that I need to rethink and revise, for example, my formal interest as a spouse? According to the logic of Atiyah, Schauer and Bankowski I will do it by suspending my role as a spouse - its exclusionary logic - and looking back to love, to see whether love dictates sticking to the exclusionary reason or not. But this is impossible for two reasons. First because as spouse I may never perceive my interests threatened (until it's too late probably) because love does not make its failures known in a way that is seen to affect interests. And more importantly because suspending the role even temporarily - looking behind the formal into the substantive - involves suspending also the very language of interests, duties, rights and so on, the very language, that is, in which a failure would have registered at all. Such suspensions are not merely improbable, they are impossible, as is the dialectic of formal and substantive. It is at this point that the theory of exclusionary reasons would benefit from systems theory. The

---

into 'variations of weighted balances of reasons' mis-reads what is specific about balances involving exclusionary reasons, where the assigning of a weight of zero is a formal property of reason, done by kind, not weight.

[16] MacCormick, 1989

[17] On this see literature on 'juridification'. For an overview, Teubner (1987).

theoretical disagreements over revisability that at present remain insoluble[18] (and the final word on which Raz has postponed to a future date in both his 'Facing Up'[19] and the postscript to his second edition of *Practical Reason*) would gain great leverage once it is understood with the help of systems theory that the variables that allow one to observe at the formal level are different and incompatible to those at the substantive level. Every role-taking is exclusionary and remains blind to every other. From the formal position of a specific role, one operates in a world that is exclusionary because as role-taker, for example, the spouse not only sees what s/he sees but also cannot see that s/he cannot see what s/he could have seen as lover. I will not say any more at this stage because we will return to love and marriage very soon.

I will not push this argument any further here however, because it will distract from points (1) & (2) that I would like to retain, and points (3) & (4) that I intend to prove:
1. That law, its rules and roles provide exclusionary reasons for action (to both the moral and political first-order reasons they entrench)
2. that exclusionary reasons are not revisable in the light of first-order reasons that they exclude
3. that as a direct consequence of (2), the containment thesis does not hold
4. that the exclusionary is the opposite of the reflexive

Let me merely recapitulate my argument about the revisability of exclusionary reasons and tie it in with my suggestion about the reflexive. This has immediate repercussions for the containment thesis. Were (legal) roles and rules as exclusionary able to allow for their own revisability in view of substantive moral and political concerns, if they could be revised in that light and their exclusionary function bracketed, diminished or dissolved, as the case may be, then containment would be possible. Because that would mean that in the balance of reasons, the second-order reason might be suspended momentarily and a glimpse allowed behind it to inquire whether the case at hand really requires the exclusionary function or whether the excluded considerations have now, for the case at hand and/or every future such case, become significant. In this way roles and rules that fix expectations in certain ways and prevent constant recourse back to the reasons for action they stand in for could be bracketed, the blocking effect suspended, the excluded, eliminated reasons rendered visible again. Were

---

[18] Also Schauer: 'The primary inconsistency appears to be in the way in which Raz takes exclusionary reasons as incapable of override ... He maintains that an uncancelled exclusionary reason will always prevail within its ambit.' (1991, 89)

[19] Raz (1989)

this possible, the containment thesis would have gained some mileage. If roles and rules are flexible in that way, then they only fix reasons under condition that there are no superior first order reasons why things shouldn't be thus fixed. If this were the case, *political reflection* and questioning of roles and rules would not be occluded or excluded in law by kind. The law would always be open to weighing up the reasons thus put forward and to suspend or revise its own exclusionary categories. But this is impossible. Of course roles and rules are revised, the exclusionary function lifted in the process. But the reasons why we may revise an exclusionary reason are not the reasons that might have outweighed it in a conflict of first- and second-order reasons. Such conflicts are impossible because of the nature of exclusionary reasons. The law does not contain the possibility of such a challenge. In being exclusionary it is not *reflexive* in the way that I will now argue politics is.

CHAPTER SIXTEEN

Theories of Political Reflexivity

Elements of political reflexivity are to be found throughout the body of political theory. I will pursue the argument about 'reflexive politics', first of all, by relying on - but also criticising - theories that, I have found, contain elements of reflexivity. This section retraces those debts.

The theorists I will focus on are four: Cover, Lyotard, Unger and Luhmann. This choice of focus leaves out many others. William Connolly, for example, has dedicated much of his recent writings to attempting to secure a space for ambiguity in democratic politics so as to prevent political practice from reproducing discourses of control, perpetuating closure around stable patterns.[1] Another of his recent books extends a more confident deconstructionist reading into the politics of identity.[2] Connolly is of course not alone in his preoccupation with political texts. Michael Shapiro explores how, in several texts he analyses, fundamental assumptions are built into narrative structures so that the purported findings are already prefigured in the texts' discursive modalities.[3] The first moment of reflexivity - that of upsetting settled meaning - is well captured in deconstruction.

Connolly's early work on 'essentially contested concepts'[4] is even more relevant to a thesis of reflexive politics. The main idea here is that concepts are not (what Lyotard would call) 'rigid designators' but are themselves ***politically negotiable***,[5] and thus are aspects of the reality they help shape. The central thesis of the book is insightful. Connolly says 'to examine and revise the terms of political discourse is not a prelude to politics but a dimension of politics itself.'[6] But this promise of a reflexive theory of politics is then more or less abandoned by Connolly. He takes his insight for granted and channels his efforts, instead, into probing the conventions governing the dominant concepts of our political discourse. There lie the limits of the value of his theory to the reflexive thesis.

---

[1] Connolly (1987)
[2] Connolly (1991)
[3] Shapiro (1988)
[4] A concept he borrows from Gallie (195?)
[5] 'Meaningfulness is constantly negotiated and is not just a simple communication of pre-existing meanings.' (Brigham, 1978, i)
[6] Connolly, 1987, 3

In many ways the reflexive thesis is a thesis about politics unbound (or 'absolute politics'.)[7] It can accommodate all challenges to existing political patterns that tend to normalise differences, but more importantly, can accommodate politics that claim new boundaries and new militancy and lay claim to new domains of the uncontested. Two elements have been mentioned so far and they will become, as re-stated in what follows, essential elements of the reflexive thesis. They are the *contingency* of possible political meanings and the notion that politics sets the *context* within which politics is possible. I take these as the two pillars of the reflexive thesis. To begin with we will draw support for both from existing theories and then attempt a re-statement from a systems-theoretical perspective.

ROBERT COVER: REFLEXIVITY AND ANARCHY

In the fourth thesis against republicanism,[8] it was argued that it is *a priori*, and thus anti-political according to the reflexive thesis, to view law as the community's definitive narrative. The republicans' assumption that law is constitutive of the texture of our communities, the language that articulates or contains political understandings and voices commitment, is thoroughly question-begging. Robert Cover's influential writings, paradoxically appealed to by the republicans themselves as a departure, anticipate a convincing critique of the containment thesis, while his anarchist strivings provide a tempting lead into the reflexive.

'We inhabit a nomos - a normative universe,' begins Cover. The nomos is normative, it is *a universe* and it is *particular*. It is normative because it is the domain of 'right and wrong, of lawful and unlawful, of valid and void.'[9] It is a universe in that we inhabit the world of meaning in the same way as we inhabit the physical world. Discourse plays the key role here for Cover. The nomos exists as discourse. Discourse creates 'history and destiny, beginning and end, explanation and purpose.'[10] Discourse cannot be private, it requires the community. For Cover 'the scope of the community of

---

[7] See Pizzorno for an attempt to define the features of "absolute politics". He says: 'Behind the idea of politics having boundaries, and of these dilating and contracting, it is not hard to discover the image of a state of affairs - and the hope of or terror of it - where no boundaries at all are set around the practice of political commitment and the exercise of political will. Everything social would then be placed *sub specie politicae*, interpreted through politics and seen as transformable by politics.' (1987, 27)
[8] Above chapter eleven
[9] Cover, 1983, 4
[10] ibid., 5

discourse defines the scope of the universe that is the nomos.'[11] At the heart of the universe lies particularity. A particular community's discourse is a narrative that produces a meaningful history, offering 'an explanation or purpose' of the social life the community has found itself leading and to have led. In the future tense, this rationalisation projects meaning into future possible trajectories.

However interesting this all is, none of it is yet particularly novel, nor is it very far from what the republicans themselves claim. Their talk of a fund of possible meanings is tied to particular communities, they too borrow terms like 'universe of meaning' and are attuned to the vocabulary of historical narratives. The novelty of Cover's work and the decisive breaking point with republicanism is the **anarchist** moment. Cover says: 'the nomos that I have described requires no state.'[12]

Cover's nomos is no state law, his community maps onto no citizenry. This underlies the inspiration of his work, and is the reason why he introduces his rather elaborate distinctions between the 'jurisgenic' (remember Michelman) and the 'jurispathic', the 'paideic' universe of the 'nomos' and the violence of the 'imperial'. For Cover, law is a 'resource of signification' but as a resource it is not yet a nomos, a community is not yet consolidable around it.[13] In a strange way the point is not to create law but to limit it. By limiting it a community articulates its own particular *nomos*. What the republicans do is understand the process as an integration, not a limiting. For them various *nomoi* are integrated as communities negotiate the meaning of state law. The citizenry becomes a community in the sharing of state law-as-nomos that integrates and thus contains the variety of particular *nomoi*. But this turns Cover's argument into its opposite, turns the 'paideic' into the 'imperialistic', the *nomos* into state law, and in the process destroys the anarchist linchpin of the theory. What the republicans would claim is integration in fact destroys what was constitutive about the way the *nomos* upheld a community (the 'paideic' function). In litigating constitutive differences, the 'jurisgenic' turns 'jurispathic'. Litigation is 'imperial' control of the anarchy of legal meaning. The fragile community exists in articulating its nomos, and, significantly, is created and dissolved at every moment of social life because the nomos that constitutes it and is constituted by it is dynamic, it exists in time. The infinitely delicate process of the production and reproduction of moral life is destroyed in the republican retelling of Cover's arguments. What is destroyed is the *reflexive* moment, that, in Cover, is tied to the anarchist moment, and to which we now turn.

---

[11] Kahn, 1989, 58

[12] Cover, 1983, 11

[13] Luhmann would express this in terms of loose and strict coupling, 1986e, 208-9

'The narratives that create and reveal the patterns of commitment, resistance and understanding ... are radically uncontrolled,' says Cover.[14] Litigating narratives does not integrate them but suppresses their wealth of possibilities. The courts' authority, he says, [15] comes from a unique power to deny other meanings. 'By exercising its superior brute force ... the agency of state law shuts down the creative hermeneutic of principle that is spread throughout our communities.'[16] Law is the violence of the 'jurispathic'. The spontaneous orders of the diverse *nomoi*, the reflexive diversity, cannot survive its passage into state law. In Cover there is a disjunction between state law and nomos where the republicans see a convergence.[17] Cover's reflexive 'hermeneutic of principle' is the moment of the coming about of community around a political/ethical understanding both capable of upholding a commitment, and dynamic, always potentially disruptable internally: and with no measure of authority, force, persuasion and violence capable of upholding it externally.

This recourse to Cover has been important for a number of reasons. First because the usurpation of his argument needs to be resisted; the republicans' unanimous allusion to him, quite strikingly, downplays the driving force of his argument. The republicans have heavily drawn on the inventory of his terms and relied on his formulations. This proximity brings out the irony. The value of Cover's theory for a theory of reflexive politics is the anarchist moment. The disjunction he describes between the anarchy of community and the function of law is evidence of the impossibility of containment of the former in the latter, ironically the very thing republicans appeal to Cover in order to establish.

JEAN-FRANÇOIS LYOTARD: REFLEXIVITY AS THE THREAT OF THE DIFFÉREND

Lyotard ties his account of the political with his notion of the différend and defines politics as 'the threat of the différend.'[18] We will revisit briefly his analysis of meaning-in-linkage and the différend as what resists this, and

---

[14] Cover, 1983, 17

[15] He stresses this particularly in 1986, 1601

[16] Cover, 1983, 44

[17] Tushnet says: 'Cover is [...] thoroughgoing in his anarchism. His argument includes the premises that law-creation is community-building and that law-creation involves violence. He fails to discuss the inference that follows from these premises: community-building involves violence too.' (1988, p155)

[18] Lyotard, 1988, 190

relate the political-as-différend with containment, on the one hand, with reflexivity on the other.

Central to Lyotard's account of politics in both (1986) and in (1988) is the notion of linkage. The meaning of a sentence, Lyotard has explained, only comes about in linkage with other event-sentences that precede it and absorb it into a genre. Meaning is in linkage and possibilities of linkage are provided in and as genres. A genre is attached to a 'goal', it is teleologically driven, and thus invites certain linkages of sentences in view of that goal. The eventhood or singularity of the sentence is destroyed in this absorption. The différend appears in Lyotard's work as the unspeakable resistance, that which cannot be addressed in itself by us competent speakers, who are always-already employing genres.

I take it from Lyotard that this is the point at which real politics begins, in standing back, before the genre, to capture the eventhood of the sentence, at the point at which the different, incongruous, heterogeneous is not yet rendered the same, congruent, homogenous. The task of politics is to uncover the logic that homogenises, the logic of absorption. Because, says Lyotard, referring to Heidegger,

'[e]very sentence is in principle what is at stake in a différend between genres of discourse. The différend proceeds from the question, which accompanies any sentence, of how to link onto it ... There are différends because, or like, there is Ereignis. But that's forgotten as much as possible: genres of discourse are modes of forgetting the occurrence, they fill the void between the sentences ...'[19]

The task that Lyotard sets for himself is that of making politics reflexive in a way that would allow the différend to surface. The first step is to incorporate the disruptive moment as essential to politics itself:

'There is no politics if there is not ... a questioning of existing institutions, a project to improve them, to make them more just. This means that all politics implies the prescription of doing something else than what is.'[20]

There is disruption here but it does not yet go deep enough; Lyotard is here still talking about prescriptions, about rationalising genres. In *Just Gaming*, Lyotard describes politics as the formulation and pursuit of prescriptions with no recourse to a metalanguage that could settle differences between prescriptions. The political, like the ethical and the aesthetic, neither admit a metalanguage above them nor are they themselves metalanguages. All three

---

[19] ibid., 188
[20] Lyotard, 1986, 23

are realms of indeterminate judgement. The idea of Justice becomes the 'multiplicity of justices' and the 'justice of their multiplicity.'[21]

With *Le Différend*, Lyotard is able to enrich and qualify his ideal of the political, through recourse to a new central category:

'Were politics a genre, and were that genre to pretend [purport?] to that supreme status, its vanity would be quickly revealed. *Politics however is the threat of the différend*. It is not a genre it is the multiplicity of genres, the diversity of ends, and par excellence, the question of linkage. It plunges into the emptiness where 'it happens that ... ' It is, if you will, the state of language but it is not a language. Politics consists in the fact that language is not a language, but sentences, or that Being is not Being, but There is's. It is tantamount to being that is not. It is one of its names.'[22]

If Lyotard founds his notion of the political on the idea of disruption, it is because he seeks a politics that can resist its confinement to a determined game. Having developed the connection between genre, linkage and the différend, he can now make more concrete the logic of disruption. His theory of politics needs to be attuned to and become attentive to the possibility of resistance to what and how things become negotiated in litigation. So politics now becomes the art of différends, and the possibilities of disruption are oriented to what is communicable as commensurable and what is suppressed as incommensurable within the communicative processes and the consequent limitations of linkage possibilities. In the process, the uncovering of the différend becomes the privileged site of politics (or philosophical politics as Lyotard occasionally terms it.) Accompanying every prescription is the awareness that things could be otherwise; but more than that, accompanying every observation or, more closely to Lyotard,[23] every representation is the awareness of what is suppressed. Politics is caught up in that necessary and impossible dilemma that we have to 'represent yet must not represent,' because to state what the case is and what must be done testifies to the suppressed différend. Politics is the openness to the différend. Thinking politically involves our constant placing of what politics means at risk. The latter is precisely what I take reflexive politics to mean. But I will turn to systems theory to provide the best defence of the thesis, because, while

---

[21] Lyotard, 1986, 100. Sam Weber, predictably to some extent, warns that Lyotard runs the risk here of superimposing the meta-prescription 'be plural' to politics and doing precisely what his own ideal of agonistics disallows (1986) Also, Nancy argues that as an idea of plurality, justice is still brought under a unifying moment. (1985, pp47-8)
[22] Lyotard, 1988, 190
[23] See his (1983)

Lyotard's formulation of the thesis is most powerful, he himself pulls the ground from underneath any possibility to achieve it. Why? Because to articulate politics always-already means having suppressed the différend. Politics is always only a potentiality; to observe and state what is political is always-already anti-political.[24]

Lyotard's politics as an art of différends becomes the very impossibility of containment of politics in law. His challenge has not gone unanswered. From the opposite direction to mine, it is Seyla Benhabib that most directly undertakes to refute Lyotard on behalf of the republicans and in favour of the containment thesis.

For Benhabib 'it is imperative that the politics of the différend not be settled beyond and at the margins of democratic politics.'[25] There is no reason, she claims, to doubt that the constitutional framework adequately provides the processes that will contain our democratic deliberation and negotiation of political statements. If Lyotard cannot see this it is because he has paid insufficient attention to the rational foundation of the democratic form of government. She accuses him of reading political phenomena through 'a limit condition: an extraordinary and foundational moment.'[26] This reading she attributes to 'a general fascination with limit situations and extremes.' Benhabib continues, quoting Richard Wolin:

'[This] is an interest in transposing the fundamental experiences of aesthetic modernity - shock, disruption, experiential immediacy ... - to the plane of everyday life.'[27]

But there is something 'remarkably brief, impatient, almost staccato' about Lyotard's 'limit situations' argues Benhabib.

'The premise of the absolute heterogeneity and incommensurability of discourses is never argued for; it is simply posited ... It is a mood of deconstruction, destabilization, rupture and fracture ... Lyotard never distinguishes between incommensurabilty, heterogeneity, incompatibility and untranslateability ...'[28]

Incommensurability is the central epistemic premise of Lyotard's philosophy of language as well as politics, and also its weakest, says Benhabib. 'Caught in that mood', she concludes,

---

[24] In a similar vein, but in relation to justice, Nancy (1985) describes Lyotard's notion of as one that cannot itself be phrased, cannot be 'brought to sentence'.
[25] Benhabib, 1994, 2
[26] ibid., 5
[27] ibid
[28] ibid.

'Lyotard disregards the institutional mechanisms whereby constitutional traditions enable democracies to correct, to limit and to ameliorate ... the arbitrary formation of normatives.'[29]

This last formulation is a moment of high republicanism, a powerful restatement of the containment thesis. Benhabib is driven by the 'imperative' to contain 'the politics of the différend' within 'democratic politics.'[30] She goes on to elaborate a theory of republican politics, wherein the deliberative processes of the public sphere 'let the différend appear, and which do not oppress and stifle it.' 'Must such politics be located ... at the margins, at the limits and extremes of the process alone?' she asks. She answers in the negative and pursues a republican theory of strong democracy[31] to answer Lyotard's politics. Enough has been said already about the republican containment thesis to merit any further comment on Benhabib's analysis here.[32]

I think that while Benhabib falls into precisely the same mistakes as the other republicans in her prescriptions for containment, she is incidentally right about one thing, and this leads to my own doubts about the value of Lyotard's account as a theory of reflexive politics. It concerns the incommensurability thesis. Whatever the *teli* that differentiate genres from each other, Lyotard does not convincingly answer why it is that they establish incommunicability between regimes of sentences and genres of discourse. But even supposing that they do, why are moral, political and legal claims driven by different *teli* (and what are they)? So while Benhabib's argument is neither very original nor convincing, she is right in querying the incommunicability thesis.

The reason for seeking to ground a theory of reflexive politics in Luhmann's rather than Lyotard's theory has, to begin with, to do with the often vague and unhelpful rendering of the question of incommensurability. Where in Luhmann the differentiation of systems is structurally grounded, in Lyotard the differentiation of genres appears haphazard. Where Luhmann's systems have specific structural possibilities of observation and structural blindspots, Lyotard's analysis of genre-specific communication may just as appropriately

---

[29] ibid., 17
[30] ibid., 3
[31] The references to 'strong democracy' here and throughout are to Benjamin Barber (1984)
[32] Incidentally only, it is because the republicans do not have a theory about structural-institutional limitations on possible deliberation, and cannot see the distinction between inertias simple and structural, that they do not also see the threat that 'limit situations' pose to their theory.

be talked about in the softer terms of facilitation and hindrance. While their accounts of meaning in linkage appear very close, in Luhmann the specific logic of linkage is more thoroughly worked out. And where Luhmann accounts for differentiation on the basis of functional imperatives, Lyotard is again caught out without a differentiating principle that would make his theory sociologically interesting.

But throughout all this, there is an even more important reason for the recourse to Luhmann. Lyotard's 'philosophical' reflexive politics can only always remain a negation of linkage. His political statement can never be brought to sentence. Because to be articulated it must link up and therefore litigate the différend. The reflexive statement must remain tentative, unsaid, if it is to be true to the contingency of the political. Politics is the struggle of différends, and, by definition, différends must resist becoming reduced to a commensurable order, because that would imply that they have already been litigated over, straightjacketed to a specific order of linkage that alone allows communicability. As an art of différends, Lyotard's politics are always disrupting their own possibilities, his reflexive politics always in the negative, a statement only in the non-statement. *In Luhmann we will seek the possibility of a statement that is stated, but stated with an eye on its own contingency.*

ROBERTO UNGER: REFLEXIVITY AS NEGATIVE CAPABILITY

In one of his more polemical moments, Unger takes issue with the 'institutional' and 'structural fetishism' of 'deep structure theory', the unshakeable assumption that 'structures are structures.'[33] Structures, on this view, fix what can be understood as conflict into inflexible patterns. As 'formative contexts' they form routines of conflict. In 'deep structure theory' the distinction between the context that forms the routine and the routinised conflict itself is rigid and allows no dialectic. Unger queries this, as well as what results from it: that political conflict is channelled into either the routine activity that takes the context for granted or becomes a conflict over the context itself. To repeat, it is in his view narrow and disabling to present politics as the mutually exclusive possibilities of revolution or conservative tinkering.

Unger's solution to this 'false' dilemma is to loosen the distinction between context and routine. Deep-structure theory has no room for the possibility of 'revisability of the context from within.'[34] He groups the

---

[33] Unger, 1987a, 13
[34] ibid.

various possible strategies of disentrenchment of the formative contexts of social life as *negative capability*[35] and concludes that given 'the range of forms of empowerment, a cumulative move toward greater revisability is possible.'[36] Formative contexts are replaceable piece-by-piece.[37]

'The fighting that goes on within a stabilized social framework is only a more truncated version of broader and more intense struggles about the framework.'[38]
'We may [thus] be able to imagine ourselves more fully as the context-bound yet context-resistant and context-revising agents we really are.'[39]

But Unger refuses to see why his 'disentrenching' politics cannot do the work he wants them to.[40] Let us see why more closely. Unger likens the 'more truncated' conflicts *within*, with conflicts *about* the context, he juxtaposes context-bound, context-resistant and context-revising. How could this be? The answer, for Unger, lies in the logic of piece-by-piece disentrenchment, where 'the means [themselves] of stabilization generate opportunities for destabilization.' This is not unfamiliar, it underlies the logic of deviationist doctrine that plays up 'opportunities' of deviant reconstruction from within the body itself of law. After all, stresses Unger, 'to conceive of the ideal, ... is to conceive it from the standpoint of variation.'[41] But this surely is the story of 'simple inertia'.[42] Variation involves varying certain variables, it is a movement away from the fixed, only in terms of which it *is* a movement, a variation. Shifting variables involves keeping others constant. Unger says this too: '[R]evisions typically destabilize some parts of the established framework while strengthening

---

[35] 'All the varieties of empowerment seem to be connected in one way or another with the mastery the concept of disentrenchment describes. I call these varieties of empowerment "negative capability"' (1987b, 279)

[36] Unger, 1987a, 156

[37] ibid., 157

[38] ibid., 161

[39] ibid., 200

[40] Of course his suggestions re. structure-denying structures, of which destabilisation rights provide the obvious example, remain problematical for other reasons too. Not only because as Yack remarks, '[i]n the end Unger does not provide a single example of a structure-denying structure," but also because of a paradox: "If the structure-denying structure succeeds in promoting its own subversion, then it will be replaced and will disappear as a force in our lives. If it fails to promote its own subversion then it becomes mere constraint and needs to be evaluated as such.' (Yack, 1988, pp 1961, 1969, 1970)

[41] Unger, 1987a, 43. That something is from the point of view of how it could be different is of course a central assumption of systems-theoretical structural observation. But variation patters are guided by the system's constitutive reductions.

[42] See chapter fourteen above

others.'[43] But by conceding this, Unger is conceding too much. Variation makes sense only in terms of respecting the integrity of the context, an integrity that is re-instated with each variation. And what is impossible is that 'in the contest between the incongruous insight and the established context, *the context may go under.*'[44] It is impossible because what is 'incongruous' just as what is a 'variation', *is* such *given* the context. The contextual reduction of possible states is constitutive of the meaning of an incongruity. Were it not, what appears incongruous would not even register as such. The context does not go under, it remains there structurally inert to make sense of incongruity, challenge, resistance and conflict, contested and re-instated at the same time. Of course things change as incongruities show up. But none of these allow for *reflexive* revisions over the context, they allow only *systemic* revisions, revisions that are, in some deep-structural way, *context-bound*. Unger's eloquent statement that 'a truth [may be revealed] in the very fields that had no room for it'[45] is fundamentally misleading, not because a field conceals the truth, but because a field organises and undergirds a certain access to truth; and what cannot be seen cannot be seen.

The reflexive thesis that I suggest both draws from and argues against Unger's prescriptions for utopian politics. I have argued that Unger's emancipatory thesis is untenable because his politics sooner or later stumble on the institutional threshold. Resistance to the context cannot be context-bound. The terms of closure cannot be resisted, since, in Luhmann's terms, it is that closure that allows cognitive openness, and thus also Unger's 'cognitive access to one another.' I have argued this above and will say nothing more on it just now. Unger himself would not be too unhappy in principle that from a systems-theoretical perspective his argument here appears unconvincing. Systems theory exhibits all the features he has attributed to 'deep-structure' theory which he vehemently rejects in favour of his own 'super-theory'. The difference between the two, as was said, turns on their respective attitudes toward the entrenched nature of institutional frameworks. Systems-theory sees conflict and change as possible only in variation from existing formative structures that reinstate the formative context even as they challenge it. In fact they are only acknowledged as challenges, as conflicts, through the structural assumptions they are meant to challenge. Unger deeply opposes this circumscription; for him the formed conflict may subvert the formative framework, and he occasionally even

---

[43] Unger, 1987a, 158

[44] ibid., 20, my emph.

[45] ibid.

talks of turning the formative structure into 'a structure of no structure.'[46] This 'transformative opportunity' I find fundamentally implausible and, with Luhmann, point again to a distinction between observers.

In all, the 'reflexivity' of Unger's politics of law remains problematical.
On the *positive* side, his theory has reflexive aspirations and his account of politics is that it is reflexive. There is, in Unger's work, an urgent emancipatory message. For Unger 'it's all politics' because society is an artefact and all that is social is contingent, challengeable, changeable. There is no aspect of social arrangements not open to revision. Even the definitions of what can be changed and the strategies we employ to effect change are in turn open to political scrutiny. 'Negative capability' underlies his radical project, as method of disentrenchment of whatever context becomes vested with false necessity. He proclaims the radical contingency of human experience and action. To understand society is to embrace that contingency, that Unger once most insightfully describes as 'seeing the settled from the side of the unsettled.'[47] (This we will soon see could be taken as the guiding distinction of reflexive politics.) In all this lies reflexivity, of which Unger's is a powerful and important re-statement. His theory aims to keep 'the context held up to light and treated for what it is: a context rather than a natural order.' His view of a political society is one in which 'people neither treat the conditional as unconditional nor fall to their knees as idolaters of the social world they inhabit.'[48] He seeks 'a society less hostage to itself.'[49] This oscillation between context-bound (the conditional) and context-challenging (refusing to be idolaters) may present a paradox: if all activity is contextual can all contexts be questioned? Unger's work can be seen as an attempt to expose this paradox as merely apparent. Because, according to Unger, all contexts can be questioned, disrupted, even overturned by activity that is both reflexive and contextual. I have argued against this possibility and treat the paradox as a real one. My suggestion is for a politics that is reflexive in a different way.[50]

---

[46] Unger, 1987a, 46 'Unger's structure-denying structures represent malleable or "plastic" constraints; but we should not confuse them with enabling constraints. His structures are, instead, self-subverting constraints. Enabling constraints increase our freedom and flexibility only if they bind us firmly in a particular sphere of activity. In contrast, Unger's structure-denying structures increase our freedom by providing a looser hold on the activities they themselves govern.' (Yack, 1988, p1968)
[47] Unger, 1987a, 18
[48] ibid., 45
[49] ibid.
[50] To all this, I suspect, Unger would say: by suggesting that the only challenge to the context can come from outside the context, you are reverting to the false necessity of revisionism or revolution. Given how systems-theory re-shuffles the coordinates of what counts as in and

My *dispute* with Unger is that in proclaiming contingency across the board he has lost sight of what makes reflexivity possible. Reflexive political contestation as such cannot be accommodated in legal indeterminacy, because what is challengeable in law is simultaneously fixed by concepts and assumptions that give rise to indeterminacies in the first place. To register as critique something must first register as information. What is contestable legally is in some part given. The improbabilities are already institutional and selections will be made within dilemmas already in place. What is context-bound is not context-resistant, what is thus fixed is not reflexive.

Our recourse to Luhmann was designed to bring the inescapable dilemma into relief. The distinction needs to be kept constantly in view, between what is inert and challengeable within the system, and what is resistant structurally and invisible to the system. As with every system there is a facilitative/confining tension here and Luhmann's redundancy/variety distinction captures precisely that tension. Unger is surely right to suggest that the facilitative/confining balance can be exploited in the direction of the former. Immanent critique makes law more aware of what is latent within it and thus less confining. But to identify the facilitative with the reflexive itself, either cloaks the confining moment which makes the theory ideological, or collapses law into politics, sacrifices the former to the latter and makes the theory, as a theory about *law*, self-defeating.

My disagreement, thus, with Unger is that in proclaiming contingency across the board he has lost sight of what makes legal as opposed to political reflexivity possible. There is deep, structural necessity in all facets of social life and at the same time there is extreme contingency. Not because, as Unger says, constraints are falsely necessary. But because what one institutional mapping of reality compels one way, another mapping allows another way. Here reside the possibilities that systems theory has to offer, and I can only begin to allude to them here. Reflexivity involves stepping out of the institutional closure and querying from an observer's position the terms of closure and the shape of contingency. Contingencies are fixed by systems but in the absence of meta-systems and privileged sites of observation, fixed contingencies appear contingent. That is what makes contingency an 'eigenvalue' of our society, as Luhmann recently put it.[51] That, I believe, is how reflexive politics would be stated from the point of view of systems theory. To understand systems theory as critical theory in this way, we will need to probe the dynamics of second-order observation. We will turn to

---

what out of the context, and given the limits of what may be challenged from within, this may not be that interesting an objection. What is interesting is how Unger's reflexive thesis may be re-stated from a systems-theoretical perspective.

[51] Luhmann, 1992a

Luhmann again to argue both with him and against him for a theory of reflexive politics that draws on the possibilities of second-order observation.

CHAPTER SEVENTEEN

LUHMANN ON POLITICAL REFLEXIVITY

The philosophers have only interpreted the world, in various ways;
the point is to change it.
(Marx)

Niklas Luhmann's systems theory may seem an unlikely basis for a theory of reflexive politics and indeed to attempt to establish him as critical theorist flies in the face of much conventional categorisation in social theory today. His writings appear deeply incompatible with utopian theorising. Where Unger proclaims his theory's deep commitment to breaking through the 'compulsive routines' that prevent us from seeing society as an artefact, Luhmann advances an unnecessary[1] contradistinction: 'If we presuppose society as it is the only thing we can do is to conserve it.'[2] There is little room for a break from political necessity here, let alone a radical break carrying the utopian vision of reflexivity. To some extent this argument is warranted, and to that extent my argument will be a critique of Luhmann's account of the political system. But it is also *from within* the theory of autopoiesis that I will argue that things could be seen differently. There is, therefore, throughout the argument **a double move**: *to draw on Luhmann and yet to contest his conclusions*. My argument for reflexive politics stands and falls on establishing this critical internal perspective, that allows systems theory to be undertaken as critical theory.

Luhmann's most consistent account of the political system can be found in his *Political Theory in the Welfare State*. Here Luhmann traces the evolution of the political system up to the current historical phase of a functionally differentiated society. The crux of his account is that the coding of power as 'Macht/Unmacht' (holding/not holding power or, governing/governed), that establishes the political system, received, under the democratic party-political pattern, a 'supercoding' in terms of a 'government/opposition' distinction. The codification was bifurcated at the top. This secondary (super-)coding historically acquired primacy over the original coding to the extent of rendering the original 'governed' a parasitic third. (Every coding is binary and cannot include third values). The

---

[1] The allusion is to Marx's 11th thesis on Feuerbach.
[2] Luhmann, 1988a, 28

'government/opposition' schema is the present historical constellation of the coding of the political system. From a difference between those who ruled and those who were ruled, the coding has shifted to a difference between those who are in government and those who seek to be, a situation further 'programmed'[3] by the structures of party politics and occasions of competition. With the shift, what can be understood as contingency in politics has also changed. The governed of the initial distinction have shifted to a position of third value that, as public opinion,[4] allows the system to 'asymmetricize' itself. As we have seen already, asymmetry is necessary to self-referential systems if they are to avoid tautologous operation. Complete self-referentiality precludes any capacity of external reference. If the system were unable to receive any stimulus from the environment it would become redundant; it would have no outward reach, nothing to permit it to get started, nothing to read as environment. In order to activate its categories (and apply its coding) it needs to sense environmental perturbations. To 'asymmetricise' is to acquire such sensitivity. Tautologous self-referentiality is refracted, 'interrupted' because through *public opinion* the system is able to establish the necessary reference to the environment (the necessary externalisation).[5] Observation of public opinion replaces any direct observation of the environment that autopoietically closed systems are not capable of. Autopoietic systems operate by projecting expectations and then reading their fulfilment or disappointment in environmental responses. Public opinion fulfils just that function for the political system. Public opinion functions as a matrix that reflects back to the political system demands to which the latter then responds. Opinion polls and electoral results measure the success of those responses. The political system 'sees' itself in the context it has itself set up as environment. Popular sovereignty, the cornerstone of constitutionalism, has never been so radically recast and so thoroughly debased. The sovereign electorate carries no will other than that, which in the institutional sites set up in official politics, 'carries itself'.

---

[3] I use the term in the technical theoretical sense it has in autopoietic theory, see 'excursus'

[4] Luhmann's analysis is in fact more complex than this (see his essay 'Political Theory in the Welfare State' (ch 2 of the book, 1990)). Here, the political system itself is internally differentiated into politics, governmental institutions and the public (citizenry, media, associations). These subsystems come to no direct contact and simply constitute environments for one another. This analysis is important because it allows us to see where this 'third value' we have been talking of, public opinion, is located precisely. It constitutes an internal environment for politics.

[5] Luhmann, 1990a, 45, 183

Having established that function for public opinion, ***democracy*** becomes, for Luhmann, the capacity of the political system to ***observe*** itself.[6] This follows unproblematically from the analysis above, if democracy is seen as providing the institutional vessel for public opinion. Indeed democracy voices that public opinion by providing the institutional transactions (elections) and other institutional means (rights of participation, freedom of the press to criticise the government, e.t.c.) of citizens' actions. Public opinion is institutionalised and reflects the message to the political system; to use Luhmann's metaphor, it holds up the mirror[7] for the political system's self-observation: '[p]olitics can only glimpse itself in the mirror of public opinion, embedded in the artificially chosen context of its own possibilities of movement.'[8] By reading in the environment a response to projected expectations (the success of a governmental program, the success of a strike against the government), the political system does more than simply evolve through a linking of real operations - it observes itself in the process. We can see this by re-emphasising the connection mentioned earlier between operation (a), observation (b) and self-observation (c). The political system submits the environment it observes (b) to real operations (a). In the process it is able to observe itself (c) (indicate itself) in those real operations, in the distinctions it employs to observe the environment. The environment (of political expectations and political action) is read through the construction of a medium in which the system reflects its own unity and identity.[9]

The inevitable conclusion that Luhmann's analysis leads us to is that the political intelligence of democracy - its sensitivity - is determined by and circumscribed by what the code 'government/opposition' can make visible. Only what affects and modifies the prospects of the government or opposition acquires political relevance. What can be politically observed is opened up and at the same time delimited by the conditioning difference. Possible movement, new

---

[6] ibid., 105

[7] For the mirror metaphor see Luhmann, 1990a, pp 176, 179, 216.

[8] ibid., 216

[9] We can recast all this in the language of 're-entry'. 'Re-entry' is the introduction of the system/environment distinction back into the system; the system is thereby capable of self-observation, of reflecting, that is, its own identity by distinguishing itself from the environment. With no external reference open to the autopoietic system, the operation is of course radically constructivist: the context in which the system situates its operation is artificial. The system reads environmental complexity and pressure in terms of public opinion, a reduction conducive to its code that allows it to (build up and) activate its categories to deal with it.

directions to be envisaged are thereby also circumscribed.[10] The political system's (self- and other-) observation is semanticised by the 'government/opposition' distinction, where public opinion provides the matrix for political reflection. Societal reactions are channelled as *stimuli*, in the sense described, and no break with this semantics can be envisaged because the political system cannot react to what it cannot see, to what it cannot give form.

Where does this leave the possibility of reflexive politics? Underlying the latter is a concern about what can and cannot be done politically, what can and cannot be challenged and changed. **Reflexive politics** proceeds on the premise that political action and political self-determination is a real possibility, not hedged in by what appears as natural, obvious or necessary. It consequently *allows a real possibility to contest what is political, to contest what is politically possible and to contest the terms themselves in which these questions are contested*. In this sense party-political democratic self-observation becomes the limiting condition; it circumscribes political communication to certain forms. The system's self-observation cannot transcend the conceptual space opened up by democracy's constitutive difference. The question for reflexive politics then becomes: can political discourse break from this limiting condition and *where will it seek the purchase point for such a task*? We saw that Luhmann painted a bleak picture in response: the conceptual space for political action is mapped out by the political system on the basis of the code; the alignment with this semantics is necessary. If we take this at face value, then the possibility of transcending the present political condition is already precluded since the contrast schema of the political code controls what is politically visible. Reflexive politics loses its defining feature if it is to be channelled into a dichotomy conducive to the perpetuation of existing schemata. The political actor's self-determination and the impetus of politics to break with constraint are countered at the root.

Once again the political language of New Social Movements provides an interesting example of reflexivity in at least the following sense: issues are now

---

[10] 'The attraction of attention, political selection and thematization of interests can be regulated only within the political system itself ... Whatever can become politically relevant results from a connection with what already possesses political relevance [the recursive linking of operations]. Whatever counts politically reproduces itself... politics conditions its own possibilities - and apparently becomes sensible [sensitive] thereby to what its environment offers or requires ... It combines sensibility to certain questions and total indifference towards everything else.' (Luhmann, 1990a, pp39-40)

being pursued as political that were previously perceived as natural, as non-political (e.g. environmental pollution and with it economic growth) and with them have emerged new forms of political mobilisation, new forms of assuming political identity, of locating the claim in a context of conflict, e.t.c. New social movements are collective actors whose repertoires of action and whose conflicts do not fit the existing channels of political organisation.[11] In this framework we will ask again: what it is that leads Luhmann to dismiss the political language of movements and consequently compels us to a restrictive framework of (means and objectives of) political action?

In *Ecological Communication* and later in *Risk* Luhmann discards even the efforts of the most moderate green pressure groups as ineffective. On the basis of his account of the differentiation in modern societies, Luhmann precludes the possibility that pressing ecological concerns, as expressed by these groups, can trigger any effective response on the part of social sub-systems. The political message cannot be picked up by the political, legal or economic subsystems because it finds no point of congruence with the semantics of functional subsystems that are geared to specific codings of communication. The discourse of movements either stimulates idiosyncratically drawn answers in the subsystems, or creates 'noise' too intense to be handled by them and thus leading to dysfunctionalities. The criterion of success is to cause 'resonance' in the political sub-system of society. On the basis of their inability to address the problems in system-specific ways, the political message of movements is deemed unsuccessful.[12] Ultimately, the reason New Social Movements fail is because they ignore functional differentiation by claiming the need to handle everything politically.

For Luhmann, who denies any primacy of the political sub-system, this 'expansive' understanding of politics may even become dangerous. It is true, says Luhmann, that traditionally it was in the political system that the possibility to represent society and to decide on behalf of society, was located. The historical transition from stratification to functional differentiation has changed all that. In the present historical condition no sub-system can be replaced or represented by any other and society is left without a centre, where political would identify with societal deliberation and where society would work out its

---

[11] See discussion in chapter thirteen
[12] For a similar discussion, see Teubner's concept of 'reflexive law'

self-determination.¹³ Functional sub-systems have made it impossible for society to maintain a discourse at its centre: to maintain, that is, a 'centering comprehension of the whole in self-knowledge.'

An attempt to reclaim primacy for the political is bound to fail in a world that has lost this site for *Vernunft* - the privileged site for self-understanding or for collective rationality (in the Habermassian vein). Such a privileged *locus* is forever undermined by the irreconcilability of differences which, as codes, allow differing system accounts of reality. Any space for political praxis as envisaged by the movements has dispersed amidst this competition of accounts of reality and 'expansive politics' are deemed unsuccessful, ridiculed and discarded by Luhmann repeatedly as defying that dispersal. He says:

'Time and time again, political theory - from Hegel through Treitschke to Leo Strauss and Hannah Arendt - has tried to counter this diagnosis [the impossibility of the representation of the whole within itself] and to conceive politics as the guiding centre for everything that occurs in and with it.'[14]

'[T]he long standing premise of a kind of supremacy of politics over society, views de-politization as a misdirection and requires a kind of re-politization, either through participation or, where necessary, through violence.[15] ... The weakness of this concept ... lies ... above all in the lack of an adequate theory of society [that could account for the fact that] the unity of society no longer appears within society.'[16]

The contention is an alarming one, for the critique of society must be carried out within society. In view of the political system's obvious inability to voice that critique, and with alternative politics disarmed, Luhmann is left with one of two options:
- to ascribe societal crises to the overloading of the political system and to attempt a correction in terms of systemic 'performance',[17] or,

---

[13] 'Like Nicholas of Cusa's god, society is omnipresent in modern society, but nowhere in a particular, privileged way' (Luhmann, 1986a, 47) Also: 'There is no specifiable standpoint left from which the whole [of society] can be accurately observed' (Luhmann, 1984, 630)

[14] Luhmann, 1990a, 32

[15] This of course is not Arendt's view. For her revolution and war are in the "domain of violence" which is *anti-political* to the extent that it rules. This is also Offe's view, below.

[16] Luhmann, 1990a, 63. Also, pp102-103, pp235ff

[17] 'There are few bases for being able to radically change whatever society one is living in. There are many bases for making better use of its possibilities.' (Luhmann, 1986a, 48)

20 'Contingent is something that is neither necessary nor improbable; that which can be as it is, but is also possible differently.' (Luhmann, 1984, 152)

- to follow his line of argument to its bitter conclusion and to concede that while political rationality may have become more urgent, it has also become less likely.[18]

I suggest a simple formula to express my internal critical stance to Luhmann's account. Luhmann raises an objection against the notion that *'politics is everything'* and raises it in a way that occludes that there is a second, different notion at stake: that *'everything is politics'*. The latter is the idea, expounded by Unger and many others before him, that society in all its aspects is an artefact open to revision. The first notion, or so Luhmann claims, is that republican 'imperialist' position in political theory that claims that all social issues can be handled by the political system. It is this position that Luhmann directs his attack to. But he does this through a comprehensive rebuttal that rejects too much having addressed too little. It is the idea that 'everything is politics' that I want to rescue from Luhmann's treatment of the political system, and attempt to ground the 'reflexivity' of this notion, possibly in spite of Luhmann, in a systems-theoretical way.

To rebut the 'imperialist' claim that everything can be handled politically, Luhmann points to the condition of dispersed episteme that accompanies functional differentiation.[19] Societies, he argues against the republican tradition, have ceased to be politically constituted systems. Expansive politics presupposes a societal apex or centre and this centre has dispersed, today, amongst functionally differentiated, autopoietic systems. Therefore, with no archimedean

---

[18] ibid., 645

[19] It is in this light that we can now assess Luhmann's appeal not to attempt what he calls 'de-differentiation'. He has shown it to be both unsuccessful and dangerous. Unsuccessful because political demands in divergent political language that does not respect the political system's encodement, cannot, as a result be picked up by the political system (they do not resound). Consequently they appear as simple negation of the political system. In this latter sense they are also dangerous; not because they could actually bring about 'de-differentiation', but simply because, as they intensify, they may de-stabilize social structures and lead to societal breakdowns. But could it be also that the claim 'do not de-differentiate' is fallible from an 'internal point of view.' Because how are we to understand the source of this normative claim? As Reiner Grundmann has argued, this threat of societal breakdown can only be perceived by society as its own catastrophe. 'Luhmann, the sociologist, seems tempted to take the standpoint of society. But if he were to, he would be attempting something which, according to his theory, is impossible.' (1990, 40) Society cannot produce true self-descriptions at the comprehensive level. Every such attempt to articulate a moral or political claim at that level, as a self-reflexion of society, is ideological. Luhmann has himself pulled away any ground from underneath his claim against 'de-differentiation'.

point left outside sub-systems, there is no vantage point from which that expansive political/societal understanding can be articulated.[20] Luhmann maintains that in our present condition of dispersed episteme, the political actor is left with no purchase point from which to articulate an overall political *logos*. I argue for a political understanding that transcends the means that democratic party-political communication provides for self-reflexion *and yet* does not seek its purchase point in transcending irreconcilable system differences. I argue for opening up the code, itself, of political communication to political questioning. My approach to Luhmann is thus both critical and internal. Critical because Luhmann discards the possibility of reflexive politics on the basis of answering a different question. Internal because I attempt to ground the possibility of the argument for reflexive politics in Luhmann's own writings.

The argument for reflexive politics does not seek to ground political praxis on an intersystemic contact, on any rationality that transcends subrationalities. My argument is that an expansive understanding of politics need not be couched in the potential of such transcendence but can be accommodated within systems theory. To this effect I will draw on the main theoretical body of systems theory and more precisely on the following as are relevant to politics: (a) on *observations* and *blindspots*, (b) on *levels of observation*, (c) on the notion of the *rejection value*, (d) on the notion of *contingency* and self-reference and (e) on Luhmann's discussion of love in his excellent *Liebe als Passion*. The next three chapters, then, seek to integrate much of what has been said so far to advance a notion of politics that is **reflexive** in that it **cannot be contained** in law's **exclusionary** language, whose radical **contingency** as the expression of our freedom is **self-referentially** determined: what is political and what is politically possible becomes a political question.

---

[20] A vast amount of critique is focused in answering these conclusions of his, not least because Luhmann's writings owe much of their influence to the reaction they have triggered in the Frankfurt camp. In this confrontation, the antithesis is cast as system/lifeworld, autopoietic closure/ collective rationality: the debate between Luhmann and Habermas can be understood as respectively denying and asserting the possibility of communication occurring across the boundaries of system rationality. Whereas for Habermas, communicative rationality brings together claims from across society, for Luhmann, such a potential is countered by the semantic closure of autopoietic systems.

CHAPTER EIGHTEEN

ON LOVE, MARRIAGE, LAW AND POLITICS

Die Liebe existiert nur im noch nicht
(Luhmann)

Overshadowed by the momentous arguments of the Storrs lectures, Ackerman's analogy between citizenship and marriage has gone almost unnoticed. The extract has attracted little or no attention in the accumulating literature on civic republicanism. The oversight is regrettable. The analogy is ingenious; it fits surprisingly well at various levels of abstraction; it illustrates and familiarises the weighty claims. Indeed Ackerman could not have drawn the symmetry with more insight. However, in its ingenuity lies its danger; it highlights all too convincingly the deep paradox of the civic republican containment thesis, namely that of leaving politics behind in the name of politics.

Imagine, writes Ackerman, a place where the legal institution of marriage was unknown; imagine the couple's agonising over their decision to live together and their struggle to communicate to themselves and to others the special meanings they attached to their relationship. The legal institution of marriage provides a symbolic medium that

'immeasurably enhances the ongoing effort at communication ... *It provides a symbolic system which ... can give special meaning to a form of interaction and thereby constitute it as a special kind of community*, distinct from the *ordinary* relations of everyday personal existence.'[1]

This is all that Ackerman says about marriage and he is quick to point out the analogy with politics: 'Constitutional dualism provides a similar symbolic system in the public realm.'[2] As in the case of marriage, citizenship is a form of community first constituted in law, first constituted as legal. It is constituted in the sharing of a symbolic medium that provides political meanings that allow Americans to see themselves as citizens rather than private individuals. It is this assimilation of citizenship to marriage as the enhancement of lower-tier politics and 'ordinary personal relations' respectively, through the medium of law, that makes this analogy so fruitful a departure into the impossible dialectic between containment and reflexivity.

---

[1] Ackerman, 1984, 1042, my emphasis
[2] ibid.

THE FACILITATIVE SIDE OF MARRIAGE

That marriage makes a difference is not in dispute. Once institutionalised in this form, the union of the two partners is taken up as such for legal purposes and economic transactions, establishing assumptions of common parenthood, or assumptions behind notions like 'constructive trust', obligations of support (and alimony), re-aligning priorities of inheritance, succession, e.t.c. I will not dispute this, not so much because it is self-evidently true, but because it is irrelevant to both Ackerman's argument and mine. Both our arguments are about the sense of identity in community that makes a difference. With Ackerman, I will argue that marriage *does* make such a difference: in providing the partners with a whole new repertoire of possibilities associated with the roles of husband and wife; and in reflecting back to them, in the way of mirror, a picture of what they stand for in their relationship, that in turn allows them to re-adjust sentiments, assumptions and expectations of behaviour.

We will explore the difference that marriage makes more systematically. What is introduced with institutionalisation is a cluster of expectations of behaviour associated with the role of spouse. Ackerman is right that it is a 'new' picture. It is also a rather rigid and inflexible picture. This is not to say that everybody understands marriage in the same way and expects the same things. But to some extent at least the institution functions as a context that sets the parameters of what can be expected of each other within the relationship, establishing core and penumbra and marking out both the scope of variety and deviations as such. However critically the institution is approached, the forms into which behaviour and role (and the related expectations) are cast and frozen cannot all be challenged at once. Some must be taken on board if only to make sense of what is challenged each time; in order, that is, to map out the critical potential that the institution can release and accommodate.

There is in all this a substantive *facilitative* potential. The union of the partners does not have to be problematised, appealed to and confirmed at every corner of everyday interaction. Externally, toward third parties, it means that the spouses do not have to act out their love at all times; their decision to be married stands in for that. More importantly, to the partners themselves, it means that every decision that involves them both, from a financial decision to the choice of film they disagree about, does not become a question of the existence of love. Marriage provides an ***exclusionary reason*** that prevents this kind of problematisation.

In what follows I will explore how the concept of an exclusionary reason ties into and illuminates the love-marriage dialectic. Furthermore, I will explore how precisely it fulfils the aforementioned 'facilitative' function and what is sacrificed in the process.

Before this can be pursued, the section to follow will take us one step back in the argument, to trace the difference and incompatibility of love and marriage.[3] Indeed the argument from exclusionary reasons can only be made if the following two points are first proven:

a) that love and marriage present the partners with *different sets of reasons* to act (otherwise the one could not be exclusionary for the other in the first place) and further,

b) that these sets of reasons are *incommensurable*.

At the outset I need to anticipate a number of very crucial objections to the approach I intend to take:

i) Not for a moment am I suggesting that love and marriage cannot co-exist or indeed anything on the lines that 'marriage kills love.' That is why the 'experience' of marriage gives us very poor purchase into the contrast that appears in both Ackerman's analogy and my argument; it is undoubtedly the case that the 'experience of marriage' is usually informed by love. The counter-position I am suggesting treats marriage and love *as symbolic systems both availing languages to talk about the intimate relationship*. In contrasting them I am suggesting that they provide incompatible symbolic media in dealing with and communicating about and consolidating community between the partners. I am also arguing that they do not combine into any more comprehensive form and that neither carries the other onto higher ground.

ii) A second objection could be that, unlike Ackerman, I am employing an *a priori* impoverished concept of marriage. This is not so, I am employing a legal one. In doing so (as is also the case for objection (i) above) I am being true to Ackerman. I am not over-reading the legal premise into his theory. He is saying that the legal insitutionalisation of intimacy brings about the difference that makes a difference. It is the entry into the language of law - into marriage in the case of love, into constitutional politics in the case of politics - that Ackerman claims 'provides us with the missing language.'

iii) Finally it is not the case that I am employing an over-idealised concept of love. It is perfectly true that love crystallises into conventions that remove its romantic edge. However the potential to retrieve that edge and question

---

[3] My analysis in this section is heavily indebted to Luhmann's *Liebe als Passion* (1982(. Luhmann however does not aim to contra-distinguish love to marriage and is careful to historicise the development of the semantics of love. In that sense my argument does his injustice.

convention in the name of love suffices to legitimate the special argument I make for love.

THE INCOMPATIBILITIES OF LOVE AND MARRIAGE

In Madame de la Fayette's tribute to love,[4] her heroine, the Princesse de Clèves, refuses to marry because she has loved too much. That she had loved a man '[qu'elle] a cru si différent du reste des hommes, qu['elle se] trouve comme les autres femmes, étant si éloignée de leur resembler.' To protect the unique, unprecedented moment of love from trivialisation, she will refuse to be united in marriage. This motive, Luhmann suggests, is a motive of love, and

'love finds the motives for decisions in itself, not in marriage. Its claim to complete individualized uniqueness can only be expressed and registered in the extra-ordinary and only in negation, in renunciation.'[5]

The example points to a radical divergence between love and marriage.[6] We will trace the incompatibilities by distinguishing, for analytical reasons, within each of the settings of love and marriage areas and operational concepts that can be contrasted. This break-up into more elementary categories is fictitious I hasten to add. Although methodologically useful, it is unsatisfactory from one substantive point of view. It does injustice to the discourse of love by severing the interdependence of these areas, an interdependence that is constitutive of and at the basis of love's self-referentiality. It is this latter perhaps that throws into sharp relief the difference to marriage, in which these areas are clearly delineated. This however remains to be shown.

1) A first difference can be formulated as a question of ***attribution***. In love, positions of harmony and conflict can be attributed to the person that is

---

[4] Madame de la Fayette, *La Princesse de Cleves*, quoted in Luhmann, 1982, 124, n5.
[5] ibid. (my trans.)
[6] Such snapshot accounts of the semantics of love, peculiar to the time and the artistic form, may be thought unsuitable for sweeping generalisations. Luhmann is careful to distance his own exploration of the semantics of intimacy by historizing his account of the forms and 'cultural norms' by which emotions were felt. I have a legitimate reason for disregarding such subtlety. As Luhmann himself concedes, in the semantics of love today, distinctions and symbols from the past are operationalised anew, re-embedded and radicalised; and in the process, love, as never before, folds into a self-referentiality of its own, uncoupled from any direct control that would dictate the conditions of entering and developing the loving relationship. (1982, 201 and ch 15 passim).

loved, in marriage to behaviour or role. Roles are mediating structures that allow conflict to be accommodated at the level of what is expected of one institutionally: 'a husband ought not to behave so', 'mutual trust is the basis of marriage'. Marriage accommodates the attribution of behaviour to roles and reproduces expectations that pertain to institutional role. It furnishes positions of conflict and harmony that are institutionally pre- programmed. It attributes action and responsibility to these institutional self-descriptions. On the basis of this it produces expectations, the fulfilment and disappointment of which allows further expectations to be projected, informed by new positions of readjustment of the structures.

No such mediating structures are operative in the relationship of love. Attribution can only be directed to the person, and that means the person as lover. No external measure of disappointment or fulfilment can be derived from role. Every action of the beloved is judged in terms of its contribution to the enhancement of love and thus every assessment has to take on board the whole disposition of that person; no intermediate level attributions, then, no avoiding the ultimate questions.

2) A second point of divergence is relative to how the relationship is thematised in marriage and love. Marriage operates a cluster of *rights*, and *interests* fulfil a double role of being both vested in those rights as well as determining how those rights are to be upheld, weighed or traded. As a legal relationship marriage can only conceptualise the relationship in terms of those categories. The partners' relationship to one another is understood in those terms. Relative positions are fixed not least by bargaining in the shadow of divorce.[7] Sexuality is thematised into marriage as a right, in the light of the invisibility (until recently in certain jurisdictions) of rape in marriage, or the grounding of a reason for divorce (in certain jurisdictions) in the case of repeated refusal of sexual intercourse. There is enough evidence in all this to avoid going into rights of access to economic finances, right of support and maintenance, rights to and of access to offspring, e.t.c.

The relationship of love is not thematised in a similar way. Interests are nonsensical concepts here or, if we *have* to speak in their terms, it is only by stretching them beyond recognition that we can identify an interest in the

---

[7] There are obvious analogies with 'limit situations' in politics (Benhabib, 1994, 17) and constitutional politics (crises of constitutional continuity - see Carl Schmitt here among others - and the question of sedition above) that I have discussed in their own right, outwith this analogy. But the 'in the shadow of divorce' argument gives us a fine opportunity to address how the *modalities of time* vary between reasons advanced from the divorce perspective and those from love. In the first case one argues from the point of view of the future pathology or end as to what constitutes a valid present reason, in the second one argues from the present with a view to a future that is always open, always tending to future expansion. The difference in time modalities can be designated as that between the present/future and the future/present.

enhancement of love. Relative positions are not fixed through interests because sacrifice (of an interest) is conducive to love for the partner performing it; the loss is then a gain as it is conducive to love in love's self-referential cycle. Also, unlike marriage, love allows no bargaining positions under the threat of termination, because such a threat to stop loving is an indication that love has already evaporated, and therefore carries no bargaining power; to take the threat seriously already presupposes accepting that the beloved no longer loves. The terms 'right' and 'interest' lose their co-ordinates and may as well be abandoned, for, in Luhmann's telling phrase, 'interests are impossible in love because both one's profits and one's losses are enjoyed.'[8]

3) Proceeding from the premise that identities are not fixed in a transcendental way, but are relational, we can formulate another important difference in **the construction of identity** in marriage and love. In marriage, identity is 'legal personality', a pivotal point for the attribution of rights and duties and the precondition for operationalising them. The legal relationship is formed along the personality/rights axis that defines both what can be done in marriage and how the subjects stand towards one another.[9]

In love, relational identity is so cast as to be absorbed into the relationship in a way that uncouples it from any external premise. As Luhmann has argued not only the beloved's action but also the beloved's experience serves as the horizon for the lover's experience and action.[10] The world makes sense to the lover in terms of the beloved's experience of it. This reliance on the partner as the mediator between the self and the world[11] radicalises the relational aspect of the construction of identity in a way that is not true for marriage. Experience of the world means experience in terms of sharing it, and as everything acquires relevance for the person in terms of it enhancing love, identity must be conceived as dynamic, as growing through love.

4) One can extend the analysis of rights to include the incompatibility of love with *duty*. Whereas the performance of duty is only the flip-side of rights and thus inherent in marriage, nothing could be further from love than to act

---

[8] Luhmann, 1982, 83
[9] See the discussion of 'roles' in chapter nine.
[10] ibid., 18, ch2 passim and ps 26ff, 219ff
[11] Of Nadja, Breton says: 'Even while I am close to her, I am closer to the things that are close to her' (Breton, *Nadja*, p104). Nadja herself becomes a sign for shifts of places and things; of Paris where she shifts from quarter to quarter with Breton, and of objects: Nadja's glove, her clothes. What is important is not that these are sites that mediate the intimacy but that they become meaningful through the intimacy they mediate; the world acquires meaning because the beloved inhabits it, and its objects become signs of that love, events increasingly over-invested with meaning as artifices of love.

towards the beloved as one would perform a duty. Also, duties are performed in compliance to rules and love provides none,[12] for it is the relationship itself that places demands, and those demands defy the duty pattern because they can only be identified through love.

Stretching this point further, one can maintain that love cannot be contracted into, even in the form of marriage. Here we have an acute incompatibility. The maxim *pacta sund servanda* that imbues the contract with permanence turns love into what it should defy if it is not to vanish: a duty. With this point we are already well within the boundaries of the question of time.

5) Love and marriage operate with different *time* horizons. Time itself may be abstracted and made uniform, even conceived along a linear pattern, but if we are to give due importance to the social construction of time and the plurality of *Temporalgestalten* of our society we need to 'disconnect time from chronology.'[13] In our case we need to seek the time that is particular to love and marriage. Suspended between beginning and end, love controls its own horizon. Love exists only in the 'not yet',[14] one can never have loved enough; love lies in the promise of future fulfilment, its actual fulfilment signals its end.[15] This can be expressed in many ways: in systems-theoretical terms it means that love's temporal modality is the present-future; if we follow Husserl in his definition of the horizon as that which is never touched, never surpassed, but helps define a situation, love *is* its own horizon. Love

---

[12] One can employ a softer term than 'rules' to claim the opposite: that love is full of **conventions**. Such conventions operate to provide visible indications of love and remove the constant recourse to the deep-level questions. Conventions provide such criteria of 'correct' loving behaviour. However, after the lover has brought the beloved flowers for the fifth consecutive anniversary, the latter may turn and say: 'flowers again! you do not love me any more.' The convention may be questioned in the name of love. This self-reflexive move on the part of love, its ultimate appeal to itself, shows that the convention holds no power in love, other than a short relief, that breaks down when it is questioned. Normative expectations from rules (the ones operative in marriage) do not 'learn' in this way. It is in view of this, that I have made no references to the operative conventions in love and that is why, therefore, my essay is sociologically so 'thin'. My interest has been to contrast love and marriage at the conceptual ('philosophical') level.

[13] In Luhmann, 1976, 135. For more on Luhmann's analysis of time see 1980, ps 235-300, and his chapter 'Struktur und Zeit' in 1984, ps 377-488. Note the proximity of this approach to time, with Castoriadis' collapse of time into its future horizon: 'à être'. 'Time is', he says, in the sense of it 'being towards'. (1975, ps293ff)

[14] 'Die Liebe existiert nur im noch nicht' (1982, 89)

[15] This gives love its specifically episodic character, in the systems-theoretical sense of episodic - as something that prepares for its own end, as Sean Smith notes in his 'The Complexities of Complex Equality', (unpublished Ms)

punctuates its time[16] and controls its time; what shows the latter to be especially true is the impossibility of binding love in the time-span of marriage. By its very nature, love exists as the possibility of its enhancement and exposes itself to its own corrosion. Binding it externally, attempting to institutionalise permanence, achieves nothing but a semblance of permanence which is intolerable to love. Indeed feigning permanence becomes itself a criterion for distinguishing between true and false love.

6) Marriage is about imbuing the relationship with permanence, countering the instability of love. At the risk of simplifying things slightly, one can say that to some extent marriage is based on repetition, unchangeability, and thematises change as a disturbance, a threat that must be overcome and restored. On the other hand, love thrives on *change*, its existence over time is dynamic, it requires 'die Formen zu wechseln und immer Neues zu verzehren.'[17] Its structures project enhancement, intensification. In contrast to marriage, immobility is likely to be thematised as indifference, repetition as reluctance to unfold love further, to exceed the limit, which in turn signals the absence of love. Because 'staying is nowhere.'[18]

7) Similarly, spontaneity and *chance* play a very different role in love and marriage. In one sense chance radicalises the improbabilities on which love relied; introducing chance into what sparks off, maintains and diminishes love, folds love back into an ultimate self-referentiality: no causal input from social structures, no dependence whatsoever on the outside.[19] There is no reason to love other than that one loves, no causality can account for its birth and maintenance, no reason for its evaporation other than that one does not

---

[16] In *Nadja* for example, very little ostensibly happens, sometimes nothing at all, yet the lover-narrator continuously brings events to our attention, momentous events capable of changing his life. These events only come about as he over-invests what happens with meaning. Without love there would have been no punctuation of the continuum, nothing to break or interrupt the flanerie in Paris or the early morning (non-)happenings at the Quai aux Fleurs (in *L'Amour Fou*) (See also the brute/institutional fact 'ontological' discussion earlier on what is 'carved out' as occurence)

[17] 'to change forms, and always to consume something new' (Luhmann, 1982, 90-1)

[18] 'Wie der Pfeil die Sehne besteht, um gesammelt im Absprung
   mehr zu sein als er selbst. Denn Bleiben ist nirgends'   (Rilke, Duineser Elegien, 8)

[19] It was pointed out to me by David Garland that it is not chance that lovers attribute their relationship to but fate, making accidents appear as necessities, coincidences as destiny, as events pre-programmed by fate. This is indeed a striking feature of the semantics of love. In Luhmann's analysis, the closure through chance of love that made it 'absolute in and of itself (in sich selbst verabsolutiert)' created the paradoxical reference to chance as 'necessity,... as fate, or even ... as freedom of the will' (1982, 181)

love any more. Love's self-referentiality is radicalised through chance[20] and expressed in spontaneity: love's expression cannot be pre-programmed because it would not be true to the sharing of the moment. Spontaneity lies in verbalising and acting out the improbable that is sparked off in the intensity of the intercourse and is true to the extent that it is not pre-meditated.

Marriage, on the other hand, firmly located in the legal system, uses structures to play down chance and envisages contingency in specific ways. It projects expectations of behaviour conducive to its self-descriptions (its operative categories of legal personality) and modifies them only to reach a new state of order, to which new deviations will again be disturbances. In brief, the institution of marriage cannot accommodate chance and spontaneity but must continuously translate them into what are its own possibilities of perception and movement.

I have gone to some length to illustrate the difference and incompatibility of the mappings of intimacy provided by love and marriage. Systems theory can give us new purchase to the question of incompatibility. Intimacy between two partners is 'structurally coupled' into both the systems of law and love. However, what this means for either of the systems is radically different. In each case intimacy is subjected to the difference that makes a difference: for law its relevance to legal and illegal action, to love its relevance to enhancing/not-enhancing love. This means that love instils occurrences of communication between the partners with information value (as signs of love) on the basis of its own distinction, geared by structures which determine what and under what terms is assigned to what part of the distinction. The same is true of law. Here too we have structures (conditional and goal programs) and values that decide what registers as information as well as how this information contributes to deeming something legal or illegal. Marriage should be understood at this level of programming of the legal system. The closure of the discourses around their codes accounts for the incompatibility of the mappings of intimacy from love and law.

I hasten to add that my list is only indicative of areas of difference, not exhaustive; it could be extended to include differences in the construction of motive, justification, etc. With Ackerman, I *reject* a weaker reading of his analogy to the effect that the semantics of love and marriage do *not* offer different answers to (a) how the partners understand their relationship, (b) how the partners understand themselves through their relationship. Too many

---

[20] This openness to risk is most prominent in *Nadja*. The submission of love to risk, to danger or to endless possibility, (or to both as in the book's final chapter's footnoted incident), is elevated here to nothing less than the condition of a love that is because it is in risk, a love that - as always tentative (never yet accomplished) - *demands more risk*, and love that *absorbs* all risk by defining what risk means self-referentially.

highly differentiated assumptions are employed for this to be true (above 1-7) and these assumptions work at the deep level of the constitution of identity, each projecting a form of community that allows identity to be shaped in specific and incompatible ways.

But Ackerman argues that marriage enhances love's potential, whereas I would like to argue that it hedges it in and impoverishes it.

I intend to pick up Ackerman's argument again at this point, to show why this is the case, so I must reiterate its main thrust: he is saying that law provides us with the missing language, the missing symbols that will accommodate a heightened form of intimacy and community. Instead of 'symbolic violence' in the legal discourse's channelling effect,[21] he sees symbolic empowerment. I will argue that he can only say that because he cannot see the exclusionary function of law. To summarise: I have attempted to show that marriage and love present (i) different and (ii) incompatible mappings of the intimate relationship. I will now (iii) advance the argument about the exclusionary function of marriage. I will conclude with an argument against Ackerman's optimistic view of the institutionalisation of community and extend it in the next section from intimacy to politics.

EXCLUSIONARY REASONS AND THE COMMUNITY OF MARRIAGE

As we have already seen the definition of an exclusionary reason is that it provides a (formal) reason for not acting on the basis of a (substantive, first-order) reason. What is the relevance of this for love and marriage? Due to the incompatibility of how the intimate relationship is envisaged by the two, one mapping can only be employed at the expense of the other. Entrenched at the formal level, reasons pertaining to rules and roles of marriage become divorced from reasons of love. On the exclusionary platform marriage presents its own exclusionary balance of reasons. Love no longer resonates here. To read and debate a relationship in terms of marriage works to occlude what can be said about it in terms of love. We have traced the incompatibility in formative assumptions regarding identity, attribution, modes of action, time, change, the role of chance, spontaneity and order in each discourse. Every reason from marriage is exclusionary to a reason from love. In the overall picture, this means that the balance of reasons informed by love is replaced - by kind, not weight - by a balance of reasons informed by marriage and ultimately, thus, sanctioned by law. The exclusionary function consists in this then: what brings one set of assumptions to the fore at the same time submerges the other.

---

[21] Legal reason constituting the 'forme par excellence da la violence symbolique legitime,' in Bourdieu, 1986, 3

Atiyah, as we saw, used the love/marriage schema too. Substantive reasons for action are temporarily, says Atiyah, 'frozen' into formal rules that facilitate decision-making. But should these formal rules cease to mirror their underlying substantive reasons, they will be revised in the light of the latter. That was, for Atiyah, the dialectic between formal and substantive as expressed in marriage.

My objection to this was that no signal could ever pierce the exclusionary veil to make the reason for revision of the exclusionary function felt. This was my revisability argument. We can see what this means more concretely now. How will I know that I need to rethink and revise my formal interest as a spouse? According to the logic of Atiyah (Schauer and Bankowski) I will do it by suspending my role as a spouse - its exclusionary logic - and looking back to love, to see whether love dictates sticking to the exclusionary reason or not. But this is *impossible* for two reasons. Because as spouse I may never perceive my interests threatened *because love does not make its failures known in a way that affects interests*; interests are nonsensical concepts in love. And because suspending the role even temporarily - looking behind marriage to love - involves suspending also the very language of marriage and its language of interests, duties, rights, motives and so on, the very language, that is, *in which a failure would have registered and in terms of which it is a failure.* From the formal position of a specific role, one operates in a world that is exclusionary because as role-player the spouse not only sees what s/he sees but also cannot see that s/he cannot see what s/he could have seen as lover.

Cast in the vocabulary of exclusionary reasons, both what is gained and what is lost by employing the 'symbolic system' of marriage can be described more precisely.

As to the 'facilitative' side first: not every decision relevant to the relationship has to be problematised on the basis of the relationship of love; not everything has to be either informed by the latter or refer back to the latter. Marriage projects in place of the excluded, its own balance of reasons particular to the institution, associated with expectations of behaviour pertaining to role. What performance is reasonably expected from spouses? This question acquires primacy in marriage and marginalises all others. And externally, towards third parties, conforming to this set of reasons removes from the spouse the burden to prove that s/he is acting out of love.

Marriage is about creating secure expectations in intimate relationships; its function to inject some measure of security into love's inherent instability. In what sense this is achieved has already been mentioned; it prevents every trivial disagreement within the marital exchange from turning into a question that engages the foundations of love. The facilitation here lies in unburdening the partners from the anxiety that their love is always at stake, or the complexity that would result from their tracing every slightest motive back to love (the complexity, more accurately of involving the world in every move). The foundations 'need not be thought about,'[22] because marriage provides for middle-range, exclusionary, reasons for not making recourse to the reasons from love. Not everything has to be thematised on the enhancement/corrosion axis of love, but can be less painfully attributed to expectations from role and performance of duty. Love's unfulfilled nature and the instability that comes from its need to develop by devouring new forms can be replaced by stability that stems from fulfilment of expectations from role. Even the lover's burden of being spontaneous, of always having to seek the new, is reduced. Unlike love with its dynamic nature, marriage does not stagnate at the absence of change. Instead, repetition creates order and allows only diversions from the pattern to appear as disturbances that register as risks. Here we have a complete reversal, for what could be more abhorrent to the lovers than the existence of such order that signals the end of spontaneity?

What is given up is the flip-side of what is gained; this is the sacrifice that the exclusionary function calls for. In the absence of exclusionary reasons no verification external to the relationship of love, no pretence of middle-range reasons could stand in the way of constant and deep re-evaluation of the relationship. The institution places a wooden hand on love. It denies love the freedom to refer to everything, to make sense of everything and to refer everything back to itself.[23]

The provision of a different - formal - level at which intimacy may be semanticised in marriage, at the expense of love's semantics of intimacy, has been shown to be exclusionary to the latter. In the new balance of reasons that furnishes the partners' positions there are considerations that need not be referred back to, reasons for action that are overruled (more accurately displaced or outweighed by kind); falling back on them may even become suspect from the vantage point of marriage. What is overruled need not be thought about. *When should not thinking about it yield to thinking about it? The question cannot be asked.* The excluded reasons cannot pierce the exclusionary veil. My own argument for reflexivity proceeds on the premise that there is great value in thinking through what 'need not be thought about.' Ackerman's analogy is important in highlighting how the republican

---

[22] See Bankowski, 1993

[23] The replacement of reasons from love with middle-range reasons from role may unburden anxiety, but for the partner who loves such recourse on the part of the beloved may become intolerable. It may even serve to increase complexity if the recourse to exclusionary reasons from role on the part of the beloved, is evaluated by the lover as hesitation to act from reasons from love.

containment thesis has lost sight of this, and how it imposes this loss in insight, this loss in reflexivity, onto politics.[24]

A great deal more can be said about what is distorted and sacrificed in the presence of the exclusionary reason. I will abandon this inquiry at this point because enough has been said to set the focal question in context. It is the question whether marriage **enhances community** between the lovers. This is the driving force of Ackerman's argument as he conceives of marriage as first 'giving meaning to a special form of interaction,' as the moment of transcending 'everyday ... ordinary ... existence,' into which he collapses ordinary love, and of 'thereby constituting a special kind of community.' My question to Ackerman is whether what was given up as ordinary love, excluded by what is now meaningful as community in the semantics of marriage, does not in fact contain the essence of what was being sought.

Why? We have already seen that love brings everything to bear on its own horizon. Everything is thematised according to what it contributes to love. Nothing is taken up a priori, not the nature of the bond, not the existence of the bond. The very nature of love, that of placing everything against its horizon, precludes all *a prioris*.[25] Love is uncovered, instantiated, rediscovered in every question, every moment of 'ordinary' interaction. On the contrary, marriage is about blocking this continual reference back to the source. It provides institutional symbols that can be checked against institutional assumptions, inhering in its structures and programs. In this sense, marriage is about introducing *a prioris*, introducing reasons 'not to think about it.' Bearing in mind that love and marriage both semanticise, i.e. give meaning and substance to the bond between the partners, and therefore both make sense of what it means for them to be-in-community, Ackerman must face the question which semantics will best do the job. He opts for marriage as the moment that empowers the bond. The trouble is that marriage prevents recourse to the deep interpretative ground and the bringing to bear of the world on the interpretative question of the existence of community. This is because marriage does not have the means to inquire into this deep premise of the existence of community; the latter's existence works as a pre-condition for the development of the semantics of marriage, and in that it

---

[24] This function remains latent, in that marriage presents its semantics, its codifications, descriptions and structures to make sense of the fluidity of love as necessary. The existence of a different semantics and their appropriateness never becomes a problem for law, because law does not posess the reflexive structure to accommodate such questions. The exclusionary reason stands in for the reasons that fall within its ambit and moreover prevents recourse to them. By presenting its own codification as necessary, law downplays its contingency, and thus its exclusion of a competing codification of love is never accounted for.

[25] Except one that is; that not everything needs to be thus problematized. Each system, Luhmann tells us, confers exclusivity to its own claim to reality.

is a blindspot. The structures of those semantics can only ask questions about fulfilment or disappointment of expectations from roles, as if the answers to this *always-already* settle the question of love and community founded on love. Marriage provides answers in the name of love, and in that '*as if*' we see the story of re-enactment played out again, as we saw it played out in conflict previously. And as we said there, what is re-enacted is not contained. But here in love, (as in politics below) there is more at stake than re-enactment. Because what the containment in law displaces are those very interpretative questions that turn love (like politics) reflexive: turn them upon themselves to ask what they are really about *in a way that at once challenges and realises them*. But by inserting law as empowering that which love like politics are uniquely suited for, Ackerman displaces the interpretative questions with exclusionary ones. His analysis takes on board community as an *a priori* by removing from community (love) the ultimate question of what community is (what does love entail); by removing the understanding of what is love, from love. This is how Ackerman creates a paradox for himself in his appeal to marriage as an enhanced community of love: 'leave love behind in the name of love.' Unlike a paradox that can be creatively unfolded, this is an oxymoron.

BACK TO POLITICS

In a strange way I have been talking about politics all along. This is due in no small measure to the power of Ackerman's analogy that draws the symmetry between marriage and citizenship with such precision. I trust that the connections with the analysis of love are obvious enough. All I have said can be carried into this context if the terms are changed: spouse for citizen, marriage for citizenship, love for politics. Then Ackerman's 'ordinary politics' like ordinary love, and 'constitutional politics' like marriage will be seen to avail (i) different, (ii) incompatible and (iii) exclusionary templates for 'semanticising' the political and the quest for community. In politics, as in love, my intention is to turn Ackerman's example against him, in order to show that what he celebrates as emancipating in fact impoverishes by channelling politics and occluding its possibilities.

As in the case of marriage, Ackerman's constitutional politics purports a transcendence of ordinary politics by offering us the language of law. Again, this is, ultimately, an argument about the enhancement of community. The constitutive moment for the community is, again, envisaged in crossing the threshold into institutionalisation. Ackerman is right in claiming, as he did for marriage, that constitutional politics provides us with a language that will furnish a debate, confrontation and eventually, definition of our political identities.²⁶ The trouble is that it is an exclusionary 'language' and its danger lies in that it cannot account for its exclusionary function. The conceptual arsenal is not innocent. It is charged with assumptions of identity and of forms of action that can accommodate that identity. Constitutional politics avails a cluster of categories to make politics possible, and there are other different, incompatible templates excluded. As is the case in marriage, in constitutional law too, there are forms of action that pertain to role. Their containment at that level is evidenced particularly when limits of rights are allegedly transcended and thus expectations from institutional structures are stretched. The 'freedoms' in the Constitutions are such structures, and instances of speech, protest, privacy, equality of protection, e.t.c., cannot escape containment in those structures, not least by being characterised as instances from a pool of such exclusive alternatives (of 'this and not another right'). We have learnt from the New Social Movements, especially feminism, the coercion that inheres in forcing social action into this template, of universalising social problems and practices through these categories.²⁷ What I am saying is that whatever answer we may want to give to this question, we must confront it as a political question against the horizon of community and we are prevented from seeing it as such if we take on board citizenship as already containing the answer to community. If we take it on board as exclusionary context, it circumscribes our possibilities of vision. But the civic republicans are happy to live with this impoverishment of the political because they are all too busy waving the flag for institutions.²⁸

The argument carries through to the republican aspiration to contain community in law. Like marriage, citizenship takes community on board as an *a priori*. For the republicans community is there by virtue of the State that circumferes political space. This circumference also provides the exclusionary reason for giving up politicising the question: 'not thinking about it' becomes unyielding. In citizenship, as in marriage, community is institutionally brought into existence and the question whether it exists, the task of retrieving it in an interpretative way at every step is left behind. In its continuous questioning of its fulfilment, love substantiated the communal

---

²⁶ Ackerman, 1984, 1072

²⁷ See chapters twelve and thirteen.

²⁸ It is interesting to contrast Ackerman's zealous celebration of the moment of constitutional politics which 'invests a certain aspect of the personality [of private citizens] with heightened significance,' as they 'say to one another "This time, we really mean it!"' (1984, 1041), with Luhmann's more cautious approach to the function of public opinion (in 1990, chs 2 & 8.) According to Luhmann, public opinion operates as a mirror for the political system, providing answers (affirmation or disappointment) to expectations projected by it. Ackerman's constitutional moments of popular mobilization are for Luhmann occasions when societal noise forces a variation in the pattern of expectations to be projected, and assures in this way a return to order.

bond, fed questions that constantly brought community to self-conscious realisation. One cannot sever the intimate dialectic between community and love as one cannot sever it between community and politics by imposing law as the mediator. If one is to give politics due significance by bringing everything to bear on politics, one has to take the ultimate step back and ask the real question about community: *locate in community the understanding of what constitutes community*. Radicalising the question in this way, releasing the variables from legally fixed positions, will create a shifting pattern of communities constellating around understandings that, for the time being, seem adequate to hold together people-in-community. To politicise the question of community is an act of faith in freedom and instability is a small price to pay.

My purpose is to suggest elements of a theory of politics, in a way that makes reflexivity its defining feature. My discussion of love was aimed at tapping the seam of a reflexivity trapped and depleted by legal institutionalisation. The reason why a discussion of love is so appropriate here is because both politics and love pivot on the reflexive moment or, what amounts to the same thing in this case, are totally self-referential. Only by loving can one know love's demands; what is politics is always politically contestable.

My thesis is that a truly emancipatory concept of politics pivots on the reflexive potential that would allow any exclusion to be reflected. The difficult question, as we shall see, is what makes this pivot possible? But I have little doubt that to do politics justice we must conceive of it at this, most abstract level; any step towards the concrete must then be thought of as the embracing of a political option, a form. If we do not accede to this we are conspiring to the poverty of politics. And we will have to invent a different word to refer back to the more abstract category that was hedged in when we decided to define politics as 'this and not that,' to refer back, that is, to the projected unity that made this distinction possible because meaningful. Any other tentative definition of politics that does not embrace this self-reflection cannot logically exhaust what the political is, however broad that definition: albeit 'participation in power,' 'the totality of actions undertaken with a view to determining the future of society' (Unger), or 'the conflictual self-reproduction of society' (Touraine), to give but a few examples. Because in each case it is a perfectly legitimate *political* question to ask 'why action?', 'why participation?', or 'why conflictual?' and politically question one definitional option against the background of other possibilities. Reflexive politics incorporates the self-reflexive, self-referential moment, so that every exclusionary form appears a negation of political possibility, not an enhancement as Ackerman would have us believe.

Before I take to systems theory one last time to draw theoretical backing for the reflexive thesis, let me discard the ***sceptic's challenge***. Why resort, the sceptic asks, to a definition of politics as reflexive and why is it, in turn, not restrictive to define politics in this way? Why does this definition, as is apparently the case for every definition, not hedge in what can be understood as politics and thus not fall into its own trap?

With the sceptic I have no dispute. To the sceptic I would respond: 'We are asking the same question; when you ask "why reflexive?" your question too is the reflexive one.'

CHAPTER NINETEEN

CONTINGENCY AS EIGEN-VALUE OF POLITICS
[REFLEXIVITY AS SECOND-ORDER OBSERVATION]

A picture kept us captive. And we could not get outside of it, for it lay in our language and language seemed to repeat it to us inexorably.
(Wittgenstein)

In Luhmann's discussion of the political system, democracy, as foil for the guiding distinction, allowed for the system's self-observation. The scope of political variability was thereby delimited, the scope of what could change arrested in that depiction. This means more than that the system sanctions a certain order of affairs. What is at stake here is meaning, the possibility that something registers as politically meaningful. For Luhmann, the 'government/opposition' distinction opens up the contingency space in politics in the sense of delimiting what can be done politically in terms of operations. In terms of observation it allows not simply an understanding of how things are but also a glimpse of how things could be different (the opposition could come to power). It is in that limiting way that the conceptual space of political possibility is semanticised.

But an observer can shift to a level where the political system's self-observation can in turn be observed. Luhmann calls this observation of observation a second-order observation. A different system now sees the initial, observing system and its environment. It is crucial for second-order observation that the observed is observed as observer in its own right.[1] Now,

'this system that observes other systems has other possibilities ... It can observe the horizons of the observed system so that what they exclude becomes evident.'[2]

'[I]n this way,' says Luhmann, "an observer can see that the observed system cannot see that it is unable to see what it cannot see. This insight marks the real epistemic gain second-order cybernetics has to offer.'[3]

What this means is that the political system's self-observation can in turn be set in context. At this level the parameters of that observation may be

---

[1] See Luhmann, 1991a, 225-6. Systems, that is, perceive each other all the time without automatically becoming second-order observers. They only become that when what one system - say law - thematises another's - say the economy - way of observing, say people as profit maximizers. It is obvious in this context why theory is the second-order observer par excellence.
[2] Luhmann, 1986e, 23
[3] Luhmann, 1990a 139

problematised. In *Political Theory in the Welfare State,* Luhmann reserves this task for political theory. With the initial distinction the discourse was structured, the political system semanticised. The meta-language of theory involves stepping back from the initial distinction and in turn setting that in the context of a further distinction. 'One can distinguish the very distinction that one had begun with and use it to generate theory.'[4] Reflection involves reflecting also on the distinction that set the co-ordinates of what was meaningful to the system. What constituted a blindspot for the system can now be observed at the meta-level of theory. As second-order observation, political theory can now inquire into what was meaningful to the self-observing system and what was invisible to that self-observation. At this level latent possibilities may be uncovered that the system's operative difference could not bring to light.[5] This does not mean that second-order observation introduces the archimedean point - the view from nowhere. Luhmann stresses that 'second-order observation is not objectively better knowledge but only a different knowledge.'[6] Moreover, it is a basic assumption of systems' theory that the system's cognition is based on a (guiding) distinction that the system cannot at once operate and query. The distinction opens up the system's conceptual space but at the same time constitutes its blindspot. Blindspots cannot be avoided at any level of observation. However at the second level (political theory) the distinction that opens up first level observation (political system) can be observed. On the basis of the political system's blindspot, a query can be articulated at the level of theory over the terms of self-observation, the terms of inclusion and exclusion of politically significant communication. My suggestion is to locate the possibility of reflexive politics on the premise that every political conceptualisation can be recast from the point of view of a different difference.[7] That, therefore, political conflict that is 'pre-programmed by the contrast set of the political code' can now be politicised. I suggest this

---

[4] Luhmann, 1990a, 168

[5] 'If a system is able to discover new "inviolate levels" that serve to deparadoxise its identity, semantic systems deemed necessary may become contingent.' (1990a 138-9)

[6] (1986e 25)

[7] Luhmann ascribes the contingency of the social world to his discussion of functional differentiation. Functionally induced reductions of social complexity compete as contingency. Luhmann says : 'die Universalität der Kontingenz an die Spezifikation der Funktionsysteme gebunden ist.' And 'In diesem Sinne ist das Beobachten zweuter Ordnung mit seiner Semantik, seinen Eigenwerten der Kontingenz, methodologisch gesprochen, eine Intervenierende Variable, die erklärt, dass die Gesellschaft in eine an Funktionen orientierer Differenzierungsform übergehen kann.' (1992a, 114, 119)

contingency[8] of possible departures as the founding principle of reflexive politics.[9]

My main suggestion for a foundation of reflexive politics lies thus in exploiting the possibilities of second-order observation; leaving open the question of which difference makes a difference in politics is a most decisive step in the direction of reflexivity.[10] This approach involves the possibility to challenge the guiding difference of the political system. The question thus turns on the 'criteriality' of the political code, in other words on the appropriateness of the specific encodement of the political discourse. In that sense Luhmann's concept of a **'rejection value'** is crucially relevant here.[11] To put it briefly, a rejection value is a third value that can be introduced into the system at the level of its code. The rejection value does not negate the values of the binary coding itself (the code is a contrast set anyway) but it negates the need 'for the [binary distinction] as the basis of choice.' The very choice is rejected. A rejection value bears on the question of the criteriality of the code and does not itself enter any question of evaluation on the basis of the code. It thus builds a reflexive structure into the system itself,

---

[8] Luhmann defines as contingent that which is neither impossible nor necessary 1984, 152. For the problems of defining the term through two negations, see 1992a pp96ff.

[9] In a previous paper (1991) I had attempted to establish a connection between first and second-observation, such as would allow the political system (first-order) to "learn from political theory. How was political theory to 'resonate' at the level of the political system?
I hesitate to follow this as a possible - or at least not incompatible with systems-theory- route. On the one hand I think, now, that this connection between levels of observation flies in the face of too much of systems theory. There cannot be an adequate feedback, recursive or not, between levels of observation. On the other hand, Luhmann recently seems to re-affirm the possibility, by treating theory not as a different system, but at the level of system's programming. "The entire system [can] operate at the level of second order observation, and only secondarily is observation of the first order activated once again ..." And " [I]n the case of self-observation of the second order [the observing system] can be the system itself." (1991a, 220, 225). I will leave the question open because given the contingency of guiding distinctions around which worlds of political action build up, a notion of reflexive politics need not seek its internal leverage from such a connection between levels of observation.

[10] In systems theory, contingency is tied to second-order observation. 'Alles wird kontingent, wenn das, was beobachtet wird, davon abhängt, wer beobachtet wird.' (1992a, 100)

[11] Luhmann takes the concept from Gunther (See Luhmann, 1986a, sections V, VII and n13). To take a simple example. The use of one system code operates as a rejection value for all other codes. Once a true/false code is opted for, given the incompatibility of encodements, the criteriality of all other codes is precluded. In the above sense, rejection values are congruent with the differentiation of autopoietic systems. Problems begin to arise when the rejection value is introduced not as the privileging of one system coding over another but internally within one and the same system, "adapting it to being three-valued, and giving it the possibility of throwing out its own code" (1986a, p24). Luhmann undertakes a complex analysis of this possibility with regard to the legal system and concludes that rejection values would require a degree of differentiation of levels that is unrealistic in the legal systems of the present day.

'adapting [the system] to being three-valued and giving it the possibility of throwing out its own code.'[12]

Even if such 'reflexive excess' (produced by three-valuedness) is a 'logical dream' for the legal system,[13] it can be well envisaged for the political system. Where for the legal system it would create an unbearable 'reflexive excess', for the political system it would significantly enhance its reflexivity, by (re-)introducing a complexity that is selective - a repertoire of possible departures from the assumed guiding difference. It can be maintained that Luhmann himself permits this in his discussion of political theory. When Luhmann brings political theory to bear on the question of the performance of the political system, he is telling the story of the rejection value. Political theory is introduced to ask the question whether a social problem should be taken up politically (or whether it should be pushed off to other sub-systems). This is a specific case of three-valuedness turned into a binary choice through a double decision, the preliminary one carrying the rejection value ('should the political code apply to this problem, or not?') Only if the rejection value were to be turned into an acceptance value (at the level of theory) would the 'political' question be asked (at the level of system).[14]

There is one problem with subscribing to the rejection value formula in this context. The challenge to settled departures, to the 'distinctions assumed in politics' is **iconoclastic**. The challenge is reactive, *the dominant image still holds defiance captive.* Applied to describe how people experience political meanings, the rejection-value formula would thus cover only the problematic of a certain form of action (extra-parliamentary) that is specifically directed against the political system, against parliamentary democracy. By bringing the question of alternative politics to bear on rejection or acceptance of the code, it again locates the code at the centre of choice, unable to account for those politics that side-step it entirely. As negation of the rejected encodement of politics, alternative politics on this account *preserves the representation space* within which the choice is made. Luhmann allows this bias to become the founding principle of protest,[15] and *does not see that resistance is not only by opposition but also by difference.*

---

[12] Luhmann, 1986a, 187

[13] ibid., 189

[14] Luhmann himself does not connect his discussion of political theory with the rejection value.

[15] This, his earlier position in (1986e) is tempered in his more recent analysis of protest movements in (1991a). Here he says: "The form of protest remains a form that presupposes the other side that is to react to the protest. The collapse of this difference entails the collapse of the protest." (1991a, 126) To the extent only that this difference refers to "the very institutions from which [the protest] is taking exception" (ibid), the difference again becomes an opposition to the political system itself. In my eyes Luhmann remains ambiguous on this point.

A reflexive understanding of politics, I argued, involves probing the limits of closure of politics with the help of other significant distinctions. What does this really mean? And, what matters most, how could it translate into a theory of political action that can carry a challenge into the naturalness and apparent closure with which politics seem vested - a closure which republicanism helps perpetuate by celebrating what is stale as new and what is limiting as empowering.

The political system precipitates action in the sense of marking out what it is possible or expectable to do politically. Human potential for action is organised by the system as the latter defines what are the issues to be pursued, the means to be employed, even the identities to be assumed. These central insights have already been well covered in previous chapters and will not be further explored here.

However, if we take the potential of the radical contingency of politics seriously, new opportunities for political action suggest themselves. These opportunities were previously precluded by the encodement of the political system, that defined for itself what was politically at stake. But positions can be assumed in defiance of the system's allocation of political roles and a new freedom for the actor to locate problems and undertake actions can be established. Luhmann says:

'The distinction [necessary/contingent] can be utilized in such a way that an observation can interpret as artificial and contingent what the system itself assumes to be natural and necessary. For example, an observer may examine how a system creates the impression of its self-determinations being natural, necessary and lacking functional alternatives.'[16]

The guiding distinction of politics can be set in context, and new distinctions, articulated at the level of second-order observation can shake received assumptions, inform political understanding and gear political action.

We can test this re-shaping of the political discourse by replacing the 'government/opposition' distinction by a different one, e.g. that of dominating/dominated. This would be re-invoking Carl Scmitt's friend/foe distinction as the *ultima ratio* of politics.[17] There is evidence that the social problematic of politics has, to an extent, shifted back to such schemata. The old critique of domination may have been displaced but is not redundant.[18]

---

[16] Luhmann, 1988a, 139
[17] Smitt, 1976
[18] Luhmann maintains that with the transition from stratification to functional differentiation, the critique of arbitrariness and despotism was made redundant.

278   CHAPTER NINETEEN

As exploitation assumes new forms and is seen to affect new subjects (the urban subproletariat, immigrant workers, women), new sites of domination have appeared and new forces have risen to counter them.[19] In the process new constituencies become political. Alternative discourses are operative in the political mobilisation of groups whose political understandings are *not* aligned to that of the political system. Issues like economic growth, corporate control over pricing and investment, the managerial asphyxiating of the workplace, were neither political *per se* nor attuned to the political system's guiding distinction; how they *became* political in spite of the political system is a problem Luhmann's theory needs urgently to address. But more significantly still, it needs to answer this: if the encodement of politics is the ultimate determinant of political meaning, how can all that defies or ignores this encodement be accounted for politically? The definition of value, the deployment of language, the commodification of ownership and association in the a-political marketplace, are all politically challenged today. The development of multinational corporations has given rise to demands for their democratic control pursued by movements and initiatives outside the nation states. Civic initiatives (in eastern Europe and elsewhere) attempt to restore the public political space both beyond the reach of the state and across state boundaries.[20] New social movements level their challenge to institutional politics. Existing channels of political participation and organisation cannot accommodate their conflicts. Institutional confinement gives way to institutional breakdown that releases political forces. The tension between confinement and breakdown is evidenced in many organisational forms: in trade unions, where, even today, the Confédération Francaise Démocratique du Travail entertains an ambiguous position between class action and reformist action.[21] We encounter it again in the

---

[19] "There is a plurality of subjects of resistance, each the product of highly differentiated social processes and exemplifying its own discrete and peculiar rationality. Their opacity and incommensurability is such that there is no privileged position from which their reactions can be predicted and channeled, least of all the institutions of parliamentary democracy. Subterranean political groupings engage in a form of guerrilla warfare against the state ... they become visible only infrequently and unexpectedly, and their relationship to the state is one of 'reciprocal incitation and struggle; less of a face to face confrontation which paralyses both sides than a permanent provocation.' [Foucault]" (Barron, 1990, 122-3)

[20] "The Nation-State has been replaced from above by a tightly interdependent system of transnational relationships and subdivided from below into a multiplicity of partial governments, defined both by their own systems of representation and decision-making and by an ensemble of interwoven organisations which combine inextricably the public and the private." (Melucci, 1988, 257)

[21] Jean-Louis Moynot, confederal secretary of the CGT and member of the communist party, urged in his writings that the party neither ignore nor take over the new social protest but try to push them beyond corporatist formulations. Similar appeals not to stifle the political

erratic behaviour of radical and 'green' parties in Italy and Germany that, at the outset at least, attempted to reconcile within themselves the radical irreconcilability between movement and institution (exhibited clearly in the confrontation between the reformist and fundamentalist wings of the party). We see the tension most vividly in the 'autogestionnaire' currents of the Polish Solidarity movement and their demand for control of the productive process, co-opted tragically by the union itself in the latter's attempt to further what Maurice Glasman has appropriately called 'market Leninism'.[22] Groups organise locally, self-help groups are set up. Urban guerrillas and anarchists take up violence, their language is political nonetheless. The discourses of all the above re-activate conflicts that remain latent in the political system's registering of conflict. This is a very different kind of politics from that which attempts to bring social problems under the Welfare State umbrella, and it is a weakness of Luhmann's - a most indicative one in fact - to treat these as demands towards the State to 'handle everything politically.'[23]

In an article written some ten years ago,[24] Claus Offe sought to address the question of the expanding boundaries of the political, as was evidenced by the emergence of new political actors and forms of political action. A new paradigm was emerging as these non-institutional collectivities, pursuing aims at the boundaries and margins of the democratic process politicised themes hitherto perceived as part of the natural order of the world, or at least of lacking a political, contestable side. And as the unquestionable became questioned, the boundaries of the political were released to constellate again around new balances and contingencies. It is perhaps paradoxical that in this situation of politics unbound, Offe attempts to fix a definition of political action. He says:

'A minimum requirement for employing the word political for a mode of action is that the actor make some explicit claim that the means of action can be recognized as legitimate and the ends of action can become binding for the larger community. Only social movements that share both these characteristics have a political quality ... Two interesting limiting cases, represented by new religious sects and by terrorism, are thus not included.'[25]

What justifies this disqualification? Offe continues:

---

dynamism of class and autogestionnaire action, were heard by the radical labour lawyers in Germany in the thirties (Fränkel) and Otto-Kahn Freund in Britain .
[22] See Glasman's excellent (1994)
[23] Luhmann, 1990a, 101
[24] Offe (1985)
[25] ibid., 69

'Terrorist groups cannot expect their violent means to be recognized as legitimate and rightful by the wider community. On the other hand, their objectives are quite conventionally (if absurdly and unrealistically) political. They consist - to take the aims of, say, the RAF or the Brigate Rosse - of an anti-imperialist revolutionary war, the outcomes of which would clearly be binding upon the entire community in quite an elementary way.'[26]

The answer to Offe brings us neatly back to the argument for reflexive politics. From this point of view one would begin to argue not for a different distribution of legitimacy between means and ends, but for a politics that includes a debate about that distribution. It is part of the reflexivity argument that distributions like the above cannot remain outside politics. To fix the boundaries of possible politics meat-politically, as Off does, is itself a silencing of politics.

Obviously activities that defy the encasement of politics at the same time create stimuli and responses to governments and oppositions. Yet such discourse talks past the political system's encodement of the political universe. The political impetus is carried elsewhere, and to attempt to read it all by driving it through the party political system may have Luhmann overtaken by the course of events, left observing a redundant politics. 'Resistance to government is actually or potentially everywhere, and yet nowhere in particular,' writes Anne Barron drawing on Foucault and Deleuze.[27] Is not the 'nowhere in particular' a sign of an inability to register resistance? Is the 'everywhere and yet nowhere in particular' a sign that the political action under observation is falling through the conceptual net we are employing? Notice the levels of resistance here: the political system itself registers resistance as support for the opposition; introducing the rejection value it acquires the ability to register resistance as iconoclastic, as its own rejection. But we need to be able to account politically for politics that resist both these reductions. Luhmann's account of politics and the normative position that underlies it is very inhibiting here. How are we for instance to understand Luhmann's deeply paradoxical worry

'whether [in the face of a rapidly changing political landscape of] reviving regionalism, experimenting with self-help groups, e.t.c., a function system for politics differentiated as democracy can carry out the process of adjustment when, at the same time, it is its victim?'[28]

---

[26] ibid., 70
[27] Barron, 1990, 122
[28] Luhmann, 1990a, 33

Luhmann's paradoxical question about democracy is whether it can include its own alternatives; he cannot say yes, he must concede the blindspot here. What he is left with, then, is a politics semanticised in spite of the political code. What conclusions are we to draw about the system that while disclosing political possibility can at the same time be superseded politically? There is a logical impasse here and it stems from the way Luhmann describes the encodement of the political system. The only way out of this impasse is to see these competing semantics as themselves the site of political struggle, and thus accept as political the struggle over the meaning of politics. This requires systems theory to embrace the reflexivity thesis. Without the guiding assumption of the contingency of possible departures that explains the incommunicability of politics, we cannot perceive what is at stake; only by allowing contingent, mutually cross-cutting and under-cutting, political guiding distinctions will we be able to understand why political struggle has become this war 'without battlelines, with neither confrontation nor retreat, without battles, even: pure strategy.'[29]

Luhmann's theory of second-order observation allows us to see how autopoietic theory can account for the very real effects and impact that non-institutional politics carry; how it can account for a political discourse that can be heard in spite of the political system. More than two decades ago, as if anticipating a politics beyond the limits of governmentality, Luhmann wrote that the basic concepts of a discipline that is willing to face up to the assumptions of a contingent world must be able to deal with the problem that 'neither concepts nor the world can be treated simply as given ... Their suitability [was to be judged] from the point of view of grasping and reducing the contingency of possible worlds.'[30] From the point of view of emancipatory politics it is here that lies the value of systems theory. The assumption of a given or natural state of the world is shaken, replaced by a picture of competing mappings that grasp the world in its radical contingency. And unlike so much (other) post-modern theory, the acknowledgement of contingency goes hand in hand with a thorough and complex account of the mechanisms and logics of closure that, as reductions on that vast contingency, compel meaning into specific templates. The acknowledgement of contingency and the theory of systemic reductions allows a theory of politics that can probe the logic of closure and challenge what appears as natural and given because it now has the keys to what closes options and what underlies necessities.

Luhmann's pre-occupation with the contingency of the world re-situates politics as lever of social life. His theory of the possibilities of second-order

---

[29] Deleuze and Guattari 1988, 353
[30] Luhmann, 1971, 21-2

observation and, more generally, the consequent freedom of possible departures is the first step to *turning politics reflexive*. Of course every departure, as guiding difference, then reduces possibilities and only thus allows for meaning. Every challenge needs to draw a boundary to acquire form and in that hedges in what could be visible as challenge otherwise. A meaningful challenge is always already a reduction. But reflexivity lies in the possibility to step back and question that reduction and the universe it has mapped out. Reflexivity is the switching of levels of observation, the freedom of choice of the guiding distinction. It is the in-built resistance to any external constraint of what is politically possible. In second-order observation inheres the potential to query the casting of the terms of self-observation and to 'de-naturalise' what the system itself perceives as necessary. There inheres the capacity to unlock political discourse from its compulsion into specific forms.[31] To acknowledge that action that side-steps the institutional paradigm may be as faithful to politics as action that takes it up is. To allow us to act on our ability to act. And to celebrate the radical contingency of possible departures as that which is specific and significant to politics, therefore to elevate contingency in the position of the 'eigen-value' of politics.[32]

Towards the end of his *Political Theory of the Welfare State* Luhmann asks two 'basic questions':

'All self-observation depends on the assertion of differences. Events can be experienced and processed as information only on the basis of differences. Therefore the basic questions are: which differences can be assumed in politics and can they be assumed in agreement?'[33]

I aim to do no more than to establish that this is itself a political question. To establish that the choice of difference that opens up political self-observation neither is nor should be a pre-political choice. The nature of politics as reflexive is situated here.

---

[31] For a defence of reflexivity as rationalization see Eder, who alludes to Habermas. Eder writes: "Reduced to its procedural form, the ultimate ground of the rationality of modernity is that we can choose our symbolic orders, that we are not stuck with any one type of rationality, and that we can at any time abandon what we have ceased to accept rationally. (1993, 34)
[32] The allusion is to Luhmann's *Kontingenz als Eigenwert der modernen Gesellschaft* (In 1992a)
[33] Luhmann, 1990a, 105

CHAPTER TWENTY

POLITICS 'AS PASSION'
[REFLEXIVITY AS SELF-REFERENCE]

If contingency, as it inheres in second-order observation, is the one pillar of reflexive politics, self-reference is the other. It is not surprising that I will seek to establish what it means for politics to be self-referential from within systems-theory; but I will attempt this analysis in a way that is novel in two respects. I will talk about self-reference in a way that makes politics self-referential as only love is. And second, *I will treat self-reference not as a limiting condition for politics, as that which underpins its closure, but as the liberating moment, as that which allows its reflexivity.* Both these arguments are internally linked and mutually constitutive.

Why is this second step, this theory of self-reference, a necassary complement to what has already been described as significant to reflexive politics, i.e. its contingency? In a nutshell, and I will explain this, it is *because if contingency is what underlies reflexivity, reflexivity is what defines politics.* I have so far dealt only with the first leg of this assertion. Dealing with the second explains why reflexive politics is not merely an alternative, but a better understanding of politics. This is not to say that this question has not been addressed at all; to treat politics as reflexive allowed us above to capture as what they are, i.e. as political, alternative forms of politics that would otherwise have been invisible. My purpose in adding self-reference as a second step towards a theory of reflexive politics is to elevate reflexivity into the defining feature of politics.

Like love, politics is completely self-referential (this allusion to Liebe als Passion is what justifies the title of this section as 'Politics as Passion'.) In the section on love and marriage we explored what this self-reference meant. What it means to love someone can only be articulated from the viewpoint of s/he who loves, and in the mirror of what it means not to love. No range of middle-range, formal, exclusionary reasons can relieve the complexity of love, the complexity of referring to everything, and referring everything back to itself. Love brings the world to bear on the interpretative question of its own existence, since reasons only become meaningful against the horizon of what it means to love. Note how interesting this is regarding freedom. Nowhere as much as in love is it as obvious that freedom is something that holds *between* people. And as love absorbs freedom, for the lover what it means to be free is paradoxically tied to the dependencies that love creates.

An understanding of politics needs to be founded on such a self-reference. Like the question of what is love cannot be removed from love, the question of what is politics cannot be removed from politics. By being reflexive, politics refers everything back to its own possibilities. Just as love thematises everything on its enhancement/corrosion axis (love's guiding distinction) and thus self-referentially refers everything back to its own enhancement, so does politics. *Something acquires meaning politically in that "it could be otherwise"*. To view something politically is to view the settled in the mirror of the unsettled, it is to view something in the light of its contingency. Because politicising means relativising givens in the light of alternatives. This is self-referential in the way love is in that *what gives something its political meaning is its placing against the horizon of the enhancement of politics* (like what made something a sign of love was its placing against the horizon of the enhancement of love.) So like love, politics refers everything back to its own potential of enhancement and only thus makes it political. And in this drive to self-enhancement politics propels itself on, bringing the world, increasingly more of it, within the ambit of political possibility. Conversely, every form, every option taken, every reduction made, brackets out alternatives and is thus, in as far as it does not acknowledge itself as artifact, a negation of political possibility.

Another way of stating the self-referentiality of love and politics is by employing the notion of 'horizon' and the dialectic between what is conditioned and what is unconditional. As horizon, the unconditional serves to situate the conditioned; at the same time every state of the conditioned alludes to, points to, transcends to the unconditioned. The conditioned becomes meaningful against its horizon, in the mirror of the unconditioned. On the other hand the unconditioned itself, as horizon, can never be determined save as conditioned. The reflexivity of both love and politics need to be seen as expressed in that dialectic between conditioned and unconditioned. What is important is that they need to be defined as the form of the distinction: both sides need to be kept constantly in sight. Love is not the conditioned moment alluding to the unconditional, the finite moment that becomes meaningful in alluding to the infinite. The meaning of love is not captured by the conditioned, enclosed in the modalities of the finite. Love is the distinction itself of the conditioned and the unconditional. *Love is its own horizon*. Love is meaningful in the mirror of the 'not yet' (one can never have loved enough) - its actual fulfilment, its circumscription in the finite, signals its end. Love crystallises in a pattern only by keeping an eye open to the revisability that alone allows it to be alive and flourish. To call "love" the crystallised pattern ignores that what makes it possible as love is that it is *at once held and suspended*. Politics, too, is the finite and the infinite, the actual and the possible, both at once visible. An actual state of affairs becomes political once it becomes possible otherwise. Reflexive politics actualises both references at once because it sees one state of affairs in the mirror of alternatives and only then deems it political. This constant setting options in further contexts underpins and defines reflexive politics : its only requirement (not vulnerable to the skeptic, as we saw) is that one remains free to contest and that the terms in which one contests remain contestable. The conditioned and the unconditional are both present in this formulation of politics. Something is political only in the mirror of the existence of alternatives (in the mirror of the 'not yet', or rather in the mirror of its revisability); what crystallises as an option in politics is only political in the mirror of alternatives not taken (in the further mirror that the constellation of those sets of alternatives are not fixed, etc.) That is how reflexivity works out its definition of politics through self-reference.

Conclusion

In an intriguing lecture presented at the 1989 IVR World Congress in Edinburgh, Jan Broekman made a case for the revolutionary. He explained that we could never understand the denunciation of the Law voiced by revolutionaries, because we have lost the means of access to their message. "When we read their texts we are already legal subjects. And we do not know what type of denunciation would have classified and qualified us legally, if we were not readers but revolutionaries. We do not know." (1989, 329) The legal person as 'performative' lends itself to our understanding of the revolutionary in such a way that the revolutionary's text is forever subverted under the legal categories we employ to interpret it. The revolutionary meaning is thus removed from view. As legal persons we could not understand revolutionary action otherwise than from the point of view of its other - Order - which is to say we cannot understand it at all.

Republicanism claims to be a theory about how to contain the political moment in law, and in containing it to empower it. Through systems theory I have attempted to show that this is impossible. I have shown how containment impoverishes the political by inserting a prioris at the sites of contestation. And I have shown how it renders invisible what it purports to accommodate. Even as merely a test case, sedition disproves containment; the revolutionary, subversive utterance cannot be captured in law except as seditious, to become, as the law links to the political and purports to "carry" politics, the sign of the abolition of politics as such.

My suggestion for a reflexive politics pivots on contingency and self-reference. It is a re-statement of politics as freedom. Because contingency is about the freedom to contest what politics is about and self-reference is the freedom to contest the terms in which that question is contested. Nothing can hedge in freedom in the name of politics. Like the distinction between freedom to love and love, that between freedom and politics collapses as it is drawn. Love and politics absorb freedom and elevate it to their constitutive moment. And at the same time they imbue it with those - reflexive - dependencies that establish freedom as a relation between people, in the intimate and public domain respectively.[1]

Reflexive politics is an invitation to resist the closure that law inflicts on the realm of politics and which prevents its constitutive contingency from

---

[1] There is another way of integrating the two moments of reflexive politics. The first involved reflexivity as the freedom to choose what politics is about. The second involved reflexivity as self-reference: what politics is about is a political question. Politics absorbs freedom in defining it against - or even as - its horizon: and yet what makes politics possible as self-referential is the freedom that inheres in reflexivity in the first sense, of the contingency of possible departures.

surfacing. Republicanism, as a variation on the old theme, renews the attempt to establish law as the centrepiece of politics. But however re-stated, the old is too old. We must resist the forms that hold the political future captive to the political present. We need to politicise and make contestable the present state of politics and we need to act upon our ability to act. No necessity compels us to close politics to the future, and without that closure - to reverse Luhmann's prediction - the future might begin.[2]

---

[2] Luhmann (1976)

BIBLIOGRAPHY

[*NB I have compiled the bibliography of Luhmann's works in the strict chronological order of the appearance of each of his texts rather than of its translation into English. I have done this for two reasons. First because Luhmann has always written in a way that continually develops and qualifies his earlier work, even at the level of its most fundamental pre-suppositions. In that sense it is important to identify each work's precise location on the trajectory. This becomes more urgent because the collections of his work in English have included articles on a haphazard basis, making it impossible to follow the continuity in his work.]

Abrams K (1988): "Law's Republicanism", in 97, *Yale Law Journal*, 1591
Ackerman B (1980): *Social Justice in the Liberal State*. New Haven: Yale University Press
   (1984): "The Storrs Lectures: Discovering the Constitution", in 93, *Yale Law Journal*, 1013.
   (1985): "Beyond Carolene Products", in 98, *Harvard Law Review*, 713
   (1988): "Transformative Appointments", in 101, *Harvard Law Review*, 1164
   (1989): "Constitutional Politics/ Constitutional Law" in 99, *Yale Law Journal*, 453.
   (1991): *We The People. Foundations*. Cambridge MA: Belknap.
Alexy R (1989): *A Theory of Legal Argumentation*. Oxford: Clarendon
Amar A (1988): "Philadelphia Revisited: Amending the Constitution Outside Article V", in 55, *University of Chicago Law Review*, 1043.
Anscombe G E M (1957): *Intention*. Oxford: Blackwell
Arendt H (1968): *The Human Condition*. Chicago: Chicago University Press
Atiyah P (1986): "Form and Substance in Legal Reasoning". In MacCormick N & Birks P (eds): *The Legal Mind*. Oxford: Clarendon
Aubert V (1983): *In Search of Law*. Oxford: Martin Robertson.
Aust S (1987): *The Baader-Meinhof Group*. Translated by Anthea Bell. London: Bodley Head.
Bailey S H, Harris D J & Jones B L (1991): *Civil Liberties: Cases and Materials*. London: Butterworths
Baker C E (1989): *Human Liberty and Freedom of Speech*. New York: Oxford University Press
Balestrini N (1987): *Les Invisibles* . Trans. C Moiroud and M Fusco. Paris: P.O.L. Editeur.

Bankowski Z (1976): *Images of Law*. London: Routledge and Kegan Paul
   (1991) Ambiguities of the Rule of Law. In Jung H, Mueller-Dietz H & Neumann U (eds) *Recht und Moral*. Baden-Baden: Nomos Verlagsgesellschaft
   (1993): "Don't Think About It: Legalism and Legality". In Karlsson et al (eds*): Law, Justice and the State*. Berlin: Duncker & Humblot
Barber B (1984): *Strong Democracy*. Berkeley: University of California Press
Barendt E (1985): *Freedom of Speech*. Oxford: Clarendon
Barron A (1990): 'The Colonization of the Self in Everyday Life.' In Carty A (ed): *Post-Modern Law*. Edinbugh: Edinburgh University Press
Barthes R (1977): "Introduction to the Structuralist Analysis of Narratives" in *Image-Music-Text*. London: Fontana
   (1983) *Selected Writings*. London: Fontana
Baudrillard J (1973): *The Mirror of Production*. St Louis: Telos Press
   (1988): *Selected Writings*. Ed. M Poster. London: Polity Press
Bellamy R (1993): "Dethroning Politics: Liberalism, Constitutionalism and Democracy in the thought of F A Hayek" (unpublished paper)
Benhabib S (1987): *Critique, Norm and Utopia*. New York: Columbia University Press
   (1994): "Democracy and Difference: Reflections on the Metapolitics of Lyotard and Derrida", in 2, *Journal of Political Philosophy*, 1
Bennington G (1988): *Lyotard. Writing the Event*. Manchester: Manchester University Press
Berger S (1987): "Religious Transformation". In Maier C (ed): *Changing Boundaries of the Political*. Cambridge: Cambridge University Press
Berlin I (1969): *Two Concepts of Liberty*. Oxford: Clarendon
Bickel A (1962): *The Least Dangerous Branch*. Cambridge MA: Harvard University Press
   (1975): *The Morality of Consent*. New Haven: Yale University Press
Bork R (1971):"Neutral Principles and Some First Amendment Principles", in 47, *Indiana Law Journal*, 1
Bourdieu P (1986):"La Force du Droit", in 64, *Actes de la Recherche en Sciences Sociales*, 3
Brest P (1988): "Toward Radical Republicanism", in 97, *Yale Law Journal*, 1623
Breton A (1928): *Nadja*. Paris: Gallimard.
Brigham J (1978): *Constitutional Language*. Westport, Conn.: Greenwood
Broekman J (1985): Law, Anthropology and Epistemology. In Bulygin E et al. (eds): *Man, Law and Modern Forms of Life*. Dodrecht: Reidel

(1989): Revolution and Moral Commitment to a Legal System. In MacCormick D N & Bankowski Z (eds): *Enlightenment, Rights and Revolution*. Aberdeen: Aberdeen University Press
Brown B (1985): "A Feminist Interest in Pornography: Some Modest Proposals", in 7, *m/f*, 5
 (1990): "Debating Pornography: The Symbolic Dimensions", in 1/2, *Law and Critique*, 131
 (1993): Feminism. In Bellamy R (ed) *Theories and Concepts of Politics*. Manchester: Manchester University Press
Brownlie I (1990): *Principles of Public International Law*. 4th ed. Oxford: Clarendon
Carter A (1973): *Direct Action and Liberal Democracy*. London: Routledge & Kegan Paul.
Castoriadis C (1975): *L'Institution imaginaire de la Société*. Paris: Seuil
Christie N (1977): "Conflicts as Property", in 17, *British Journal of Criminology*, 1
Christodoulidis E A & Veitch T S (1994): "Terrorism and Systems Terror", in 23, *Economy and Society*, 459
Christodoulidis E A (1991): 'A Case for Reflexive Politics: Challenging Luhmann's Account of the Political System', in 20, *Economy and Society*, 381
 (1994): 'The Suspect Intimacy between Law and Political Community: The Case of *Law's Empire*', in 80, *ARSP*, 1
 (1996): 'The Inertia of Institutional Imagination: A Reply to Roberto Unger', in 59, *Modern Law Review*, 377
Connolly W (1974): *The Terms of Political Discourse*. Lexington, Mass.: Heath
 (1987): *Politics and Ambiguity*. Madison: University of Wisconsin Press
 (1991): *Identity/Difference*. Ithaca: Cornell University Press
Cornell D (1988) 'Institutionalization of Meaning. Recollective Imagination and the Potential for Transformative Legal Interpretation', 136, *University of Pennsylvania Law Review*.
Coser L (1950): "Review of Parsons' 'Essays'," in 55, *American Journal of Sociology*, 502
 (1956): *The Functions of Social Conflict*. New York: The Free Press
 (1962): 'Some Functions of Deviant Behavior and Normative Flexibility', in 68, *American Journal of Sociology*, 172
 (1967): *Continuities in the Study of Social Conflict*. New York: The Free Press
Cotterrell R (1984): *The Sociology of Law*. London: Butterworths
Cover R (1983): "Nomos and Narrative", in 97, *Harvard Law Review*, 4

(1986): "Violence and the Word", in 99, *Yale Law Journal*, 1601
Craig P P (1990): *Public Law and Democracy in the UK and the USA*. Oxford: Clarendon.
   (1993): "Public Law, Sovereignty and Citizenship". In Blackburn R (ed) *Rights of Citizenship*. London: Mansell
Crick B (1971): 'Politics as Freedom.' In *Political Theory and Practice*. London: Allen Lane.
Dahrendorf R (1968): "Homo Sociologicus", in *Essays in the Theory of Society*. Palo Alto: Stanford University Press
Dan-Cohen M (1989): "Law, Community and Communication", in *Duke Law Journal*, 1654
Davidson D (1980): *Essays on Actions and Events*. New York: Oxford University Press
Davies P L & Freedland M (1984): *Labour Law: Texts and Materials*. 2nd ed. London: Weidenfeld & Nicholson
Deleuze G & Guattari F (1988*)*: *A Thousand Plateaus*. London: Athlone
Donzelot J (1984): *L'Invention du Social*. Paris: Fayard
Dorsen N & Friedman L (1973): *Disorder in the Court*. New York: Pantheon Books
Dummett A & Nicol A (1990): *Subjects, Citizens, Aliens and Others: Nationality and Immigration Law*. London: Weidenfeld & Nicholson
Dworkin R (1978): *Taking Rights Seriously*. London: Duckworth
   (1989): 'Liberal Community', in 77, *California Law Review*, 479
   (1986): *Law's Empire*. London: Fontana
Edelman B (1979): *Ownership of the Image*. London: Routledge and Kegan Paul
Eder K (1993): *The New Politics of Class*. London: Sage
Edmundson W (1993): "Rethinking Exclusionary Reasons", in 12, *Law and Philosophy*, 329
Ely J H (1975): "Flag Desecration: A Case Study in the Roles of Categorization and Balancing in First Amendment Analysis", in 88, *Harvard Law Review*, 1482
   (1978): "Toward a Representation-reinforcing Model of Judicial Review" in 37, *Modern Law Review*, 51
   (1980): *Democracy and Distrust*. Cambridge MA: Harvard University Press.
Farmer L (1992): "The Genius of Our Law", in 55, *Modern Law Review*, 1
Feinberg J (1980): *Rights, Justice and the Bounds of Liberty*. Princeton: Princeton U. P.
Feldman S (1992): "Republican Revival, Interpretive Turn," in *Wisconsin Law Review*, 679

Festiner W, Abel R & Sarat A (1980): "The Emergence and Transformation of Disputes: Naming, Blaming, Claiming ...", in 15, *Law & Society Review*, 49

Finn J (1991): *Constitutions in Crisis*. New York: Oxford University Press

Finnie W (1990) "Old Wine in New Bottles? The Evolution of Anti-Terrorist Legislation", in 35, *Juridical Review*, 1.

Fischer R (1964): Fractionating Conflict. In Fisher R (ed): *International Conflict and Behavioral Science. The Craigville Papers*. New York: Basic Books

Fish S (1982) "Working on the Chain Gang. Interpretation in Law and Literature", in 60, *Texas Law Review*, 551

Foerster H von (1981): *On Observing Systems*. Seaside California: Intersystems

Foner E (1988): *Reconstruction: America's Unfinished Revolution*. New York: Harper & Row.

Freund J (1974): "Le droit comme motif et solution de conflicts", in *ARSP* Beiheift 8, 47

Fusco M (1987): "Introduction". In Balestrini N: *Les Invisibles*. Paris: P.O.L. Editeur.

Gallie W B (1956): 'Essentially Contested Concepts', in *Proceedings of the Aristotelian Society*, vol. 56, London

Gardner J (1992): "The Failed Discourse of State Constitutionalism," in 90, *Michigan Law Review*, 761

Gearty C (1993): "Citizenship and Freedom of Expression". In Blackburn R (ed) *Rights of Citizenship*. London: Mansell

Geertz C (1973): *The Interpretation of Cultures*. New York: Basic Books

Gellhorn W (1976): *The States and Subversion*. Ithaca: Cornell University Press

Gey S (1993): "The Unfortunate Revival of Civic Republicanism", in 141, *University of Pennsylvania Law Review*, 801

Glanville R (1981): 'The Same is Different'. In Zeleny M (ed) *Autopoiesis: A Theory of Living Organisation*. New York: Elsevier

Glasman M (1994): "The Great Deformation", in 205, *New Left Review*, 59
 (1996): *Unnecessary Suffering: Managing Market Utopia*. London: Verso

Goodhart J (1935): 'Newspapers and Contempt of Court', in *Harvard Law Review*, 885

Gouldner A (1973): *For Sociology: Renewal and Critique in Social Theory*. London: Allen Lane

Greenawalt K (1989): *Speech, Crime and the Uses of Language*. New York: Oxford University Press

Grundmann R (1990): "Luhmann Conservative, Luhmann Progressive". EUI Working Paper LAW 90/7 : Florence
Günther K (1993): *Sense of Appropriateness*. Albany: SUNY Press
Gusfield J (1963): *Symbolic Crusades: Politics and the American Temperance Movement*. Urbana, Ill: University of Illinois Press
Habermas J (1962): *Strukturwandel der Öffentlichkeit*. Darmstadt: Luchterhand.
   (1972): *Knowledge and Human Interests*. London: Heineman
   (1974): "The Public Sphere: An Encyclopaedia Article", in 3, *New German Critique*, 49
   (1987a): *The Theory of Communicative Action*. Cambridge: Polity Press
   (1987b): *The Philosophical Discourse of Modernity*. Boston: Beacon Press
   (1992a): "Citizenship and National Identity: Some Reflections on the Future of Europe", in 12, *Praxis International*, 1
   (1992b): *Faktizität und Geltung*. Frankfurt: Suhrkamp
Hall S & Held D (1989): "Citizens and Citizenship", in Hall & Jacques (eds): *New Times*. London: Lawrence and Wishart.
Hayek F A (1979): *The Political Order of a Free People*. London: Routledge
Heater D (1991): "Citizenship: A Remarkable Case of Sudden Interest", in 44, *Parliamentary Affairs*, 140
Heller T (1987): Accounting for Law. In Teubner (ed): *Autopoietic Law: A New Approach to Law and Society*. Berlin: de Gruyter
Herzog D (1986): "Some Questions for Republicans", in 14, *Political Theory*, 473
Hoffman A (1970): *The Trial of the Chicago Seven*. New York: Dial Press
Hohendal P (1974): "Habermas: The Public Sphere", in 3, *New German Critique*, 45
Horowitz I L (1962): "Consensus, Conflict and Cooperation: A Sociological Inventory," in 41, *Social Forces*, 177
Hunt A (1992): "Law's Empire or Legal Imperialism?" In Hunt A (ed): *Reading Dworkin Critically*. New York: Berg
Jordan G (1993): The Pluralism of Pluralism: An Anti-Theory? In Richardson J (ed): *Pressure Groups*. Oxford: Oxford University Press
Kahn P (1989): "Community in Contemporary Constitutional Theory", in 99, *Yale Law Journal*, 1
Kalven H (1966): *The Negro and the First Amendment*. Chicago: University of Chicago Press
Kamenka E & Tay A (1976): "Beyond Bourgeois Individualism: The Crisis in Law and Legal Ideology". In Kamenka E and Neale R (eds): *Feudalism, Capitalism and Beyond*. London: Edward Arnold

Kingdom E (1991): *What's Wrong With Rights: Problems for Feminist Politics of Law.* Edinburgh: Edinburgh University Press

Klarman M (1992): "Constitutional Fact/ Constitutional Fiction: A Critique of Ackerman's Theory of Constitutional Moments", in 44, *Stanford Law Review*, 759.

Koestler A (1978): *Janus.* New York: Random Books

Kymlicka W (1991): *Liberalism, Community and Culture.* Oxford: Oxford University Press

Leubsdorf D (1987): "Deconstructing the Constitution", in 40, *Stanford Law Review*, 181.

Lobban M (1992): "From Seditious Libel To Unlawful Assembly", in 10, *Oxford Journal of Legal Studies*, 307

Luhmann N (1967): "Positive Law and Ideology". Included in *The Differentiation of Society.* New York: Columbia University Press

(1971): "Meaning as Sociology's Basic Concept". Included in *Essays on Self-reference.* Columbia University Press (1990)

(1972): *The Sociological theory of Law.* Translated by E King-Utz and M Albrow. London: Routledge and Kegan Paul. [original: *Rechtsoziologie.*]

(1975a): "Interaction, Organization and Society". Included in *The Differentiation of Society.* New York: Columbia University Press

(1975b): "The Self-Thematization of Society". Included in *The Differentiation of Society.* New York: Columbia University Press

(1975c): *Soziologische Aufklarung 2.* Opladen: Westdeutcher Verlag.

(1976a): "The Furure Cannot Begin: Temporal Structures in Modern Society", in 43, *Social Research*, 130

(1976b): "Generalized Media and the Problem of Contingency". In Loubser J et al. (eds): *Explorations in the General Theory of the Social Sciences: Essays in Honour of Talcott Parsons.* New York

(1977): "The Differentiation of Society." Included in *The Differentiation of Society.* New York: Columbia University Press

(1980): Temporalisierung von Komplexität. In *Gesellschaftstruktur und Semantik.* vol.1. Frankfurt: Suhrkamp

(1981): *Ausdifferenzierung des Rechts: Beitrage zur Rechtssoziologie und Rechtstheorie.* Frankfurt: Suhrkamp

(1982): *Liebe als Passion.* Frankfurt: Suhrkamp

(1984): *Soziale Systeme.* Frankfurt: Suhrkamp

(1985a): "Complexity and Meaning" in *The Science and Praxis of Complexity.* Tokyo: United Nations University Press

(1985b): "Some Problems with Reflexive Law". In Teubner G & Febbrajo A (eds): *State, Law, Economy as Autopoietic Systems.* Milano: Giuffré

(1986a): "The Coding of the Legal System". In Teubner G & Febbrajo A (eds): *State, Law, Economy as Autopoietic Systems*. Milano: Giuffré

(1986b): "The Self-Reproduction of Law and its Limits". In Teubner G (ed): *Autopoietic Law: A new Approach to Law and Society*. Berlin: de Gruyter

(1986c): "The Autopoiesis of Social Systems". In Geyer F & van der Zouwen J (eds): *Sociocybernetic Paradoxes; Observation, Control and Evolution of Self-Steering Systems*. Beverly Hills, California: Sage

(1986d): "The Individuality of the Individual: Historical Meaning and Contemporary Problems". In Heller T, Sosna M & Wellbery D (eds): *Reconstructing Individualism*.

(1986e): *Ecological Communication*. Cambridge: Polity Press.

(1986f): "Distinctions Directrices: Uber Codierung von Semantiken und Systems". in Neidhardt, Lepsius, Weiss (eds): "Kultur und Gesellschaft" (special issue), 27, *Kolner Zeitschrift fur Soziologie und Sozialpsychologie*, 145

(1988a): "Tautology and Paradox in the Self-Descriptions of Modern Society". Included in *Essays on Self-reference*. Columbia University Press

(1988b): "The Unity of the Legal System". In Teubner G (ed): *Autopoietic Law: A New Approach to Law and Society*. Berlin: de Gruyter

(1988c): "The Third Question: the Creative Use of Paradoxes in Law and Legal History", in 15, *Journal of Law & Society*, 153

(1989): "Law as a Social System", in 83, *Northwestern University Law Review*, 136

(1990a) *Political Theory in the Welfare State*. Berlin: de Gruyter

(1990b) *Soziologische Aufkrarung 5*. Frankfurt: Suhrkamp

(1990c) "Verfassung als evolutionare Errungenschaft", in 9, *Rechtshistorisches Journal*, 176

(1990d) 'Interesse und Interessenjurisprudenz im Spannungsfeld von Gesetzgebung und Rechtsprechung' in *Zeitschrift für Neuere Rechtsgeschichte*, 1

(1991a): *Risk: A Sociological Theory*. Translated by R Barret: Berlin: de Gruyter

(1992a): *Beobachtungen der Moderne*. Opladen: Westdeutcher Verlag

(1992b): "The Concept of Society", in 31, *Thesis Eleven*, 67

(1992c): "Operational Closure and Structural Coupling: the Differentiation of the Legal System", in 13, *Cardozo Law Review*, 1434

(1993): *Das Recht der Gesellschaft*. Frankfurt: Suhrkamp

(1995): "Legal Argumentation: An Analysis of Its Form," in 58, *Modern Law Review*, 285

Lukes S (1991): 'The Principles of 1989: Reflections on the Political Morality of the Recent Revolutions'. In *Moral Conflict and Politics*. Oxford: Clarendon

Lyotard J-F (1984): *The Postmodern Condition*. Manchester: Manchester University Press.

(1983): *Des Dispositifs Pulsionnels*. 2nd ed.. Paris: Christian Bourgeois

(1988): *The Differend*. Manchester: Manchester University Press.

MacCormick D N & Weinberger O (1968): *An Institutional Theory of Law*. Dodrecht: Reidel

MacCormick D N (1974): "Law as Institutional Fact", in 90, *Law Quartely Review*, 102

(1989): "Legalism". In 2, *Ratio Juris*

(1993): "Beyond the Sovereign State", in 56, *Modern Law Review*, 1

(1993): Constitutionalism and Democracy. In Bellamy R (ed): *Theories and Concepts of Politics*. Manchester: Manchester University Press

Macedo S (1990): *Liberal Virtues*. Oxford: Clarendon

MacKinnon C (1983): *Feminism Unmodified*. Cambridge MA: Harvard University Press

(1992): "Pornography, Civil Rights and Speech". In Itzin C (ed): *Pornography*. New York: Oxford University Press

Maier C (1987): "Introduction". In Maier C (ed): *Changing Boundaries of the Political*. Cambridge: Cambridge University Press

March J & Simon H (1958): *Organizations*. New York: Wiley

Marshall T H (1950): *Class, Citizenship and Social Development*. New York: Doubleday

Mathiesen T (1974): *The Politics of Abolition*. Oslo: Universitetsforlaget.

McIntyre A (1977): "Epistemological Crises, Dramatic Narrative and the Philosophy of Science", in 60, *The Monist*, 453

(1981): *After Virtue*. London: Duckworth

Melucci A (1982): "Reponse à Alain Touraine", in Touraine A (ed): *Mouvements Sociaux d'aujourd'hui*. Paris: Editions ouvrières

(1988) "Social Movements and the Democratisation of Everyday Life". In Keane J (ed): *Civil Society and the State*. London: Verso.

(1989): *Nomads of the Present*. London: Hutchinson Radius.

(1992): "Challenging Codes: Framing and Ambivalence in the Ideology of Social Movements", in 31, *Thesis Eleven*, 131

Michelman F (1986): "Foreword: Traces of Self-Government", in 100, *Harvard Law Review*, 4

(1988): "Law's Republic", in 97, *Yale Law Journal*, 1493

Miller C J (1989): *Contempt of Court*. 2nd ed. Oxford: Clarendon
Miller M (1987): Argumentation and Cognition. In: Hickmann M (ed) *Social and Functional Approaches to Language and Thought*. New York: Academic Press
  (1992): "Discourse and Morality- Two case studies of Social Conflicts", in 33, *Arch. europ. sociol.*, 3
  (1994) "Intersystemic Discourse and Co-ordinated Dissent: A Critique of Luhmann's Concept of Ecological Communication", in 11, *Theory, Culture and Society*, 101
Minow M (1987): "Justice Engendered", in 101, *Harvard Law Review*, 10
Murphy W T (1984): "Modern Times: Niklas Luhmann on Law, Politics and Social Theory", in 47, *Modern Law Review*, 603
  (1994): "Systems of Systems: Some Issues in the Relationship Between Law and Autopoiesis", in 5, *Law and Critique*, 1
Mydral F (1944): *An American Dilemma*. New York: Harper Bros.
Nancy J-L (1985): "Dies irae", in Lyotard J-F (ed) *La Faculté de Juger*. Paris: Minuit.
Neisser U (1976): *Cognition and Reality*. San Fransisco: W H Freeman
Nowak J & Rotunda R (1991): *Constitutional Law*. St Paul: West Pub. Co
Offe C (1985): "Challenging the Boundaries of Institutional Politics", in 52, *Social Research*
Oldfield A (1990): "Citizenship: An Unnatural Practice?", in *Political Quarterly*, 319
Parsons T & Shils E (1951): *Toward a General Theory of Action*. Cambridge MA: Harvard University Press
Parsons T (1951): *The Social System*. London: Routledge and Kegan Paul
Perry S (1987): "Judicial Obligation, Precedent and the Common Law", in 7, *Oxford Journal of Legal Studies*, 215
Picciotto S (1979): "The Theory of the State, Class Struggle and the Rule of Law". In Fine R (ed) *Capitalism and the Rule of Law*. London: Hutchinson.
Pitkin H (1984): *Fortune is a Woman; Gender and Politics in the Thought of N Machiavelli*. Berkeley: University of California Press
Pizzorno A (1987): 'Politics Unbound'. In Maier C (ed): *Changing Boundaries of the Political*. Cambridge: Cambridge University Press
Pocock J G A (1975): *The Macchiavellian Moment*. Princeton N.J.: Princeton University Press
  (1981): "The Machiavellian Moment Revisited", in 53, *Journal of Modern History*, 70
  (1985): *Virtue, Commerce and History*. Cambridge: Cambridge University Press

Poggi G (1979): "Luhmann's Neo-Functionalist Approach". Introduction to Luhmann's *Trust and Power*. Chichester: Wiley

Pope J G (1990): "Republican Moments; The Role of Direct Popular Power in the American Constitutional Order", in 139, *University of Pennsylvania Law Review*, 287

Postema G (1987): "Protestant Interpretations and Legal Practices", in 6, *Law and Philosophy*, 283

(1989): In Defence of 'French nonsense': Fundamental Rights in Constitutional Jurisprudence. In MacCormick D N & Bankowski Z (eds): *Enlightenment, Rights and Revolution*. Aberdeen: Aberdeen University Press

Poulantzas N (1973): *Political Power and Social Classes*. London : New Left Books

Powell H J (1988): "Reviving Republicanism", in 97, *Yale Law Journal*, 1703

Pranger R (1968): *The Eclipse of Citizenship*. New York: Holt, Reinhart & Wilson

Preuss U (1995): "Citizenship and Identity: Aspects of a Political Theory of Citizenship". In Bellamy et al (eds): *Democracy and Constitutional Culture in the Union of Europe*. London: Lothian Foundation

Raschke J (1980): "Politik und Wertwandel in den Westlichen Demokratien", in 36, *Aus Politik und Zeitgeschichte*, 23

Rasmussen D (1990): *Reading Habermas*. Oxford: Blackwell

Rawls J (1971): *A Theory of Justice*. Cambridge MA: The Belknap Press

Raz J (1979): *The Authority of Law*. Oxford: Clarendon

(1986): *The Morality of Freedom*. Oxford: Clarendon

(1989): "Facing Up: A Reply", in 62, *S California Law Review*, 1153

(1990): *Practical Reason and Norms*. 2nd ed. Princeton: Princeton University Press

Rex J (1961): *Key Problems of Sociological Theory*. London: Routledge and Kegan Paul

(1981): *Social Conflict*. New York: Longman

Ricoeur P (1986): *Lectures on Ideology and Utopia*. N.York: Columbia University Press

Rosenblum N (1994): "Democratic Character and Community", in 1, *The Journal of Political Philosophy*, 67

Rottleutner H (1987): "Biological Metaphors in Legal Thought". In Teubner G (ed): *Autopoietic Law: A new Approach to Law and Society*. Berlin: de Gruyter

(1989b): 'A Purified Sociology of Law', in 27, *Law and Society Review*, 779

Sandel M (1982): *Liberalism and the Limits of Justice.* Cambridge: Cambridge University Press
  (1985): "The State and the Soul", in 19, *The New Republic*, 39.
  (1988): "Democrats and Community", in 22, *The New Republic*, 20
Sartre J P (1976): *The Critique of Dialectical Reason.* Trans. A Sheridan-Smith. 2nd ed. London
Saussure de F (1973): *Cours de Linguistique Générale.* Paris: Payot
Schauer F (1982): *Free Speech: A Philosophical Enquiry.* Cambridge: Cambridge University Press
  (1991): *Playing by the Rules.* Oxford: Clarendon
Shapiro M (1988): *The Politics of Representation.* Madison: University of Wisconsin Press
Shiner R (1992): "Exclusionary Reasons and the Explanation of Behaviour", in 5, *Ratio Juris*, 1
Simmel G (1955): *Conflict.* Trans. K Wolff. New York: The Free Press
Simon J (1992): "Columbus in the Twilight Zone: B Ackerman's "Discovery" of the Constitution", in 17, *Law and Social Inquiry*, 501
Skilling H G (1988): "Parallel Polis, or an Independent Society in Central and Eastern Europe", in 55, *Social Research*, 211
Smart C (1986): "Feminism and Law", in 14, *International Journal of the Sociology of Law*, 109
Smith A (1986): *The Ethnic Origins of Nations.* Oxford: Blackwell
Smith S A de (1985): *Constitutional and Administrative Law*, 5th ed. by Street H and Brazier R. Harmondsworth: Penguin Books.
Smith S C (1990): "Dworkin's Imperialism and Socio-Legal Empiricism", 17, *Journal of Law and Society*, 263
  (1991): "Beyond 'Mega-Theory' and 'Multiple Sociology': A Reply to Rottleutner", in 19, *International Journal of the Sociology of Law*, 321
  (1995): The Redundancy of Reasoning. In Bankowski Z & White I (eds): *Informatics and the Foundations of Legal Reasoning.* Dodrecht: Kluwer
Schmitt C (1976): *The Concept of the Political.* New Brunswick: Rutgers University Press
Spencer Brown G (1972): *Laws of Form.* New York: Julian
Sullivan K (1988): "Rainbow Republicanism", in 97, *Yale Law Journal*, 1713
Sunstein C (1985): "Interest Groups in American Public Law", in 38, *Stanford Law Review*, 29
  (1986): "Legal Interferences with Naked Preferences", in *University of Chicago Law Review*, 1129.

(1988): "Beyond the Republican Revival", in 97, *Yale Law Journal*, 1539

(1996): *Legal Principles and Political Conflict*. New York: Oxford University Press

Tannenbaum F (1924) : *Darker Phases of the South*. New York: G P Putnam's Sons.

Tassopoulos I (1993): *The Constitutional Problem of Subversive Advocacy in the USA and Greece*. Athens: Sakkoulas

Taylor C (1989): 'Cross-purposes; the Liberal-Communitarian Debate.' In Rosenblum N (ed): *Liberalism and the Moral Life*. Cambridge MA: Cambridge University Press

Teubner G (1983): "Substantive and Reflexive Elements in Modern Law", in 17, *Law & Society Review*, 239

(1987): Juridification: Concepts, Aspects, Limits, Solutions. In Teubner G (ed): *Juridification of Social Spheres*. Berlin: de Gruyter

(1988a): "Enterprise Corporatism: New Industrial Policy and the "Essence" of the Legal Person", in 36, *The American Journal of Comparative Law*, 130.

(1988b): "Hypercycle in Law and Organization. In *The European Yearbook of the Sociology of Law*. Milano: Giuffré

(1989): "How the Law Thinks: Towards a Constructivist Epistemology of Law", in 23, *Law & Society Review*, 727

(1991): Regulatorisches Recht: Chronik eines angekündigten Todes. In P Koller, O Weinberger (eds) *Grundlagen der Rechtspolitik*. Wiesbaden

(1992): "The Two Faces of Janus: Rethinking Legal Pluralism", in 13, *Cardozo Law Review*, 1419

(1993a): *Law as an Autopoietic System*. Oxford: Blackwell

(1993b): "The "State" of Private Networks: The Emerging Legal Regime of Polycorporatism in Germany", in 2, *Brigham Young University Law Review*, 553

Therborn G (1980): *The Ideology of Power and the Power of Ideology*. London: Verso

Thompson E P (1978): *The Poverty of Theory and Other Essays*. London: Merlin Press

Thompson J (1984) *Studies in the Theory of Ideology*. Cambridge: Polity Press

(1993): "The Theory of the Public Sphere", in 10, *Theory*, Culture and Society, 173

Touraine A (1974): *The Post-Industrial Society: Tomorrow's Social History*. New York: Random House

(1977): *The Self-Production of Society.* Chicago: Chicago University Press

(1981): *The Voice and the Eye: An Analysis of Social Movements.* Cambridge: Cambridge University Press.

Townsend C (1993): *Making the Peace.* Oxford: Oxford University Press

Tribe L (1985): *Constitutional Choices.* Cambridge MA: Harvard University Press

Turner B (1986): *Citizenship and Capitalism.* London: Allen and Unwin

(1990): "Outline of a Theory of Citizenship", in 24, *Sociology*, 189

Tushnet M (1988): *Red, White and Blue: A Critical Analysis of Constitutional Law.* Cambridge, MA: Harvard University Press

Unger R M (1976): *Law in Modern Society: Toward a Criticism of Social Theory.* New York: Free Press

(1983): *The Critical Legal Studies Movement.* Cambridge MA: Harvard University Press

(1987a): *Social Theory: Its Situation and Its Task.* Vol. 1 of *Politics: A Work in Constructive Social Theory.* Cambridge MA: Cambridge University Press

(1987b): *False Necessity: Anti-Necessitarian Social Theory in the Service of Radical Democracy.* Vol. 2 of *Politics: A Work in Constructive Social Theory.* Cambridge MA: Cambridge University Press

(1996): 'Legal Analysis as Institutional Imagination' in 59, *Modern Law Review*, 1

Virally M (1960): *La Pensée Juridique.* Paris: L.G.D.J.

Walker C (1985): "Scandalising in the 80s", in 101, *Law Quartely Review*, 359

Walzer M (1970): The Obligation to Live for the State. In *Obligations.* Cambridge MA: Harvard University Press

(1991): "The Idea of Civil Society", in *Dissent*, 293

Warren M (1989): "Liberal Constitutionalism as Ideology", in 17, *Political Theory*, 511

Weber N (1984): "Afterword". In Lyotard J-F & Thebaud J-L, *Just Gaming.* Translated by W Godzich. Manchester: Manchester University Press

Weick K (1979): *The Social Psychology of Organizing.* New York: Random House

White S (1988): *The Recent Work of Jürgen Habermas.* Cambridge: Cambridge University Press

Willener A (1970): *The Image-Action of Society.* London: Tavistock

Williams D (1967): *Keeping the Peace.* London: Hutchinson

Wolfe A (1989): *Whose Keeper?* Berkeley: University of California Press

Wolin S (1960): *Politics and Vision.* Boston: Little, Brown & Co

Yack B (1988): 'Toward a Free Marketplace of Social Institutions: Roberto Unger's "Super-liberal" theory of Emancipation', in 101, *Harvard Law Review*, 1961

Young I (1989): "Polity and Group Difference: A Critique of the Ideal of Universal Citizenship," in 99, *Ethics*, 250

Zolo D (1992): The Epistemological Status of the Theory of Autopoiesis and its Application to the Social Sciences. In Teubner G, Febbrajo A (eds): *State, Law, Economy as Autopoietic Systems*. Milano: Giuffré

INDEX

—A—

Ackerman, B, 15, 16, 18, 29, 31-39, 43, 45, 48, 49, 60, 67, 70, 162, 164, 202, 205, 210, 256-258, 264-271
Action,
  theory, 75, 77, 90
  collective, 25, 166
  communicative action, 23-27, 40, 113,
  concept of, 105, 227-232
  political, 250, 251, 260, 275-286
  strategic, 26, 27
Alexy, R, 40
Arendt, H, 7, 16, 17, 39, 253

—B—

Baader-Meinhof, 175-6, 181
Bankowski, Z, 90, 177, 227, 229, 230, 231, 266, 267
Barthes, R, 59
Berlin, I, 37
Bickel, A, 14
Bork, R, 165, 166, 181
Breton, A, 261,
Broekman, J, 215, 286

—C—

citizenship, 3, 5, 6, 7, 8, 11, 12, 16, 34, 37, 42, 50, 51, 62, 63, 69, 70, 161, 163-4, 177, 186, 203-4, 210, 256, 269, 270
Civil Society, 4, 5, 19, 29
coding, 82, 88-96, 151, 159-160, 178-9, 213
Communitarianism, 4, 8, 11, 12, 16, 38
Critical Legal Studies, 65, 159, 211-224
community, 3, 4, 6, 7, 8, 10, 11, 12, 14, 15, 16, 17, 18, 31, 33, 34, 35, 36, 37, 38, 39, 41, 42, 43, 45, 46, 47, 48, 49, 50, 51, 53, 54, 55, 56, 57, 58, 59, 60, 61, 62, 63, 64, 65, 66, 67, 69, 70, 137-141, 145, 193, 195, 201-211, 219, 235, 236, 237, 256, 257, 258, 265, 268, 269, 270, 279, 280
communication theory, 20-30, 73-77, 113,
complexity, 29
conflict, 56, 70, 227, 228, 230, 233, 242, 244, 251, 259, 269, 274, 279
  class, 97, 99, 177, 195-6, 199, 208,
  communal/non-communal, 200-7,
  constitutive, 96, 194-199
  phenomenal, 96, 194-199
  staging of, 139
  symbolic, 190-3
  theory, 102-3
  finite, 110, 140, 141-3,
  infinite, 140, 141-4,
Connolly, W, 19, 234-235
consensus, 8, 13, 27-30, 102, 105, 110, 123, 141-4
  theory, 102
  ideal, 27-28
constitutionalism, 3, 5, 8, 10, 14, 20, 22, 23, 24, 31, 43, 69, 161, 163-4, 249
Contempt of Court, 173-86
contingency, 28, 56, 70, 106-8, 111, 112, 116, 129, 136, 179, 186, 213, 221, 235, 242, 245, 246, 249, 255, 264, 268, 273, 274, 275, 277, 281, 283, 284, 286
  double, 102-115, 116, 119, 123, 124, 126, 128, 131, 132, 134, 213, 223
Counter-majoritarian Paradox *see Judicial review*

Coser, L, 96, 102, 136, 137, 140, 141, 144, 145, 193, 199, 200, 201, 204
Cover, R, 39, 201, 203, 234 - 237

—D—

Davidson, D, 75, 153
democracy, 6, 14, 24-28, 163-4, 170
  associational, 4-9
  discursive, 20-30
différend, 176-186
differentiation
  functional, 29-30, 84-87, 107, 117-9, 241, 252, 254, 274, 275, 277
  discourse, 6, 17, 19, 21, 25, 26, 27, 28, 29, 35, 40, 42, 49, 51, 54, 64, 142, 164, 167, 185, 234, 235, 238, 241, 251, 252, 259, 265, 274, 275, 277, 280, 281, 282
  rational, 19-30
distinctions, 78, 82, 88-96, 138
  directrices *or* guiding, 88-96, 207,
  form of, 84
Dworkin, R, 10, 11, 12, 15, 18, 24, 29, 43, 46, 47, 48, 51, 53, 54, 55, 56, 57, 58, 59, 60, 61, 66, 70, 138, 139, 141, 143, 144, 146, 157, 202, 205, 206, 210, 211, 217, 223
Durkheim, 98, 105-6

—E—

Edelman, B, 149
Eder, K, 86, 199, 282
Ely, J, 15, 16, 28, 32, 171
empathy, 3, 40, 41, 70, 113, 181, 185
event, 45, 128, 179, 217, 238
  individuation of, 75,
exclusionary reasons, 138, 140, 185, 227, 228, 229, 230, 232, 255, 257, 258, 265, 266, 267, 268, 269, 270, 271, 283
expectations, 7, 137, 221, 223, 232, 249, 250, 257, 260, 262, 264, 266, 269, 270
  normative/cognitive, 121, 128

legal, 116-128, 129, 139
variation of, *see Evolution*
retention of, *see Evolution*
stabilisation of, *see Evolution*
generalisation of, 120-8, 134, 213
immunisation of, 213-224

—F—

Feminism, 157-163, 190-1
function,
  law's, 2, 14, 16, 27-28, 116, 117-120,
  equivalents (functional), 117, 119, 205,
  functionalism, 137

—G—

Gallie, W B, 19, 234
Glasman, M, xiii, 205
Gusfield, J, 191

—H—

Habermas, J, 3, 7, 8, 10, 17, 19, 20, 21, 22, 24, 25, 26, 27, 28, 29, 39, 40, 41, 42, 65, 75, 87, 97, 105, 113, 141, 142, 203, 217, 254, 282
horizon, 84, 124, 261, 262, 268, 270, 283, 284

—I—

identity, 12, 13, 34, 35, 38, 39, 42, 47, 48, 49, 58, 59, 60, 62, 65, 66, 67, 69, 70, 143, 147, 192-8, 200, 234, 250, 251, 257, 261, 265, 270, 274
  collective, 193-8, 199
  politics of, 193-8, 205, 206-8
ideology, 21, 163, 185, 194, 207, 209, 224
inertia
  simple/structural, 212, 218-224
information, 76-7, 90, 103, 106, 218, 224,
institutionalisation, 8, 107, 123-4, 129, 133, 198, 213,

institutional and brute fact, 125, 153, 155, 163, 184,
integrity, 23, 28, 46, 53, 55, 56, 57, 58, 59, 60, 145, 244
interaction, 36, 48, 104-6, 111-2, 116, 123-4, 132, 136-7, 143, 152, 154, 216-7, 254, 282
interests, 4, 13, 149, 156-163,

—J—

judicial review, 14-19
juridification, 22, 23, 96-101, 231

—L—

legitimation, 21, 158, 185, 207,
lifeworld, 20-2, 97
liberalism, 4, 8, 11, 12, 13, 17, 20-22, 32, 37, 167
love, 283-285
   love/marriage, 127-8, 154-6, 256-273
Luhamnn, N, 29, 54, 73, 74, 75, 76, 77, 78, 79, 80, 81, 82, 83, 84, 85, 86, 87, 88, 89, 90, 91, 92, 93, 94, 95, 102, 103, 104, 105, 106, 107, 108, 109, 110, 111, 113, 116, 117, 118, 119, 120, 121, 122, 123, 124, 125, 126, 128, 129, 130, 131, 132, 133, 134, 136, 137, 140, 141, 142, 145, 147, 149, 150, 151, 153, 154, 155, 156, 157, 159, 160, 180, 189, 208, 213, 214, 215, 216, 217, 219, 220, 221, 222, 234, 236, 242, 244, 246, 248, 249, 250, 251, 252, 253, 254, 255, 256, 258, 259, 261, 262, 263, 268, 270, 273, 274, 275, 276, 277, 278, 279, 280, 281, 282, 287
Lukes, S, 4
Lyotard, J-F, 177, 183, 184, 185, 234, 237, 238, 239, 240, 241, 242

—M—

MacKinnon, C, 158, 159, 191
Marxism, 164, 171, 201, 208, 209, 209, 248

McIntyre, A, 39, 59, 205
Melucci, A, 68, 188, 193, 194, 195, 196, 198, 199, 278
Miller, M, 108, 109, 141, 142, 143, 144, 174
MacCormick, N, 6, 15, 21, 25, 153, 231
Michelman, F, 16, 17, 18, 29, 36, 37, 38, 39, 40, 41, 42, 43, 44, 45, 46, 47, 48, 49, 50, 51, 60, 63, 64, 65, 69, 70, 143, 144, 146, 182, 202, 203, 204, 206, 207, 210, 211, 216, 217, 223, 236

—N—

narrative, 15, 18, 38, 46, 47, 48, 59, 60, 146, 147, 203, 205, 208, 234, 235, 236, 237

—O—

Offe, K, 166, 253, 279, 280

—P—

Parsons, T, 75, 89, 103, 104, 105, 106, 108, 121, 130, 137
person, legal, 124, 192, 205, 208, 209,
pluralism, 4, 5, 11, 12, 13, 14, 18, 37, 38, 66
popular sovereignty, 6, 10, 14, 24, 29, 170, 180-1
pornography, 158-163, 170, 190-3
Postema, G, 54, 65, 138
programming, 91-93, 107, 125, 139, 149, 155-6, 159-160, 178-9, 213, 264, 275
   conditional and goal-oriented, 155-6,
public
   sphere, 8, 17, 19-30,
   opinion, 6, 23-30

—R—

Rawls, J, 24,
Raz, J, 12, 227, 229, 230, 232
reduction, 25, 139, 141, 147, 159-160, 180-1, 212, 218, 221, 244, 250, 282, 284
   of complexity, 83-4, 94, 106-8, 114, 116, 124, 126, 133, 184,
   achievement, 92, 213, 224
reference
   external, 74, 81, 82, 153-4,
   internal, 74, 81, 154,
   self-, 106, 109, 111, 116, 149, 153, 157, 160, 161, 177-8, 185, 196, 219,
   referrer/referred, 155, 178, 182-5,
reflexivity, 103, 110, 113, 115, 120, 164, 178, 201,
   reflexive politics, 161, 186, 206, 212-3
   conflict, 134-5
Rex, J, 102
rights, 3, 6, 14, 28, 32, 33, 36, 38, 65, 68, 163-4, 180, 185, 192, 198, 208, 231, 243, 250, 260, 261, 266, 270
   freedom of speech, 6, 10, 20-30, 157-163, 169-86, 190
   political, 163-168, 201-7,
role, 85, 108, 123, 125, 147, 149, 154, 200
   theory, 108-9
Rottleutner, H, 73, 90, 92, 151, 152, 216

—S-

Sandel, M, 5, 12, 39, 50
Sartre, J-P, 194
scandalising (the Court), 173-4, 182
Schauer, F, 23, 120, 170, 229, 230, 231, 232, 266
Schmitt, C, 260
sedition, 163-86, 260, 286
Simmel, G, 96, 102, 141, 145, 159, 193, 199, 200
Smith S C, 54, 87, 91, 92, 121, 152, 165, 169, 191, 220, 262
social movements, 100, 147, 193-4
solidarity, 3, 190, 192, 198, 200, 205, 206
speech,
   political, 6, 8, 10, 20, 21, 23, 25, 28, 40, 149,
   freedom of, see Rights
State, 4, 5, 7, 8, 13, 19, 21, 23, 33, 38, 50, 51, 66, 68,171, 176, 208,
   Welfare State, 3, 22, 97-8,
structure, 15, 19, 70, 86, 111, 119, 167, 199,
   structuralism, 90, 94
   structural articulation, 179-180, 185,
   structural coupling, 22, 98, 119, 191, 221, 236
   structural inertia, 212-24
Sunstein, C, 11, 17, 18, 29, 36, 37, 38, 39, 40, 41, 42, 43, 44, 45, 49, 50, 61, 65, 70, 114, 157, 182, 210, 223
System
   closure, 118, 119, 130, 215
   complexity, 83-4, 103-4, 106, 131, 160, 213, 229, 250, 267, 274, 276, 283
      reduction of see Reduction
   contingency, 88, 91, 132,
   environment, 74, 77-81, 84, 86, 179, 181, 207, 213,
   evolution, 131, 212-24
   identity, 86, 89, 93-4, 116, 128
   observation, 78-96, 107, 124, 126, 128, 136, 138, 149, 152, 185, 189, 209, 222, 239, 241, 243, 246, 249, 250, 251, 255, 273, 274, 275, 277, 280, 281, 282, 283
      and blindspots, 162, 165, 181, 184, 190, 222
   operation, 74-8, 81 91, 108, 130, 151, 160, 249, 250

'order from noise', 83, 90, 122,
redundancy, 219-220
re-entry, 79, 82
unity, 58, 80, 85, 87, 94-5, 106, 111, 117, 250, 253, 271
variety, 219-220

—T—

Taylor, C, 7, 8, 39
terror, 177-186, 235
  terrorism, 171-180
Teubner, G, 81, 86, 88, 89, 95, 97, 98, 99, 100, 101, 112, 119, 134, 140, 141, 149, 150, 151, 152, 153, 157, 197, 216, 217, 218, 219, 222, 231, 252
thematisation, 107, 112, 151, 156-163, 184, 191
time, 84, 94, 105-6, 130, 137, 152, 188, 205, 210, 217
  temporal dimension, 121-2, 127, 213

Touraine, A, 96, 193, 194, 195, 196, 197, 198, 199, 208, 271
Turner, B, 7, 199
Tushnet, M, 12

—U—

Unger, R, 10, 64, 65, 98, 212, 213, 219, 221, 223, 224, 225, 234, 242, 243, 244, 245, 246, 248, 253, 271

—V—

value, 125, 149, 155-6
  negation value, 89, 91, 103,
  rejection value, 255, 275, 276, 280
Varela, F, 81, 82, 73

—W—

Walzer, M, 3, 4
Weber, M, 75, 105-6, 239
Wolin, S, 7, 212, 240,
Willener, A, 194

Law and Philosophy Library

25. S. Urbina: *Reason, Democracy, Society.* A Study on the Basis of Legal Thinking. 1996
    ISBN 0-7923-4262-3
26. E. Attwooll: *The Tapestry of the Law.* Scotland, Legal Culture and Legal Theory. 1997
    ISBN 0-7923-4310-7
27. J.C. Hage: *Reasoning with Rules.* An Essay on Legal Reasoning and Its Underlying Logic. 1997
    ISBN 0-7923-4325-5
28. R.A. Hillman: *The Richness of Contract Law.* An Analysis and Critique of Contemporary Theories of Contract Law. 1997
    ISBN 0-7923-4336-0
29. C. Wellman: *An Approach to Rights.* Studies in the Philosophy of Law and Morals. 1997
    ISBN 0-7923-4467-7
30. B. van Roermund: *Law, Narrative and Reality.* An Essay in Intercepting Politics. 1997
    ISBN 0-7923-4621-1
31. I. Ward: *Kantianism, Postmodernism and Critical Legal Thought.* 1997
    ISBN 0-7923-4745-5
32. H. Prakken: *Logical Tools for Modelling Legal Argument.* A Study of Defeasible Reasoning in Law. 1997
    ISBN 0-7923-4776-5
33. T. May: *Autonomy, Authority and Moral Responsibility.* 1998   ISBN 0-7923-4851-6
34. M. Atienza and J.R. Manero: *A Theory of Legal Sentences.* 1998   ISBN 0-7923-4856-7
35. E.A. Christodoulidis: *Law and Reflexive Politics.* 1998   ISBN 0-7923-4954-7
36. L.M.M. Royakkers: *Extending Deontic Logic for the Formalisation of Legal Rules.* 1998
    ISBN 0-7923-4982-2

KLUWER ACADEMIC PUBLISHERS – DORDRECHT / BOSTON / LONDON

Printed in the United Kingdom by
Lightning Source UK Ltd., Milton Keynes
138744UK00001B/27/A